Concept, Image, and Symbol

Cognitive Linguistics Research
1

Editors

René Dirven
Ronald W. Langacker

Mouton de Gruyter
Berlin · New York

Concept, Image, and Symbol

The Cognitive Basis of Grammar

Ronald W. Langacker

1991
Mouton de Gruyter
Berlin · New York

Mouton de Gruyter (formerly Mouton, The Hague)
is a Division of Walter de Gruyter & Co., Berlin

∞ Printed on acid-free paper
which falls within
the guidelines of the ANSI
to ensure permanence and durability

Library of Congress Cataloging in Publication Data
Library of Congress Catalog Current Number 90-48063

Die Deutsche Bibliothek — Cataloging in Publication Data

Langacker, Ronald W.:
Concept, image, and symbol : the cognitive basis of grammar /
Ronald W. Langacker. — Berlin ; New York : Mouton de
Gruyter, 1991
(Cognitive linguistics research ; 1)
ISBN 3-11-012863-2
NE: GT

Printing: Ratzlow-Druck, Berlin
Binding: Dieter Mikolai, Berlin
Printed in Germany

Contents

Preface

A symposium organized by René Dirven and held in Duisburg in the spring of 1989 marked the birth of cognitive linguistics as a broadly grounded, self-conscious intellectual movement. At that conference, initiation of the journal *Cognitive Linguistics* was announced and plans were made to form the International Cognitive Linguistics Association. Additionally, agreement was reached to launch the monograph series Cognitive Linguistics Research, and I was prevailed upon to prepare the first volume in that series. The result is before you.

My own self-conscious efforts at formulating a cognitively realistic linguistic theory began precisely thirteen years prior to the Duisburg symposium. Within a few years these efforts gave rise to a coherent conceptual framework, originally called "space grammar" and later rechristened as "cognitive grammar", that I have continued to refine, develop, and articulate ever since. This work has led to the publication of quite a number of articles, each exploring some aspect or application of the theory in considerable detail. Naturally these articles are scattered about in many places; most linguists would not have occasion to come across more than a few in the course of their normal reading. Yet an accurate appreciation of the framework is best derived from their cumulative impact--from seeing how the model represents an integrated view of the many facets of linguistic organization, and how it accommodates a diverse array of phenomena. The purpose of the present book is therefore to make this possible by assembling a variety of papers and revising them as needed. It differs from my two-volume monograph (Langacker 1987a; *to appear*) by virtue of being considerably shorter and more accessible, and also by treating particular problems in greater depth and breadth.

Though hardly self-explanatory, the title *Concept, image, and symbol* reflects the theory's central claims about the nature of grammatical structure. The word concept alludes to the claim that meaning resides in conceptualization (in the broadest sense of that term). Semantic structures are simply the conceptual structures evoked by linguistic expressions, and viable semantic analysis ultimately reduces to conceptual analysis. However, an expression's meaning consists of more than just conceptual content--equally important to linguistic semantics is how that content is shaped and construed. There are many different ways to construe a given body of content, and each construal represents a distinct meaning; this is my intent in saying that an expression imposes a particular image on the content it evokes. The word symbol refers to the basic claim that grammar is inherently symbolic. That is, all valid grammatical elements and constructs are held to be symbolic in the sense of having both conceptual and phonological import. Grammar can thus be seen as forming a continuum with lexicon. By their very nature, grammatical structures impose specific images on the conceptual content supplied by lexical items and provide a way of symbolizing (i.e. signaling phonologically) the construals thus effected.

The twelve chapters have all appeared (or been submitted) elsewhere in one form or another. However, they are not just reprinted here without modification. To varying extents they have been revised and tailored to avoid excessive redundancy and to make them fit together as a single coherent work. There is no denying that they still read more like a collection of articles than a monograph written *de novo*; given the original materials it could hardly be otherwise. Hence for the most part the chapters do retain their textual and thematic cohesiveness and could if desired be read independently. I believe the book does however constitute a unified *oeuvre* whose components are neither disjoint nor unduly repetitive, but are instead complementary and mutually supporting.

The most obvious changes have been mechanical. These include updating the references and assembling them in a single bibliography; converting everything to a common format; avoiding the repetition of identical or equivalent diagrams; and adjusting as needed the numbering of diagrams, examples, sections, and footnotes. Modifications to the text itself range from minimal to fairly substantial. They consist primarily in the deletion or compression of passages that overlap too extensively with material presented elsewhere. Other changes have been made to provide continuity, and to a lesser extent by way of updating and refinement.

Too numerous to mention individually are the various people who have contributed in one way or another to this volume. They include the family who supported my research for so many years; the professional scholars who offered comments and criticisms; the students who were willing to take these ideas seriously and worked to apply them; and not least, those who helped on countless occasions--for both the original papers and the present volume--in matters of publication, editing, technical advice, and clerical assistance. All of them have my full and warm appreciation.

Chapter 1. Introduction

Despite the diversity of contemporary linguistic theory, certain fundamental views are widely accepted without serious question.* Points of widespread agreement include the following: (i) language is a self-contained system amenable to algorithmic characterization, with sufficient autonomy to be studied in essential isolation from broader cognitive concerns; (ii) grammar (syntax in particular) is an independent aspect of linguistic structure distinct from both lexicon and semantics; and (iii) if meaning falls within the purview of linguistic analysis, it is properly described by some type of formal logic based on truth conditions. Individual theorists would doubtlessly qualify their assent in various ways, but (i)-(iii) certainly come closer than their denials to representing majority opinion.

Since 1976, I have been developing a linguistic theory that departs quite radically from these assumptions. Called "cognitive grammar" (alias "space grammar"), this model assumes that language is neither self-contained nor describable without essential reference to cognitive processing (regardless of whether one posits a special *faculté de langage*). Grammatical structures do not constitute an autonomous formal system or level of representation: they are claimed instead to be inherently symbolic, providing for the structuring and conventional symbolization of conceptual content. Lexicon, morphology, and syntax form a continuum of symbolic units, divided only arbitrarily into separate components; it is ultimately as pointless to analyze grammatical units without reference to their semantic value as to write a dictionary which omits the meanings of its lexical items. Moreover, a formal semantics based on truth conditions is deemed inadequate for describing the meaning of linguistic expressions. One reason is that semantic structures are characterized relative to knowledge systems whose scope is essentially open-ended. A second is that their value reflects not only the content of a conceived situation, but also how this content is structured and construed.

Cognitive grammar is therefore quite distinct from any version of generative theory. Moreover, it departs from most varieties of traditional and formal semantics, as well as the newer "situation semantics" of Barwise and Perry (1983), by equating meaning with conceptualization (or cognitive processing). It agrees in this regard with the "procedural semantics" of Miller and Johnson-Laird (1976) and Johnson-Laird (1983), and with the linguistic theories of Chafe (1970) and Jackendoff (1983); however, it is very different from all of these in its conception of grammatical organization and its specific proposals concerning semantic structure. Although cognitive grammar is not a direct outgrowth or a variant of any other linguistic theory, I do consider it compatible with a variety of ongoing research programs. Among these are Lakoff's work on categorization (1982, 1987); Fauconnier's study of mental spaces (1985); Haiman's ideas on iconicity and encyclopedic semantics (1980, 1983, 1985); Talmy's research on spatial terms, force dynamics, and the meanings of grammatical elements (1975, 1977, 1978, 1983, 1985a, 1985b, 1988a, 1988b); the proposals of Moore and Carling concerning the nonautonomy of linguistic structure (1982); Fillmore's conception of frame semantics (1982); Wierzbicka's insightful investigation into the semantics of grammar (1988); the growing body of research on metaphor and image schemas (Johnson 1987; Lakoff & Johnson 1980; Lakoff & Turner 1989; Sweetser 1984, 1987); recent studies of grammaticization (Bybee 1988; Kemmer 1988; Sweetser 1988; Traugott 1982, 1986, 1988); and the rich, multifaceted work in a "functional" vein by scholars too numerous to cite individually (though Givón [1979, 1984, 1989] must certainly be mentioned).

This first chapter affords an overview of cognitive grammar as I myself conceive it. The topics it briefly covers will all be taken up again in later chapters and examined in greater detail. Readers interested in still further discussion and illustration of the theory will find it in the following works: Casad 1982, 1988; Cook 1988a, 1989; Hawkins 1984, 1988; Janda 1984, 1988, to appear; Langacker 1981, 1982, 1985, 1987a, 1988a, 1988b, to appear; Lindner 1981, 1982; Poteet 1987; Rice 1987a, 1987b, 1988; Smith 1985a, 1985b, 1987, 1989; Tuggy 1980, 1981, 1986, 1988, 1989; Vandeloise 1984.

1. Linguistic semantics

Meaning is equated with conceptualization. Linguistic semantics must therefore attempt the structural analysis and explicit description of abstract entities like thoughts and concepts. The term conceptualization is interpreted quite broadly: it encompasses novel conceptions as well as fixed concepts; sensory, kinesthetic, and emotive experience; recognition of the immediate context (social, physical, and linguistic); and so on. Because conceptualization resides in cognitive processing, our ultimate objective must be to characterize the types of cognitive events whose occurrence constitutes a given mental experience. The remoteness of this goal is not a valid argument for denying the conceptual basis of meaning.

Most lexical items have a considerable array of interrelated senses, which define the range of their conventionally sanctioned usage. These alternate senses are conveniently represented in network form; Figure 1 depicts a fragment of the network associated with the noun *ring*. Certain senses are "schematic" relative to others, as indicated by the solid arrows. Some represent "extensions" from others (i.e. there is some conflict in specifications), as indicated by the dashed-line arrows. The nodes and categorizing relationships in such a network differ in their degree of entrenchment and cognitive salience--for instance, the heavy-line box in Figure 1 corresponds to the category prototype. The precise configuration of such a network is less important than recognizing the inadequacy of any reductionist description of lexical meaning. A speaker's knowledge of the conventional value of a lexical item cannot in general be reduced to a single structure, such as the prototype or the highest-level schema. For one thing, not every lexical category has a single, clearly determined prototype, nor can we invariably assume a high-level schema fully compatible with the specifications of every node in the network (none is shown in Figure 1). Even if such a structure is posited, moreover, there is no way to predict precisely which array of extensions and elaborations--out of all those that are conceivable and linguistically plausible--have in fact achieved conventional status. The conventional meaning of a lexical item must be equated with the entire network, not with any single node.

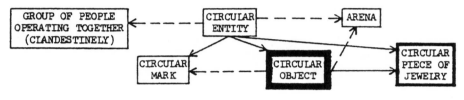

Figure 1.

Because polysemy is not our central concern, we will nevertheless focus on individual nodes. What is required to adequately characterize any particular sense of a linguistic expression? Specifically rejected is the idea that a semantic structure reduces to a bundle of features or semantic markers (cf. Katz & Fodor 1963). Rejected as well is the notion that all meanings are described directly in terms of semantic primitives. It is claimed instead that semantic structures (which I call "predications") are characterized relative to "cognitive domains", where a domain can be any sort of conceptualization: a perceptual experience, a concept, a conceptual complex, an elaborate knowledge system, etc. The semantic description of an expression therefore takes for its starting point an integrated conception of arbitrary complexity and possibly encyclopedic scope. The basic observation supporting this position is that certain conceptions presuppose others for their characterization. We can thus posit hierarchies of conceptual complexity, where structures at a given level arise through cognitive operations (including simple coordination) performed on the structures at lower levels. Crucially, the cognitive domains required by linguistic predications can occur at any level in such hierarchies.

Consider some examples. The notion *hypotenuse* is readily characterized given the prior conception of a right triangle, but incoherent without it; *right triangle* therefore functions as the cognitive domain for *hypotenuse*. Central to the value of *elbow* is the position of the designated entity relative to the overall configuration of the human arm (try explaining what an elbow is without referring in any way to an arm!), so *arm* is a domain for *elbow*. Similarly, *tip* presupposes the conception of an elongated object, and *April*, of the calendrical cycle devised to plot the passage of a year. A meaningful description of *shortstop* or *sacrifice fly* is possible only granted substantial knowledge of the rules and objectives of baseball. The implications of this position are apparent: the full and definitive characterization of a semantic structure must incorporate a comparable description of its domain, and ultimately of the entire hierarchy of more fundamental conceptions on which it depends. Pushing things to their logical conclusion, we must recognize that linguistic semantics is not an autonomous enterprise, and that a complete analysis of meaning is tantamount to a complete account of developmental cognition. This consequence is terribly inconvenient for linguistic theorists imprinted on autonomous formal systems, but that is not a legitimate argument against its validity.

What occupies the lowest level in conceptual hierarchies? I am neutral as to the possible existence of innately specified conceptual primitives. It is however necessary to posit a number of "basic domains", i.e. cognitively irreducible representational spaces or fields of conceptual potential. Among these basic domains are the experience of time and our capacity for dealing with two- and three-dimensional spatial configurations. There are basic domains associated with the various senses: color space (an array of possible color sensations), coordinated with the extension of the visual field; the pitch scale; a range of possible temperature sensations (coordinated with positions on the body); and so on. Emotive domains must also be assumed. It is possible that certain linguistic predications are characterized solely in relation to one or more basic domains, e.g. time for *before*, color space for *red*, or time and the pitch scale for *beep*. However most expressions pertain to higher levels of conceptual organization and presuppose nonbasic domains for their semantic characterization.

Most predications also require more than one domain for their full description, in which case I refer to the set as a "complex matrix", as illustrated for *knife* in Figure 2. One dimension of its characterization is a shape specification (or a family of such specifications). Another is the canonical role of a knife in the process of cutting. Additional properties are its inclusion in a typical place setting with other pieces of silverware; specifications of size, weight, and material; information about the manufacture of knives; the existence of knife-throwing acts in circuses; and so on indefinitely. Obviously these specifications are not all on a par. They differ greatly in their degree of "centrality", i.e. the likelihood of their activation on a given occasion of the expression's use. Moreover, some are probably incorporated as components of others--for instance, Figure 2 plausibly suggests that a shape specification is typically included in the conceptions constituting other domains of the complex matrix. I do however adopt an "encyclopedic" view of semantics (Haiman 1980). There is no sharp dividing line such that all specifications on one side are linguistically relevant and all those on the other side clearly irrelevant. Any facet of our knowledge of an entity is capable in principle of playing a role in determining the linguistic behavior of an expression that designates it (e.g. in semantic extension, or in its combination with other expressions).

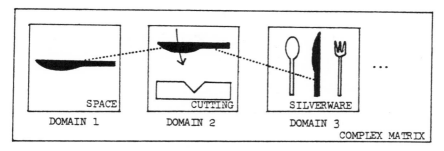

Figure 2.

If we succeed in identifying and describing the domain or complex matrix invoked by a linguistic predication, we have not yet finished its characterization. Equally significant for semantic structure is the "conventional imagery" inherent in the meaning of an expression. By imagery, I do not mean sensory images à la Shepard (1978) or Kosslyn (1980), though sensory images--as one type of conceptualization--are quite important for semantic analysis. I refer instead to our manifest capacity to structure or construe the content of a domain in alternate ways. This multifaceted ability is far too often neglected in semantic studies. Let us explore its dimensions and briefly note their grammatical significance.

2. Dimensions of imagery

The first dimension of imagery, observed in every linguistic predication, is the imposition of a "profile" on a "base". The base of a predication is its domain (or each domain in a complex matrix). Its profile is a substructure elevated to a special level of prominence within the base, namely that substructure which the expression "designates".[1] Some examples are sketched in Figure 3, with the profile given in heavy lines. The base (or domain) for the characterization of *hypotenuse* is the conception of a right triangle; for *tip*, the base is the conception of an elongated object; and for *uncle*, a set of individuals linked by kinship relations. The base is obviously essential to the semantic value of each predication, but it does not per se constitute that value: a hypotenuse is not a right triangle, a tip is not an elongated object, and an uncle is not a kinship network. The meaning of *hypotenuse*, *tip*, and *uncle* is in each case given only by the selection of a particular substructure within the base for the distinctive prominence characteristic of a profile. An expression's semantic value does not reside in either the base or the profile individually, but rather in the relationship between the two.

Some further examples will demonstrate both the descriptive utility and the

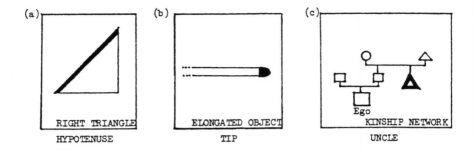

Figure 3.

grammatical import of these constructs. The predications in question represent specific senses of *go*, *away*, and *gone*, namely those illustrated in (1):

(1) a. *I think you should go now.*
    b. *China is very far away.*
    c. *When I arrived, he was already gone.*

Consider first the particular sense of *go* that is diagramed in Figure 4(a). This is a relational rather than a nominal predication, i.e. it profiles the "interconnections" among conceived entities; these interconnections are indicated in Figure 4 by the heavy dashed lines. The relevant domains are space and time. With the passage of time, one individual, referred to here as the "trajector" (tr), moves from a position within the neighborhood of another individual, the "landmark" (lm), to a final position outside that neighborhood. Only four states of the process are shown explicitly, but they represent a continuous series. The dotted lines indicate that the trajectors "correspond" from one state to the next (i.e. they are construed as identical), as do the landmarks. *Away* profiles a relationship that is identical to the

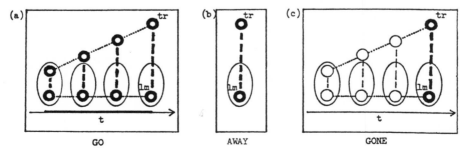

Figure 4.

final state of *go*: the trajector is situated outside the vicinity of the landmark. Observe now that the participle *gone* profiles this same relationship, but it does so with respect to a different base. The base for *away* is simply the spatial domain, but the base for *gone* is the process profiled by *go*--something cannot be *gone* except by virtue of the process of going. The semantic contribution of the past participial inflection is to restrict the profile of the stem, in this case *go*, to its final state. *Gone* thus differs from *go* by virtue of its profile, and from *away* by virtue of its base.

A second dimension of imagery is the "level of specificity" at which a situation is construed. For example, the same situation might be described by any of the sentences in (2):

(2) a. *That player is tall.*
　b. *That defensive player is over 6' tall.*
　c. *That linebacker is about 6' 5" tall.*
　d. *That middle linebacker is precisely 6' 5" tall.*

Each of these sentences can be regarded as schematic for the one that follows, which elaborates its specifications and confines their possible values to a narrower range. It is well known that lexical items form hierarchies with respect to level of specificity, e.g. *animal* → *reptile* → *snake* → *rattlesnake* → *sidewinder*. Relationships of schematicity are also important for grammatical structure. Consider the combination of *break* and *the cup* to form the composite expression *break the cup*. As part of its internal structure, the predicate *break* makes schematic reference to two central participants. The combination of *break* and *the cup* is effected through a correspondence established between one of these participants (its landmark) and the entity profiled by *the cup*, which is characterized with far greater specificity. One of the component expressions thus elaborates a schematic substructure within the other, as is typically the case in a grammatical construction.

A third dimension of imagery pertains to the "scale" and "scope of predication". The scope of a predication is the extent of its coverage in relevant domains. A predication's scope is not always sharply delimited or explicitly indicated, but the construct is nonetheless of considerable structural significance (cf. Chapter 2). Consider the notion *island* with respect to the various scopes indicated in Figure 5. The outer box, scope (a), is presumably sufficient to establish the land mass as an island, but scope (b) is at best problematic. There is no precise requirement on how extensive the body of water surrounding an island must be, but the narrow strip of water included in (b) does not have the necessary expanse (e.g. it could simply be a moat, and the land inside a moat is not thought of as an island). Similarly, the finger of land projecting out into the water qualifies as a *peninsula* given scope (c), but not (d); only from the former can we determine that the overall land mass is quite large relative to the finger-like projection. We can see that predications often imply a particular scale by noting the infelicity of using *island* to designate a handful of mud lying in the middle of a puddle. In my own speech, *bay* and *cove* are quite comparable in meaning except that *bay* specifies the requisite configuration of land and water on a larger scale.

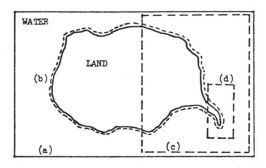

Figure 5.

Body-part terms illustrate the semantic and structural significance of these constructs. Essential to the characterization of terms like *head, arm*, and *leg* is the position of the profiled entity relative to the body as a whole, whose conception thus functions as their domain and immediate scope of predication. Each of these designated entities functions in turn as immediate scope of predication for other body-part terms defined on a smaller scale, e.g. *hand, elbow*, and *forearm* in the case of *arm*. *Hand* then furnishes the immediate scope of predication for *palm, thumb*, and *finger*, on a still smaller scale, and *finger* for *knuckle, fingertip*, and *fingernail*. This hierarchical organization has structural consequences. For example, sentences like those in (3), where *have* pertains to part-whole relationships, are most felicitous (other things being equal) when the subject designates the immediate scope of predication for the object (cf. Bever & Rosenbaum 1970; Cruse 1979).

(3) a. *A finger has 3 knuckles and 1 nail.*
    b. *??An arm has 14 knuckles and 5 nails.*
    c. *???A body has 56 knuckles and 20 nails.*

A similar restriction can be observed with noun compounds. We find numerous terms like *fingertip, fingernail, toenail, eyelash*, and *eyelid*, where the first element of the compound constitutes the immediate scope of predication for the second.[2] Compare this to the nonexistence and oddity of expressions like *bodytip, *armnail, *footnail, *facelash*, and *headlid* to designate the same entities.

In certain grammatical constructions the scope of predication plays a specific structural role. A case in point is the "nested locative" construction exemplified in (4).

(4) a. *The quilt is upstairs in the bedroom in the closet on the top shelf behind the boxes.*
   b. *The rake is in the yard by the back fence near the gate.*

Each locative expression confines the subject to a specific "search domain", which then constitutes the scope of predication for the locative that follows. Thus in (4a) the locative *upstairs* confines the quilt to an upper story, and *in the bedroom* is construed relative to this restricted region--only an upstairs bedroom need be considered. The search domain imposed by this second locative functions in turn as the scope of predication for *in the closet*, and so on. Formally, these relationships are handled by positing a correspondence between the search domain of each locative and the scope of predication of its successor. Apart from the abstractness of the entities concerned, this correspondence is just like that found in any instance of grammatical combination (e.g. between the landmark of *break* and the profile of *the cup* in *break the cup*).

The relative salience of a predication's substructures constitutes a fourth dimension of imagery. Salience is of course a very general notion, so its descriptive significance depends on our ability to sort out the various contributing factors. One factor is the special prominence associated with profiling (considered previously). A number of others can be discerned, but only two will be discussed: the relative prominence of relational participants, and the enhanced salience of elements that are explicitly mentioned.

Relational predications normally manifest an asymmetry in the portrayal of the relational participants. This asymmetry is not strictly dependent on the content of the predication, and is consequently observable even for expressions designating symmetrical relationships, e.g. *resemble*. I maintain that *X resembles Y* and *Y resembles X* are semantically distinct (even granting their truth-conditional equivalence): the former characterizes X with reference to Y, and the latter describes Y with reference to X. We can similarly employ either *X is above Y* or *Y is below X* to describe precisely the same conceived situation, but they differ in how they construe this situation; in the former, Y functions as a point of reference--a kind of landmark--for locating X, whereas the latter reverses these roles. The subtlety of the contrast with predications like these hardly diminishes its significance for linguistic semantics and grammatical structure. The asymmetry is more apparent in cases like *go*, *hit*, *enter*, and *approach*, where one participant moves in relation to another (which is stationary so far as the verb itself is concerned), but its characterization must be abstract enough to accommodate the full range of relational expressions.

I attribute this inherent asymmetry to figure/ground organization (for discussion, see Langacker 1987a, chapter 6). A relational predication elevates one of its participants to the status of figure. I refer to this participant as its "trajector";

other salient participants are referred to as "landmarks". This terminology is inspired by prototypical action verbs, where the trajector is usually the initial or primary mover, but the definitions make no specific reference to motion and are therefore applicable to any relational expression. The trajector/landmark asymmetry underlies the subject/object distinction, but the former notions have considerably broader application. In particular, a schematic trajector and landmark are imputed to a relational predication's internal structure, regardless of whether these entities receive (or are capable of receiving) separate expression. The verb *read* consequently has a trajector and a landmark in all the sentences of (5), despite the fact that both are made explicit (by elaborative noun phrases) only in (5a):

(5) a. *David read a new book.*
   b. *David is reading.*
   c. *The best way to learn is to read.*

The terms subject and object are generally reserved for overt noun phrases that elaborate a relational trajector and primary landmark at the clausal level. By contrast, trajector/landmark asymmetry is characteristic of relational predications at any level of organization, even if left implicit.

The enhanced salience of explicitly mentioned elements can be illustrated by the semantic contrast between pairs of expressions like the following: *father* vs. *male parent*; *pork* vs. *pig meat*; *oak* vs. *oak tree*; *triangle* vs. *three-sided polygon*; and *sink* vs. *passively descend through a medium under the force of gravity*. I am not concerned here with differences in connotation or information content--for sake of discussion, let us accept the members of each pair as equivalent in these respects. My claim is that the paired expressions nevertheless contrast semantically because the second expression in each case explicitly mentions certain semantic components and thereby renders them more prominent than they would otherwise be. Even for a speaker who knows perfectly well that pork comes from pigs, the expression *pig meat* renders this provenience more salient than does *pork*, simply because the former incorporates a symbolic unit that specifically designates this source. In similar fashion, the inclusion of the designated entity in a broader class of geometrical figures is highlighted by *three-sided polygon*, but remains latent in the case of *triangle*.

A linguistically appropriate characterization of meaning should accommodate such differences. Cognitive grammar defines the meaning of a complex expression as including not only the semantic structure that represents its composite sense, but also its "compositional path": the hierarchy of semantic structures reflecting its progressive assembly from the meanings of component expressions. Let us assume, for example, that the composite semantic values of *pork* and *pig meat* are identical. As an unanalyzable morpheme, *pork* symbolizes this notion directly, so its compositional path consists of the single semantic structure [PORK]. However *pig meat* is "analyzable", i.e. speakers recognize the semantic contribution of its component morphemes. The meaning of *pig meat* therefore incorporates not only the composite structure [PORK], but also the individually symbolized components [PIG] and [MEAT], together with the relationship that each of them bears to the composite value. The two expressions arrive at the same composite value through different compositional paths (a degenerate path in the case of *pork*), with the consequence that they differ in meaning.

Besides accounting for the semantic contrast between simple and composite expressions, this conception of meaning has the advantage of resolving a classic problem of truth-conditional semantics. The problem is posed by semantically anomalous expressions, e.g. **perspicacious neutrino* and **truculent spoon*, which lack truth conditions and thus ought to be meaningless and semantically equivalent. Not only is this counterintuitive, but it also predicts--quite incorrectly--the semantic anomaly of sentences like those in (6), which contain anomalous constituents.

(6) a. *There is no such thing as a perspicacious neutrino.*
    b. *It is meaningless to speak of a truculent spoon.*

In the present framework, anomalous expressions are indeed both meaningful and nonsynonymous. Though a coherent composite conceptualization fails to emerge for **perspicacious neutrino*, it has a semantic value, consisting of the meanings of its components together with their specified mode of combination (as determined by the grammatical construction). The same is true for **truculent spoon*, and because its components are different from those of **perspicacious neutrino*, so is its semantic value. Lacking a coherent composite sense, these meanings are defective, but they are meanings nonetheless. Sentences like (6) are semantically well-formed precisely because they comment on the anomaly of a constituent.

I will mention two more dimensions of imagery only in passing, though each is multifaceted and merits extended discussion. One is the construal of a situation relative to different background assumptions and expectations. To take just one example, either (7a) or (7b) might be used to describe the same state of affairs:

(7) a. *He has a few friends in high places.*
    b. *He has few friends in high places.*
    c. *Few people have any friends in high places.*
    d. **A few people have any friends in high places.*

Intuitively, the difference between *few* and *a few* is that the former is somehow negative, and the latter more positive. This is corroborated by (7c) and (7d): *any*, which requires a negative context (cf. Klima 1964), is compatible with *few*, but not with *a few*. Analytically, I suggest that *few* construes the specified quantity as being less than some implicit norm, whereas *a few* construes the quantity relative to a baseline of zero. These respective predications therefore indicate departure from an implicit reference point in a negative vs. a positive direction.

The final dimension of imagery is perspective, which subsumes a number of more specific factors: orientation, assumed vantage point, directionality, and how objectively an entity is construed. Orientation and vantage point are well known from the ambiguity of sentences like (8a). The contrast between (8b) and (8c) shows the importance of directionality, even for situations that appear to involve no motion.

(8) a. *Brian is sitting to the left of Sally.*
   b. *The hill falls gently to the bank of the river.*
   c. *The hill rises gently from the bank of the river.*
   d. *The balloon rose swiftly.*

I suggest, though, that (8b)-(8d) all involve motion in an abstract sense of the term (see Chapter 5). Described in (8d) is physical motion on the part of a mover construed "objectively", by which I mean that it is solely an object of conceptualization, maximally differentiated from the conceptualizer (i.e. the speaker and/or hearer). Motion along a similar trajectory is implied in (8c), but in this case the movement is abstract and the mover is construed "subjectively": the mover is none other than the conceptualizer, in his role as the agent (rather than the object) of conceptualization. Gradations between physical and abstract motion on the one hand, and between objective and subjective construal of conceived entities on the other, are important to the analysis of numerous linguistic phenomena.[3]

3. Grammar as image

Lexicon and grammar form a continuum of symbolic elements. Like lexicon, grammar provides for the structuring and symbolization of conceptual content, and is thus imagic in character. When we use a particular construction or grammatical morpheme, we thereby select a particular image to structure the conceived situation for communicative purposes. Because languages differ in their grammatical structure, they differ in the imagery that speakers employ when conforming to linguistic convention. This relativistic view does not per se imply that lexicogrammatical structure imposes any significant constraints on our thought processes--in fact I suspect its impact to be rather superficial (cf. Langacker 1976). The symbolic resources of a language generally provide an array of alternative images for describing a given scene, and we shift from one to another with great facility, often within the confines of a single sentence. The conventional imagery invoked for linguistic expression is a fleeting thing that neither defines nor constrains the contents of our thoughts.

The most obvious contribution of grammar to the construal of a scene pertains to designation. Grammatical constructions have the effect of imposing a particular

Nice example

profile on their composite semantic value. When a head combines with a modifier, for example, it is the profile of the head that prevails at the composite structure level. Consider a simple situation in which a lamp is suspended over a table. Starting from such simple expressions as *the lamp, the table, above,* and *below,* we can combine them in alternate ways to form composite expressions that profile different facets of the scene. *The lamp above the table* naturally designates the lamp. By choosing *the table* for the head, and appropriately adjusting the prepositional phrase modifier, we obtain instead *the table below the lamp,* which profiles the table. Another option is to add the proper form of *be* to the prepositional phrase, converting it into a process predication designating the extension of the locative relationship through a span of conceived time, e.g. *is above the table.* When a subject is then supplied, the resulting sentence *The lamp is above the table* also profiles the temporally extended locative relationship.

Let us further explore the sense in which grammar embodies conventional imagery by considering the semantic contrast between (9a) and (9b).

(9) a. *Bill sent a walrus to Joyce.*
    b. *Bill sent Joyce a walrus.*

The standard transformational analysis of these sentences treats them as synonymous and derives them from a common deep structure; depending on the particular choice of deep structure, *to* is either deleted or inserted transformationally, and the nonsubject nominals are permuted in the course of deriving the surface form of either (9a) or (9b). Cognitive grammar does not posit abstract deep structures, and neither sentence type is derived from the other--they are claimed instead to represent alternate construals of the profiled event. Examples (9a) and (9b) differ in meaning because they employ subtly different images to structure the same conceived situation.

The essentials of the analysis are sketched in Figure 6, where the small circles represent Bill, Joyce, and the walrus; the large circles stand for the regions over which Bill and Joyce exercise dominion; and heavy lines indicate a certain degree of relative prominence. Up to a point the sentences are semantically equivalent. Each symbolizes a conception in which a walrus originates in the domain under Bill's control and--at Bill's instigation--follows a path that results in its eventual location within the region under Joyce's control. The semantic contrast resides in the relative salience of certain facets of this complex scene. In (9a), the morpheme *to* specifically designates the path followed by the walrus, thereby rendering this aspect of the conceptualization more prominent than it would otherwise be, as indicated in Figure 6(a). In (9b), on the other hand, *to* is absent, but the juxtaposition of two unmarked nominals (*Joyce* and *a walrus*) after the verb symbolizes a possessive relationship between the first nominal and the second. Consequently (9b) lends added prominence to the configuration that results when the walrus completes its trajectory, namely that which finds it in Joyce's possession, as indicated in Figure 6(b).

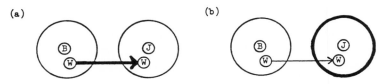

Figure 6.

All of the content present in one conception may be presumed to figure in the other as well--what differs is the relative salience of substructures. This subtle difference in imagery has an impact on the felicity of using *to* or the double-object construction for certain types of situations.[4] Consider the data in (10):

(10) a. *I sent a walrus to Antarctica.*
   b. *?I sent Antarctica a walrus.*
   c. *I sent the zoo a walrus.*

Example (10a) is fully acceptable because *to* emphasizes the path traversed by the walrus, and a continent can perfectly well be construed as the endpoint of a path. However, it is harder to construe a continent as a possessor exercising control over other entities, so (10b), which specifically places Antarctica in a possessor role, is felt to be marginal. The status of (10c) depends on the construal of *zoo*. If the zoo is simply construed as a place, it is difficult to view it as a possessor, and (10c) is questionable for the same reason as (10b). But a zoo is also an institution, and it is conventional in English to treat institutions as being analogous to people, which allows them to function linguistically as agents, possessors, and so forth. Example (10c) is consequently well formed to the extent that this second construal prevails. As viewed in the present framework, then, judgments of well-formedness often hinge on the interplay and compatibility of images, and are influenced by subtle shifts in context, intended meaning, or how a speaker chooses to structure and interpret a situation.

The examples in (11)-(13) provide further illustration.

(11) a. *I gave the fence a new coat of paint.*
   b. *?I gave a new coat of paint to the fence.*

(12) a. *I cleared the floor for Bill.*
   b. *?I cleared Bill the floor.*
   c. *I cleared Bill a place to sleep on the floor.*

(13) a. *I baked her a cake.*
   b. ?*I mowed her the lawn.*

It is conventional in English to employ possessive locutions for part-whole relations, so construing a fence as the possessor of a new coat of paint, in the manner of (11a), is quite natural. It is more difficult to envisage a coat of paint moving along a path to the fence; (11b) is thus a bit less natural, because *to* renders the path more prominent than the eventual possessive relationship.[5] The sentences in (12)-(13) bring out another consequence of the analysis. Because the two constructions are claimed to be parallel (i.e. neither is derived from the other) and semantically distinct, it is to be expected that the double-object construction-- having no intrinsic connection with *to*--might serve as an alternative to other prepositions also. It is well known from transformational studies (where the fact has long been problematic) that the double-object construction alternates with *for* as well as *to*. With *for* also the double-object construction is restricted to instances where the first object is plausibly construed as winding up in possession of the second. In (12), for example, Bill does not come to possess the floor just because I clear it for him, so (12b) is peculiar; (12c) is perfectly acceptable, however, since the additional context provided by the second nominal (*a place to sleep on the floor*) makes it apparent that the spot in question effectively comes under Bill's control and lies at his disposal by virtue of the act of clearing it. The data in (13) is similarly explained. Baking someone a cake puts the cake at that person's disposal, but mowing a lawn can hardly have a comparable effect under normal circumstances.

4. Grammatical organization

The ultimate goal of linguistic description is to characterize, in a cognitively realistic fashion, those structures and abilities that constitute a speaker's grasp of linguistic convention. A speaker's linguistic knowledge is procedural rather than declarative, and the internalized grammar representing this knowledge is simply a "structured inventory of conventional linguistic units". The term "unit" is employed in a technical sense to indicate a thoroughly mastered structure, i.e. one that a speaker can activate as a preassembled whole without attending to the specifics of its internal composition. A unit can therefore be regarded as a cognitive routine. The inventory of conventional units is "structured" in the sense that some units function as components of others (i.e. they constitute subroutines).

I speak of an "inventory" of conventional units to indicate that a grammar is nongenerative and nonconstructive. That is, I reject the standard notion that a grammar is properly conceived as an algorithmic device giving a well-defined class of expressions ("all and only the grammatical sentences of a language") as output. This conception is viable only if one imposes arbitrary restrictions on the scope of linguistic structure and makes gratuitous assumptions about its character. It is commonly assumed, for example, that judgments of grammaticality are categorical rather than matters of degree; that figurative language is properly excluded from the domain of linguistic description; and that a motivated distinction can be made between semantics and pragmatics. Although such assumptions support the notion that language is self-contained and cognitively autonomous, there is little factual basis for their adoption.

Instead, I conceive the grammar of a language as merely providing the speaker with an inventory of symbolic resources, among them schematic templates representing established patterns in the assembly of complex symbolic structures. Speakers employ these symbolic units as standards of comparison in assessing the conventionality of novel expressions and usages, whether of their own creation or supplied by other speakers. The novel symbolic structures evaluated in this fashion are not a well-defined set and cannot be algorithmically derived by the limited mechanisms of an autonomous grammar. Rather their construction is attributed to problem-solving activity on the part of the language user, who brings to bear in this task not only his grasp of linguistic convention, but also his appreciation of the context, his communicative objectives, his esthetic sensibilities, and any aspect of his general knowledge that might prove relevant. The resulting symbolic structures are generally more specific than anything computable from linguistic units alone, and often conflict with conventional expectations (e.g. in metaphor and semantic extension). Assessing their conventionality (or "well-formedness") is a matter of categorization: categorizing judgments either sanction them as elaborations of schematic units or recognize them as departing from linguistic convention as currently established.

Only three basic types of units are posited: semantic, phonological, and symbolic. A symbolic unit is said to be "bipolar", consisting of a semantic unit defining one pole and a phonological unit defining the other: [[SEM]/[PHON]]. That lexical units have this bipolar character is uncontroversial; *pencil*, for example, has the form [[PENCIL]/[pencil]], where capital letters abbreviate a semantic structure (of indefinite internal complexity), and a phonological structure is represented orthographically. A pivotal claim of cognitive grammar is that grammatical units are also intrinsically symbolic. I maintain, in other words, that grammatical morphemes, categories, and constructions all take the form of symbolic units, and that nothing else is required for the description of grammatical structure.

Symbolic units vary along the parameters of complexity and specificity. With respect to the former, a unit is minimal (a "morpheme") if it contains no other symbolic units as components. For instance, despite its internal complexity at both the semantic and the phonological poles, the morpheme *sharp* is minimal from the symbolic standpoint, whereas *sharpen, sharpener,* and *pencil sharpener* are progressively more complex. With respect to the second parameter, symbolic units run the gamut from the highly specific to the maximally schematic. Each sense of *ring* depicted in Figure 1, for example, combines with the phonological unit [ring] to constitute a symbolic unit. Some of these senses are schematic relative to others, so the symbolic units in question vary in their level of specificity at the semantic pole. Basic grammatical categories (e.g. noun, verb, adjective, adverb) are represented in the grammar by symbolic units that are maximally schematic at both the semantic and the phonological poles. A noun, for instance, is claimed to instantiate the schema [[THING]/[X]], and a verb the schema [[PROCESS]/[Y]], where [THING] and [PROCESS] are abstract notions to be described later, and [X] and [Y] are highly schematic phonological structures (i.e. they specify little more than the presence of "some phonological content").

A grammatical rule or construction is represented in the grammar by a symbolic unit that is both complex and schematic. For example, the morphological rule illustrated by the deverbal nominalizations *teacher, helper, hiker, thinker, diver,* etc. consists in a complex unit that incorporates as components the verb schema [[PROCESS]/[Y]] and the grammatical morpheme [[ER]/[er]] (i.e. the suffix *-er,* which is attributed substantial though schematic semantic content). This unit further specifies how the component structures are integrated, conceptually and phonologically, to form a composite symbolic structure. Using "-" to indicate this integration (examined later), we can write the constructional schema as follows: [[[PROCESS]/[Y]]-[[ER]/[er]]]. Its internal structure is exactly parallel to that of an instantiating expression, e.g. [[[TEACH]/[teach]]-[[ER]/[er]]], except that in lieu of a specific verb stem it contains the schema for the verb-stem category.

One constructional schema can be incorporated as a component of another. In the top portion of Figure 7(a), the schema just described combines with the noun schema [[THING]/[X]] to form a higher-order constructional schema, which speakers presumably extract to represent the commonality of *pencil sharpener, lawn mower, mountain climber, back scratcher, taxi driver,* and so on. The lower portion of 7(a) represents the lexical unit *pencil sharpener,* which conforms to the specifications of this schema but elaborates it greatly. The arrow labeled (a) indicates that the upper structure as a whole is judged schematic for the overall expression; this categorizing relationship is what specifies the membership of the expression in the class that the schema characterizes. This global categorizing relationship is based on local categorizations between component structures: relationship (b) identifies *pencil* as a member of the noun class; (c) categorizes *sharpener* as a deverbal nominalization derived by *-er*; and (d) classes *sharpen* as a verb.[6] The full set of categorizing relationships of this sort constitutes the expression's "structural description". Observe that *pencil sharpener* has a conventional meaning which is considerably more specific than anything derivable compositionally from the meanings of its parts--a pencil sharpener is not simply 'something that sharpens pencils'. Given the nonconstructive nature of the present model, we can nevertheless accept the expression as a valid instantiation of the construction in question, without relegating the unpredictable semantic specifications to the realm of extralinguistic knowledge. The constructional schema is not responsible for assembling the expression, but only for its categorization.

(a)   (b)

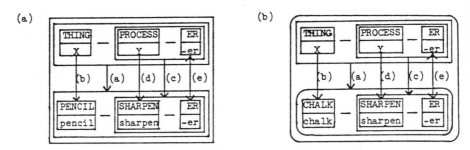

Figure 7.

All of the structures and categorizing relationships in Figure 7(a) have the status of units, which I indicate by enclosing them in boxes or square brackets. What about a novel expression on the same model, for example *chalk sharpener*? Its organization is sketched in Figure 7(b), where a closed curve (as opposed to a box) indicates a structure that does not yet constitute a unit. The assembly of this novel symbolic structure is largely prefigured by existing units, including the constructional schema, the components *chalk* and *sharpener*, and the categorization of *chalk* as a noun. Taken as a whole, however, neither the full expression *chalk sharpener* nor its categorization by the constructional schema (relationship (a)) has unit status. It does not matter for our purposes whether a speaker employs the existing units to construct or simply to understand the novel expression--in either case, all of the structures and relationships in 7(b) figure in its composition and structural description, and in either case its contextual meaning may incorporate specifications that are obvious from the situation being described (which functions as the domain for the composite expression) but are not supplied by the conventional meanings of its components. Despite this lack of full compositionality, the expression may well recur with sufficient frequency to become established as a conventional unit parallel to *pencil sharpener*, *lawn mower*, etc. If so, its contextual meaning (in an appropriately schematized form) becomes the conventional meaning of the new lexical unit. Full semantic compositionality is therefore not a hallmark of either novel expressions as they are actually understood or the fixed expressions which result from their conventionalization.

This conception of grammar makes it possible to impose the following restriction on linguistic analyses: the only units permitted in the grammar of a language are (i) semantic, phonological, and symbolic structures that occur overtly in linguistic expressions; (ii) structures that are schematic for those in (i); and (iii) categorizing relationships involving the structures in (i) and (ii). I call this the "content requirement", and consider it to be intrinsically more restrictive (at least in a certain, possibly nontechnical sense) than the constraints generally imposed on algorithmic models. Essentially, it rules out all arbitrary descriptive devices, i.e. those with no direct grounding in phonetic or semantic reality. Among the devices excluded are contentless features or arbitrary diacritics; syntactic dummies with neither semantic nor phonological content, introduced solely to drive the formal machinery of autonomous syntax (cf. Perlmutter 1978); and the derivation of overt structures from abstract, underlying structures of a substantially different character (e.g. the derivation of passives from actives--see Chapter 4 for an alternative account).

5. Grammatical classes

The content requirement proscribes the use of diacritic features. How, then, does a grammar indicate the behavior and class membership of conventional units? Some classes are characterized on the basis of intrinsic semantic and/or phonological content. In this event, a schematic unit is extracted to represent the shared content, and class membership is indicated by categorizing units reflecting the judgment that individual members instantiate the schema. The vowel [i], for example, is classed as a high vowel by virtue of the categorizing unit [[HIGH VOWEL]→[i]], where [HIGH VOWEL] is a schematic phonological structure which neutralizes the properties that distinguish one high vowel from another. Similarly, among the categorizing units depicted in Figure 7(a), relationships (b) and (d) identify *pencil* and *sharpen* as a noun and a verb respectively, whereas relationship (a) identifies *pencil sharpener* as an instance of the grammatical construction characterized by the overall schema. Only symbolic structures with actual semantic and phonological content figure in these relationships.

Obviously, though, the membership of many grammatical classes is not fully predictable on the basis of semantic or phonological properties, e.g. the class of nouns that voice *f* to *v* in the plural (*leaf/leaves*, but *reef/reefs*), or the class of verbs that conventionally occur in the double-object construction described earlier (cf. Green 1974; Oehrle 1977). The fact that morphological and syntactic behavior is often not fully predictable is generally taken as establishing the independence of grammar as a distinct aspect of linguistic structure. However, this conclusion does not actually follow from the observation--the tacit reasoning behind it confounds two issues that are in principle distinct: (i) what KINDS of structures there are; and (ii) the PREDICTABILITY of their behavior. The present framework accommodates unpredictable behavior without positing arbitrary diacritics or rule features. To say that *leaf* (but not *reef*) voices *f* to *v* in the plural is simply to say that the composite symbolic structure *leaves* (but not *reeves*) is included among the conventional units of the grammar. Similarly, to say that *send* participates in the double-object construction amounts to positing the constructional schema [send

NP NP], where the verb is specific but the two noun phrases are characterized only schematically. The nonoccurrence of *transfer* in this construction is reflected in the grammar by the nonexistence of the parallel symbolic unit [transfer NP NP].[7]

Crucial to the claim that grammatical structure resides in symbolic units alone is the possibility of providing a notional characterization of basic grammatical categories, nouns and verbs in particular. The impossibility of such a characterization is a fundamental dogma of modern linguistics, but the standard arguments that appear to support it are not immune to criticism. For one thing, they presuppose an objectivist view of meaning, and thus fail to acknowledge sufficiently our capacity to construe a conceived situation in alternate ways. Consider the argument based on verb/noun pairs which refer to the same process, e.g. *extract* and *extraction*. Such pairs demonstrate the impossibility of a notional definition only if one assumes that they are semantically identical, yet this is not a necessary assumption when meaning is treated as a subjective phenomenon. It is perfectly coherent to suggest that the nominalization of *extract* involves a conceptual reification of the designated process, i.e. the verb and noun construe it by means of contrasting images. Another type of argument against a notional characterization pivots on the confusion of prototypes with abstract schemas. In the case of nouns, for instance, discussions of notional definitions generally focus on physical objects (or perhaps "persons, places, and things"), which are clearly prototypical; the existence of nouns like *extraction*, which do not conform to this prototype, is then taken as demonstrating that nouns are not a semantic class. Obviously, a schematic characterization of the class--one compatible with the specifications of all class members--cannot be identified with the category prototype representing typical instances. If a schematic characterization is possible at all, it must be quite abstract, accommodating both physical objects and many other sorts of entities as special cases.

Cognitive grammar posits a number of basic classes that differ in the nature of their profile (see Chapter 3 for extensive discussion). As previously indicated, a noun is a symbolic structure that designates a thing, where "thing" is a technical term defined as a "region in some domain"; in the case of count nouns, the profiled region is further specified as being "bounded". Because physical objects occupy bounded regions in three-dimensional space, expressions which designate such objects qualify as count nouns, but the definition does not specifically refer to them or to the spatial domain in particular. Examples of count nouns characterized with respect to other domains include *moment* (a bounded region in time), *paragraph* (a delimited portion of a written work), and *B-flat* (a minimal, point-like region on the musical scale). Observe that the bounding implied by a count noun need not be sharp or precise, and it may be imposed as a matter of construal when objective factors do not suggest any demarcation. Where, for instance, does one's *midriff* begin or end?

Contrasting with nouns are "relational" expressions, which profile the "interconnections" among conceived entities. The term "entity" is employed in a maximally general way, and subsumes anything we might have occasion to refer to for analytic purposes: things, relations, boundaries, points on a scale, and so on. Interconnections can be regarded as cognitive operations that assess the relative position of entities within the scope of predication. It is speculated that only four basic types of assessment are necessary, provided that cognitive domains have been properly described: inclusion (INCL), coincidence (COINC), separation (SEP), and proximity (PROX). Significantly, the interconnecting operations defining a relational conception commonly associate entities other than the major relational participants (trajector and primary landmark), or associate selected facets of these participants rather than treating them as undifferentiated wholes.

By way of illustration, consider the predicate [ABOVE], sketched in Figure 8. Its domain is space organized in terms of vertical and horizontal dimensions, including an implicit reference point O_v (the vertical origin). The major relational participants are both things, characterized only schematically; one is further identified as the trajector (relational figure).[8] Among the entities invoked by specifications of this predicate are the horizontal and vertical projections of the trajector (h_t, v_t) and of the landmark (h_l, v_l). The expression *above* is optimally employed when the horizontal projections of the trajector and landmark coincide, i.e. [h_t COINC h_l], but is tolerated so long as they remain in proximity to one another: [h_t PROX h_l]. With respect to the vertical dimension, on the other hand, their projections must not coincide--the specification [v_t SEP v_l] is obligatory. The pivotal specification of [ABOVE] is provided by an operation interconnecting two entities that are still more abstract. Let [$O_v > v_t$] be the operation which registers the displacement of the trajector from the vertical origin, and [$O_v > v_l$] that of the landmark. The specification in question resides in a higher-order operation assessing the relative magnitudes of the component operations: [($O_v > v_t$) INCL ($O_v > v_l$)].

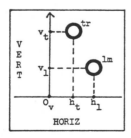

Figure 8.

Interconnecting operations of roughly this sort must somehow figure in the cognitive representation of a relational notion (though I take no position on the specifics of their implementation). [ABOVE] is a "simple atemporal relation" (or "stative" relation), in the sense that its specifications portray a single, internally consistent configuration. We must also recognize "complex" atemporal relations, where such is not the case. Consider the contrast between (14a) and (14b).

(14) a. *There is a bridge across the river.*
     b. *A hiker waded across the river.*

Distinct senses of *across* are involved, diagramed in Figures 9(a) and (b). In 9(a), the trajector (in this case the bridge) simultaneously occupies all the points on a path leading from one side of the primary landmark (the river) to the other. In 9(b), on the other hand, the trajector still occupies all the points on the path leading from one side of the landmark to the other, but does so only successively through time. The profiled relationship involves indefinitely many distinct configurations (or states), of which only a few are represented diagramatically. This sense of *across* is consequently a complex atemporal relation.[9]

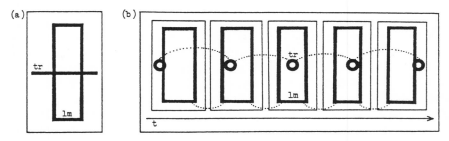

Figure 9.

Atemporal relations contrast with "processes", which define the class of verbs. I will argue in Chapter 3 that the distinction between a process and a complex atemporal relation involves the contrast between "sequential" and "summary scanning". Sequential scanning is the mode of processing we employ when watching a motion picture or observing a ball as it flies through the air. The successive states of the conceived event are activated serially and more or less instantaneously, so that the activation of one state begins to decline as that of its successor is initiated; essentially, we follow along from one state to the next as the event unfolds.[10] On the other hand, summary scanning is what we employ in mentally reconstructing the trajectory a ball has followed (e.g. in identifying a pitch as a curve, fastball, or slider and diagraming its degree of curvature). The component states are activated successively but cumulatively (i.e. once activated they remain active throughout), so that eventually they are all coactivated as a simultaneously accessible whole. The difference between a complex atemporal relation (like *across*) and the corresponding verb (*cross*) is therefore attributed not to their intrinsic content, but rather to the mode of scanning employed in their activation--a matter of conventional imagery.

Abbreviatory notations for the basic classes of predications are presented in Figure 10. A circle is the natural choice to represent a thing. A simple atemporal (or stative) relation profiles the interconnections between two or more conceived entities, where an entity can be either a thing or another relation. (Dashed lines represent these interconnections, and by convention the uppermost of the interconnected entities will be taken as the trajector unless otherwise indicated.) A complex atemporal relation consists of a sequence of stative relations scanned in summary fashion. A process is comparable to a complex atemporal relation in profiling a sequence of relational configurations, but has certain other properties as well: (i) the component states are conceived as being distributed through time; (ii) these states are scanned in sequential fashion; and (iii) the trajector is always a thing (never a relation). The arrow in Figure 10(e) stands for conceived time, and the heavy-line bar along this arrow indicates that the component states are scanned sequentially through processing time.

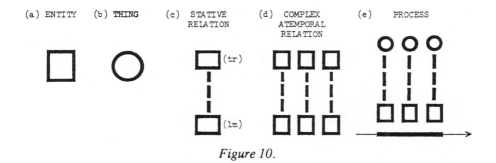

Figure 10.

6. Grammatical constructions

Grammar resides in patterns for the successive combination of symbolic structures to form more and more elaborate symbolic expressions. It is described by a structured inventory of "grammatical constructions", each of which specifies the relation between two or more "component" structures and the "composite" structure resulting from their integration. The essential structures and relationships in a grammatical construction are spelled out in Figure 11, where $[SEM_3/PHON_3]$ is the composite structure formed by integrating the component expressions $[SEM_1/PHON_1]$ and $[SEM_2/PHON_2]$. The two diagrams are notational variants: 11(b) is an "exploded" version of 11(a); it shows the component and composite structures separately at each pole.

Four symbolic relationships are indicated in Figure 11. The ones labeled s_1 and s_2 hold between the semantic and the phonological poles of each component

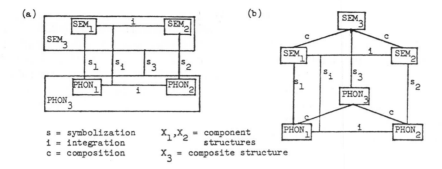

Figure 11.

expression, whereas s_3 indicates that the composite phonological structure symbolizes the composite semantic structure. The fourth relationship, s_i, reveals an important sense in which grammar is said to be inherently symbolic: the integration of component structures at the phonological pole serves to symbolize the integration of the corresponding component structures at the semantic pole. Consider the plural noun *walls*. At the phonological pole, the component structures are integrated by the suffixation of *-s* to *wall*, which involves the appropriate temporal sequencing, syllabic organization, and minor phonetic adjustments. It is precisely the fact that *-s* suffixes to *wall* (and not to some other noun stem) which symbolizes the fact that the plurality it expresses is predicated of the notion *wall* in particular (rather than the thing designated by some other noun in the sentence). Or to put it in other terms, the symbolic association s_i does not hold between a semantic and a phonological structure per se--instead it associates the RELATIONSHIPS between two semantic and two phonological structures.

Integration and composition work in essentially the same way at the phonological pole and the semantic pole, but we will confine our attention to the latter. I suggest that the integration of two component structures always involves "correspondences" being established between certain of their substructures. The corresponding substructures provide points of overlap between the component predications, which are necessary if a coherent composite conception is to emerge. The composite structure is obtained by superimposing the specifications of corresponding substructures. In those instances where there is some conflict in their specifications, a fully consistent composite notion cannot be formed, and the result is what we perceive as semantic anomaly (or the violation of "selectional restrictions").

The semantic pole of a typical construction is sketched in Figure 12(a), which diagrams the integration of *above* and *the table* to form the prepositional phrase *above the table* (I will ignore the semantic contribution of the definite article).

[ABOVE] profiles a stative relation in oriented space between two things, each characterized only schematically. [TABLE] profiles a thing characterized in far greater detail with respect to numerous domains; purely for sake of diagramatic convenience, it is represented by a mnemonic shape specification. The integration of these component predications is effected by a correspondence established between the landmark of [ABOVE] and the profile of [TABLE] (correspondences are represented by dotted lines). By superimposing the specifications of these corresponding substructures, and adopting the relational profile of [ABOVE], we obtain the composite predication (ABOVE-TABLE), which designates a stative relation involving a schematic trajector and a specific landmark. Note that the compositional process results in "vertical" correspondences between elements of the component and composite structures, in addition to the "horizontal" correspondence(s) linking the components.[11]

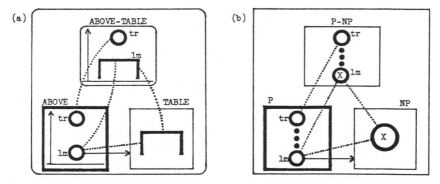

Figure 12.

Semantics is not fully compositional. When first assembled, an expression's composite structure may invoke a domain or incorporate specifications (e.g. the orientation of the table) that are not predictable from the component structures or other conventional units. Because such specifications are part of how the expression is actually understood in context, and may well be included in its conventional semantic value should the expression be established as a unit, it is arbitrary to exclude them from the purview of semantic analysis. There are nevertheless conventional patterns of composition that determine central aspects of a composite structure's organization. These are represented in the grammar by constructional schemas, whose internal structure is parallel to that of the specific expressions which instantiate them. For example, the grammar of English includes a schema for the prepositional-phrase construction. Its phonological pole specifies the contiguity and linear ordering of the preposition and its noun-phrase object; its semantic pole, given in Figure 12(b), is precisely analogous to 12(a) except that the component and composite structures are schematic rather than specific. The first component is schematic for the class of prepositions. Basically, it is identified only as a stative relation whose trajector and primary landmark are both things. The other component is the noun-phrase schema: it profiles a thing, and implies additional content (labeled X), but does not itself specify the nature of this content. As in the specific structure 12(a), a correspondence holds between the landmark of P and the profile of NP, and the composite structure is formed by superimposing the specifications of these correspondents (and adopting the relational profile of P). Speakers can employ this constructional schema in the computation and evaluation of novel expressions. It serves as the structural description of any expression which it categorizes when so employed.

This construction has various properties that can be regarded as prototypical. There are just two component structures, one of them relational and the other nominal. A correspondence holds between two highly prominent substructures: the profile of the nominal predication, and the primary landmark (one facet of the profile) of the relational predication. Moreover, there is a substantial asymmetry in the degree of specificity at which the predications characterize the corresponding elements--the landmark of [ABOVE] is quite schematic, whereas by comparison the profile of [TABLE] is specified in considerable detail. I have indicated this diagramatically by an arrow (standing for a relationship of schematicity) between [ABOVE]'s landmark and the other predication as a whole. Finally, it is the relational predication which lends its profile to the composite structure (i.e. *above the table* designates a stative relation, not a thing). I thus refer to [ABOVE] in 12(a) as the construction's "profile determinant", and make this role explicit by putting the box enclosing this predication in heavy lines.

None of the properties just cited is invariant except the existence of at least one correspondence between substructures of the components. By recognizing these properties as prototypical rather than imposing them as absolute requirements, we obtain the flexibility needed to accommodate the full range of attested construction types. It is probably necessary, for example, to allow more than just two component structures at a particular level of constituency (e.g. for coordinate expressions such as *X, Y, and Z*). It need not be the case that one component structure is relational and the other nominal--in fact, there need be no relational component at all. Appositional constructions involving two nominal predications, e.g. *my good friend Ollie North*, are straightforwardly accommodated in this framework by means of a correspondence established between the nominal profiles. In all the examples cited so far, the corresponding elements have been things that either constitute or are included within the profile of the component structure. Often, however, the correspondents are relational substructures, and they need not be in profile. Consider once more the sense of *gone* diagramed in Figure 4(c). The component structures are [GO], which designates a process, and one particular semantic variant of the past-participial morpheme. This particular predication profiles the final state of an otherwise unprofiled process that constitutes its base. The participial morpheme itself characterizes this process quite schematically; only in combination with a verb stem is the nature of the process made specific. Their integration is effected by a correspondence between the specific process profiled by [GO] and the schematic process functioning as the base within the participial predication. By superimposing their specifications, and adopting the profile contributed by the grammatical morpheme, we obtain a composite structure that profiles just the final state of the process [GO].

A factor we have not yet considered is "constituency", which pertains to the order in which symbolic structures are progressively assembled into larger and larger composite expressions. Clearly, the composite structure resulting from the integration of component structures at one level of organization can itself be employed as a component structure at the next higher level, and so on indefinitely. In Figure 13, for example, the composite structure (ABOVE-TABLE) from Figure 12(a) functions as a component structure, combining with [LAMP] to derive the composite semantic value of the noun phrase *the lamp above the table*. At this second level of organization, it is the schematic trajector of the relational predication that is put in correspondence with the profile of the nominal predication; moreover, it is this latter which functions as the construction's profile determinant. The composite structure (LAMP-ABOVE-TABLE) consequently designates the lamp, not its locative relationship vis-à-vis the table, though this relationship is included as a prominent facet of its base.

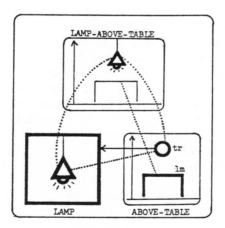

Figure 13.

Some grammatically significant observations can be made on the basis of these examples. For one thing, we see that either a relational or a nominal predication is capable of serving as the profile determinant in a construction. In Figure 12, it is the relation [ABOVE] which contributes the profile of the composite expression, whereas in Figure 13 it is the nominal [LAMP]. Moreover, the constructs now at our disposal permit workable and revealing characterizations of certain fundamental grammatical notions that have long been problematic, namely "head", "modifier", and "complement". At a given level of organization, a construction's head can be identified with its profile determinant. *Above* is thus the head within the prepositional phrase *above the table*, whereas *lamp* is the head within the noun phrase *the lamp above the table*. In appositional expressions like *my good friend Ollie North* there is no real basis for singling out either component noun phrase as the head. But that is precisely what we expect: because their profiles correspond, and each corresponds to the profile of the composite structure, it is arbitrary to say that the latter inherits its profile from either one of the component structures (as opposed to the other).

To the extent that one component structure, taken as a whole, serves to elaborate a salient substructure within the other, I will speak of the elaborating component as being "conceptually autonomous", and the elaborated component as "conceptually dependent". In Figure 12(a), then, [TABLE] is conceptually autonomous with respect to [ABOVE] because it elaborates the latter's schematic landmark. In Figure 13, similarly, [LAMP] is autonomous by virtue of elaborating the schematic trajector of the dependent predication (ABOVE-TABLE). The notions modifier and complement can now be characterized explicitly in a way that reconstructs the normal usage of these traditional terms: a "modifier" is a conceptually dependent predication that combines with a head, whereas a "complement" is a conceptually autonomous predication that combines with a head. *The table* is consequently a complement (or "argument") of *above* in *above the table*, and this entire prepositional phrase functions as a modifier of *lamp* in *the lamp above the table*. What about appositional constructions? Because there is no basis for recognizing either component structure as the head (and often no autonomous/dependent asymmetry), the definitions are correctly found to be inapplicable. In *my good friend Ollie North*, neither *my good friend* nor *Ollie North* is considered a modifier or a complement of the other.

This conception of grammatical structure has numerous descriptive advantages, only a few of which will be noted at this juncture. One advantage is that it readily accommodates variability of constituency, which is in fact quite common. The present framework does not posit phrase trees of the sort familiar from generative studies, nor does it rely on phrase structure configurations for the definition of grammatical relations. Constituency is simply the sequence in which component symbolic structures are progressively assembled into more and more elaborate composite expressions. Though a specific order of assembly commonly becomes conventionalized as the sole or default-case sequence, the choice is not inherently critical in this model, because alternate constituencies often permit the same composite structure to be derived. Moreover, because grammatical relations are not defined in configurational terms, a unique constituency is not essential. What identifies *the table* as the object of *above* in *above the table*, for example, is the fact that the noun phrase elaborates the preposition's landmark. Though constituency happens to be invariant in this case, the critical factor in defining the prepositional-object relation is the correspondence established between the landmark of the preposition and the profile of the noun phrase.

We can better appreciate these points with regard to sentences like the ones in (15).

(15) a. *Alice likes liver.*
　　 b. *Liver Alice likes.*
　　 c. *Alice likes, but most people really hate, braised liver.*

Sentence (15a) exhibits the normal, default-case NP + VP constituency of English clauses: *liver* elaborates the schematic landmark of *likes* at the first level of constituency, yielding a processual predication with a specified landmark and schematic trajector; *Alice* then elaborates the trajector of *likes liver* at the second level to derive a process predication whose trajector and landmark are both specific. It should be apparent, however, that the same composite structure will result if the constituents combine in the opposite order, with *Alice* elaborating the schematic trajector of *likes*, and then *liver* the schematic landmark of *Alice likes*. This alternative constituency is available for exploitation, with no effect on grammatical relations, whenever special factors motivate departure from the default-case arrangement. Two such factors are illustrated here. In (15b) we observe the topicalization of the direct-object noun phrase, normally described as a movement transformation. There is no need in this framework to derive this sentence type by transformation--it can be assembled directly through the alternate compositional path. The second type of situation arises in conjoined structures when two verbs have different subjects but share the same object, as in (15c). In lieu of the transformational process of "Right Node Raising", which supposedly derives this type of sentence from conjoined clauses of normal NP + VP constituency, we can once again assemble the overt structure directly. The two subject-verb constituents are put together first and then combined in a coordinate structure. A direct object NP is subsequently added, being integrated simultaneously with each conjunct through a correspondence between its profile and the conjunct's relational landmark.

Also eliminable in this framework is the raising rule needed in certain transformational accounts (e.g. Keyser & Postal 1976) to handle agreement between a subject and an auxiliary verb, as in (16).

(16) *The lamp is above the table.*

The rationale for a raising rule goes something like this: (i) a verb is assumed to agree with its own subject; (ii) *the lamp* is not the logical subject of *be*, which--if anything--has a clause for its underlying subject; (iii) hence, to account for agreement, some rule must raise *the lamp* from its position as subject of *above* and make it the subject of *be*. However the need for such a rule is obviated given a proper analysis of *be* and a suitably flexible conception of grammatical constructions.

The semantic pole of (16) is outlined in Figure 14.[12] Pivotal to the analysis is the semantic value attributed to *be*, of which three main features are relevant. First, *be* is a true verb, i.e. a symbolic expression that profiles a process. Second, all the component states of the designated process are construed as being identical; this is indicated by the dotted correspondence lines internal to [BE] that link the three states which are explicitly represented (additional correspondence lines specify that the trajector is the same from one state to the next, as is the landmark). Third, apart from this specification of identity, the profiled process is maximally schematic. *Be* is one of numerous verbs in English which designate a process consisting of the extension through time of a stable situation (see Chapter 3)-- others include *have, resemble, like, know, contain, slope, exist,* and so on--but it abstracts away from the specific content that distinguishes these predications from one another. In summary, [BE] follows through time, by means of sequential scanning, the evolution of a situation that is construed as being stable but not further specified (except for its relational character).

Any single component state of [BE] constitutes a schematic stative relation. At the first level of constituency in Figure 14, the more specific stative relation (ABOVE-TABLE) is put in correspondence with a representative state of [BE], the latter serving as profile determinant. The result is the composite predication (BE-ABOVE-TABLE), which is like [BE] except that all the specifications inherited from (ABOVE-TABLE) are attributed to the situation followed sequentially through time. Observe that the landmark of (BE-ABOVE-TABLE) is now specific, whereas its trajector remains schematic. At the second level of constituency, this schematic trajector is elaborated by [LAMP] to derive the composite structure (LAMP-BE-ABOVE-TABLE), which represents the composite meaning of the full sentence. It profiles the extension through time of a stable situation in which the lamp and the table participate in a particular locative relationship.

Observe that the sentence is assembled directly, in accordance with its surface constituency. In particular, there is no "raising" rule which derives it from a hypothetical underlying structure by changing the grammatical relation of the subject NP. But does *the lamp* function as the subject of *be*, as their agreement presumably requires? It certainly does, given the way grammatical relations are defined in this framework. A subject NP is one which elaborates the schematic trajector of a relational predication by virtue of a correspondence established between that trajector and its own profile. With respect to Figure 14, note first that [BE] does in fact have a schematic trajector, characterized as both a thing (not a clause) and a relational participant. Moreover, [BE]'s trajector does correspond to the profile of *the lamp*, when both horizontal and vertical correspondences are taken into account: the profile of [LAMP] corresponds to the trajector of

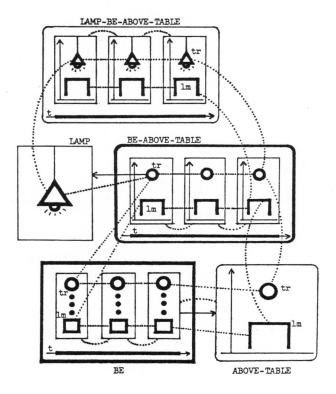

Figure 14.

(BE-ABOVE-TABLE), which in turn corresponds vertically to the trajector of [BE]. It is simply incorrect, in this analysis, to claim that *be* has no nonclausal subject, or that *the lamp* is not its "logical" subject in (16). With no special apparatus, the analysis establishes a relationship between *the lamp* and *be* which is perfectly adequate as a basis for agreement.

Finally, the analysis permits a simple and natural account of sentences like (17b), in which an auxiliary verb functions as a pro form:

(17) a. Q: *What is above the table?*
    b. A: *The lamp is.*

As highly schematic process predications, auxiliary verbs are perfectly suited to this role, and sentences of this type are derivable without any deletion operation. Because constituency is potentially variable in this framework, we can derive

(17b) just by combining *the lamp* and *be* directly. A correspondence is established between the profile of the former and the schematic trajector of the latter. *Be* is the profile determinant, so the composite structure designates a process involving the evolution of a stable situation through time. Apart from its trajector, identified as the lamp, this situation is characterized only schematically.

7. Conclusion

This initial presentation of cognitive grammar has itself been quite schematic. I do however hope to have shown that currently predominant linguistic theories do not represent the only possible way of conceiving the nature of language structure and linguistic investigation. By taking a radically different perspective on questions of meaning and grammar, it is possible to formulate a coherent descriptive framework which promises to be both cognitively realistic and linguistically well-motivated. The remaining chapters will each elucidate certain aspects of the framework in greater depth and detail. Let us begin in Chapter 2 with a case study illustrating the cognitive grammar conception of linguistic semantics.

Chapter 2. Inside and outside in Cora

Cora grammar is striking in its profusion of devices for marking location.*[1]
Besides postpositions, these devices include locative particles and an elaborate set
of verb prefixes. Central to this locative system is a basic 'inside'/'outside'
contrast symbolized respectively by the morphemes *u* and *a*, one of which is found
in virtually every particle and prefix combination in the system. The sentences in
(1) are typical examples.[2]

(1) a. *ka-pú=a-t^{y}é-n^{y}eeri'i*   *m-a-a*   *haa-ta'a*
    not-it=outside-in:middle-be:visible MED-outside-foot:of:slope water-in
    'The river is muddy'

  b. *u-ká-taa-sin*   *mí*   *kantiira*
    inside-down-burn-DUR ART candle
    'The candle is burning'

The purpose of this chapter is to present and explicate some of the subtleties of the
u/*a* contrast, as well as to illustrate certain constructs and fundamental principles of
cognitive semantics.

On first examination, a unified and coherent account of *u* and *a* does not seem
possible, for these prefixes appear to be used in inexplicable, inconsistent, or
directly contradictory ways. The sentences in (2), for instance, have the same
translation and can be employed to describe precisely the same objective situation.

(2) a. *u-h-kí-t^{y}a-pu'u*
    inside-face:of:slope-short-in:middle-planted
    'Its [dog's] tail is chopped short'

  b. *a-h-kí-t^{y}a-pu'u*
    outside-face:of:slope-short-in:middle-planted
    'Its [dog's] tail is chopped short'

Examples like (3) display the 'outside' prefix when 'inside' would seem to be
called for.

(3) *a-t^{y}á-suuna*   *káasu* *hece*
    outside-in:middle-pour basin in
    'The water is pouring into the basin/pan'

There is no apparent basis for the 'inside'/'outside' contrast in (4) or in (5):

(4) a. *pu'u=rí=u-kda-n^{y}e*   *y-ú*   *aᵗ^{y}e'e*
he=now=inside-down-arrive   PROX-inside   along:river
'He has now arrived here alongside the river'

   b. *mu'u=rí=a-kda-ki*   *ša'iču'i   iri   hece*
they=now=outside-down-go:PL   barely   hill   at
'They have just now come down off the hill'

(5) a. *y-ú*   *n^{y}a-wari-ta'a*
PROX-inside   my-back-in
'right here in back of me'

   b. *y-é^3*   *n^{y}a-híise-'e*
PROX-outside   my-eyes-in
'right here before my eyes'

Finally, note the unexpected pattern of acceptability in (6):

(6) a. *ú*   *čah-ta'a*
inside:DIST   home:area-in
'there in town'

   b. **m-ú*   *čah-ta'a*
MED-inside   home:area-in
'right here in town'

   c. *íiy-a*   *čáh-ta'a*
PROX-outside   home:area-in
'right here in town'

   d. **íiy-u*   *čáh-ta'a*
PROX-inside   home:area-in
'right here in town'

It would be wrong to conclude from facts like these that the distribution of *u* and *a* is determined grammatically rather than semantically. Though conventionality is definitely an important factor, a clear semantic rationale for the choice can almost invariably be found. Further, though *u* and *a* have a multiplicity of different values not all necessarily compatible with a simple 'inside' or 'outside' gloss, it would also be wrong to conclude that either morpheme must be resolved into a number of unrelated homophones.[4] Let us start by reviewing certain theoretical assumptions presented in Chapter 1.

1. Theoretical preliminaries

Cognitive grammar makes a number of theoretical assumptions considered self-evident, though some of them conflict with prevailing views. First, it assumes that a frequently-used morpheme or lexical item has a variety of interrelated senses. They can be thought of as forming a network, where some senses are prototypical, and others constitute either extensions or specializations of a prototypical value or of one another. The grammar of a language must give a full account of conventional usage. Thus it must map out the complete network of conventionally established senses for a lexical item, describing each of them individually together with the relations they bear to others. Part of this network will take the form of schemas, more abstract representations that embody whatever generalizations can be extracted from an array of specific senses.[5] In describing this network the analyst therefore achieves a unified account of the meaning of a lexical item, and captures whatever generalizations are plausibly attributed to speakers, but avoids the misguided reductive approach which ignores the essential problem of conventional usage.

Second, it assumes that meanings are always characterized relative to cognitive domains, i.e. knowledge structures or conceptual complexes of some kind. The putative difference between linguistic and extralinguistic knowledge, or between a dictionary-type account of the meaning of lexical items and an essentially encyclopedic account, is illusory. Neither language in general nor semantics in particular is an autonomous system or a separate module that can be characterized in isolation from other aspects of cognition. There is no nonarbitrary distinction between semantics and pragmatics, hence semantic analysis ultimately presupposes the characterization of conceptualization and knowledge structures to whatever degree of precision and detail is necessary for the description of specific linguistic elements. Obviously the problems in accomplishing this are enormous, but there is little point in avoiding them by imposing aprioristic (and eventually untenable) compartmentalizations on the data.[6]

Third, it assumes that the meaning of an expression is not fully given by an objective characterization of the scene it describes. People have the capacity to construe a scene by means of alternative images, so that semantic value is not simply received from the objective situation but instead is in large measure imposed on it. The term imagery is understood here as referring to such phenomena as the following: certain facets of the scene can be rendered more salient than others, e.g. by being explicitly symbolized rather than left implicit; the situation can be described at varying levels of specificity; alternate figure/ground alignments can serve to organize it; to the extent that the scene has a visual aspect, it can be portrayed as if observed from different vantage points and orientations; and so on.[7] Two linguistic expressions can therefore designate the same objective situation yet differ substantially in their semantic import because they structure it through different images. Consider (2) as a specific example (every expression cited in this chapter--in relation, say, to its English translation--would serve equally well to illustrate the point). For one thing, with *tʸa-pu'u* 'be planted in the middle', the Cora expressions emphasize certain facets of the situation not directly symbolized in *The dog's tail is chopped short*, in particular the location of the tail (the 'planted' entity) in the middle of an extended area (the rump). More important here, though, is the fact that (2a) and (2b) presuppose different perspectives on the scene: (2a) would be said if the dog were seen from behind, and (2b) if it were seen from the side (later we will find out why). In accordance with the conventions of Cora grammar, then, (2a) and (2b) construe the same objective situation in terms of contrasting images, neither of which is equivalent to that of the English translation, which makes no explicit reference at all to vantage point.

With these various claims and assumptions about meaning, we can begin to make sense of the Cora locative system. Our specific objective here is to characterize in preliminary terms the networks representing the conventionally established meanings of *u* and *a*. Presumably their prototypical values pertain to the notion of containment in physical space, as sketched in Figure 1. The term trajector (tr) refers here to the entity being located relative to others in a relational predication; a landmark (lm) is a point of reference for computing the position of the trajector. For notational simplicity, heavy lines are used to identify the trajector throughout this chapter.[8]

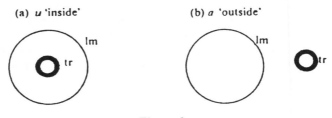

Figure 1.

The sentences in (7) illustrate this prototypical sense of *u* and *a*.

(7) a. *m-ú*   *wa-tʸé-ča-sɨ*   *m-ú*   *či'i-ta*
      MED-inside EXT-in:middle-move-PAST MED-inside house-in
      'Stand right there inside the house'

   b. *m-á*   *wa-tʸé-ča-sɨ*   *pua'ake   či'i-hece*
      MED-outside EXT-in:middle-move-PAST outside   house-at
      'Stand right there outside near the house'

In these examples the house functions as the landmark relative to which 'inside' and 'outside' relations are calculated. But what is the trajector? Though it could be taken as the addressee, one can equally well argue that the verbal process of 'standing' serves as trajector and is situated with respect to the confines of the house. The matter is perhaps indeterminate,[9] but it is suggested that the locative specifications treated here are primarily adverbial in nature and have for their trajector a process or other verbal relationship of some kind (observe that in a number of cases--e.g. $n^y eeri'i$ 'it be all lit up' in (1a)--it is difficult to distinguish between the verbal process itself and any other entity that could be construed as its subject). One additional point of clarification is necessary. For the most part an attempt is made only to characterize the meanings of locative expressions, so what is considered to be the trajector is the trajector of these locative expressions alone. This is to be distinguished from the trajector (subject) of the verb or the sentence as a whole--in fact, it is the process designated by the verb or sentence that is considered to be the trajector of the locative expressions. In (7), for instance, the process of standing is taken as the trajector of *mú, má,* and the other locatives, which are consequently adverbial, but this process itself involves a trajector (subject) equated with the addressee.

2. Enclosure

The prototypical senses of *u* and *a*, sketched in Figure 1, predicate that the trajector is contained within a physical landmark of some kind or is external to it, respectively. Certain other senses also involve physical enclosure and are straightforwardly regarded as developments from the prototype. The first of these represents the special case where the trajector is in contact with a surface of the landmark, an inner surface for *u* and an outer surface for *a*, as shown in Figure 2. Because these senses are fully compatible with those in Figure 1, we can regard this as a case of specialization rather than extension.[10] Though Figure 2 depicts

(a) *u* 'on inner surface'   (b) *a* 'on outer surface'

Figure 2.

only a single point of contact between the trajector and the landmark, the extent of contact is quite variable; note the following sentences:

(8) a. *u-h-t^{y}ee*   *m-ú*   *či'i-ta*
      inside-face:of:slope-long MED-inside house-in
      'It's a long ways up to the ceiling inside that house'

    b. *a-h-t^{y}ee*   *mí*   *či'i*
      outside-face:of:slope-long ART house
      'That's a tall house'

Considerations of length preclude a full description of every sentence presented in this chapter, but a relatively complete analysis of at least one sentence may serve to clarify the nature of the elements and constructions we are dealing with. It is claimed that grammatical structure can be exhaustively described in terms of symbolic units, which include the morphemes and larger lexical items overtly present in linguistic expressions as well as schematic symbolic units describing patterns for combining them. Patterns for combining symbolic units specify how component symbolic structures are integrated to form a composite symbolic structure; starting from lexical units, the successive integration of progressively larger symbolic structures yields higher-order constituents such as phrases, clauses, and sentences. The integration of two symbolic structures is defined by correspondences between substructures, with respect to both their semantic and their phonological representations. Let us take their phonological integration for granted here and concentrate on the integration of semantic representations, which is sketched for (8a) in Figure 3.

The semantic representations of component morphemes are given along the top row in Figure 3; the informal notation should be self-explanatory. The correspondences established between semantic substructures are indicated by dotted lines. Thus the trajector of *u* is put in correspondence with that of *h*, and the vertical surface functioning as the landmark within *h* corresponds to one of the surfaces of the landmark within *u*. Similarly, the trajectors of *m* and *u* are equated, and the entity designated by *či'i* corresponds to the landmark of *-ta*. By superimposing corresponding entities we obtain the composite semantic structures shown in the second row. The prefix combination *uh* locates its trajector on a vertically oriented surface; *mú* situates its trajector internally to a landmark at a medial distance from the speaker (S); and *či'ita* places its trajector within the confines of a house.

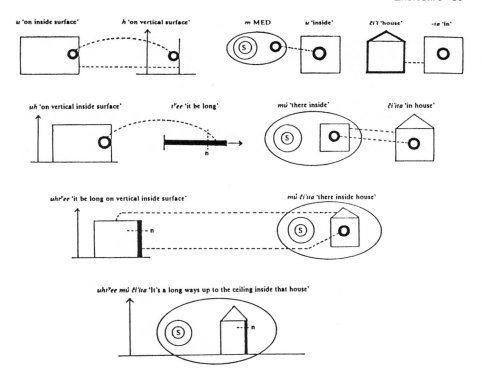

Figure 3.

Integration of this sort continues at higher levels of constituency. The trajector of *uh* is equated with the relationship designated by the verb stem *t^{y}ee*, which describes an entity surpassing the norm (n) along a scale of length. The trajectors of *mú* and *či'ita* correspond, and the enclosure implied by the former also corresponds to the house that figures in the latter. The results of these integrations are the higher-order composite structures shown in the third row of Figure 3, namely *uht^{y}ee* 'it be long on a vertical inside surface' and *mú či'ita* 'there inside the house'.[11] Finally, these two composite structures function as components at the last hierarchical level, where their trajectors are put in correspondence as well as their enclosures, yielding the semantic structure of the sentence as a whole, given at the bottom. Observe that the trajector of all the locative expressions, both simple and composite, is eventually equated by correspondences with the verbal relationship *t^{y}ee* 'it be long'.

The notion 'contact with a surface', which is shared by the values of *u* and *a* depicted in Figure 2, is pivotal to understanding the extension giving rise to the senses represented in Figure 4. Since *u* and *a* function quite consistently as a contrasting pair, it is to be expected that the 'inside'/'outside' contrast might in some cases be relative rather than absolute. Thus, while *u* 'deep penetration to interior' could conceivably be considered a specialization of the previous sense 'on inner surface', the extension of *a* from 'on outer surface' to 'shallow penetration to interior' preserves the exteriority of *a* only by comparison to *u*--deep penetration and shallow penetration are both 'inside' notions, but if one of the two is to be construed as an 'outside' relationship, the latter is the obvious candidate. Note that in Figure 4(b) the entire trajector remains roughly contiguous to the surface, which is the interface between the 'inside' and 'outside' regions.[12]

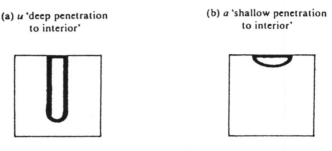

(a) *u* 'deep penetration to interior'

(b) *a* 'shallow penetration to interior'

Figure 4.

Examples of these extended meanings of *u* and *a* are given respectively in (9) and (10).

(9) a. *u-tʸé-nee-ri-'i*   *ú*   *či'i-ta*
     inside-in:middle-visible-APPLIC-STAT inside house-in
     'It's all lit up inside the house [by light visible through the windows]'

     b. *nʸa-ru-'u-tʸá-muuku'u-s-te-'e-sin*
       I-him-inside-in:middle-hat-(?)-make-APPLIC-DUR
       'I'm going to put his hat on him'

(10) a. *a-tʸá-suuna*   *áa*   *ti*   *háh-mʷaa*
      outside-in:middle-pour outside:DIST SUBR water-lay:flat
      'Water is pouring into the pond [from waterfall]'

      b. *ra-'a-tʸe-veîča-hraa*   *mí*   *kiye*
       it-outside-in:middle-cut:out-PAST ART log
       'He hollowed out a log to make a dugout canoe'

The processes in (9) involve penetration of some entity essentially all the way through the interior of an enclosure from the surface (e.g. the head penetrates the plane defined by the brim of the hat and more or less fills the crown region), while processes at the surface of an enclosed area (the pond or log) figure much more prominently in (10). Clearly, though, the distinction is relative instead of absolute, and there is no precise dividing line between the 'shallow penetration' and 'deep penetration' configurations--the choice depends on convention or on how a given speaker decides to construe the situation. It is a matter of conventional imagery.

The hypothesized contrast between deep and shallow penetration is confirmed by the distinction between (11), with *u*, and (3) above, with *a*.

(11) *u-t^y á-suuna*   *ša' ari cahta' a*
  inside-in:middle-pour pot   inside
  'The water is pouring into the storage jar'

The enclosure in (11) is a storage jar, a relatively deep container, while in (3) it is a basin or pan, a much shallower container. Even though the water presumably reaches the bottom of the container in both instances, there is a clear sense in which the penetration is deeper in the former instance. The problem posed by (3) at the outset is now solved: the locus of the water pouring counts as an 'outside' region because the container is shallow, consequently its penetration is shallow-- and close to the outside surface--compared to that of water pouring into a storage jar (and comparable receptacles). Observe that in (11) and (3) the outer surface from which the penetration occurs is virtual rather than actual. Strictly speaking, then, the semantic values of *u* and *a* in these sentences constitute extensions from those in Figure 4. These extensions are given in Figure 5.

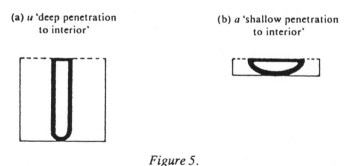

(a) *u* 'deep penetration to interior'   **(b)** *a* 'shallow penetration to interior'

Figure 5.

3. Topographical domain

Figures 2, 4, and 5 represent extensions from the prototypical values of *u* and *a* (Figure 1) along one path of development. We turn now to a second course of development from the prototype, observed in a system of locative particles evolved to deal with topographical relationships in mountainous terrain. The notion of enclosure remains, but is characterized relative to a more complex situation and involves a more abstract type of landmark.

Representative examples of these topographical particles are given in (12).

(12) a. *mah* 'away up there to the side in the face of the slope'

> m-á-h   tu wá-ta-t^{y}auu
> MED-outside-face:of:slope we COMPL-REFL-find
> 'We found each other right up there on the side of the hill'

b. *yuu* 'right here at the foot of the slope'

> y-ú-u   pu ú-čap^{w}a
> PROX-inside-foot:of:slope it that:way-footprint
> 'A string of footprints goes right along here'

c. *an* 'away up there on top of the slope'

> á-n   pú a-'u-h-n^{y}eh-sin
> outside:DIST-top:of:slope it away-inside-face:of:slope-arrive-DUR
> 'He's going up to the top of the hill'

These particles are essentially regular combinations of three morphemes each; all combinations occur except **yun*, **mun*, and **un* (i.e. 'inside on top' is excluded, for a reason to become apparent below). The initial morpheme is a deictic predication indicating distance from the speaker (S), as shown in Figure 6. The final morpheme describes the position of the trajector relative to the contour of the slope; observe Figure 7. Sandwiched between the two is *u/a*. Presumably they mean 'inside'/'outside', but what is the boundary relative to which these relations are calculated?

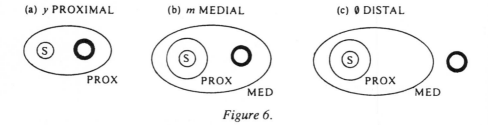

(a) *y* PROXIMAL   (b) *m* MEDIAL   (c) Ø DISTAL

Figure 6.

(a) : 'foot of slope'   (b) *h* 'face of slope'   (c) *n* 'top of slope'

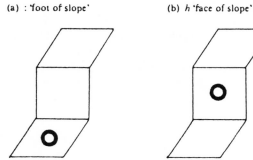
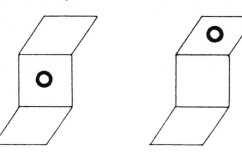

Figure 7.

As it turns out, a conceived situation of some complexity is required for its characterization. This situation (a "nonbasic domain"[13]) is sketched in Figure 8(a). It involves a vantage point (VP) somewhere in the area at the foot of a slope; when no semantic conflict results, this vantage point is generally equated with the position of the speaker. From this vantage point a viewer (normally the speaker) is presumed to be looking directly up the face of the slope. The dashed arrow in 8(a) represents the viewer's line of sight in relation to the slope; observe that this line of sight runs from the foot of the slope, along the face, up to the horizon line between the face and top, but does not curve to include the region on top. The landmark enclosure for *u/a* is defined relative to this line of sight: it includes a narrow region along either side of the line as well as a restricted area at the foot of the slope surrounding the vantage point. 'Inside' and 'outside' pertain to this abstract enclosure in the obvious way, as shown in 8(b)-(c). It should now be evident why the forms *yun*, *mun*, and *un* are excluded: they imply a location that is both 'inside' and 'on top', but the landmark region for 'inside' terminates at the skyline.[14]

(a) ABSTRACT DOMAIN   (b) *u* 'in line of sight'   (c) *a* 'outside line of sight'

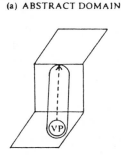

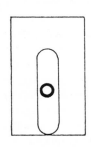
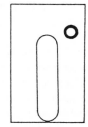

Figure 8.

Figure 9 depicts the semantic value of the topographical particles given in (12). In 9(a) the trajector is located simultaneously at a medial distance from the speaker (*m*), outside the speaker's line of sight up the slope (*a*), and in the face of the slope (*h*). In 9(b) the trajector is proximate to the speaker (*y*), and inside the landmark enclosure (*u*) at the foot of the slope (:). In (c) the trajector is at a distal location from the speaker (∅) on top of the slope (*n*), hence outside the line of sight area (*a*).

(a) *mah* (b) *yuu* (c) *an*

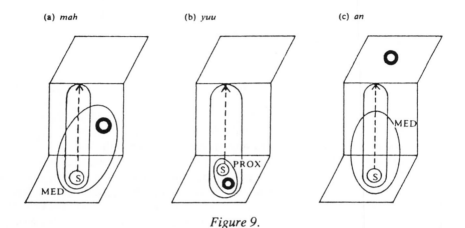

Figure 9.

Presumably these topographical variants of *u* and *a* were extended from the more basic, nontopographical senses of Figure 1. It appears, though, that certain verb prefixes and prefix combinations represent the subsequent extension of topographical predications back into nontopographical domains. The prefix combinations *uh-* and *ah-*, previously exemplified in (2) and (8), are a case in point. Their value in (8), roughly 'on a vertical inside/outside surface' (cf. Figure 3), does not pertain in any way to a line of sight, so they do not necessarily have a topographical origin.[15] On the other hand, a topographical origin is the only plausible means of accounting for their semantic contribution in (2), which does indeed involve a line of sight, as indicated in Figure 10.

The block shape in Figure 10 stands for the body of a dog. Recall that (2a), with *uh-*, describes a dog's tail being chopped short when the dog is viewed from behind, while (2b), with *ah-*, describes the same objective situation when the dog is viewed from the side. The basis for this marking is now apparent. With a hind view, represented in 10(a), the dog's rump is a vertical surface analogous to the face of a slope, and the locus of the verbal relationship (the tail being cut short) lies in the narrow region defined by the line of sight along this surface. With a side view like that in 10(b), by contrast, the dog's flank is functionally equivalent to the slope's face, and the locus of the verbal relationship is consequently off to the side and external to the line of sight region. Another of the apparent problems cited at the outset is therefore resolved.

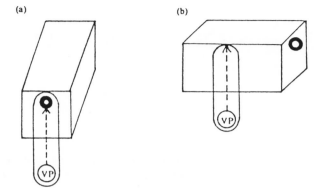

Figure 10.

4. Accessibility

We have now traced two paths of evolution leading from the prototypical values of *u* and *a* depicted in Figure 1: one path includes the meanings represented in Figures 2, 4, and 5, and the other those represented in Figures 8 and 10. Yet a third path of extension can be observed. It stems from the pragmatic consideration sketched in Figure 11, namely that an enclosure often serves as a barrier to perception, or to access more generally. From an external vantage point, an entity that bears an 'inside' relation to another is commonly inaccessible to view, while one that bears an 'outside' relation remains accessible. It is therefore natural that the *u/a* contrast should be extended to mean 'inaccessible'/'accessible', primarily (though not exclusively) with respect to vision. The vertical line in Figure 12 stands for a barrier to perception (or access), and the accessibility of the trajector depends on whether or not it is on the same side of the barrier as the vantage point.

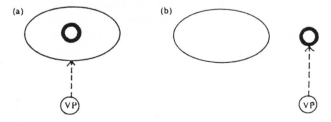

Figure 11.

(a) *u* 'inaccessible'   (b) *a* 'accessible'

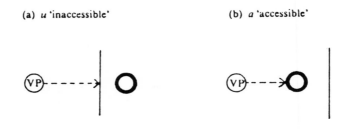

Figure 12.

An example of this semantic contrast is provided by instances where a topographical expression combines with *tavan* 'across the river', as illustrated in (13).

(13) a. *ú-tavan*   *téepi*
    inside:DIST-across:river Tepic
    'off yonder over the river in Tepic'

   b. *á-tavan*   *sáa-ta'a*
    outside:DIST-across:river sand-in
    'off yonder on the beach on the other side of the river'

Once again the *u/a* contrast is defined relative to an abstract domain of some complexity, in this case the one introduced by *tavan*, shown in Figure 13(a). From a vantage point on one side of a river, the viewer's line of sight extends across the river as far as the horizon, which constitutes (by definition) the limit of visual accessibility.[16] The trajector is therefore inaccessible if it lies over the horizon, as in example (13a) (Figure 13(b)), and accessible otherwise, as seen in example (13b) (Figure 13(c)).

One facet of imagery (as previously defined) is our ability to conceive and portray a scene as it appears from different vantage points. The importance of vantage point for linguistic predications is made strikingly clear when the values of *u* and *a* in combination with *tavan* are compared to their values in independent topographical particles (e.g. (13) and (12), respectively). In both instances the *u/a* contrast hinges on position with respect to a line of sight that terminates at the horizon, as shown in Figures 13(a) and 8(a). Yet on first examination, the use of *u* and *a* in the two domains appears to be contradictory: with *tavan*, a trajector that falls within the line of sight is accessible to vision, hence *a* is chosen (cf. Figure 13(c)); however it is *u* that occurs in an independent topographical particle when the trajector occupies the line of sight (cf. Figure 8(b)). This apparent

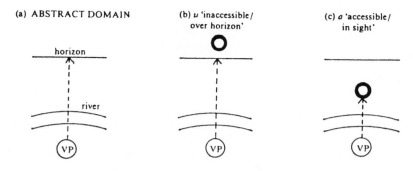

Figure 13.

contradiction is explained by the role that vantage point plays in the two kinds of predication. In particular, the presumed vantage point can itself be either internal or external to a bounded region that constitutes some kind of barrier to perception (or more generally, that delimits the perceptual field in some way). With the independent topographical particles, the vantage point is assumed to be internal to the bounded region. In fact the region is defined in terms of the line of sight from the presumed vantage point, hence everything within the region is accessible to view. The *tavan* expressions, by contrast, presuppose an external vantage point of the sort illustrated in Figure 11, such that something internal to the bounded region is blocked from view. Whether *u* 'inside' corresponds to the trajector being accessible or inaccessible to view therefore depends on whether or not the viewer is also construed as being inside the bounded region (and hence on the same side of the boundary as the trajector).[17]

Accessibility may be one factor motivating the *u/a* contrast in certain examples analyzed previously in terms of 'deep penetration' vs. 'shallow penetration'. In (9b) and (11), *u* could be construed as indicating either that the verbal process (a head filling the crown of a hat, water pouring into a storage jar) penetrates deeply into an enclosure, or else that aspects of the process are hidden from view.[18] In (10) and (3), on the other hand, *a* can be construed as indicating either that the verbal process (water pouring into a pond or basin, hollowing out a log) makes only shallow penetration into an enclosure, or that the entire process is accessible to view. For the most part the two will tend to be correlated, since deep penetration most likely decreases perceptual access. This is further illustrated in (14):

(14) a. *u-ká-kun*
    inside-down-hollow
    'There is a small, deep well there'

b. *a-tʸá-kun*   *m-é*   *čuaa-ta'a*
outside-in:middle-hollow MED-outside dirt-in
'There is a wide-mouthed well dug into the ground there'

The penetration of a hollow area into the ground is clearly involved in both examples, and deepness of the penetration is a far more salient property in the sentence with *u* than the one with *a*.[19] At the same time, though, visual (and other) access to the interior of a wide-mouthed well is considerably greater than for a narrow-mouthed one. A third factor may be involved as well, namely shape. Observe the cultural correlation between containers that are shallow and wide on the one hand, and on the other, containers that are roundish and have only a small opening at the top. Extension of *u/a* to indicate a 'restrictive'/'expansive' contrast with respect to some area is attested elsewhere in the Cora locative system.[20] In cases like this, the *u/a* contrast is therefore motivated by more than one independently established factor, either of which can function separately from the others. It would be pointless to force a choice among them, for it is perfectly plausible to assume that speakers might be influenced by more than one. To insist on a single motivating factor would be gratuitous.

In the examples considered so far, accessibility to view has been controlled by the presence or absence of some kind of boundary or barrier to perception. A further extension along this path is obtained by making accessibility depend instead on the direction in which the viewer is facing. This gives rise to the senses in Figure 14, where the front of the viewer (V) is defined as that side which is oriented to his line of sight. This extension immediately accounts for the expressions in (5) ('right here in back of me' vs. 'right here before my eyes') and therefore resolves another matter that initially seemed problematic. Note that the viewer need not be equated with the speaker, as was the case in (5), but can be some other participant in the scene.

(a) *u* 'inaccessible/in back'   (b) *a* 'accessible/in front'

Figure 14.

We are also in a position now to explicate the sentences in (4), which were problematic because the same general kind of motion along a downhill trajectory can be marked by either *u-* or *a-* on the verb.[21] What proves to be crucial is the verb stem itself: in this particular context involving a downhill path (though not in every context), the prefix combination *u-kda-* is consistently required by *nʸe* 'arrive', while *kɨ* 'go (PL)' consistently takes *a-kǎa-*. The hypothesis to be suggested thus hinges on the semantic contrast between 'arrive' and 'go'. Both involve spatial motion along a path--represented by the heavy arrow in Figure 15--but 'arrive' focuses on the goal or endpoint of the overall trajectory, while 'go' either focuses on its origin or else is neutral in this regard. In Figure 15 an ellipse indicates the focal area of the verbal predication.

(a) *nʸe* 'arrive'   (b) *kɨ* 'go (PL)'

Figure 15.

The basis for the *u/a* choice with these verbs becomes apparent in Figure 16. The arrow at the left in 16(a) and 16(b) simply stands for the vertical axis (relevant because downhill motion in particular is involved). The heavy arrow represents the downhill motion; it is the verbal process in (4), hence it functions as the trajector for the locative prefix combinations *u-kǎa-* and *a-kǎa-*. The mover is both the subject of the sentence (the trajector of the verbal process) and the viewer in terms of which accessibility is assessed. The mover is therefore labeled V in 16, and the dashed arrow indicates his line of sight, which has the same direction as the path of motion. The *u/a* contrast can now be explicated in the following way.

(a) *u-kǎa-nʸe*   (b) *a-kǎa-kɨ*

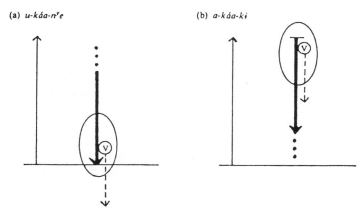

Figure 16.

The pertinent values of *u* and *a* are those in Figure 14, namely 'inaccessible/in back of viewer' vs. 'accessible/in front of viewer', and they pertain to the position of the trajector relative to the viewer while the viewer/mover occupies the focal area within the verbal trajectory. While the viewer is in the focal area of the 'arrive' trajectory, i.e. near the endpoint of the path, most of the verbal trajectory (motion down the hill) lies behind him, and since the verbal process is itself the trajector for the locative prefixes, *u* 'inaccessible/in back of viewer' is the appropriate choice. The situation is reversed when the viewer is in the focal area of the 'go' trajectory, so *a* 'accessible/in front of viewer' is employed because most of the downhill trajectory lies ahead.[22] These examples are rather complex, but it can be seen that our analysis accounts for the *u/a* contrast by means of independently established factors in a way that is fully consistent with the behavior of these elements in other contexts.

The sentences in (15) exemplify yet another sense of *u/a*.

(15) a. *nu-'u-t^{y}í-'aca*   *y-ú*   *n^{y}a-kíca-ta'a*
I-inside-up-have:ulcer PROX-inside my-buttocks-in
'I have a sore right here on my buttock'

   b. *na-'a-rá-'aca*   *y-é*   *n^{y}a-hiise-'e*
I-outside-facing:out-have:ulcer PROX-outside my-eyes-on
'I have a sore right here on my eyelid'

From their value in Figure 14, namely 'in back of viewer'/'in front of viewer', they have been extended to mark the contrast between something being 'on the back side' of some landmark vs. being on its 'face' or 'front'. These meanings are depicted in Figure 17. Sentence (15b) confirms that this semantic extension has indeed occurred and that the meanings in Figure 17 are established by conventional usage as distinct from those in Figure 14 (though closely related to them). A viewer does not have visual access to something on his eyelid, so this location cannot be regarded as a special case of 'accessible/in front of viewer', though their close connection is apparent. For this reason the designation V (viewer) is parenthesized in Figure 17: the role of the landmark as viewer relates not so much to the possibility of the landmark perceiving the trajector on his face or back as it does to the fact that a viewer's 'face' is defined in part as the surface from which his gaze is directed outward.

But objects other than potential viewers can be construed as having a face and hence a front/back alignment. The 'face' of an object can be the side that other entities typically interact with, and in particular the side to which external viewers have canonical visual (and other) access. In the case of humans the two criteria dovetail, since face-to-face interaction is prototypical. To the extent that the landmark is incapable of perception, or incapable of perceiving a given trajector, the characterization of front/back alignment shown in Figure 17 gives way to that

(a) *u* 'on back side'   (b) *a* 'on face/front'

Figure 17.

in Figure 18, where external viewers play a predominant role. There is no necessary conflict between the two, and in many instances they may both be operative. In (15a), for example, the locus of the ulceration can be considered inaccessible to both the subject (who happens to be the speaker) or to some other potential viewer; thus it is on the subject's back side by the criterion of either Figure 17 or Figure 18, and in addition can be considered 'inaccessible' or 'in back' in accordance with the specifications of Figure 14. Once again it would be pointless to choose among these multiple sources of motivation.

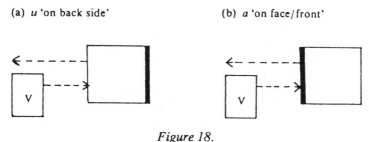

(a) *u* 'on back side'   (b) *a* 'on face/front'

Figure 18.

5. Scope

All of the problematic examples presented at the outset have now been accounted for, with the exception of those in (6). Why should the predication 'there in town' be acceptable with an 'inside' deictic particle when marked distal (*uǐ čahta' a*) but not when marked medial (**mǔ čahta' a*)? And why should the proximal 'right here in town' require an 'outside' form (*ǔya čáhta' a*; **ǔyu čáhta' a*)? An explanation is available, though at this point it must be regarded as tentative in certain respects.

To understand the data, we must first establish two points. One of them has already been touched on, namely the unmarked character of *a* as opposed to *u*. Previous examples indicate that *u* is the marked member of the pair and only occurs when all its conditions are fully satisfied; *a* prevails in neutral or indeterminate cases. This was first observed in regard to (4) and Figure 16: *u* is used for motion when the goal in particular constitutes the focal area, and *a* for neutral motion predications as well as when the origin is in focus. It can also be observed in relation to the topographical particles (cf. Figure 8). We noted that the line of sight up the face of a slope cannot take in the area on top; an 'inside'/'outside' contrast is therefore possible with respect to the line of sight area only when the trajector is at the foot or in the face of the slope. One might expect, then, that the 'inside'/'outside' distinction would not be indicated at all for 'on top' locations, but in fact *a* is always used. The 'outside' region is much more extensive than the 'inside' region and includes even those areas where the possibility of an 'inside'/'outside' contrast does not arise.

The second point to make is that any linguistic predication has a scope, i.e. it pertains to a particular conceived situation or scene that is somehow delimited and restricted in its coverage, whether implicitly or explicitly. The scope may be sharply delimited or only vaguely so, it may be large or small, but only a restricted area within our conceptual universe is included. For example, (13a) situates its trajector in a distant town over the horizon, hence its scope is quite broad, while (13b) locates something on the bank of a river within the line of sight, so its scope may well be restricted to whatever is in view together with the immediate surroundings. The scope of predication is far greater in talking about the position of planets in the solar system than in discussing the arrangement of furniture in a room, even though one might use the same locative predications in each.[23]

Scope will naturally tend to correlate in certain ways with deictic predications of distance from the speaker (Figure 6). With a proximal expression, where something is located in the immediate vicinity of the speaker, the scope of predication is quite likely to be restricted to include the speaker and his near surroundings (there need be no sharp dividing line). On the other hand, scope must be fairly broad (in relative terms) to accommodate a distal predication, and since removal from the speaker is the pivotal notion, scope in a distal predication may extend indefinitely (note (13a)). Obviously there is nothing absolute or fully predictable about these matters, but it is quite possible for natural tendencies like these to become frozen in linguistic convention in various ways. The data in (6) can be explained along these lines.

The distal predication (6a) *ú čahta'a* 'there in town' is sketched in Figure 19(a). The trajector is situated in a town which lies at a distal location from the speaker; this entire configuration falls within the scope of predication. Why is this not also possible when the trajector is medial or proximal to the speaker? 'Inside' predications are not in general precluded at nondistal locations--note *mú či'ita* 'right there (MED) inside the house' in (7a), for instance. The crucial factor is apparently the massive size of a town in relation to the normal scale of human activities. When dealing with a trajector that is immediately adjacent to the speaker (PROX), or only a short distance away (MED), the scope of predication is sufficiently limited that the boundaries of the town essentially fade out of the picture: either they overflow the scope of predication as shown in 19(b), or else they are outside the scope altogether, as in 19(c). Because the trajector fails to be enclosed within a landmark whose boundaries are wholly in the scope of predication, the conditions for an 'inside' relation are not fully and saliently met. Consequently (by default) the unmarked 'outside' relation is invoked, as in (6c) *íiya čáhta'a* 'right here in town'. Only when a town is quite far from the speaker do its boundaries become sufficiently prominent for it to be construed as a clearly delineated enclosure capable of defining an 'inside' relation completely contained within the scope of predication.[24]

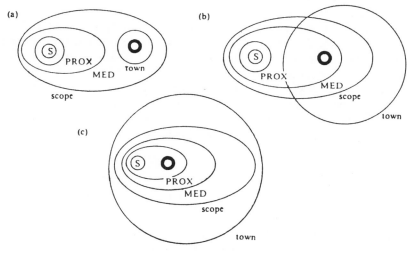

Figure 19.

Corroboration of this analysis is provided by the data in (16).

(16) a. *m-ú-tavan*   *či'i-tá*
      MED-inside-across:river house-in
      'right there across the river inside the house'

   b. **m-ú-tavan*   *ví'ira'a-ta'a*
      MED-inside-across:river cornfield-in
      'right there across the river in the cornfield'

In each case the trajector is to be construed as being across the river from the viewer but on the same side of the horizon and consequently in view. The trajector is therefore 'accessible' and 'in sight' according to the characterization given earlier in Figure 13(c), so *a* 'outside' might be expected instead of *u* 'inside'. *a* can in fact be used, and both expressions in (16) are well formed if *mátavan* is substituted for *mútavan*. Our problem here, then, is to determine why *mútavan* is possible at all in this context, and why it makes a difference whether the trajector is in a house or a cornfield.

The acceptability of (16a) is straightforwardly accounted for by assuming that the prototypical sense of *u* 'inside' (Figure 1) is sometimes permitted in combination with *tavan*, even though the extended sense 'inaccessible/over horizon' (Figure 13) has become established in such expressions. The *u* of (16a) therefore simply means 'inside' and takes the house for its landmark, as shown in Figure 20(a). Why, then, is this not possible in (16b)? The difference derives from the interaction of scope with the boundaries of the landmark, as in the previous example. Because *tavan* serves to locate something more or less directly across the river from the viewer, the scope of predication with *tavan* expressions tends to be a fairly narrow region along the line-of-sight axis, as suggested by the box in Figure 20. A house is reasonably compact, so its boundaries are easily included in a narrow region of this kind and the conditions for an 'inside' relation are fully satisfied. However, a cornfield resembles a town in being broadly extended; its boundaries therefore overflow a narrowly construed scope of predication, as seen in 20(b), making its relation to the trajector an 'outside' one.[25]

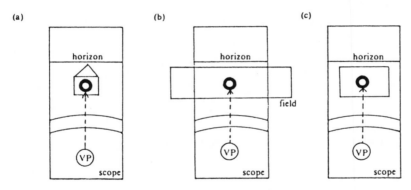

Figure 20.

This analysis makes certain empirical predictions. For example, suppose the viewer is far enough back from the river that the entire cornfield falls within the narrow scope region along the line of sight, as in 20(c). In this event the cornfield becomes equivalent to a house as a compactly bounded region and (16b) should be acceptable. This is indeed the case. The judgment of deviance for (16b) was based on canonical distances and relative sizes and disappears in the more atypical situation where a cornfield can be construed holistically as a compact enclosure. The analysis further predicts that a landmark which extends indefinitely far in either direction cannot give rise to an 'inside' predication in this context regardless of how far back the viewer stands. This prediction is borne out by (13b) *átavan sáata'a* 'off yonder on the beach on the other side of the river'. The 'beach' is a strip of sand along the bank of the river that has no clearly defined endpoints and essentially continues indefinitely. Therefore, even when the viewer (speaker) is far enough back from the river to necessitate a distal predication, as in (13b), the beach still overflows the scope boundaries, resulting in an 'outside' relationship.

6. Implications

We have traced the extension of *u/a* along three distinct paths starting from the presumably prototypical sense of 'inside'/'outside' with respect to a physically bounded landmark of some kind. Along one path we observe specialization to indicate location on an inner vs. outer surface, and then extension to mark deep vs. shallow penetration to the interior (where the surface from which the penetration is made can be actual or only virtual). Another path begins with the adoption of a more abstract landmark region defined in reference to the line of sight up the face of a slope. The resulting 'inside'/'outside' values are then generalized to accommodate the line of sight along any kind of vertical surface. The third path is based on the contrast 'inaccessible'/'accessible', which is related to 'inside'/'outside' by the fact that an entity is often hidden from view when contained inside another. Inaccessibility to view can be due to the presence of some kind of barrier or line of demarcation (e.g. the horizon) beyond which perception is impossible. It can also be due to the orientation of the viewer, so that 'inaccessible'/'accessible' is extended to 'in back'/'in front', where the front/back alignment may be determined with reference to the line of sight of either the landmark itself or an external viewer. A number of points have arisen in the course of this discussion that have general descriptive and theoretical interest. Let us examine some of them briefly by way of conclusion.

To the extent that the analysis is considered appropriate and illuminating, the assumptions outlined in section 1 must be recognized for making it possible. It seems undeniable that the *u/a* contrast must be described in terms of a network of distinct but related senses established by conventional usage and bearing specifiable relationships to one another. It is most improbable that a single abstract meaning can be found that would be schematic for all of the specific values attested for *u* and *a*, and even if one were found it would also be schematic for indefinitely many values that *u* and *a* happen not to have. A linguistic description that limited itself to stating a single meaning for *u* and *a*--whether an all-subsuming schema or the prototypical sense--would therefore fail to provide an explicit account of the facts of the language, in particular the range of conventionally established senses and usages characteristic of these morphemes.[26] Nor is it plausible to treat the various senses as representing distinct, homophonous lexical items. Not only would this fail to account for the parallel grammatical behavior of these putative homophones, but it would also amount to the highly dubious claim that speakers perceive no relations among the various meanings and consider them totally separate lexical items. These are hardly hypothetical alternatives: it is common for linguists to assume (often tacitly) that all the meanings of a lexical item must be predictable from a single basic sense, and that separate lexical items must be posited when no such meaning can be found. This is an unwarranted assumption that creates more problems than it solves. The network model is far more realistic and descriptively adequate, for it permits and in fact requires all of the following: (i) a statement of the full array of conventionally established usages; (ii) a characterization of the relations between individual senses; and (iii) a description (in the form of schemas) of whatever generalizations can be extracted from sets of particular senses. Searching for a single schematic value compatible with all the specific senses of a lexical item is a worthwhile enterprise, but the existence of such a value is by no means a *sine qua non* for a unified and motivated analysis, nor does it obviate the need to describe the full network.

The data presented here is also pertinent to discussions concerning the nature of linguistic semantics. For one thing, it is claimed that meanings are always characterized relative to domains, i.e. knowledge systems or conceived situations of any degree of complexity. For example, the landmark of *u/a* in topographical particles has no objective existence and presupposes for its description the conception of a viewer looking straight up the face of a slope from a position at its foot. Only by evoking this entire complex scene can *u* and *a* be given any value at all in the topographical domain. Moreover, the data illustrates in a sometimes striking manner the importance of imagery in semantic structure: the relative salience of different facets of a scene, the level of specificity at which it is characterized, the figure/ground organization imposed on it, the vantage point from which it is viewed, etc. The meaning of an expression is not given solely (if at all) by the objective properties of the situation it describes--rather it is a function of how speakers construe the situation and structure it by means of specific images. Semantic structure is therefore language-specific to a considerable degree, for the choice of images is a matter of linguistic convention. Every Cora example cited can be shown to differ semantically from its English translation despite their functional equivalence, not least because of the prevalence in Cora of 'inside'/'outside' specifications enhancing the prominence of various relationships that the conventions of English allow one to leave implicit.

Finally, let us review some of the specific descriptive constructs we have found it necessary to invoke. One of these is the notion of correspondences between substructures, permitting the integration of two component semantic structures to form a composite structure in a grammatical construction (cf. Chapter 6). We have seen that numerous linguistic predications, including individual morphemes, presuppose a particular vantage point on the scene they describe as a crucial facet of their inherent semantic value. This vantage point is typically equated with the position of the speaker (where this is possible with no inconsistency), but it need not be in all cases. We further noted that a number of otherwise puzzling examples receive a very natural explanation if one postulates a restricted scope of predication for certain expressions; a landmark entity that overflows the scope boundaries apparently does not sufficiently delimit a bounded region to permit an 'inside' predication relative to it. Lastly, we have found instances where the choice of *u* or *a* can be motivated by more than one factor and taken as instantiating more than one semantic value in the network uniting its various senses. Multiple sanction of this sort is quite common, and it would be misguided to insist that a particular occurrence necessarily reflects one value to the exclusion of all others.

3. Nouns and verbs

Are notional definitions possible for basic grammatical categories?* In particular, can such fundamental categories as "noun" and "verb" be attributed universally valid semantic characterizations? The judgment of contemporary linguistic doctrine on this matter is strongly and unequivocally negative. Textbook writers consequently feel obliged to demolish the naive contrary view,[1] and to establish that such constructs must be defined on grammatical rather than notional grounds. Nevertheless, standard arguments against the possibility of a semantic definition are superficial, and are critically dependent on certain tacit but dubious assumptions. I will try to show that notional descriptions of basic grammatical categories are well within the realm of plausibility, granted an appropriate view of linguistic semantics.

1. Issues

Several points of clarification must preface the main discussion. First, I do not hold that all grammatical classes are strictly definable in notional terms: the claim is specifically made only for nouns, verbs, and their major subcategories (count vs. mass nouns, and the corresponding aspectual subclasses for verbs). The membership of many grammatical categories (e.g. the class of morphologically irregular verbs in English) is essentially arbitrary from a semantic standpoint, and in many other cases meaning is only one of the factors involved, or is less than fully predictive.[2]

To be clear about the intended claim, we must briefly examine alternate models of categorization. Traditionally dominant has been the view that a category is defined by a set of criterial attributes, i.e. necessary and sufficient conditions for class membership. This model is assumed in truth-conditional semantics, which seeks an objective characterization of meaning independent of human conceptualization and cognitive processing. Despite its prevalence, the criterial attribute model has no apriori claim to psychological validity. In fact, recent findings by cognitive psychologists strongly favor an alternative conception: categorization by prototypes, where membership in a category is determined by perceived resemblance to typical instances. Categorization is then a matter of human judgment, and no attributes need be shared by all class members.[3] My own model is a synthesis of categorization by prototypes and by schemas. A schema is an abstract template representing the commonality of the structures it categorizes, which thus elaborate or instantiate it; e.g. the concept [TOOL] bears a relationship of schematicity to such notions as [HAMMER] and [SAW]. A schema differs from a list of criterial attributes in being an integrated concept in its own right--it is simply characterized with lesser specificity and detail than its instantiations.

A semantic definition of the noun or the verb class overall is clearly unattainable if only objective, truth-conditional factors are considered. But the possibility of semantic characterizations limited to the category prototypes is hardly controversial; a number of scholars have suggested that physical objects are prototypical for nouns, and overt physical actions for verbs (cf. Lyons 1968: 318; Givón 1984 (chapter 3); Hopper and Thompson 1984, 1985; Bates and MacWhinney 1982). Though I accept this analysis, and the importance of prototypes in general, I claim that nouns and verbs also lend themselves to schematic semantic characterization--this is the novel (and surely controversial) aspect of the following proposals. More precisely, I maintain that all members of the noun class (not just central members) instantiate an abstract noun schema, while all verbs elaborate an abstract verb schema.

If the schematic characterizations to be proposed are essentially correct, they are no doubt universal rather than language specific. It has of course been questioned whether the noun/verb distinction is valid for all languages, but this is really a nonissue. Even if a language has a single class of stems that function as either nouns or verbs, a stem nevertheless takes on the differentiating properties of one class or the other whenever it is employed in a particular construction. Nothing more is at stake than whether there are grounds for believing that one categorization is "primary" for a given expression.[4]

Finally, there are methodological issues to address. In the orthodox view, basic grammatical categories are defined for a particular language according to their morphosyntactic behavior (e.g. the class of verbs in English might be identified by their ability to inflect for tense and for subject agreement). This is eminently reasonable as a matter of analysis and practical description, since it is the parallel grammatical behavior of a set of expressions that alerts us to their status as a category. However the behavioral properties responsible for our initial discovery of a category must be distinguished from its ultimate characterization. I maintain that the grammatical behavior of the noun or verb class is best regarded as SYMPTOMATIC of its semantic value, not the sole or final basis for a criterial definition.

A fair evaluation of the notions proposed below must consider the coherence and descriptive value of the overall system in which they function. One cannot reasonably expect that the import and motivation of a particular point will be evident when it is examined in isolation, or require that independent psychological evidence must establish the cognitive reality of each individual construct (no linguistic theory satisfies such demands). The semantic contrasts dealt with here are subtle, and are explicated in terms of cognitive operations to which we have no direct or intuitive access. Thus, when I claim that the adjective *like* designates a relation construed atemporally, while the verb *resemble* (or the phrase *be like*) scans this same relationship sequentially through conceived time, there is no way I can prove this claim directly or autonomously. What I can and will argue is that this analysis is part and parcel of a comprehensive descriptive framework in which a substantial array of semantic and grammatical phenomena receive a natural, unified, and revelatory account.

2. Basic concepts

Let us first review some basic concepts. A fundamental claim of cognitive grammar is that all valid grammatical constructs are symbolic in nature. Lexicon, morphology, and syntax form a continuum of symbolic units, each residing in the association of a semantic and a phonological structure. Generalizations are embodied by schematic symbolic structures, which are characterized at varying levels of abstraction and coexist in the linguistic system with any specific structures mastered as familiar units. Schemas are extracted from more specific structures. They categorize such structures through relations of elaboration or extension, and are used for the computation of novel instantiating expressions.

Meaning is equated with conceptualization (in the broadest sense); semantic structures are thus conceptualizations shaped in accordance with linguistic convention. Semantic structures (of any size) are referred to as predications. They are characterized relative to cognitive domains, some of which are basic in the sense of being cognitively irreducible (e.g. our experience of time and space, or fields of perceptual potential such as the range of possible color sensations), while others involve cognitive structures of indefinite complexity. Any cognitive structure--a novel conceptualization, an established concept, a perceptual experience, or an entire knowledge system--can function as the domain for a predication.

Meaning is therefore sought in the realm of cognitive processing. It does not reside in objective reality, nor is the problem of semantic description revealingly formulated in terms of truth conditions. Even expressions describing an objective situation may differ in meaning depending on how the situation is construed. Thus a speaker who accurately observes the spatial distribution of certain stars can describe them in many distinct fashions: as a *constellation*, as a *cluster of stars*, as *specks of light in the sky*, etc. Such expressions are semantically distinct; they reflect the speaker's alternate construals of the scene, each compatible with its objectively given properties. An expression is said to impose a particular image on its domain. The conventionalized images embodied by the symbolic units of a language (both lexical and grammatical) are crucial to their semantic value.

Various dimensions of imagery (i.e. construal) must be recognized, the most significant being the profile/base distinction. The base for a linguistic predication is its domain, i.e. the cognitive structures it presupposes; its profile is a substructure of the base that is elevated to a distinctive level of prominence as the entity which the expression designates. Expressions often invoke the same domain but contrast semantically by choosing alternate profiles within this common base. For instance, the conception of a body of land completely surrounded by water can function as the base for a variety of expressions, simple and composite, that profile (i.e. designate) different aspects of it: *island* profiles the land mass; *the water near the island* designates a portion of the water; *shoreline* profiles the boundary between the two; and so forth.

The scope of a predication is that portion of relevant domains which it specifically invokes and requires for its characterization. Scope boundaries need not be sharply defined: the relevance of domain features may simply fall off gradually the farther they lie from the profiled element. Often, however, their diminution in salience appears to be quantized, occurring in discrete steps. Thus the conception of a finger provides the immediate scope of predication for *knuckle*, since the designatum of *knuckle* is identified in large measure by its position within a finger; the conception of a finger in turn evokes that of a hand (as its own immediate scope), which evokes that of an arm, and so on. It would be incorrect to say that the conception of a hand, an arm, or the body as a whole is irrelevant to the meaning of *knuckle*, but there is a clear intuitive sense in which the conception of a finger comes into play more directly and prominently.

A predication typically invokes multiple domains, which characterize different aspects of the profiled entity. Semantic contrasts often hinge on the inventory of domains, as well as their ranking for relative prominence. For instance, the physical specifications of *bay* and *harbor* are quite comparable, but *harbor* evokes more saliently than *bay* its role as a haven for ships. *Roe* and *caviar* both designate a mass of fish eggs. Granted the encyclopedic view of meaning, part of the overall sense of *roe* is that the profiled substance is sometimes processed to make caviar, while part of the meaning of *caviar* is that it is made from fish eggs. However, the two predications differ in the ranking of their shared domains: the knowledge system relating to fish reproduction is a "primary" domain for *roe*, while *caviar* gives higher rank to domains pertaining to food, consumption, and social status.

Other dimensions of imagery can be briefly noted. One is the level of specificity at which a predication characterizes a scene. The central parameter here is "grain" or "resolution": a schema describes a structure with lower resolution (coarser grain) than do its instantiations (e.g. *tree* vs. *eucalyptus*). Another dimension of imagery is the impact of explicit mention on the relative prominence of substructures; in *pig meat*, for example, the overt occurrence of *pig* renders this notion more salient than it is in *pork* (though it is included in both). A third dimension is figure/ground organization, which I impute to the subject/object distinction and other grammatical phenomena (cf. Talmy 1978; Wallace 1982). It is thus a primary factor in the contrast between pairs like *above* and *below*, or between an active and a passive clause (Chapter 4). Further dimensions of imagery include presumed vantage point (e.g. *come* vs. *go*); construal relative to different background assumptions and expectations (*half empty* vs. *half full*); and the subjective directionality manifested in contrasting sentences like *The roof slopes upward* vs. *The roof slopes downward.*

In the context of a conceptualist semantics which accommodates conventional imagery, standard arguments against the semantic basis of fundamental grammatical classes lose most of their force. One such argument is that either a noun or a verb can be used to describe the same event (e.g. *explode* and *explosion*). Tacitly but crucially assumed is the objectivist view that the meaning of an expression is independent of human conception, being fully determined by the situation it describes. Rejecting this view, one can argue that the noun and verb construe the event with contrasting images and are therefore semantically distinct (i.e. nominalization involves some type of conceptual reification). I will later give this claim some substance with reference to plausible assumptions about cognitive processing.

Another standard argument runs as follows: "If the class of nouns is semantically defined, what might the definition be? The only obvious possibility is that nouns are the names of physical objects (alternatively: people, places, and things). However, many nouns do not name physical objects or anything even remotely resembling them. A notional definition is therefore unworkable." The difficulty with this line of argument is that it confuses different models of categorization. Physical objects represent the noun category prototype; a description based on the prototype cannot be expected to apply without modification to both central and peripheral members. A characterization directly applicable to all class members will necessarily be highly schematic, accommodating physical objects as a special (though privileged) case. Proposing such a characterization will be our first order of business.

3. Bounding

As a first approximation, I offer the schematic characterizations in (1).

(1) a. A "noun" designates a "region" in some domain.
  b. A "count noun" designates a "bounded region" in some domain.

Observe that these descriptions make no reference at all to physical objects. Such objects are bounded in space, and hence qualify as count nouns under (1b), but there are indefinitely many other domains in which bounding can occur. The basic plausibility of defining count nouns in this fashion can be established by considering some representative examples (for mass nouns, see section 5).

Some count nouns are defined relative to basic domains. *Moment, instant,* and *period* are reasonably described as designating bounded regions in time. Among the many nouns that profile bounded regions in two-dimensional space are *point, line, circle, triangle, rectangle,* and the more schematic *polygon*; comparable terms for three-dimensional space include *sphere, cube, cylinder, cone, pyramid,* etc.[5] In certain nominal uses (e.g. *Blue is my favorite color*), color expressions designate bounded regions in color space. *Streak, spot, splotch,* and *blur* refer to visual configurations of limited expanse; their primary domain is the extensionality of the visual field.

A noun like *beep, blip,* or *flash* requires a combination of basic domains. A *beep* involves both time and pitch, and is bounded in both domains: it must be quite short, and it must to some degree approximate a pure tone (white noise would not qualify). Time, color space, and the visual field all figure in *blip* and *flash,* which contrast in regard to their bounding in these domains. A blip is fairly sharply bounded in the visual field, but its temporal limits are less precise; while certainly judged to be a transient event, for some speakers it may endure for a considerable length of time. A flash, on the other hand, must be virtually instantaneous, hence sharply bounded in time. However it need not be bounded at all in the visual field. A brief light sensation which totally suffuses the visual field--so that no boundaries at all are perceived in this domain--can nevertheless be recognized as a flash.

We learn from this contrast that a count noun need not specify bounding in every prominent domain. If the bounding required for count-noun status is an index of primacy, then time ranks above the visual field for *flash*, while the visual field is primary for *blip*. Nor do count nouns necessarily specify bounding in every dimension of their primary domain. A *line*, for instance, is severely bounded along one axis of two-dimensional space, but along the other axis it extends indefinitely. Similarly, a *stripe, horizon, road, river, edge, boundary,* or *shore* is unproblematically identified as such even when no endpoints are apparent, i.e. when it extends beyond the scope of predication in both directions of its long axis. This is quite analogous to the light sensation of a flash totally suffusing the visual field.

Instructive in another way are terms like *arc* and *hypotenuse*. What is their domain? We cannot describe them directly with respect to undifferentiated two-dimensional space: an arc cannot be identified as such except with reference to a circle, and a line segment must be construed in relation to a right triangle before it constitutes a hypotenuse. The respective domains for *arc* and *hypotenuse* are consequently the concept of a circle and of a right triangle; each expression profiles a bounded region within this conceived entity. Because the presupposed entities are themselves two-dimensional configurations, there is a sense in which an arc or hypotenuse also inhabits the spatial domain--but this relationship is mediated by the conception of a circle or right triangle, which constitutes the primary domain and immediate scope of predication.

Analogous cases abound. Nouns like *January, Tuesday, hour, month,* and *year* are not characterized directly with respect to the basic domain of time. Instead they designate bounded regions in nonbasic domains consisting of abstract constructs (e.g. the calendrical cycle) which are devised to track and measure its passage. Similarly, the domain for a term like *C-sharp, B-flat,* or *F* is not to be equated with the basic pitch domain per se, but rather with a musical scale constructed with reference to this basic domain.[6] We have already seen that *knuckle, finger, hand, arm,* etc. receive their primary value by virtue of their position within a more inclusive portion of the body (or the body as a whole). They constitute bounded regions in three-dimensional space only derivatively, via the status of the body as a physical object.

A few more examples from nonbasic domains will suffice. The performance of a play provides the domain for count nouns such as *act, scene, line, prolog,* and *intermission.* Terms like *chapter, page, paragraph,* and *sentence* designate bounded regions within a written work. For restricted portions of athletic events, we have the expressions *period, quarter, half, inning, round, frame,* and *down.* Nouns like these could be proliferated indefinitely. They refer not to physical objects, but rather to more abstract entities that are nevertheless bounded regions in an intuitively obvious sense.

Several points must be made concerning bounding. For one thing, the bounding that defines a count noun cannot be merely the default-case limitation resulting from a restricted scope of predication. To illustrate this, let us assume that the frame *I see NP* imposes on the direct object nominal a local scope of predication that coincides with the extension of the visual field. Suppose, first, that I am looking at a white wall some 30 feet away, and that painted on this wall is a solid-red circle about 5 feet in diameter. In this context I can felicitously say *I see a red spot,* for I see not only the region painted red but also the background of white that defines its boundaries. The fact that these boundaries are included within the scope of predication (i.e. the visual field) is responsible for my construing the red sensation as a bounded region (rather than simply a region); the count noun *spot* is thus appropriate. But suppose, now, that I stand right up against the wall and stare at the middle of the red-painted region, so that I can see no white at all--the red sensation totally fills my visual field. In this situation I cannot felicitously say *I see a red spot.*[7] Instead I would say *I see (nothing but) red* (where *red* functions as a mass noun). The color sensation is limited by the extent of my visual field, but this is not itself sufficient to qualify it as a bounded region. Bounding WITHIN (not just BY) the scope of predication therefore appears to be pivotal for the count/mass distinction.

A second point is that the bounding implied by a count noun need not be precise or sharply defined. *January* is more precisely bounded than *season,* and *navel* more precisely than *midsection,* but all of these impute boundaries of at least a fuzzy sort to their profiled regions. This type of imprecision in bounding must be distinguished from another, which results from schematicity. Observe, for instance, that *note* is schematic and *F-sharp* is specific, but both are construed as points on a musical scale and thus have precise boundaries. The difference is that only those of *F-sharp* are identified (i.e. a particular point on the scale is singled out). Compare this contrast with the one between *center (of the room)* and *place (within the room).* Here both predications have fuzzy boundaries--in fact, the designated region is quite variable in extent, ranging from a point to an area including well over half the reference object (room)--but this region is limited nonetheless. Despite this flexibility, *center* is fairly specific (only a particular class of regions qualify), while *place* is schematic (any location is permitted).

Finally, I must emphasize that bounding is a function of how we construe the conceived entity, and is not invariably motivated by objective considerations. A *spot on the rug* may be delimited perceptually as a region of discoloration, but when *spot* simply means 'location' the same expression designates an area whose bounding need have no objective basis whatever. The boundary implied by a count noun may therefore, at the extreme, be "virtual" in its entirety--it is imputed rather than observed. Less drastically, the "closure" phenomenon is often responsible for completing a boundary that is only partially suggested by objective factors. In Figure 1(a), for example, we see that virtual bounding (indicated by the dashed line) defines one side of the region designated by *bump* (cf. *bulge, protrusion, welt, hump, mound*, and so on). The same is true for *dent*, sketched in 1(b) (also for terms like *hole, depression, pit, cavity, cave*, and many others). Nouns for containers (*jar, pot, tub, vat, box*, etc.) are frequently construed with a virtual boundary in a way that permits the use of *in* for the configuration of 1(c) (cf. Herskovits 1985, 1986, 1988; Vandeloise 1984). Finally, the closure indicated in 1(d) effects the bounding that figures in *archipelago* and similar expressions (e.g. *forest, orchard, swarm*).

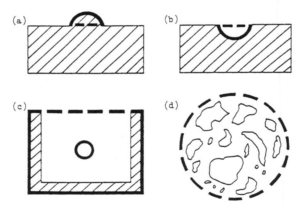

Figure 1.

4. Interconnection

While the proposed definition straightforwardly accommodates a vast array of count nouns, there are others to which its application seems problematic. For example, in what sense does a *team* constitute a bounded region? A team can be recognized as such even if its members are scattered about the playing field and intermingled with the opposition. Similarly, a *constellation* need not consist of stars that are spatially contiguous: they can be distributed over a substantial reach of the nighttime sky and interspersed with extraneous stars. If an *alphabet* is construed as a bounded region, what is it bounded from?

The term bounded region has a spatial origin, which naturally colors our intuitive understanding of the notion. What examples like *team, constellation*, and *alphabet* show is that a quasi-spatial construal will not in general prove adequate for count nouns. We must therefore define the term explicitly in a way that transcends the limitations suggested by its provenience. At the requisite level of abstraction, a region need not have the continuous extensionality of space, nor does bounding necessarily imply anything like a shape.

To achieve a workable definition, we must consider not only conceptualization per se, but also the cognitive processing responsible for it. I assume that any mental experience is constituted by the occurrence of some "cognitive event"--i.e. some pattern of neural activation--which may be novel, or may represent the activation of an established cognitive routine. I further assume that cognitive events can be coordinated to form higher-order events, and that events of arbitrary complexity can be progressively assembled in this fashion. Thus, when I conceive of a star in the sky (whether through perception, recall, or imagination), some kind of cognitive event occurs that constitutes this mental experience. When I conceive of two stars in spatial proximity to one another, the responsible event is more complex: two events of the first type occur, together with a coordinating operation that registers their spatial divergence and assesses its magnitude.

I will speak of conceived entities being "interconnected" when the cognitive events that constitute them are coordinated as components of a higher-order event. The stars in a constellation are therefore interconnected, not by virtue of any objective relationship, but rather because some observer executes a cognitive routine that construes them as points in the outline of a fancied schematic image. The letters in an alphabet are similarly interconnected: both locally, via our knowledge of successor relations (e.g. one's ability to give B as the successor of A resides in a cognitive routine incorporating the conceptions of A and B as subroutines); and more globally, through our well-rehearsed ability to recite various hierarchically organized strings of letters, including the alphabet as a whole.

We may now define a "region" as a set of interconnected entities. A region is "bounded" (along a certain dimension) when there is a limit to the set of participating entities (i.e. it does not extend indefinitely). A constellation is thus a region because its component stars are interconnected through a cognitive routine effecting their coordination as points in a schematic image. It is a bounded region because only a particular, limited set of stars are incorporated in the figure--spatial contiguity is incidental, and other stars in the same area of the sky are excluded.

The members of a team are interconnected by virtue of their role as participants in the conceived relationship of cooperative effort toward a common goal. Though lacking a shape in the spatial sense, a team is bounded because its members are specifically conceived only as cooperating with one another (not necessarily with other individuals). An alphabet is bounded because particular letters are designated as the initial and final elements of the sequence; reference to external entities is not essential.

There are many other count nouns of this sort: *orchestra, trio, family, place setting, jigsaw puzzle, corporation, deck (of cards), set (of tools), litter (of kittens), fleet (of ships), audience, (professional) society,* etc. Each profiles a limited collection of discrete elements that cohere as a region because they are conceived as interacting parts of a larger entity deriving its unitary character through functional (rather than structural) considerations.

One might object that the proposed characterization is impermissibly broad. After all, a set of entities need only co-occur in some conceptualization to be interconnected and thus established as a region; virtually anything has the potential to be so construed. This abstract definition of a region, however, is not per se intended to be either restrictive or predictive for the class of nouns. While every noun is claimed to profile a region in some domain, not every potential region is specifically recognized as such or achieves any substantial cognitive salience. The likelihood of a given region being singled out for special prominence as the profile of a noun is presumably determined by a variety of additional factors, e.g. optimality as a region (based on density and minimal distance of interconnections),[8] communicative utility, and approximation to the category prototype.

How does this abstract definition of a region apply to the examples considered above? Two points are essential. First, the term "entity" is used in a maximally general way, as a cover term for anything we might conceive of or have occasion to refer to for analytical purposes: things, relations, sensations, interconnections, points on a scale, locations in the visual field, etc. Crucially, when I describe something as an entity I do not thereby imply that it is discrete, that it is separately recognized, or that it achieves any substantial cognitive salience. Consider again a red spot painted on a white wall. The entities that constitute the spot are color sensations associated with various locations in the visual field, but it is not suggested that the viewer perceives an array of individual red dots at any stage or level of processing.[9] I merely claim that input from throughout the visual field is coordinated in some fashion to yield the spatially extended color sensation.

Second, I assume that any concept involving continuous extension along some parameter intrinsically requires a train of cognitive events whose sequenced occurrence constitutes the conception of this extensionality. Thus the conception of a line is said to incorporate, at some level of processing, a sequence of events representing its continuous one-dimensional extensionality, and the perception of a red spot includes chains of events establishing the omnidirectional continuity of the red sensation throughout a region of the visual field. Though I refer to these event chains as "scanning" operations, they do not necessarily define the focus of conscious attention. I regard them instead as relatively low-level operations, essentially automatic and ubiquitous in active domains.

Granted these notions, we can readily describe the count nouns of section 3 as designating sets of interconnected entities. The entities comprising a *beep*, for example, are sound sensations distributed through a limited period of time. They are interconnected by virtue of the perceptual operations that render them a unified auditory experience, i.e. a continuous sound episode (as opposed to unrelated sound fragments). The conceptualization of a physical object involves some reference to the continuous spatial extension of its material substance. By assumption, such reference is provided by scanning chains: they trace the spatial expanse of the object's substance, and in fact their very occurrence constitutes the conception of its continuity and extensionality. When one conceives the spatial expanse of a *dent, cavity*, or *pit*, or the temporal expanse of an *intermission*, scanning chains trace the extensionality of a more abstract entity, namely the absence of a certain substance or activity.

5. Count vs. mass nouns

We have seen that the bounding which establishes a given predication as a count noun may be limited to a particular domain (or even a particular dimension in a domain), and further, that the relevant boundary must fall within the scope of predication. Definition (1b) can therefore be revised as (2a), and (2b) can be suggested for mass nouns.

(2) a. A "count noun" designates a region that is bounded within the scope
    of predication in its primary domain.
  b. A "mass noun" designates a region that is NOT specifically bounded
    within the scope of predication in its primary domain.

This concept of mass nouns is, I believe, valid. Recall the situation where a large red spot is seen from up close (so that red totally fills the visual field); (2b) correctly predicts the appropriateness of expressions like the following, with a mass noun as direct object: *I see ({nothing but/a lot of}) red*. The designated color sensation is unbounded within the visual field, which is both the primary domain and the scope of predication.

For purposes of count/mass categorization, the primary domain is that in which different instantiations of the category can occur and be identified; it is also the domain of quantification. For physical substances (our immediate focus of attention), the primary domain is space. It is important to observe, moreover, that the definitions in (2) apply at the level of the lexical head, not that of the noun phrase as a whole. Spatial bounding is therefore not precluded for the substance designated by a mass noun: (2b) implies only that the noun itself does not impose it. The noun *water*, for instance, profiles a substance of indefinite spatial expanse, but whether this absence of bounding survives at the noun-phrase level depends on other factors. When nothing in the linguistic or situational context suggests any limitations on the extent of the designated mass, the result is a generic construal, as in (3a) (cf. Smith 1964):

(3) a. *Water is the topic of her term paper.*
   b. *I drank water with lunch yesterday.*

More commonly, though, the noun phrase designates a limited volume of the substance. This interpretation can be imposed by quantifiers (*some water; a lot of water; two gallons of water*), by definite determiners and modifiers (*this water; the water in that pond*), or by pragmatic considerations, as in (3b).

Thus count nouns specify bounding in their primary domain, while mass nouns lack this stipulation. Bounding, however, is only one of several factors that distinguish count and mass nouns: others include "homogeneity", "expansibility/ contractibility", and "replicability". These factors are interdependent, and can in fact be regarded as different manifestations of the same fundamental contrast. I will begin by arguing that the substance designated by a mass noun is construed as being internally homogeneous.

The bounded region profiled by a count noun is typically heterogeneous. This is not, however, an invariant feature of the class: in cases like *spot, beep, pond, bump, intermission*, etc., the designated region may well display internal uniformity out to its boundaries. The differences among count nouns in this regard correlate with different ways in which their bounding is achieved. For expressions like *bicycle, cat, pencil, piano*, and *constellation*, internal configuration alone imposes limitations on the constitutive set of interconnected entities; e.g. a bicycle has distinct parts arranged in a specific fashion, and its identification is crucially dependent on the satisfaction of these specifications. The same cannot be true when the designated region is homogeneous. In the absence of distinguishing internal features, the major burden of delimitation necessarily falls on contrast with surroundings (e.g. silence in the case of *beep*).

The homogeneity of mass-noun referents is not self-evident, since even collections of heterogeneous objects are tolerated as class members (e.g. *livestock, furniture*). At issue, though, is conceived (rather than objective) homogeneity. Speakers aware of the internal diversity of a substance are nevertheless capable of construing it as homogeneous, and the resulting image can be conventionalized as the semantic value of a predication. Two dimensions of imagery are especially relevant: scope of predication, and level of schematicity.

The substances designated by mass nouns vary with respect to the individuation and salience of their constitutive entities. At one extreme are essentially continuous substances, where any individuation is purely extrinsic: *water, glue, aluminum, glass, air,* etc. Other substances are composed of many individual particles, all of which are basically identical. The salience of these constitutive particles increases with size: *dust, sand, buckshot, corn, grass, gravel, asparagus, tile, cattle, timber.* The individuation is greatest in cases like *equipment, livestock,* and *furniture,* where the component elements are not only quite large, but also of diverse character.

Objectively, no two constituents of a substance are ever identical down to the smallest detail. Sufficiently close examination will always reveal some point of difference between any two drops of water, grains of sand, kernels of corn, blades of grass, head of cattle, or pieces of furniture. Often, though, we remain unaware of such differences, or else we ignore them for linguistic purposes. We generally conceive of such entities schematically, i.e. at a level of abstraction that neutralizes their distinguishing properties. A schematic characterization of this sort is possible even for examples like *furniture*: the component elements fall within a certain size range (e.g. a typical ashtray is too small to qualify); they are permanent artifacts in a dwelling; they are potentially movable, rather than intrinsic parts of the dwelling itself (a bookcase is a piece of furniture, but built-in shelves are not); there is a certain commonality in their function (e.g. tools are excluded); and so on.

The constitutive elements of a mass are therefore equivalent when construed at an appropriate level of schematicity, and a mass noun characterizes them at such a level. Observe, however, that the identity of component elements does not guarantee strict homogeneity: this requires continuity, which is precluded by any notable degree of individuation. In a patch of *grass*, for example, there are spaces between the individual blades, so that random sampling at different locations does not yield uniform results. We can resolve this apparent problem by attributing to the noun a scope of predication that is sufficiently large in relation to individual members of the mass. *Grass* evokes the conception of an extremely large number of blades distributed quite densely and more or less evenly over an extended area. This mass is homogeneous in the sense that any reasonably-sized subregion selected for examination will itself be filled with many blades distributed in comparable fashion. The categorization of *grass* as a mass noun derives from this canonical conception, which emphasizes the uniformity that emerges when the mass is examined on a particular scale.

Because of its conceived homogeneity, the substance designated by a mass noun can be expanded or contracted indefinitely without affecting its class membership. Down to some lower limit (beyond which the integrity of the substance is not preserved), any portion of a mass qualifies as a valid instance of the category (cf. Carlson 1981). The substance that fills a bay is *water*, but so is any subpart I select for examination (e.g. a bucketful scooped out at random) or a more inclusive mass like the ocean as a whole. By contrast, it is not generally true that any subpart of a count-noun referent is itself an instance of the nominal category. The tail of a cat is not a cat, a piece of pencil lead is not a pencil, and the sequence MNOPQ is not the alphabet.

For the instantiation of a count-noun category, incrementation is achieved by the addition of discrete instances. I refer to this property as replicability; its linguistic reflexes include countability and pluralization.[10] The bounding of count nouns, whether achieved through internal configuration or contrast with surroundings, is responsible for their replicability: because there is some limit to the set of interconnected entities constituting the designated region, there is a point at which one instance of the category is exhausted, so that further incrementation results in the initiation of another instance. Mass nouns are nonreplicable (do not pluralize) because there is no such limit, i.e. they are indefinitely expansible. Incrementing a valid instance of a mass-noun category does not serve to initiate a second, distinct instance, but simply to make the first instance larger. Thus we speak of *more sand* but *another hammer*. Note also *the water in those two lakes*, where *water* remains singular when *lake* undergoes replication.

The relatedness of the four distinguishing properties should now be apparent. Bounding prevents indefinite expansion, and also contraction (since the boundary itself is necessary to an instance of a count-noun category). Heterogeneity forecloses the possibility of any subpart being equivalent to any other, and thus rules out expansibility/contractibility. Heterogeneity can itself be crucial to bounding; even in cases like *spot*, which shows internal homogeneity, the line of contrast that delimits the boundary can be regarded as introducing a measure of heterogeneity. Finally, replicability depends on bounding, and is incompatible with indefinite expansibility.

Supporting the definitions in (2) are nouns of dual categorization which differ in semantic value according to their count- or mass-noun status. The mass noun *rock*, for instance, names a substance of indefinite expanse, while *a rock* designates a discrete, bounded object composed of this substance. Other examples of this type include *brick, stone, fur, hide, glass, cloth, rope, wire, diamond, cake, meatloaf, steak,* and so on. *Tile* is particularly instructive, having three common values: (i) as the name of an undifferentiated substance, it functions as a mass noun; (ii) as a count noun, it designates a relatively small, discrete object composed of that substance; and (iii) by putting together a large number of such objects, we obtain a material of indefinite expanse that is also called *tile* in a mass-noun use. Since each sense presupposes and incorporates the one that precedes, I will say that they represent different "levels of conceptual organization". Our capacity for entertaining conceptions involving multiple levels of organization will be crucial in later discussion.

Given proper circumstances, almost any count noun can be construed as designating a homogeneous, unbounded mass and thereby come to function as a mass noun grammatically. Consider these examples:

(4) a. *After I ran over the cat with our car, there was cat all over the driveway.*
   b. *I don't like shelf--I'd rather eat table.*
   c. *When he finished using his knife to tunnel through the stone wall, it had very little blade left.*

In (4a), the unfortunate cat loses its structural integrity through the accident, being converted into an effectively homogeneous substance. (Though a single cat will yield only a limited quantity of this substance, the internal properties of the mass do not impose any inherent limit on its potential expanse.) Example (4b), it has been noted, would be conceivable if uttered by one intelligent termite to another. Here the mass-noun status of *shelf* and *table* reflects both function and scope of predication. For purposes of consumption, the overall configuration of a shelf or a table is less important than the qualitative properties of the substance comprising it. Moreover, a termite is so small relative to such objects that their boundaries can be expected to fall outside the scope of predication, if this latter is adjusted to the typical scale of termite experience. Finally, (4c) is less concerned with the blade as an integral, functional whole than with its diminishing size. In effect its spatial expanse is construed as a quantifiable substance.

Also compatible with (2) is a familiar pattern whereby the mass-noun term for a beverage is employed as a count noun designating a limited quantity (single serving) of that beverage: *I'll have a {beer/whisky/ginger ale/gin and tonic}*. Another familiar pattern of extension permits the term for a substance to function as a count noun indicating a particular type or brand of that substance: *a fine wine; a hard steel; a good glue; a tasty beer*. This second pattern merits closer scrutiny, since the count-noun status of such examples does not reflect the imposition of any quantitative limits or spatial bounding. The present framework nevertheless affords a natural and revealing analysis.

A term like *wine*, which designates a physical substance, obviously requires numerous domains for its semantic characterization. Its primary domain is space --note that quantifying expressions (*some, a lot of, more*, etc.) pertain to its physical volume. *Wine* is categorized as a mass noun, then, because the designated substance is indefinitely expansible (hence unbounded) in this domain. To be sure, a substance like *wine* is bounded in the sense of being distinguished from other kinds of substances. It is convenient in this regard to speak of "quality space", defined as those domains responsible for the qualitative differentiation of one substance from another. In the case of liquids, for example, the domains of quality space include such parameters as viscosity, color, degree of transparency, dimensions pertaining to taste and smell, etc. The notion of quality space is schematized in Figure 2(a). Only three parameters are explicitly indicated, labeled P_1, P_2, and P_3. A particular type of substance, such as wine, is limited to a certain range of values along each parameter, given here as W_1, W_2, and W_3. Collectively these values define a bounded region W in quality space that characterizes the permissible range of variation for the category and sets it apart from other substances.

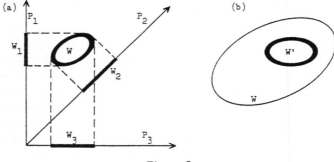

Figure 2.

A substance term like *wine*, in its basic mass-noun sense, therefore manifests a disparity between its primary domain (physical space) and the set of domains for which intrinsic bounding can be posited (quality space). Given this description, how can we characterize the semantic extension giving rise to the count-noun sense wherein *wine* means something akin to 'brand/type of wine'? Two factors figure in this extension. First, there is a reranking of domains; because the extended sense focuses on qualitative concerns, it is reasonably described as elevating quality space to the status of primary domain.[11] Second, there is a shift in profiling and scope of predication, as sketched in Figure 2(b). The region W profiled by *wine* in its basic sense is adopted as the immediate scope of predication for its extended value. The profile is an arbitrary bounded region W' that is properly included within this immediate scope W. The resulting sense of *wine* designates a bounded region within the scope of predication in the primary domain, making it a count noun in accordance with (2a). Moreover, since W' is arbitrarily chosen, there are many subregions of W that might be intended as the designatum on a given occasion (i.e. there are many possible types or brands of wine). Since W' is not unique, *wine* in this count-noun sense is a common rather than a proper noun and behaves accordingly (e.g. it pluralizes and occurs with determiners).

6. Relations

Most broadly, the meanings of linguistic expressions divide themselves into "nominal" vs. "relational" predications. These two types do not necessarily differ in the nature of their intrinsic content (consider *circle* and *round*, or *explode* and *explosion*), but rather in how this content is construed and profiled. A nominal predication presupposes the interconnections among a set of conceived entities, and profiles the region thus established. On the other hand, a relational predication presupposes a set of entities, and profiles the interconnections among these entities.

For illustration, consider the contrast between the relational predication *together* and the nominal predication *group*. Let us assume that both are construed as involving precisely three individuals, whose togetherness or status as a group is based on spatial proximity. By assumption, then, the conceptual content of *together* and *group* is essentially the same; the semantic distinction between them (and hence their membership in different grammatical categories) depends on the contrasting images they impose on this content, notably with respect to profiling.

Let $[e_1]$, $[e_2]$, and $[e_3]$ stand for those cognitive events whose occurrence constitutes the conception of the three participating individuals (taken separately). Further, let $[e_4]$, $[e_5]$, and $[e_6]$ stand for the coordinating operations responsible for establishing interconnections between each pair of participating individuals; in the present case, these operations amount to assessments of spatial proximity--e.g. $[e_4]$ is the cognitive operation that registers the spatial proximity of the individuals whose conception resides in the occurrence of $[e_1]$ and $[e_2]$. Figure 3(a) then diagrams the essential conceptual content shared by *together* and *group*, expressed in terms of the requisite cognitive events. This entire complex of events figures in the conceptualization of either notion.

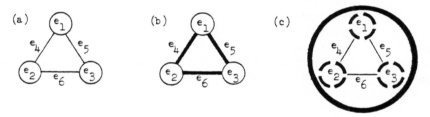

Figure 3.

As a relational predication, *together* presupposes the entities corresponding to $[e_1]$, $[e_2]$, and $[e_3]$, and profiles the interconnections among them. The special prominence characteristic of profiling--indicated by heavy lines--is accorded in Figure 3(b) to the coordinating operations $[e_4]$, $[e_5]$, and $[e_6]$, which represent the pairwise assessments of spatial proximity. By definition, these interconnections establish a region comprising $[e_1]$, $[e_2]$, and $[e_3]$. It is precisely this region that the nominal predication *group* puts in profile, as shown in Figure 3(c): the interconnecting operations are incorporated as unprofiled facets of the base, while $[e_1]$, $[e_2]$, and $[e_3]$ receive the heightened prominence of profiling. However, they achieve this salience collectively, not individually; the dashed-line circles indicate that they are profiled only as facets of region $[[e_1][e_2][e_3]]$, which is depicted by the solid-line circle and constitutes a higher level of conceptual organization.

Relational predications are therefore not distinguished by their inherent conceptual content, but rather by their profiling of interconnections. We can think of interconnections as cognitive operations that assess the relative magnitude or position of conceived entities within a domain. Consider the adjective *parallel* (as in *A is parallel to B*). Our conception of the profiled relationship must incorporate cognitive events that register the spatial discrepancy between two lines. We may speculate that the requisite events include at least the following: scanning operations, which assess the distance between pairs of directly opposite points on the two lines; and comparison of these scanning operations with respect to their magnitude, which proves the same for every sampled pair. But whatever its actual character, this complex of events is virtually instantaneous, and we experience our conception as a single gestalt.

Recall that every relational predication shows an asymmetry in the prominence accorded the entities that participate in the profiled interconnections: some participant is singled out and construed as the one whose nature or location is being assessed. This participant is called the trajector (tr) and analyzed as the figure within the relational profile.[12] The term landmark (lm) is applied to other salient participants, with respect to which the trajector is situated. The choice of trajector is not mechanically determined by a predication's content, but is rather one dimension of conventional imagery. Indeed, the asymmetry is observable even for expressions that designate a symmetrical relationship. Thus *X resembles Y* and *Y resembles X* are not semantically equivalent: in the former, Y (the landmark) is taken as a standard of reference for evaluating X (the trajector); in the latter these roles are reversed.

Participants which represent different levels of conceptual organization are capable of functioning as trajectors. In *A is parallel to B*, scanning operations presumably associate particular points along the two lines, but one of the lines as a whole, namely A, achieves the status of relational figure. Now by definition, the profiled interconnections establish A and B as a higher-level region, [AB], with the potential to be recognized as such for linguistic purposes. This happens in sentences of the form *A and B are parallel*: region [AB] is not only the profile of the subject nominal *A and B*, but also the trajector of *(are) parallel*. As a consequence, the interconnections profiled by the latter do not hold between the trajector [AB] and some external landmark--instead they associate subparts of the trajector. The same is true of many relational predications, most obviously shape expressions. The adjective *square*, for instance, invokes the conception of four line segments (A, B, C, and D) joined pairwise at their endpoints, and profiles the interconnecting operations that register their parallelism, perpendicularity, and equal length. The adjectival trajector is the higher-level region [ABCD] established by these operations, which therefore relate various subparts of the trajector to one another. The noun *square* has the same conceptual content as the adjective, but instead of the interconnections it profiles region [ABCD].

The trajector and landmark of a relational predication can be of various sorts.

Consider the boldface expressions in (5):

(5) a. *The chandelier is **above** the buffet table.*
   b. *Some guests left **before** the dancing started.*
   c. *Timothy really works **fast**.*

In (5a), the trajector and landmark of *above* are both regions, and are thus instantiated by nominal expressions (*the chandelier* and *the buffet table*, respectively). The profiled interconnections specify that the trajector is displaced farther from the vertical origin than is the landmark, while their horizontal projections roughly coincide.[13] In (5b), *before* designates a relationship of precedence in the temporal domain between two events, which are represented by finite clauses. Hence its trajector (*some guests left*) and landmark (*the dancing started*) are themselves both relational. The domain for *fast* in (5c) is the conception that activities vary along the parameter of rate. Its trajector (*works*) profiles an activity and is therefore relational. This trajector is situated within a landmark that is not specifically named, but is identifiable as that portion of the rate scale which lies beyond an implicit norm.

Relations are either "simple" or "complex", depending on whether or not their profile reduces to a single, consistent configuration. Such a configuration is reasonably called a "state", so a simple relation can also be termed "stative". The italicized words in (5) all profile stative relations, as does *across* in (6a); by contrast, the same preposition is complex in (6b):

(6) a. *There is a road across the desert.*
   b. *The troops marched across the desert.*

These two senses of *across* were respectively diagramed in Figures 9(a) and 9(b) of Chapter 1. Both senses specify that the trajector occupies a path leading from one side of the landmark to the other. The relation in (6a) is stative: since the trajector is an elongated object that simultaneously occupies the entire path, the profiled interconnections amount to a single configuration. In (6b), however, the trajector is small compared to the path, and thus occupies the points along it successively rather than simultaneously. This implies a continuous sequence of distinct configurations, each of which finds the trajector in a slightly different position vis-à-vis the landmark. The relation is therefore complex. It is internally coherent because the component states are conceived as being distributed along the temporal axis.

7. Processes

Relational predications are divided into those that profile "processes", and those that designate "atemporal relations". The set of processual predications is coextensive with the class of verbs. By contrast, atemporal relations correspond to such traditional categories as prepositions, adjectives, adverbs, infinitives, and participles. The nature of the intended distinction requires explicit characterization, since it is not at all self-evident. What do I take to be a process? In what sense do I say that a verb is temporal, while other relations are atemporal?

If a verb is characterized semantically by the profiling of a process, we cannot simply define this notion as a relationship involving time: even a stative relation (e.g. *before*) can profile a configuration in the temporal domain. Nor is a process just a sequence of relational configurations, since that does not distinguish it from a complex atemporal relation. It does not even suffice to combine the two specifications, and describe a process as profiling a sequence of relationships distributed through time; this latter definition is perfectly compatible with one sense of *across* (as in (6b)), which is not a verb but a preposition. What, then, can we single out as a possible conceptual basis for the semantic contrast between a complex atemporal relation like *across* and an obviously related verb like *cross*? The difference must be quite subtle. I suggest that it does not pertain primarily to the content of the predications, but rather to how this content is construed through cognitive processing.

Two preliminary distinctions are necessary. The first is between "conceived time" (*t*) and "processing time" (*T*), i.e. between time as an OBJECT of conceptualization and time as the MEDIUM of conceptualization. Any conception whatever requires a certain span of processing time for the requisite cognitive operations. *A fortiori*, processing time is needed to conceptualize the passage of time, or to mentally follow the temporal evolution of a situation. Except in cases of immediate experience, there is no restriction that a span of conceived time must coincide in length with the span of processing time required for its conception; we have the mental capacity, in recalling or imagining a sequence of events, to either "speed them up" or "slow them down". For example, I can mentally run through the steps involved in changing a tire, reviewing them all in a matter of seconds, but the physical implementation of these procedures takes considerably longer.

I further distinguish two modes of cognitive processing: "summary" vs. "sequential scanning". In summary scanning, the various facets of a situation are examined in cumulative fashion, so that progressively a more and more complex conceptualization is built up; once the entire scene has been scanned, all facets of it are simultaneously available and cohere as a single gestalt. With respect to the cognitive events which constitute this experience, we can suppose that, once activated, events that represent a given facet of the scene remain active throughout. By contrast, sequential scanning involves the successive transformation of one scene into another. The various phases of an evolving situation are examined serially, in noncumulative fashion; hence the conceptualization is dynamic, in the sense that its contents change from one instant to the next. At the level of cognitive events, we can suppose that events which represent a given scene remain active only momentaneously, and begin to decay as the following scene is initiated. These respective modes of scanning can be illustrated by our abilities to study a photograph and to watch a motion picture. Summary scanning is suited by nature to the conception of static situations, while sequential scanning lends itself to the conception of changes and events. We nevertheless have the conceptual agility to construe an event by means of summary scanning. Thus we can watch the flight of a ball and then mentally reconstruct its trajectory, which we can even visualize as a line with a definite curvature. In terms of the photographic analogy, employing summary scanning for an event is like forming a still photograph through multiple exposures.

To make these notions explicit, I define the "construal relation" as the relationship between a conceptualizer and his conceptualization. In speech, the relevant conceptualizers are the speaker and addressee, and the relevant conceptualization is the meaning of a particular linguistic expression. The formulaic representation in (7a) indicates that conceptualizer C carries out conceptualization Q at point T_i of processing time.

$$(7)\ a.\ \begin{bmatrix} Q \\ C \end{bmatrix}_{T_i}$$

$$b.\ \begin{bmatrix} a \\ C \end{bmatrix}_{T_1} > \begin{bmatrix} b \\ C \end{bmatrix}_{T_2} > \begin{bmatrix} c \\ C \end{bmatrix}_{T_3} > \begin{bmatrix} d \\ C \end{bmatrix}_{T_4}$$

$$c.\ \begin{bmatrix} a \\ C \end{bmatrix}_{T_1} > \begin{bmatrix} a \\ b \\ C \end{bmatrix}_{T_2} > \begin{bmatrix} a \\ b \\ c \\ C \end{bmatrix}_{T_3} > \begin{bmatrix} a \\ b \\ c \\ d \\ C \end{bmatrix}_{T_4}$$

Formulas (7b) and (7c) then represent the construal of an event by means of sequential and summary scanning, respectively. Consider the conception of an object falling to the ground, as sketched in Figure 4(a), where *a-d* label component states.[14] Formula (7b) indicates that these states are accessed serially through processing time: C activates a at T_1, b at T_2, etc. When summary scanning is employed for the same event, as in (7c), the active conceptualization grows progressively more elaborate: a is activated at T_1 and remains active throughout; the activation of b is added at T_2; and so on. Summary scanning thus involves a "build-up phase", which continues until all the component states are simultaneously active and manipulable as a single gestalt. In the present example, the build-up phase results, at T_4, in the composite conception depicted in Figure 4(b). In effect, all the component states are superimposed in a single image. The directionality of the conception--i.e. its construal as an object falling to the ground rather than rising from it--is attributable to how it is built up state by state.

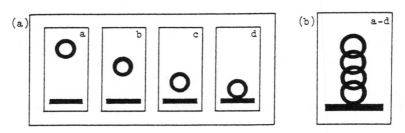

Figure 4.

The distinction between sequential and summary scanning provides a natural basis for the contrast between processes and complex atemporal relations. Under this analysis, for instance, the verb *cross* and the preposition *across* may share the same conceptual content (Figure 9(b) of Chapter 1) but differ in how the component states of this complex relationship are accessed. A verb is thus a "temporal" predication in the sense of following a situation state by state as it evolves through conceived time; its "dynamic" character reflects the successive transformations deriving each component state from its predecessor. The corresponding atemporal relation employs summary scanning for the same series of states. Though it accesses these states in sequence during the build-up phase (which accounts for its directionality), the cumulative result is a complex conception in which all the component configurations are superimposed and simultaneously active.

We can now attempt an explicit description of the schema for processual predications. Let r_i stand for a stative relation, t_i for a point in conceived time, and $[r_i]/t_i$ for their coincidence. Formula (8a) thus indicates that conceptualizer C activates at point T_i of processing time the conception of relation r_i, and further situates this relation at point t_i of conceived time.

(8) a.
$$\begin{bmatrix} [r_i]/t_i \\ C \end{bmatrix}_{T_i}$$

b.
$$
\begin{bmatrix} [r_1]/t_1 \\ C \end{bmatrix}_{T_1} > \begin{bmatrix} [r_2]/t_2 \\ C \end{bmatrix}_{T_2} > \begin{bmatrix} [r_3]/t_3 \\ C \end{bmatrix}_{T_3} > ... > \begin{bmatrix} [r_n]/t_n \\ C \end{bmatrix}_{T_n}
$$

A process is then characterized by formula (8b). A processual predication involves a continuous series of states r_1, r_2, r_3, ..., r_n, each of which profiles a relation; it distributes these states through a continuous span t_1, t_2, t_3, ..., t_n of conceived time; and it employs sequential scanning for accessing this complex structure. A process contrasts with the corresponding atemporal relation by having a "temporal profile", defined as the span of conceived time through which the profiled relationship is scanned sequentially.

By way of summary, every predication profiles some entity (recall that this notion is maximally inclusive, subsuming both regions and relations as special cases). A simple atemporal (or stative) relation profiles the interconnections between two or more entities and reduces to a single, consistent configuration (state). A complex atemporal relation profiles a series of relational configurations and scans them in summary fashion, so by definition it has no temporal profile (even if the states are distributed through conceived time). A process involves a series of relational configurations that necessarily extend through conceived time and are scanned sequentially (thus defining its temporal profile). Abbreviatory notations for these notions were given in Figure 10 of Chapter 1.

8. Motivation

I have no direct proof that formula (8b) is correct as the semantic characterization of verbs. Several considerations do however suggest its potential viability. First, it satisfies certain intuitions, accounting for both the dynamic character of verbs and their obvious association with time. Second, it relies only on constructs established independently (notably profiling, conceived time, and sequential scanning). Third, I have shown that a semantic definition of the verb class--if possible at all--must resemble (8b) in abstractness, and also in referring to cognitive processing; conceptual content is less important than how this content is construed and accessed. Finally, a strong claim of descriptive adequacy can be made for the overall analysis: it revealingly distinguishes the various types of relational predications, captures important grammatical generalizations, and explains certain peculiarities of verbal expressions in English.

Relational predications as a class are distinguished from nominal predications by their profiling of interconnections. Within this class, sequential scanning accounts for the fundamental distinction between processes and atemporal relations, some of which are verb-like in content (i.e. they profile a sequence of relational configurations extending through conceived time). How do infinitives and participles fit into this scheme? Though sometimes called "nonfinite verb forms", they are not in fact verbs by my definition--instead they designate atemporal relations.[15] They nevertheless derive from verbs, so the profiled relation is characterized with reference to a process; this sets infinitives and participles apart from other atemporal relations. More specifically, the process designated by the verb stem functions as the base for the infinitival or participial predication overall. The semantic value of the derivational morphology (*to, -ing, -ed*) resides in the effect it has on the process introduced by the stem: each derivational morpheme profiles a schematically characterized atemporal relation, and imposes its atemporal profile on the processual base provided by the stem.

In brief, the morphemes deriving infinitives and participles have the semantic effect of suspending the sequential scanning of the verb stem, thereby converting the processual predication of the stem into an atemporal relation. Where these morphemes differ is in the additional effect they have on the processual notion that functions as their base. I analyze the infinitival *to* as having no additional effect whatever: in *the first person to leave* or *Jack wants to leave*, the infinitive *to leave* profiles the same sequence of relational configurations as the verb stem *leave*, but construes them by means of summary scanning as a single gestalt. Observe that the diagram for an infinitival predication, Figure 5(a), is the same as that for a process (Figure 10(e) of Chapter 1) except for the absence on its time arrow of the heavy-line marking which indicates sequential scanning. The morpheme deriving past participles has several semantic variants, only two of which are noted here (see Chapter 4). One variant, diagrammed in Figure 5(b), profiles only the final state of the base process; the resulting predication (e.g. *broken* in *broken leg*) is stative, because it profiles only a single relational configuration. Another variant derives the participles that appear in passives; as seen in Figure 5(c), it profiles all the component states of the base process, but imposes on the composite predication a different choice of trajector (relational figure).[16] Finally, the *-ing* predication has several effects that are discussed in section **10**: besides the suspension of sequential scanning, it imposes on the base process a restricted immediate scope of

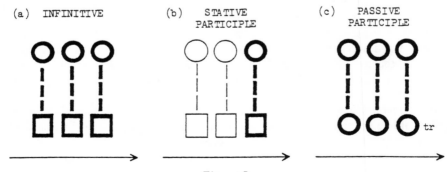

Figure 5.

predication, confines the profile to the component states within this immediate scope, and construes these states as homogeneous.

Without attempting any detailed justification of these analyses, I note that the constructs of cognitive grammar enable us to distinguish infinitives and participles from both verbs and other atemporal relations, and to elucidate their subtle semantic contrasts. Moreover, the proposed taxonomy of relational predications has considerable descriptive import. I believe the following generalizations to be valid for English (and possibly universally):

(9) a. A finite clause always profiles a process.
    b. A noun modifier is always atemporal.[17]

As implemented in English, (9a) requires that every finite clause contain a verb to function as clausal head, in the sense that its processual profile is inherited by the clause as a whole. Interpreted as full sentences, the expressions in (10) are consequently deviant, since they contain no verb to furnish the requisite profile:

(10) a. *The boy tall(s)*.
    b. *The lamp above(s) the table.*
    c. *A man strolling along the beach.*
    d. *The rock star pursued by wild teenagers.*
    e. *It already broken when I found it.*
    f. *They to leave tomorrow.*

Observe that participles and infinitives behave the same as adjectives and prepositions in this regard, just as we expect given their categorization as atemporal relations. It is possible, of course, to render these sentences grammatical simply by adding *be*:

(11) a. *The boy is tall.*
    b. *The lamp is above the table.*
    c. *A man is strolling along the beach.*
    d. *The rock star was pursued by wild teenagers.*
    e. *It was already broken when I found it.*
    f. *They are to leave tomorrow.*

This phenomenon is explained by generalization (9a), together with the semantic properties of *be*.

In numerous previous publications (e.g. 1981, 1982), I have argued that the auxiliary verbs *be, have*, and *do* designate highly schematic processes, i.e. they have little content beyond that which characterizes verbs as a class, as formulated in (8b). The semantic contrasts distinguishing *be, have*, and *do* are not essential here--we need only consider their common status as schematic processual predications. This special semantic value suits them for particular grammatical roles, one of which, illustrated in (10)-(11), is to furnish the temporal profile required for a finite clause whose major content is supplied by an atemporal predication. *Be* is processual, hence eligible to serve as clausal head, but it is only a "skeletal" process, for its component states are not identified (apart from being relational). An adjective, preposition, participle, or infinitive puts "flesh" on the skeleton: it designates one or a sequence of relational configurations specified in substantial detail; when it combines with *be*, these relations are equated with *be*'s component states. The resulting composite expression (e.g. *be tall*; *be above*; *be pursued*) inherits *be*'s processual profile and therefore designates a specified process. The atemporal predication thus elaborates the schematic content of *be*, while *be* extends the atemporal relation through conceived time and imposes on it the sequential scanning necessary for a finite clause.

More generally, this analysis offers a principled explanation for a striking organizational feature of the English auxiliary, namely the dependency between *have* or *be* on the one hand, and the participial morphemes on the other (cf. Chomsky 1957). In a full finite clause, *-ing* demands the co-occurrence of *be*, while the past-participial morpheme requires either *be* or *have* (for its passive and perfect variants, respectively). These dependencies reflect the interaction of generalization (9a) with the semantic value of the participial inflections. These inflections suspend the sequential scanning of the verb stem, thus deriving an atemporal predication; hence *be* or *have* must be added to "retemporalize" the expression before it can function as clausal head. In a complex verb group, several cycles of suspension and reimposition of sequential scanning can be observed, e.g. *criticize* (processual) > *criticized* (atemporal) > *be criticized* (proc.) > *being criticized* (atemp.) > *be being criticized* (proc.) > *been being criticized* (atemp.) > *have been being criticized* (proc.). Tense and agreement are manifested on the verb which supplies the processual profile at the highest level of organization.

The auxiliary verbs can also stand alone as clausal heads, in which case they are commonly regarded as pro forms, and the resulting sentences as elliptical:

(12) a. *Sally is.*
    b. *Joe has.*
    c. *Larry did.*

I would simply say that these expressions are highly schematic (to the extent of being uninformative except in referring back to some previously identified process). *Be*, *have*, and *do* are true verbs, and can therefore function as clausal heads despite their skeletal character. Moreover, being processual predications they have a trajector (see Figure 10(e) of Chapter 1) which can be instantiated by a subject noun phrase. Hence *Sally* is the actual semantic and grammatical subject of *be* in (12a), just as it is in *Sally is happy* or *Sally is running*.

Generalization (9b) specifies the atemporality of noun modifiers. This is a natural restriction, since nouns themselves employ summary scanning and are thus atemporal. Adjectives, prepositions, participles, and infinitives can all be used to modify nouns:

(13) a. *the **tall** boy*
 b. *the lamp **above** the table*
 c. *a man **strolling** along the beach*
 d. *a rock star **pursued** by wild teenagers*
 e. *a **broken** vase*
 f. *the first person **to leave***

What (9b) specifically rules out is the use of simple verbs in this capacity. The noun phrases in (14) are thus ill-formed.

(14) a. **a man **stroll** along the beach*
 b. **a **break** vase*
 c. **the first person **leave***

The analysis further explains why atemporal predications do not tolerate *be* when functioning as noun modifiers, as in (15), though they require it in the verb group of a finite clause.

(15) a. **the **be** tall boy*
 b. **the lamp **be** above the table*
 c. **a rock star **be** pursued by wild teenagers*

9. Perfective vs. imperfective processes

The most fundamental aspectual distinction for English verbs is between what I call "perfective" vs. "imperfective" processes.[18] Perfectives and imperfectives can be identified by well-known grammatical criteria; e.g. imperfectives occur in the simple present tense, but not in the progressive:

(16) a. *Harry resembles his father.* a′. **Harry is resembling his father.*
 b. *Paul knows the answer.* b′. **Paul is knowing the answer.*

By contrast, perfectives do occur in the progressive, but not in the simple present:

(17) a. **Tom builds a canoe.* a′. *Tom is building a canoe.*
 b. **Tom learns the answer.* b′. *Tom is learning the answer.*

Sentences like (17a) and (17b) are of course acceptable with a special interpretation (e.g. habitual, historical present), but not when they indicate one instance of the designated process situated at the time of speaking. Though such differences alert us to the existence of an aspectual contrast, I do not regard them as definitions for the perfective and imperfective classes, but rather as symptomatic of an underlying semantic distinction. The classification does not, in any case, amount to a rigid partitioning of the verbal lexicon. Some verbs function comfortably in either class, while verbs that normally belong to one are often shifted to the other by a complement or adverb. Moreover, there are patterns of semantic extension which effect a change in category without marking it overtly (e.g. a perfective can be construed as habitual, hence imperfective).

I have argued previously (e.g. 1982) that a perfective process portrays a situation as changing through time, while an imperfective process describes the extension through time of a stable situation.[19] My definition of a process, (8b), does not specify change; it requires only that a series of profiled relations be distributed through conceived time and scanned sequentially. The analysis therefore predicts the existence of imperfective processes: they constitute a limiting case, where all the component states happen to be identical. The presence vs. the absence of change is nevertheless a significant qualitative distinction. It proves responsible for the contrasting behavior of perfectives and imperfectives.

An examination of typical instances provides initial support for the characterization. Canonical perfectives (e.g. *jump, kick, learn, explode, arrive, cook, ask*) clearly involve some change through time. By contrast, imperfectives (e.g. *resemble, have, know, want, like*) are plausibly interpreted as describing the perpetuation through time of a static configuration. More instructive, perhaps, are cases where the same verb instantiates both categories. For example, the verbs in (18) are imperfective (as shown by their occurrence in the simple present), while in (19) the same verbs are used perfectively (as witnessed by their occurrence in the progressive):

(18) a. *An empty moat surrounds the old castle.*
 b. *His parents have a lovely home in the country.*
 c. *Roger likes his new teacher.*

(19) a. *The soldiers are surrounding the old castle.*
 b. *His parents are having a violent argument.*
 c. *Roger is liking his new teacher more and more every day.*

The situations described in (18) are potentially quite stable; certainly these sentences do not portray them as changing in any way. By contrast, the sentences in (19) are specifically concerned with changing configurations: the soldiers move into position around the castle, the parents carry out an activity, and Roger's opinion of his teacher becomes more favorable.[20]

Various scholars (e.g. Mourelatos 1981) have noted a similarity between the perfective/imperfective (or active/stative) contrast for verbs and the count/mass distinction for nouns. I will go one step further, and claim that the perfective/imperfective and count/mass distinctions are precisely identical, when due allowances are made for the intrinsic difference between verbs and nouns. The basis for comparing the two distinctions is spelled out in (20):

(20) a. The component states of a process (each profiling a relation) are analogous
   to the component entities constituting the region profiled by a noun.
   b. For a process, time is the primary domain with respect to which the
   presence vs. the absence of bounding is determined.

Once these identifications are made, it is readily seen that the various properties distinguishing count and mass nouns, reviewed in (21), are mirrored in full detail by the respective properties in (22), which I claim to be valid for the contrast between perfective and imperfective processes.

(21) a. The region profiled by a mass noun is construed as being internally
   homogeneous.
   b. A mass is indefinitely expansible/contractible (any subpart is itself
   a valid instance of the category).
   c. The region profiled by a count noun is specifically bounded within
   the scope of predication in its primary domain.
   d. Replicability (pluralizability) is possible for count nouns.

(22) a. The component states of an imperfective process are construed as all
   being effectively identical.
   b. An imperfective process is indefinitely expansible/contractible (any
   series of component states is itself a valid instance of the category).
   c. A perfective process is specifically bounded in time within the scope
   of predication.
   d. Replicability (repetitive aspect) is possible for perfective processes.

For verbs as well as nouns, the properties of homogeneity, expansibility, bounding, and replicability are intimately related. Expansion or contraction does not affect the identity of a process if all its component states are identical (since any series of states is then qualitatively the same as any other). Internal homogeneity precludes distinctive initial and final states; it thus removes the most obvious basis for bounding, which is necessary for replicability. Moreover, indefinite expansibility/contractibility is incompatible with both bounding and replicability.

The contrast between perfective and imperfective processes is sketched in Figure 6. Each profiles a sequence of relational configurations distributed through conceived time. These component states are represented by a wavy line for the perfective process, to indicate change through time, and by a straight line for the imperfective, to indicate constancy through time. A perfective process is so called because it is bounded, i.e. its endpoints are included within the scope of predication in the temporal domain. No such specification of bounding is made for an imperfective process; it profiles a stable situation that may extend indefinitely far beyond the scope of predication in either direction, although--by definition--the profile is confined to those component states that fall within this scope.[21] For each process, the heavy-line segment of the time arrow marks the temporal profile, characterized by sequential scanning through the profiled states.

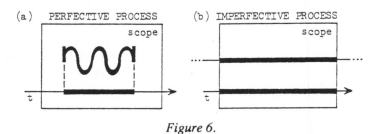

Figure 6.

This characterization of perfective and imperfective processes accounts straightforwardly for their contrastive grammatical behavior. One such difference is alluded to in (22d), namely the occurrence of perfectives (but not imperfectives) with repetitive aspect. We can force a repetitive construal by means of the adverb *again and again*:

(23) a. *Harry played the tune again and again.*
    b. **Harry resembled his father again and again.*

There are of course contexts where (23b) might be acceptable--e.g. the speaker may mean that Harry went through several distinct stages where he resembled his father, though he failed to resemble him at other times. Observe, however, that this interpretation implies a nonconventional construal of *resemble*, whereby it designates a limited episode of resemblance, including both the initiation and the termination of this relationship. This bounding renders it perfective, hence replicable.

Perfectives and imperfectives also behave differently in sentences like the following, where the first clause is in the past tense, while the second clause specifies the continuation of the designated process through the present:

(24) a. **Paul learned the answer--in fact he still does.*
    b. *Paul knew the answer--in fact he still does.*

The imperfective *know* is acceptable in such sentences, but the perfective *learn* is precluded (barring some special interpretation, e.g. habitual). An explanation requires an explicit description of the present and past tenses in English. The one I propose could hardly be more straightforward:

(25) a. Present: A full instantiation of the profiled process occurs and precisely coincides with the time of speaking.
   b. Past: A full instantiation of the profiled process occurs prior to the time of speaking.

Although these definitions may appear naive, they are sufficient for the purpose at hand. I believe, in fact, that they are perfectly valid for English.[22]

Given the definition of a perfective process, the deviance of (24a) can now be explained. A perfective is bounded, so a full instantiation includes its endpoints. The past-tense marking on *learn* thus implies that the entire bounded process--including its endpoints--is situated prior to the time of speaking. This situation is diagramed in Figure 7(a), where the box with zigzag lines indicates the speech event. It is immediately apparent that this configuration is incompatible with continuation of the profiled process through the time of speaking. But that is precisely what the second clause specifies, so (24a) is anomalous. By contrast, (24b) is acceptable by virtue of the expansibility/contractibility of imperfectives. Suppose that Paul's knowledge of the answer continues through the present, as indicated by the upper line in Figure 7(b); the specifications of the second clause are thus satisfied. What about the first clause? The past-tense marking on *know* demands a full instantiation of this process prior to the time of speaking. The demand is satisfied by the profiling indicated in 7(b): for imperfectives, any

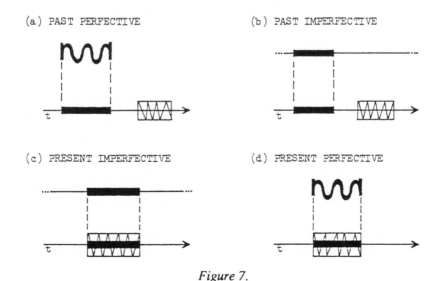

(a) PAST PERFECTIVE   (b) PAST IMPERFECTIVE

(c) PRESENT IMPERFECTIVE   (d) PRESENT PERFECTIVE

Figure 7.

sequence of component states constitutes a valid instance of the category, so the profiled segment of the overall process is itself a full instantiation of *know*.

This same property of imperfectives explains their occurrence in the simple present, as defined in (25a). Whenever an imperfective process includes the time of speaking within its temporal extension, as diagramed in Figure 7(c), we can confine the profile to that segment of the overall process which precisely coincides with the speech event, and we will still have a valid instance of the process in question. I assume that the present-tense predication achieves this effect by imposing, on the process designated by the verb stem, an immediate scope of predication that is temporally coextensive with the time of speaking. But though the profile is necessarily limited to the immediate scope of predication, the overall process referred to by the stem is still evoked as the base (and maximal scope of predication) for a present-tense verb.

Why do perfectives not occur in the present without a special interpretation? There is nothing intrinsically anomalous about the configuration that this implies, which is sketched in Figure 7(d). The difficulty is rather that circumstances normally prevent this situation from arising. For one thing, the span of time required for a bounded process to occur has no inherent connection with the time required for a speech event describing it. Even if the profiled process were the right length, the speaker could hardly describe it with a precisely coincident speech event: to do so, he would have to begin his description at exactly the instant when the process is initiated, before he had a chance to observe its occurrence and identify it. Once he observes a full instantiation of the process (including its endpoint), it is too late to initiate a temporally coincident description. Striking confirmation of this explanation is provided by the one notable exception to the generalization that perfectives do not occur in the simple present, namely that of explicit performatives:

(26) a. *I order you to put that rifle down!*
   b. *I promise that I will behave.*

Performative verbs are perfective, and by definition they occur in the simple present as characterized in (25a). Obviously this is a motivated exception: in a performative sentence the profiled process is identified with the speech event itself, so it is not only possible but actually necessary for the two to coincide.

When a perfective other than a performative occurs with present-tense form, it receives some "special" interpretation that avoids the problems cited above. In some languages, the corresponding morphology is polysemous, indicating present tense with imperfectives but recent past with perfectives. For English, a sentence like (27a) will most likely be construed as habitual, hence imperfective; the act of drinking two martinis for lunch is portrayed as a regular practice whose institutionalization is stable through conceived time.

(27) a. *Ralph drinks two martinis for lunch.*
   b. *The expedition leaves tomorrow at noon.*
   c. *This sleazy character walks up to me on the street yesterday and*
      offers to make me rich.
   d. *Bird passes to McHale. McHale shoots. He scores!*

The "imminent future" interpretation of (27b) is perhaps to be analyzed in parallel fashion; i.e. the stable situation extending through the present is not the act of leaving, but rather that of the leaving being "scheduled" for tomorrow at noon. The historical present, illustrated in (27c), involves a type of mental transfer, whereby a past event is described as if it were unfolding at the moment of speaking. The event's temporal extension is made to coincide with that of the speech event by means of an ability noted previously (section 7): our capacity, in recalling or imagining an event, to "speed it up" or "slow it down" as desired. Finally, present-tense perfectives are used in the "play-by-play" mode of speech, as in (27d), which can be regarded as a special adaptation of the historical present. The time-lag between the reported event and the speech event is as short as the announcer can make it, and the audience accepts their coincidence as a convenient fiction (cf. Langacker 1982).

10. Progressives

One last grammatical difference is the occurrence of perfectives, but not of imperfectives, in the *be...-ing* progressive construction. The basic reason is simply that the progressive is imperfectivizing, hence its occurrence with imperfectives would be superfluous. To be sure, the restriction does not follow as an inevitable consequence--languages do sometimes evolve redundant constructions--but it is nonetheless natural in functional terms.

The progressive construction is semantically quite regular, given independently established values of *be* and *-ing*. The semantic effect of adding *-ing* to a verb stem is to convert a process into an atemporal relation; by the generalizations in (9), the participle so derived can serve as a noun modifier, but not as the head of a finite clause. The function of *be* is to retemporalize the participial predication, deriving a higher-order verb (e.g. *be learning*) capable of occurring as clausal head. *Be* does so by imposing its own processual profile (including sequential scanning) on the composite expression.[23]

Constructs already at hand permit a precise semantic description of *-ing* and the progressive construction overall. From a perfective verb stem, as diagramed in Figure 6(a), *-ing* derives an atemporal relation with the properties indicated in Figure 8(a). The process designated by the stem constitutes the base and scope of predication for the participle. Within this base, *-ing* imposes a restricted immediate scope of predication comprising an arbitrary sequence of internal states (i.e. the initial and final states are excluded). By definition, the profile is confined to this immediate scope--hence the commonplace intuition that the progressive takes an "internal perspective" on the action described by the verb stem. The profiled series of states is represented by a straight (rather than a wavy) line to indicate that it is construed as homogeneous. The component states are not identical in any strict sense, but their degree of divergence depends on the level of schematicity at which they are viewed. I propose that the participle focuses on the commonality of the profiled states as component members of the same base process, and portrays them as a homogeneous set on the basis of this abstract similarity.[24]

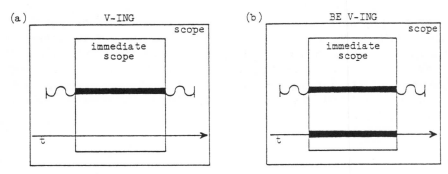

Figure 8.

In addition, *-ing* atemporalizes the base process by suspending sequential scanning, so the temporal profile of Figure 6(a) is absent in 8(a). The semantic contribution of *be* is to reinstitute sequential scanning of the profiled relationship, and thus to restore its processual character at a higher level of organization. The composite expression *be V-ing* is therefore processual, as shown in Figure 8(b), but the process it designates is not precisely the same as the process profiled by the verb stem. With respect to the perfective process *V*, the composite expression *be V-ing* defines a higher-order process that is limited to some internal portion of *V*, and construes the profiled states at a level of schematicity which renders them effectively identical. This process is imperfective because the profiled relationship is portrayed as stable through time (within the limits implied by its base).

We must now consider sentences like those in (28), which appear to be counterexamples to the claim that the progressive only occurs with perfectives:

(28) a. *He is sleeping.*
　　　b. *He is wearing a sweater.*
　　　c. *He is walking.*

Sleep and *wear a sweater* do not suggest any substantial change through time, and there is an obvious sense in which *walk* is internally homogeneous, even though physical activity is involved.[25] If we classify these processes as imperfective because of their homogeneous character, then their occurrence in the progressive is exceptional. I will argue, however, that the verbs in question are in fact perfective.

The comparison of count and mass nouns proves instructive. The region designated by a mass noun is internally homogeneous and unbounded within the immediate scope of predication; that profiled by a count noun is necessarily bounded, and is typically heterogeneous. However, internal diversity is neither prerequisite for bounding nor an obligatory feature of count nouns: a count noun like *spot* is bounded by contrast with surroundings, not by internal configuration, and the profiled region is homogeneous out to its boundary. I am claiming that the count/mass and perfective/imperfective distinctions are precisely identical, given the correspondences spelled out in (20). The overall analysis therefore predicts the existence of perfective processes analogous to *spot*, which are internally homogeneous but nevertheless construed as being bounded. This is what I propose for verbs like *sleep, wear (a sweater), walk, swim, dream, perspire,* etc.

Processes like these typically occur in "bounded episodes" rather than continuing indefinitely. Their episodic nature is evidently incorporated as part of the conventional value of these verbs, and is responsible for their categorization as perfectives.[26] We thus find the distinctions diagrammed in Figure 9, where (a) represents a canonical perfective like *jump*, (c) a canonical imperfective like *resemble*, and (b) a verb like *sleep*. Within the class of perfectives, verbs of type (b) are a limiting case, in which the degree of internal variation approximates zero. These processes are nevertheless bounded, as some limit is imputed to the set of component states which constitutes the processual profile. From another perspective, we can say that the change implied by type-(b) perfectives is confined to the initiation and the termination of the process.

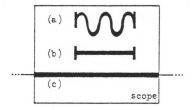

Figure 9.

Strongly corroborating this analysis are instances where the same lexeme has variants of types (b) and (c):

(29) a. *A statue of George Lakoff stands in the plaza.*
    b. *This machine lacks a control lever.*

(30) a. *A statue of George Lakoff is standing in the plaza.*
    b. *This machine is lacking a control lever.*

Since they occur in the simple present, the verbs in (29) are imperfective, whereas those in (30), with the progressive, must be type-(b) perfectives. My analysis claims that each verb stem in (29) construes the designated situation as extending indefinitely through time, while in (30) it portrays the same situation as constituting a bounded episode. This is evidently so: (29a) suggests that the plaza is the permanent home for Lakoff's statue, while (30a) either indicates that the statue is there only temporarily, or else reports on someone's immediate (hence temporary) perception of its location. Similarly, (29b) suggests that the absence of a control lever is part of the machine's design, whereas (30b) intimates a contingent situation finding the machine in need of repair. The analysis further predicts such judgments as the following:

(31) a. *Belgium lies between Holland and France.*
    b. **Belgium is lying between Holland and France.*

(32) a. **Peter lies on the beach right now.*
    b. *Peter is lying on the beach right now.*

Belgium's position vis-à-vis Holland and France is permanent for all intents and purposes, but a person generally lies on the beach only in bounded episodes.

Properly interpreted, I believe this analysis to be compatible with the seemingly very different one proposed by Goldsmith and Woisetschlaeger (1982), which explicates the contrast between the simple present and the present progressive in terms of a distinction between "structural" and "phenomenal" knowledge. In judging a property to be structural (i.e. a matter of "how the world is made"), we portray it as something that will endure until the world itself changes; we thereby lend it an intrinsic permanence that precludes its occurring in bounded episodes. Of course, what constitutes the "world" is subject to variable construal (cf. Fauconnier 1985), and a process is imperfective only with respect to a given scope of predication. At one extreme, the world can be equated with the physical or mathematical universe. If we define the relevant scope of predication as the full temporal expanse of human experience, the situations described in (33) are stable throughout and unbounded within this scope:

(33) a. *Water consists of hydrogen and oxygen.*
  b. *Two plus two equals four.*

(34) a. *Thelma dyes her hair.*
  b. *Thelma is dyeing her hair (these days).*

However, to explicate the contrast in (34) we must narrow our horizons considerably. The "world" is essentially limited to Thelma and her activities, and the scope of predication is a vaguely delimited portion of her lifespan, sufficiently long for behavioral patterns to be established and identified. In (34a), the practice of hair-dyeing is portrayed as a stable part of Thelma's behavioral repertoire throughout this span of time. In contrast, (34b) depicts this practice as being only temporary: Thelma regularly dyes her hair at present, but this has not always been her practice, nor is it expected to continue indefinitely. Regular recourse to hair-dyeing constitutes only a bounded episode within the overall period of Thelma's life that concerns us.

The interaction between aspect and scope of predication is further illustrated in (35):

(35) a. *A truly great linguist is sitting there.*
  b. *There sits a truly great linguist!*

Sit is normally perfective; though internally homogeneous, the process it designates is construed as occurring in bounded episodes. The progressive is therefore required to describe a single instance of this process that temporally includes the speech event, as in (35a). The simple present nevertheless appears in (35b), suggesting an imperfective construal that allows the profiled process to coincide precisely with the time of speaking. This special construal arises because (35b) represents a marked grammatical construction with inherent semantic import. The construction is strongly deictic, as witnessed by the preposing of *there*. Its effect, intuitively, is to spotlight a particular facet of immediate experience: it directs all attention to whatever is presently occurring in the region pointed to by *there*. With respect to the temporal domain, the effect of this focusing operation is diagrammed in Figure 10. The full episode of sitting constitutes the base, so the boundaries of this episode are included in the overall scope of predication. However, the focusing operation imposes on this base a restricted immediate scope of predication, the temporal extension of which is centered on the speech event, and which does not include the boundaries of the full sitting episode. Since the profile is necessarily confined to the immediate scope, where bounding does not occur, the designated process is imperfective.

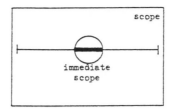

Figure 10.

In (36) we observe an interesting variation on this theme:

(36) a. *This road winds through the mountains.*
    b. *This road is winding through the mountains.*

Speakers agree that the sentences are appropriate in different contexts: (36a) might be used in planning a trip or examining a road map, while (36b) reports on what one actually experiences while driving along the road. I therefore analyze these sentences as differing in their scope of predication, particularly as it applies to *road*. We can once more employ Figure 10 to diagram this essential contrast-- we need only apply it to space (not time), and interpret the bounded line segment as the road (not the process). In (36a), the spatial scope of predication affords an overview of the entire complex configuration; a long expanse of road is presented in a single gestalt, in relation to the contours of the mountains. The subject nominal thus profiles the entire road, which corresponds to the full line segment in Figure 10. Example (36b) takes this overall configuration as its base, but imposes on it an immediate scope of predication which encompasses only what the passengers can see at one time. The immediate scope delimits the profile, so what counts as the road in (36b) is that segment of road which is visible at a given moment. How *road* is construed determines the aspectual value of *wind* (as reflected in the choice of simple present vs. progressive). The holistic construal in (36a) renders *wind* imperfective: viewed as a whole, the road does not change position vis-à-vis the mountains; the overall configuration is constant as it is scanned sequentially through conceived time. But when *road* is construed restrictively, to include only what is immediately visible, then *wind* becomes perfective: the road (so identified) no longer occupies a constant position in relation to the mountains; *wind* therefore designates a change through time rather than a stable situation.

We saw earlier that the difference between a simple and a complex atemporal relation may hinge on the size of an object relative to a path it occupies (cf. Figure 9 of Chapter 1). The perfective/imperfective contrast in (36) is similarly dependent on the relative sizes of the trajector--as determined by the immediate scope of predication--and the full trajectory it follows. Shifts in the scope of predication are not always responsible for contrasts involving this size factor. Consider (37):

(37) a. *Tom is going from Dallas to Houston.*
  b. *This road goes from Dallas to Houston.*

Tom is small in relation to the distance between Dallas and Houston, while a road is potentially long enough to occupy the full path simultaneously. *Go* is thus perfective in (37a) because it describes a change, but imperfective in (37b) because it describes a stable situation with indefinite temporal extension. These two senses of *go* make precisely the same locative specifications (the trajector occupies all the points along a path), but differ in their distribution through conceived time. In the perfective variant, the trajector occupies just one point in the path for each component state. The imperfective variant essentially telescopes the component states of the perfective into a single, more elaborate configuration, which is then followed holistically through conceived time as a stable situation.

The aspectual properties of a verb can also be influenced by the temporal extension of its object. *See* is normally imperfective and hence occurs in the simple present, as in (38a):

(38) a. *I see a rhinoceros.*
  b. **I see a flash.*
  c. **I am seeing a flash.*

A typical rhino has sufficient object permanence to support an imperfective predication; i.e. the circumstance of someone seeing it is potentially stable for a period at least long enough to include the entire time of speaking, as the simple present requires (cf. Figure 7(c)). A flash, however, is instantaneous. Its temporal duration is simply not long enough for seeing it to be construed as a stable situation extending through time. *See a flash* is therefore perfective, and (38b) is ill-formed when given a simple-present interpretation. We normally resort to the progressive in describing one present-time instance of a perfective process, but (38c) shows that this too is precluded with *see a flash*. My characterization of *-ing* and the progressive construction (Figure 8) affords a ready explanation: *-ing* imposes on a process a restricted immediate scope of predication comprising an arbitrary sequence of internal states, and it portrays as homogeneous the profiled situation thus selected. This is hardly possible with a punctual process like *see a flash*, which basically consists of just the onset and offset of a visual sensation--there is nothing in between to construe as an ongoing situation.

11. Abstract nouns

Abstract nouns and nominalizations have always been considered problematic for a notional account of basic grammatical categories. In large measure the difficulties stem from an objectivist view of linguistic semantics; they seem far less formidable when meaning is equated with cognitive processing and conventional imagery is properly accommodated. The following remarks are brief and selective, but may at least indicate that abstract nominals are amenable to this type of analysis.

The verb *explode* and its nominalization *explosion* can both be used to describe the same event (*Something exploded!*; *There was an explosion!*). An objectivist might conclude that the verb and noun are semantically identical, with the consequence that the grammatical category of an expression cannot be predicted from its meaning. My own claim is that *explode* and *explosion* contrast semantically because they employ different images to structure the same conceptual content: *explode* imposes a processual construal on the profiled event, while *explosion* portrays it as an abstract region. Nominalizing a verb necessarily endows it with the conceptual properties characteristic of nouns.

My analysis straightforwardly accommodates the reification implied by deverbal nouns like *explosion*. The verb stem designates a process, comprising a series of component states scanned sequentially through conceived time. Each component state can be regarded as an entity (recall that this notion is maximally inclusive). Moreover, the very fact that these states are coordinated (through sequential scanning) as facets of an integrated, higher-order conception is sufficient to establish them as a set of interconnected entities, and hence as a region. Every process therefore defines an implicit region consisting of its component states. A nominalization like *explosion* simply raises this region to the level of explicit concern as the profile of the composite predication.

The semantic contrast between a verb and its nominalization is schematized in Figure 11. Diagram (a) is simply the abbreviatory notation adopted earlier for processes, except that I have added a dashed-line ellipse to indicate the implicit region defined by the interconnection of its component states. Within the verb itself, this latent region has no particular salience; standing in profile are the relational configurations of the individual states, not the region per se, which pertains to a higher level of conceptual organization. The effect of the nominalization is to shift the profile to this higher level: it takes the process designated by the verb stem as its base, and within this base it selects for profiling the higher-order region comprising the component states. These states are profiled only collectively, as facets of the abstract region, so despite their individual status as relations the overall predication is nominal (cf. Figure 3(c)).

Explosion is one of many deverbal nominalizations that designate a single instance of the perfective process indicated by the verb stem: *an explosion, a jump, a throw, a yell, a kick, a walk*, etc. That the derived form is in each case a count noun follows directly from the proposed analysis: a perfective process is bounded, i.e. there is some limit to the set of component states; the region profiled by the nominalization takes these states for its constitutive entities, so it is bounded as well (cf. (20a)). With imperfective processes, the set of component states is not inherently limited. A parallel type of nominalization, namely one that simply profiles the component states as an abstract region, therefore yields a mass noun;

(a) VERB 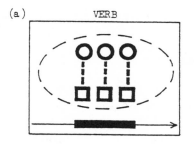 (b) NOMINALIZATION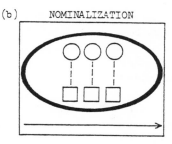

Figure 11.

examples include *hope, fear, love, desire, belief,* and *admiration.* There are of course other patterns of nominalization (e.g. count-noun variants of *hope, fear,* and *belief* designate the object of the imperfective process, not the reified process itself). And there are abstract nouns with comparable value that are not derived from verbs (e.g. *wit, chastity, woe, faith*).

Perfective processes also give rise to nominalizations that function as mass nouns: *jumping, yelling, walking, procrastination, sleep,* etc. Several considerations suggest that the difference between the corresponding count and mass nouns, e.g. between *jump* and *jumping,* is analogous to that between *lake* and *water*: just as a lake is a circumscribed body of water, so can *a jump* be regarded as a bounded instance of the abstract "substance" *jumping.* For one thing, a noun like *jumping* does not describe a single episode of the base process, but instead refers to it in a generalized, even generic fashion (e.g. *Jumping is hard on the knees*); similarly, a mass noun like *water* receives a generic interpretation unless there is some reason to construe it more narrowly. Moreover, *a jump* is one specific event bounded in time (the primary domain for processes), and *a lake* is one body of water bounded in space (the primary domain for physical substances). By contrast, neither *jumping* nor *water* is continuous or bounded in its primary domain, though each inhabits this domain. *Jumping* shows discontinuous distribution through time (as well as space), being instantiated whenever some instance of the process *jump* occurs. In similar fashion, *water* lies scattered about in lakes, rivers, puddles, drops, and oceans; the category is instantiated wherever there occurs some quantity of a substance with the requisite properties. Finally, neither *jumping* nor *water* qualifies as a region on the basis of distribution in its primary domain, but rather by virtue of qualitative homogeneity. The qualitative unity of *water*'s scattered instantiations derives from their common location in quality space (section 5). *Jumping* is homogeneous in the sense that all instantiations reside in the occurrence of a single type of process.

Though abstract nominals pose many subtle problems that have barely been explored, I feel the present approach provides important tools for the eventual resolution of these problems. I further expect the schematic characterizations proposed for count and mass nouns to prove adequate for all members of these classes, both concrete and abstract.

12. Conclusion

The noun and verb categories are universal and fundamental to grammatical structure. That such a distinction should have a conceptual basis is, on the face of it, hardly surprising. Why, in fact, would anybody believe (or want to believe) otherwise? Nonetheless, informed opinion and theoretical orthodoxy overwhelmingly support the contrary position (indeed, the presumed impossibility of a notional characterization is critical to sustaining the autonomy of grammatical structure). I have tried to show that the usual arguments for this position are crucially dependent on certain assumptions about the nature of meaning and linguistic semantics.[27] The validity of these assumptions cannot be accepted apriori. Even the staunchest advocate of objectivist semantics would not pretend that it offers a convincing account of linguistic meaning in all its varied aspects.

Cognitive grammar makes radically different assumptions, and arrives at very different conclusions. By adopting a conceptualist, imagist view of linguistic semantics, it is possible (at least in principle) to achieve a notional characterization of the noun and verb classes, as well as their major subclasses. Why, though, should these characterizations--couched as they are in terms of such mysterious entities as cognitive events--be given any credence? There are two basic reasons. First, this approach has led to a highly coherent and (I hope) revealing analysis. It accounts in unified fashion for an extremely broad array of data, and affords a natural explanation for many puzzling phenomena. Second, it invokes only constructs that are either well-attested independently or have prima facie cognitive plausibility: processing time, event coordination, relative prominence, figure/ground alignment, levels of organization, sequential scanning, bounding, degrees of schematicity, scope of predication, effective homogeneity, etc. Though linguistic theorists seldom deal with such notions, I see little reason to doubt their psychological validity or their potential relevance to linguistic semantics.

At the very least, I have indicated what a notional characterization of basic grammatical categories must look like, if any is possible at all. There is no real hope of finding universally valid definitions based on objective factors, or even on conceptual content alone; the critical factor--to be addressed at the level of cognitive processing--is how this content is accessed and construed. As linguists, we can hardly concern ourselves with specific neural circuits or the firing of individual neurons. We can, however, make plausible assumptions about the functional architecture of the complex cognitive events responsible for particular types of mental experience. Such attempts are surely speculative, and possibly premature. But they are hardly avoidable in the long run if one is serious about treating language as a psychological phenomenon.

4. The English passive

In wide sectors of the theoretical linguistic community, general agreement has been reached on certain broad and fundamental points.* The theses listed in (1) amount to a deeply ingrained, almost archetypal view of grammar which is accepted virtually without question by many theorists, and which serves as implicit frame of reference for much contemporary theoretical discourse:

(1) a. Economy is to be sought in linguistic description. Specifically, particular statements are to be excised if the grammar contains a general statement (rule) that fully subsumes them.
   b. Linguistic structure can be resolved into numerous separate, essentially self-contained components.
   c. As a special case of thesis (b), syntax is an autonomous component distinct from both semantics and lexicon.
   d. Supporting (c), it can be presumed that semantic structure is universal, while grammatical structure varies greatly from language to language.
   e. In accordance with theses (c) and (d), syntactic structure relies crucially on "grammatical morphemes", which are often meaningless and serve purely formal purposes.
   f. Syntactic structure is abstract. Surface structures often derive from deep structures which are significantly different in character, and contain elements (grammatical morphemes) that have no place in underlying structure.
   g. Syntax consists primarily of general rules. It is to be distinguished sharply from lexicon, the repository for irregularity and idiosyncrasy.[1]

The archetypal viewpoint is a coherent one that has enjoyed considerable descriptive success in narrowly circumscribed areas. However, it is not the only conceivable view. Nor can established theories claim such decisive triumphs across the entire range of linguistic phenomena awaiting explication that one can justifiably allow the archetype to stand as a definitive characterization of the parameters of viable linguistic inquiry. In attempting to formulate a more natural and broadly-grounded conception of linguistic structure, I have found reason to reject all the above theses. Cognitive grammar maintains the contrasting theses outlined in (2):

(2) a. Economy must be consistent with psychological reality. The grammar of a language represents conventional linguistic knowledge and includes all linguistic structures learned as established "units". "Content units" coexist in the grammar with subsuming "schemas".

b. Only "semantic", "phonological", and bipolar "symbolic" units are posited. Sharp dichotomies are usually found only by arbitrarily selecting examples from opposite endpoints of a continuum.

c. Syntax is not autonomous, but "symbolic", forming a continuum with lexicon and morphology. Syntactic units are "bipolar", with semantic and phonological poles.

d. Semantic structure is language specific, involving layers of "conventional imagery". "Semantic structure" is conventionalized conceptual structure, and "grammar" is the conventional symbolization of semantic structure.

e. Grammatical morphemes are meaningful, and are present because of their semantic contribution.

f. Grammatical structure is almost entirely overt. No underlying structures or derivations are posited.

g. Lexicon and grammar form a continuum of symbolic structures. This continuum contains no sharp dichotomies based on generality, regularity, or analyzability.

My purpose in this chapter is to map out this alternative conception of linguistic structure in sufficient detail to establish its initial plausibility, suggesting thereby that the various theses constituting the archetype are neither self-evident nor beyond the pale of legitimate skepticism. Preliminary discussion will lay the groundwork for a detailed example, namely an analysis of the English passive construction.

1. Grammar and analyzability

Let us begin by examining at greater length the theses listed in (2).

1.1. Economy

Cognitive grammar seeks an accurate characterization of the structure and organization of linguistic knowledge as an integral part of human cognition. In this context, the question of whether the grammar of a language should include both general statements and particular statements subsumed by them is a factual rather than a methodological issue. If speakers in fact master and manipulate both lists (particular statements) and rules (general statements) from which these lists could be predicted, a truthful description of their linguistic knowledge must contain both the lists and the rules. We have every reason to believe that general and particular statements do in fact coexist in the psychological representation of linguistic knowledge.

The proper domain of linguistic description, as conceived in cognitive grammar, is conventional linguistic knowledge. It is assumed that this knowledge takes the form of conventional "units"; a unit is defined as a structural complex that has achieved "unit status", by which I mean that it has been mastered by a speaker to the point where he can easily manipulate it as a whole, without attending specifically to its internal parts or their relation to one another. It comes "prepackaged", as it were, constituting an established routine that no longer requires a "constructive effort" for its assembly and use. For example, most linguists can pronounce the word *metathesis* with ease. It rolls off the tongue as a familiar, established articulatory routine. But a nonlinguist unfamiliar with the term will be able to pronounce it only through a conscious constructive effort, paying careful attention to all the syllables and their sequencing.

Among the units that embody linguistic knowledge are both "content units" (corresponding to particular statements) and "schemas" (corresponding to general statements). The notation A → B indicates that A is schematic for B; equivalently, we can say that B instantiates or elaborates A, meaning essentially that B specifies A in finer detail. We can think of a schema as mapping a structural complex on a coarse grid, spelling out only the essentials or gross features; a content unit instantiating it maps the same complex on a fine grid, specifying detail that the schema abstracts away from. A schematic unit defines a category, representing (at a higher level of abstraction) the content shared by its various instantiations, each of which elaborates it in different ways, specifying it in finer detail along one or more dimensions.

A schema embodies the generalization which speakers extract from an array of content units. The distinction between schematic and content units is of course relative; we can posit "schematic hierarchies", which are capable of considerable complexity and often impose intersecting class memberships on content units. Thus the concept [TOOL] is schematic for more highly elaborated notions such as [HAMMER], [SAW], and [SCREWDRIVER]; each of these is in turn schematic relative to more specific concepts (e.g. [HAMMER] → [CLAW HAMMER]); and so on. Similarly, the vowel [i] elaborates both the [FRONT VOWEL] and the [HIGH VOWEL] schemas, both of which instantiate the more abstract schema [VOWEL]. The evolution of schematic hierarchies such as these supports the view that general and particular units coexist in cognitive structure. Consider a person who first grasps the similarity among such previously established concepts as [HAMMER], [SAW], and [SCREWDRIVER], extracting the schema [TOOL] to represent their commonality. It is totally implausible to suppose that [HAMMER], etc. immediately lose their unit status (cease to be established concepts) as soon as [TOOL] gains it. We have good reason to suppose, moreover, that speakers master particular sounds, such as [i], and manipulate them as units, while also having access to more abstract structures such as the schemas which define the [FRONT VOWEL] and [VOWEL] categories. The coexistence of schematic and content units can scarcely be considered controversial in cases like these.

I see no reason to suppose that the same is not true with respect to grammatical constructions. To take the simplest sort of case, consider the pattern of English plural formation using -*s* ([z]), e.g. *dogs, beds, pins*, etc. From some such array of previously established units, the learner of English is able to extract a schema that we can abbreviate *N-s*, i.e. a representation of the pattern whereby adding -*s* to a noun forms the plural of that noun. It is hard to see how such a schema could be extracted without some array of content units from which to extract it. It is even harder to see why we should believe that such previously mastered complexes are somehow unmastered as the schema emerges, losing their unit status and having to be computed henceforth as novel complexes requiring a constructive effort.

The grammar of a language is conceived in this framework as a structured inventory of conventional linguistic units.[2] For a given speaker, this inventory defines the boundaries of established linguistic convention as he knows it. Schematic units coexist in the grammar with content units that elaborate them. Their relation is dynamic and interactive. On the one hand, a schema commonly derives from an array of previously established content units; extracting the schema amounts to perceiving the similarities which unite these units and abstracting away from their points of divergence. It should be noted that schemas are the only abstract descriptive devices posited in cognitive grammar. They are the functional equivalent of rules, and embody generalizations, but are highly constrained in that they must always and only bear schematic relations to content structures.[3] On the other hand, because schemas are abstract, they project to novel instances. Thus, given the *N-s* schema based on familiar content units, the speaker of English can readily determine that novel configurations such as *quagmires* or *larders* meet all the specifications of the schema, and therefore fall within the bounds of established convention. To the extent that a speaker can judge a novel structure (e.g. *quagmires*) to be a valid instantiation of a schema like *N-s*, we can say that the schema "sanctions" this nonunit element as a well-formed extrapolation from established convention; such extrapolation is the basis for linguistic creativity. Of course, nonunit elements can quickly gain unit status once the speaker has occasion to employ them. As they do, they become by definition conventional linguistic units and are included as part of the grammar of the language.

1.2. Components

The archetypal view holds that language can be divided felicitously into numerous, essentially self-contained components. This is true for various levels. At the highest level, it is assumed that a fairly clear distinction can be made between competence and performance. At an intermediate level, it is assumed that an account of linguistic structure per se can be distinguished from supplementary accounts of such matters as discourse, pragmatics, and perhaps usage. Within linguistic structure, such domains as semantics, syntax, morphology, lexicon, and phonology are commonly conceived as separate, autonomous components.

I am dubious about all these distinctions, but we are concerned here only with the usual segregation of linguistic structure into separate semantic, syntactic, morphological, lexical, and phonological components. My position differs in that I posit only three broad facets of linguistic structure--semantic, phonological, and symbolic--represented in the grammar by corresponding units. However, symbolic structure is not distinct from semantic or phonological structure. Symbolic units are "bipolar": they consist of a semantic unit, at one pole, in symbolic association with a phonological unit, at the other. Lexicon, morphology, and syntax are all treated in cognitive grammar as symbolic in nature, forming a continuum of symbolic units. This view, of course, requires some elaboration. Let us begin with simple lexical units, proceeding along the continuum to simple morphological and then syntactic structures.

1.3. The symbolic nature of grammar

We begin with "minimal symbolic units", i.e. morphemes. No one, I take it, would seriously challenge the claim that morphemes are symbolic in nature, or that they associate phonological and semantic representations. Consider the morpheme *dog*. At the phonological pole, it is complex, being assembled out of the smaller phonological units [d], [ɔ], and [g]. We can represent this complex phonological unit as [[d]-[ɔ]-[g]], where hyphens between the components indicate that these smaller units combine "syntagmatically" to form the complex, higher-order phonological unit represented by the outermost set of square brackets.[4] The semantic pole of *dog* is similarly complex, but for now I will simply abbreviate it as [DOG]. The morpheme as a whole, then, is a higher-order symbolic unit formed by putting [DOG] and [[d]-[ɔ]-[g]] in symbolic association, i.e. [[DOG]/[[d]-[ɔ]-[g]]]. Both poles are internally complex, but each has unit status and can be manipulated as a whole. Only at the level of the whole do they enter into a symbolic relationship (i.e. *dog* is not analyzable into smaller meaningful parts).

If it is accepted that morphemes are symbolic, what about simple grammatical constructions? For instance, what about the morphological construction whereby the syntagmatic combination of a noun and the plural morpheme yields a plural noun? Consider all the individual statements that will have to be made somewhere in the grammar to give a full account of the internal structure of *dogs*. First, of course, must be a statement of the symbolic relationships defining each of the component morphemes: [[DOG]/[dɔg]]; [[PL]/[z]]. Next, we must state precisely the nature of the syntagmatic combination at each pole: how the component structures combine with one another to form a composite structure; how the parts are integrated to form a coherent higher-order system. At the semantic pole, we must specify how the concepts [DOG] and [PL] combine and integrate to yield the composite semantic unit [DOG-PL]; we will consider such semantic integration later in some detail. At the phonological pole, we must specify how [z] combines and integrates with [dɔg] to yield [dɔg-z]. This specification will say, roughly, that [z] is integrated as the outermost consonant in the cluster rhythmically associated with the preceding syllabic nucleus [ɔ]. Thus, alongside the symbolic units [[DOG]/[dɔg]] and [[PL]/[z]], the grammar must contain the complex syntagmatic units [[DOG]-[PL]] and [[dɔg]-[z]].

These units are correct and necessary for a full account of the structure of *dogs*, but by themselves they are insufficient. Nothing thus far indicates how the various specifications are coordinated--in particular, nothing reveals the crucial connection between the integration of semantic components and the integration of phonological components. To see this, we can observe that the analysis so far presented would be consistent with the claim that, in the sentence *My dogs have fleas*, the ending *-s* on *dog* symbolizes the plurality of *flea*, while the ending *-s* on *flea* symbolizes the plurality of *dog*. To avoid this absurdity, we need the additional statement that the composite semantic structure [DOG-PL], as a whole, stands in a symbolic relation with the composite phonological structure [dɔg-z]. In other words, when *-s* is added to *dog*, it symbolizes plurality specifically with respect to the concept that *dog* symbolizes, not the concept symbolized by some other stem.

Figure 1 summarizes all the information needed for a full, accurate characterization of this morphological construction (see also Figure 11 of Chapter 1). There are symbolic relationships between [DOG] and [dɔg], between [PL] and [z], and between the composite structures [DOG-PL] and [dɔg-z]. Syntagmatic relations, involving the integration of component structures, exist between [DOG] and [PL] at the semantic pole, and between [dɔg] and [z] at the phonological pole. Relations of componentiality also exist between each composite structure and the components out of which it is assembled. Because each composite structure, [DOG-PL] and [dɔg-z], is defined by the syntagmatic integration of its components, the symbolic relation between these composite structures is effectively a symbolic relation between their defining syntagmatic relationships; i.e. a particular mode of integration (between [DOG] and [PL]) at the semantic pole is coordinated with and symbolized by a particular mode of integration (between [dɔg] and [z]) at the phonological pole. Because both poles are crucially involved, by any reasonable definition this grammatical construction is therefore symbolic in nature, and I claim that this is true for morphological structures generally.[5]

This example clearly shows the importance for morphological structure of "analyzability": the salience of the relation between a composite structure and its components. The key to correct characterization of the plural construction exemplified by *dogs* is the specification that, when *-s* is added to a stem, it

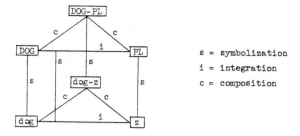

Figure 1.

symbolizes the plurality of the concept symbolized by that particular stem, not some other stem randomly chosen; and this specification presupposes the symbolic relations of the component morphemes in determining the symbolic relation between the composite structures. Analyzability is obviously a matter of degree, e.g. the components within *swimmer* are much more salient than those within *propeller*. Most symbolic units in language are analyzable to some degree, and this, rather than the nonanalyzability of single morphemes, should be taken as the norm. The difference between a complex form like *dogs*, representing a grammatical construction, and a simple form like *dog* can therefore be seen as a matter of their location on a scale of analyzability: *dogs* is near one extreme (full analyzability), while *dog* is at the other extreme, representing the limiting case (full lack of analyzability).

Analyzability, largely neglected in linguistic theory, is pivotal in one of the central claims of cognitive grammar, namely that the meaning of a symbolic expression is not the composite semantic structure alone, but is rather the composite structure in relation to all the components out of which it is built. In terms of Figure 1, the semantic structure of *dogs* includes not only the composite structure [DOG-PL], but also the components [DOG] and [PL], and the relation that each of these bears to the composite structure. Thus [DOG] and [PL] are considered active parts of the semantic structure of *dogs*: at some level, speakers perceive the semantic contribution of the individual components, in addition to dealing with the composite structure as an integrated whole. Speakers are thus attributed a kind of semantic "depth perception", and the semantic structure of *dogs* consists of the entire configuration at the top in Figure 1. As a notational device, I will use internal brackets to indicate analyzability. Thus [[DOG]-[PL]] is a "compacted" representation of the semantic structure of *dogs*, a notational equivalent of the "exploded" representation in Figure 1. Neither is equivalent to [DOG-PL], which stands for the composite structure alone, in isolation from any consideration of possible components.[6]

Given the apparatus introduced thus far, we can now describe the semantic difference between such pairs as *father* and *male parent* (ignoring all but their strict kinship values). At one level, they are semantically equivalent, and this is represented by attributing to them the same composite structure. The semantic difference which we feel intuitively reflects the fact that *male parent* is compositional in nature, with [MALE] and [PARENT] as active semantic components, while *father* is noncompositional and hence unanalyzable. *Male parent* can thus be represented as ([MALE]-[PARENT])--where parentheses are used to bracket the overall structure, on the presumption that this expression lacks unit status for a typical speaker--but *father* can be represented simply as [MALE-PARENT]. Though the two expressions have the same composite structure, they arrive at this structure through different compositional paths (a zero path in the case of *father*).

It has been argued that morphological constructions are symbolic in nature, with a particular mode of integration between phonological components standing in a symbolic relation to a particular mode of integration between semantic components. It is not hard to see that the same is true of basic syntactic constructions. Consider adjective-noun combinations such as *big dog*. The discussion for *big dog* is exactly parallel to that for *dogs* above, differing only in specifics. The expression is clearly analyzable, and the semantic integration of the concepts [BIG] and [DOG] to form [BIG-DOG] is symbolized by the integration of their phonological representations. The phonological integration is looser than in the case of a morphological construction, but no less crucial. To indicate that [BIG] modifies [DOG] in particular, rather than some other nominal concept, *big* must precede *dog*, being immediately contiguous to it, but as a separate word rather than an affix. This is not untypical of the integration found at the phonological pole of composite syntactic structures. It is commonly observed that elements of language which belong together semantically usually occur together syntactically. It can be seen that this phenomenon is a fairly direct consequence of the present framework--in particular of the claim that grammar, both morphology and syntax, is symbolic (cf. Langacker 1987a: 361f).

1.4. Semantic structure

It follows from the previous discussion of semantic structure that, in large measure, semantic structure is language specific rather than universal. I make a terminological distinction between ''semantic structure'' and ''conceptual structure''. Conceptual structure is the ongoing flow of cognition: any thought or concept, whether linguistic or nonlinguistic. Semantic structure is specifically linguistic, referring to the semantic pole of linguistic expressions (fixed or novel). Semantic structures are conceptual structures established by linguistic convention --the form which thoughts must assume for purposes of ready linguistic symbolization. Thus semantic structure is conventionalized conceptual structure.

We can assume that conceptual structure (or at least basic conceptual ability) is universal without entailing that semantic structure also is. The reason is simply that different languages often code the same conceptual structure by means of substantially different images.[7] This can mean various things. If the conventional expressions used to code the scene have the same composite structure, they may arrive at it by different compositional paths and thus differ semantically in terms of analyzability, as seen above with *father* and *male parent*. But they need not even have the same composite structure. The conventional expressions for a given conceptual scene may structure this scene in alternate ways--taking different perspectives on it, highlighting or omitting different facets. For example, (3a) and (3b) can both be used to describe the same situation as conceived in purely objective terms, but they mean very different things, highlighting different facets of the situation:

(3) a. *The glass is half empty.*
    b. *The glass is half full.*

Similarly, all the sentences in (4) could be used to describe the same configuration, but each does it through a different image. Note that a particular image and expression may be required by the conventional usage of a given language.

(4) a. *The statue is on the pedestal.*
    b. *The pedestal is under the statue.*
    c. *The statue is standing on the pedestal.*
    d. *The statue is sitting on the pedestal.*
    e. *The statue is resting on the pedestal.*
    f. *The pedestal is sitting under the statue.*
    g. *The pedestal is supporting the statue.*

In (5) we see English renditions of the conventional comparative constructions of many languages. Despite their functional equivalence, I would argue that the four expressions differ semantically.

(5) a. *The boy is taller than the girl.*
    b. *The boy is above the girl in height.*
    c. *The boy is beyond the girl in height.*
    d. *The boy is tall, the girl is not tall.*

Semantic identity can be asserted in such cases only by denying imagery and analyzability--by claiming that only composite semantic structures count as the semantic value of expressions, and that individual components (e.g. the morphemes *sit, rest, support, above, beyond,* and *not*) make no active contribution to the meaning of the sentences. Such a conception of meaning is too narrow and impoverished to be of much interest for linguistic purposes.[8]

To see more concretely the linguistic significance of analyzability and conventional imagery, let us compare and contrast the expressions *peas* and *corn*. The notions they designate, at the purely conceptual (nonlinguistic) level, are quite comparable. Both involve a mass of kernel-like objects, and the individual objects are reasonably similar in size, discreteness, etc. We can say that their conceptual structures are quite parallel. Their semantic structure is another matter, since they differ in "level of lexicalization". That is, *peas* lexicalizes its conceptual structure at the level of the individual kernel-like object, and the notion of a mass object is derived by combining this with the plural concept, whereas *corn* lexicalizes its conceptual structure at the level of the mass. Semantically, then, *peas* is composite, having the structure [[PEA]-[PL]], but *corn* is unanalyzable, with the structure [CORN]. The semantic unit [PEA] is an active part of the semantic structure of *peas*, but there is nothing comparable in the case of *corn*. Thus, since [PEA] is a semantic component, the individual kernel-like objects have a greater degree of cognitive salience for *peas* than for *corn*; the expressions employ different conventional imagery, highlighting different facets of the conceptual structures. This has linguistic consequences, since certain grammatical phenomena--such as plural number agreement, plural demonstratives, and certain quantifiers--are sensitive to the difference between mass objects with salient components vs. mass objects construed as though they were continuous:[9]

(6) a. *The peas are cold.*   a'. *The corn is cold.*
   b. *I like these peas.*   b'. *I like this corn.*
   c. *He ate many peas.*   c'. *He ate much corn.*
   d. *Seven peas got squashed.*   d'. **Seven corn got squashed.*

1.5. Grammatical morphemes

One aspect of the autonomous syntax hypothesis is the claim that grammatical morphemes are for the most part meaningless, being inserted for purely formal or grammatical purposes. This claim is almost a necessary one, since the autonomy of syntax would appear very dubious if we admitted that grammatical markers are meaningful, and that their syntactic use is determined by the meanings they convey.

The distinction between lexical and grammatical morphemes represents an artifactual dichotomization based on sharp differences between examples selected from the endpoints of what is really a continuum. It is easy and tempting, for instance, to contrast lexical units like *ostrich* and *brick* with grammatical markers like *of* and *be*; with just this array of data, it is hard to deny that we are dealing with two very different sorts of entities. In reality, however, both lexical and grammatical morphemes vary along a continuum in regard to such parameters as the complexity and abstractness of their semantic specifications. While so-called lexical morphemes tend to cluster near the complex/concrete end of the continuum, we see a clear gradation in series of forms like *ostrich--bird--animal--thing*. So-called grammatical morphemes tend to cluster near the simple/abstract end of the continuum, but here too we observe a gradation: *above--may--have--of*. The scales clearly overlap; e.g. *thing* can hardly be considered more complex semantically (or even more concrete) than *above*. I thus contend that most if not all grammatical morphemes are meaningful, and make active semantic contributions to the expressions in which they appear.

Let us consider the morpheme *of* as a test case. In transformational accounts, it is common to find *of* inserted by means of a rule such as (7), illustrated by the examples in (8).

(7) N NP ===> N *of* NP

(8) a. *a friend of Bill*
   b. *the shooting of the hunters*
   c. *the bottom of the jar*
   d. *a kernel of corn*
   e. *some of the peas*

That is, *of* is treated as a meaningless morpheme inserted for purely formal purposes, to break up the sequence N-NP.[10] I claim, however, that *of* makes a semantic contribution in these expressions, and is included in large part for that very reason. I do not claim that all instances of *of* are necessarily identical in meaning: like lexical morphemes, grammatical morphemes often have a variety of interrelated senses. The particular variant of *of* to be considered here is the one represented in (8c)-(8e). The unit [OF] predicates a relation between two entities, in which one is an inherent and restricted subpart of the other. One entity, corresponding to the prepositional object, represents an integrated whole; the other entity is arrived at by following an inward path from the external boundaries of the first.

For (8c), the appropriateness of this characterization should be evident. The relation which *bottom* bears to *jar* is that of a restricted inherent subpart in a very direct and concrete sense. Observe that *of* joins with other prepositions such as *on* and *to* to form a paradigm of relationships:

(9) a. *the bottom of the jar* b. *?the bottom on the jar* c. *??the bottom to the jar*
   a'. *?the label of the jar*   b'. *the label on the jar*   c'. *??the label to the jar*
   a''. *?the lid of the jar*   b''. *the lid on the jar*   c''. *the lid to the jar*

On is used here in a basic locative sense, predicating a relation between two objects conceived as distinct. *To* is used in a sense derivative of its locative-path sense: it describes the relation between two distinct objects which, though separate or separable, are conceived as belonging together in an integrated assembly. The intuitive judgments indicated in (9) are all to be expected if the three prepositions are attributed the meanings suggested. For the (a) examples, *the bottom of the jar* is slightly more natural than either *the label of the jar* or *the lid of the jar*, since labels and lids are not integral parts of jars to the same degree as their bottoms are. In the (b) examples, *the bottom on the jar* is somewhat odd, since *on* suggests two distinct objects rather than an integral part/whole relationship. But *the label on the jar* and *the lid on the jar* are both fine, though the label and lid must actually be attached to the jar for the expressions to be appropriate. Finally, in the (c) examples, *the lid to the jar* is felicitous, suggesting that the lid and jar are separated but belong together; however *the bottom to the jar* and *the label to the jar* both pose difficulties, since in normal circumstances the bottom and label of a jar are not readily separated from the remainder. I do not feel that the meaning attributed to *of* is any more problematic than the ones attributed to *on* and *to*, and it is hardly more abstract than the latter.

Example (8d), *a kernel of corn*, is also compatible with the characterization offered for [OF]. *Corn* specifies a mass entity, and *kernel* designates a restricted inherent subpart of this mass. The case of quantifiers is quite parallel. With respect to a mass, given here as *peas*, the quantifier designates a restricted inherent subpart the size of which depends on the semantic value of the quantifier. In the case of (8e), *some of the peas*, the size is left quite vague.

This analysis is not merely compatible with the data; it also explains a fact that would be totally arbitrary given the transformational analysis in (7). As (10) shows, *of* can be omitted from a quantifier expression with *all*, so that *all of the peas* has *all the peas* as a variant. However, other quantifiers do not permit *of*'s omission:

(10) a. *all of the peas*
　　 b. *all the peas*
　　 c. *{most/some/many/seven} of the peas*
　　 d. **{most/some/many/seven} the peas*

With the transformational insertion analysis, we would have to say that the meaningless *of* is inserted only optionally in some cases; it would be totally accidental that the optionality should be tied to *all*, rather than to some other quantifier. With my analysis, however, this peculiarity of *all* has a ready explanation: [OF] predicates a relation between a reference object and a restricted inherent subpart of it. In the case of *all*, but with none of the other quantifiers above, the restrictive nature of the subpart is vacuous. That is, if one follows the restricting path from reference object to the subpart, it is a zero path--the limiting or degenerate case--just when the quantifier happens to be *all*. Because of the vacuity of the notion of restrictiveness with *all*, it is easy to see why English would evolve or tolerate an alternate construction in which *of* is omitted. The analysis is corroborated by the following:

(11) a. *both of the peas*
   b. *both the peas*

The only other quantifier for which *of* is optional is *both*, which is clearly equivalent to *all* in relevant respects; *both*, if you like, is simply the dual version of *all*.[11]

I claim that (10a) and (10b) are semantically distinct. Though they have the same composite structure, they arrive at that structure by alternate compositional paths and convey different images. By virtue of the semantic contribution which *of* makes, *all of the peas* explicitly portrays the entity designated by *all* as a restricted subpart of the reference mass, though the degree of restriction just happens to be zero. *All the peas* does not even bring the notion of a restricted inherent subpart into the picture. The two expressions thus have different semantic structures.

1.6. Overtness of grammatical structure

Cognitive grammar does not posit deep or underlying syntactic structures which are distinct from surface structures. By and large, the morphemes overtly present in an expression coincide with the semantic units which determine its meaning, and their combination into complex formal structures at the phonological pole is symbolic of their semantic integration to form complex representations at the semantic pole.[12]

The statement that cognitive grammar does not permit underlying syntactic structures or derivations must be clarified, since it has certain features that might initially be confused with these devices. One such feature is the positing of schemas in addition to content units. Thus, besides the content unit [[[DOG]-[PL]]/[[dɔg]-[z]]] (Figure 1), the grammar of English contains a schematic unit which we can represent as [[[COUNT N]-[PL]]/[[X]-[z]]], the former constituting an elaboration of the latter.

Schemas, by definition, are abstract in relation to content units or actual expressions, but the nature of this abstractness is quite different from that of deep structures in the archetypal view. A deep structure can be quite distinct in organization from its surface manifestation (consider the derivation of passives from active structures), but a schema can differ from instantiating content structures only in degree of specificity, and can never be substantially different in kind. Moreover, deep structures and their surface descendants are both fully specified: they are underlying and superficial content structures (related by transformations or equivalent statements), and together constitute a multilevel SYNTAGMATIC structure. By contrast, schemas are more closely analogous to rules and grammatical classes than to deep structures; they bear a relation to their instantiations that can be considered PARADIGMATIC. A schema captures a generalization and categorizes a series of content structures which are parallel in formation; it does not relate one content structure to another, except in the sense of expressing their similarities. Thus the elaborative relation between the schema [[[COUNT N]-[PL]]/[[X]-[z]]] and the content unit [[[DOG]-[PL]]/[[dɔg]-[z]]] serves only to categorize the latter, and to group it with other instantiations as manifestations of the same general pattern.

The step-by-step derivation of surface structures from underlying representations in archetypal syntax is vaguely similar in certain ways to another device in cognitive grammar, namely "constituency trees". Constituency trees simply represent the order in which simple structures combine to form progressively more complex composite structures. Figure 1 is a bipolar constituency tree involving only one layer of syntagmatic combination and componentiality; but as a general matter there will be numerous such layers, with a composite structure at one level functioning as a component at the next higher level of organization. For example, the constituency tree for *most of the pins* is sketched in Figure 2.[13] Several notational devices should be noted. The composite structures (MOST-OF-THE-PIN-PL) and (OF-THE-PIN-PL) are given in parentheses, on the presumption that they lack unit status; all the other constituents are included in square brackets and presumed to be units.[14] At each level in these hierarchies, one of the components combined syntagmatically is said to be dependent, and the other autonomous; syntagmatic combination is indicated here by an arrow leading from the dependent component to the autonomous one. Moreover, one of the two components is usually singled out as the profile determinant, indicated here by underscores.

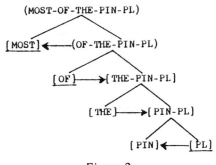

Figure 2.

The constituency trees of cognitive grammar vaguely resemble transformational derivations in the following way. As one follows the assembly of a complex expression, starting from the autonomous component at the lowest level and proceeding up the constituency tree to reach the topmost composite structure, the nature and categorization of the composite structure can vary from one level to the next. Thus the autonomous unit [PIN] is categorized as a count noun, but it combines with the dependent [PL] to yield a composite structure, [PIN-PL], which functions as a mass noun. Combining this composite mass noun with [THE] at the next hierarchical level yields a mass noun that is "grounded" (Chapter 12), making it an instance of the "nominal" (i.e. noun phrase) category. But (OF-THE-PIN-PL) is a prepositional phrase, and finally, (MOST-OF-THE-PIN-PL) is again a nominal.[15]

The most fundamental contrast with a transformational derivation should be readily apparent. Such a derivation typically relates structures of roughly the same size, for instance deriving one type of clause from another. However, a cognitive-grammar constituency tree specifies how a complex structure is built up by successive accretion of smaller components. A transformational derivation relates a set of fully-formed constituency (or phrase-structure) trees to one another, whereas the sense in which we can speak of a "derivation" in cognitive grammar pertains instead to the composition of a single constituency tree.

1.7. Continuum of lexicon, morphology, and syntax

Constituency trees like that in Figure 2 show rather concretely the continuum posited in cognitive grammar to unite lexicon, morphology, and syntax. In the "derivations" they represent, leading from simple to successively more complex structures, a single tree unites nonanalyzable lexical units (e.g. *pin*), found at the bottom; then, higher up, structures (e.g. *pins*) which are considered morphological because their integration at the phonological pole is internal to a single word; and finally, at the top, structures (e.g. *the pins; of the pins; most of the pins*) which are considered syntactic because their phonological integration is above the word level.

As we go from bottom to top along these symbolic hierarchies, the structures tend to become progressively more "diffuse" or loosely integrated with respect to various parameters. For one thing, the phonological integration becomes looser--ranging from maximal compactness at the bottom (a single, indivisible morpheme), through complex words (in which affixes tend to be less tightly bound to the stem as one goes from the root outward), to structures in which the components form phrases of varying degrees of rhythmic cohesiveness. Moreover, as we proceed from bottom to top, the likelihood increases that a structure will be analyzable, will exemplify a productive pattern, and will be regular in formation instead of idiosyncratic.

My only concern here is to point out that all these factors are matters of degree, and that, to the extent that natural divisions can be found along a parameter, the divisions do not coincide neatly from one parameter to the next in such a way that we would be justified in carving up the lexicon-morphology-syntax spectrum into discrete components. For example, if we distinguish between morphology and syntax on the basis of intraword vs. interword phonological integration, we find that this boundary has no strict correlation with basic divisions along the other parameters.[16] Words tend to be fixed units, and larger expressions tend to be novel, but there are both phrases with unit status and novel words. Words tend to be less analyzable than larger expressions, but many words are fully analyzable, and larger units often less so (consider idiomatic phrases). Though syntactic patterns tend to be more productive than morphological ones, we find the full gamut of possibilities in both domains (consider lexically-governed transformations). Regularity--the degree to which a composite structure has the properties which one would expect, given its components and a schema specifying their mode of integration--is also variable in both domains; again, however, it tends to be greater in syntactic combinations. The correlations are no better starting with any other parameter. Hence we must recognize these as essentially independent dimensions along which symbolic structures may vary continuously.

2. Descriptive framework

As preface to our analysis of the English passive, we need to review and elaborate the descriptive framework that it presupposes. Let us first consider the overall organization of a linguistic system. We will then examine the nature of syntagmatic combination and grammatical constructions.

2.1. Linguistic organization

The grammar of a language is defined as a structured inventory of conventional linguistic units. This inventory is structured in the sense that some units function as components of others. Thus [d] is a component of the composite phonological unit [dɔg], which in turn is a component of the minimal symbolic unit [[DOG]/[dɔg]], which itself is a component of the composite symbolic unit [[[DOG]-[PL]]/[[dɔg]-[z]]], etc. A unit (e.g. [d]) clearly can function as a component of many different higher-order units ([dɔg], [bɛd], [lɪd], etc.). The grammar of a language must therefore be conceived as a vast network of intersecting componential hierarchies.

A unit is always characterized relative to some domain. Most broadly, I assume that it is reasonable to speak of "phonological space" and "semantic space" as two facets of cognitive organization; jointly they define an abstract, bipolar "symbolic space". Phonological, semantic, and symbolic units are characterized relative to these respective domains. The list is exhaustive: every linguistic unit is phonological, semantic, or symbolic.

The notion of components joining to form more elaborate structures is quite general. Within the confines of this general notion, several types of componentiality must be recognized. One type is symbolization, as in [[DOG]/[dɔg]], involving only the establishment of a conventional correspondence between units in the two poles of symbolic space. A second type is syntagmatic combination, exemplified by [[DOG]-[PL]]; here a unit in semantic, phonological, or symbolic space is integrated with one or more additional units from the same domain. A third type is the joining of schematic and content units in a relation of schematicity; e.g. the categorization of [DOG] as a member of the [COUNT N] category is conceived as the formation of a complex semantic unit of the form [[COUNT N] → [DOG]]. The complex structures formed in this way are paradigmatic rather than syntagmatic, and occupy the "schematic plane" of relationships (as opposed to the "content plane") in semantic, phonological, or symbolic space. Schematic hierarchies are regarded as summaries of sets of individual schematic relationships of the form [[A] → [B]].

An elaborate and dynamic conception of relationships in the schematic plane is required. For one thing, the difference between schematic and content units is only relative. Speakers have the ability to conceptualize a situation at varying levels of abstraction, and a concept like [DOG], which appears as a content unit in contexts like (12a), serves as a schema (with categorizing function) in a context demanding greater specificity, as in (12b):

(12) a. *The Aztecs ate dogs.*
     b. *Dachshunds are funny dogs.*

Beyond this, it must be recognized that schematic relationships are dynamic reflections of the interplay between established convention and the pressures of ongoing language use. The forms they take are thus produced by the specific linguistic experience of individuals, starting during primary language acquisition and continuing throughout life. As a result, they are continually evolving structures that must vary somewhat from speaker to speaker, particularly at lower hierarchical levels (cf. Ferguson & Farwell 1975).

Schematic hierarchies, based on strictly elaborative relations of the form [[A] → [B]], are actually special cases of a broader class of relationships between units in the schematic plane. This broader class is most familiar in the domain of lexicon --specifically in the network of interrelated senses that is characteristic (as a dictionary readily shows) of virtually any lexical item in common use. In cognitive grammar, each of these senses of a lexical item is recognized as a separate semantic unit; together with the shared phonological unit, it defines a "semantic variant" of the lexical item. The variants of a lexical unit are therefore linked together at the semantic pole in a network of relationships which reflects their internal structures and the connections that speakers establish among them. It is important that we examine briefly the nature and evolution of these networks.

The conventional units of the grammar furnish the speaker with the means for assessing the status of novel expressions vis-à-vis established norms and expectations. This is done in accordance with the following general principle:

(13) Unit [A] sanctions a nonunit structure (B) as well-formed with respect to
    [A] to the extent that [A] is judged schematic for (B).

In other words, a novel structure (B) is an acceptable extrapolation from established convention, as represented in [A], if (B) elaborates [A] and therefore potentially instantiates the category that [A] defines. The status of (B) as a nonunit structure instantiating category [A] can be symbolized as ([A] → (B)). The overall status of a nonunit expression with respect to the conventions of a language is a function of its status with respect to all the units from which sanction is sought (see Chapter 10). The set of such units in the schematic plane, together with their relations to one another and to the expression being evaluated, constitute the "structural description" of this expression.

Application of principle (13) in actual language use leads to the growth of lexical networks through semantic specialization and extension, as illustrated in Figure 3, representing different senses of the lexical item *dog*. We start with a speaker (or learner) who has only the conception of a prototypical dog; this concept is given as [DOG], and we assume that our speaker has mastered the symbolic unit [[DOG]/[dɔg]]. When first exposed to a beagle, this speaker will probably have little trouble deciding that *dog* is an appropriate term for it, even though the concept and this usage are novel, since it is easy to construe (BEAGLE) as an elaboration of the prototypical conception [DOG]; ([DOG] → (BEAGLE)) represents this categorial judgment. Since (BEAGLE) is judged to be an elaboration of the concept [DOG], the symbolic structure ((BEAGLE)/[dɔg]) is seen to constitute an elaboration (specifically at the semantic pole) of the symbolic unit [[DOG]/[dɔg]]: the former is sanctioned by the latter in accordance with (13), and this sanctioning or categorial relationship is embodied in the structure ([[DOG]/[dɔg]] → ((BEAGLE)/[dɔg])). With a certain amount of practice, all these structures will gain unit status and be added to the speaker's version of the grammar of English, so that [BEAGLE] becomes an established semantic unit. The new symbolic unit [[BEAGLE]/[dɔg]] represents an item of conventional usage, namely that beagles are among the types of creatures called *dogs*. The classificatory unit [[[DOG]/[dɔg]]   →   [[BEAGLE]/[dɔg]]] functions in the schematic plane as part of a lexical network uniting different variants of the lexical item *dog*.

This case of specialization, based on "full schematicity", contrasts with semantic extension, which is based on "partial schematicity" and hence partial sanction. I say that [A] is only partially schematic for (B) when [A] can be

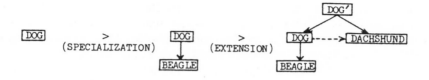

Figure 3.

construed as schematic for (B) only with a certain amount of "strain--e.g. because [A] and (B) have conflicting specifications, or because some substructure within [A] is missing from (B). I symbolize this relation with a dashed arrow: ([A] ---> (B)). It can be illustrated by the case of speakers familiar only with prototypical dogs (including beagles) who encounter a dachshund for the first time. The novel concept (DACHSHUND) can be judged an elaboration of [DOG] only with strain, since its shape specification (in particular the ratio of body length to height) falls outside the general range specified in the prototypical conception. The novel symbolic expression ((DACHSHUND)/[dɔg]) therefore receives less than full sanction from [[DOG]/[dɔg]]. Our speakers are nevertheless likely to refer to the dachshund as a *dog*, even though the usage is technically ill-formed with respect to their linguistic system, because the strain is very slight and well within the tolerances of normal language use.[17] As this usage becomes familiar, [[DACHSHUND]/[dɔg]] gains unit status and is incorporated into speakers' grammars as a conventional unit, as does the categorizing structure [[[DOG]/[dɔg]] ---> [[DACHSHUND]/[dɔg]]], the semantic pole of which is depicted in the last diagram of Figure 3. At this point the usage ceases to be ill-formed: it has become part of linguistic convention, and hence self-sanctioning.

Figure 3 also shows a schema [DOG'] superordinate to both [DOG] and [DACHSHUND]. This more abstract conception represents their commonality, i.e. the similarity between them (at an appropriate level of abstraction) that permits the semantic extension uniting them; it will be almost identical to the prototype [DOG], different only in having a less precise specification for length-to-height ratio. As a term is extended to designate a wider array of interrelated concepts, the emergence of a more abstract, more highly-schematic unit representing their commonality is facilitated.[18]

These notions do not apply just to the meanings of lexical items but to all facets of linguistic structure (Chapter 10). Semantic, phonological, and symbolic structures all give rise--by processes of schematization, specialization, and extension--to categories which are "complex" in the sense that their characterization requires a network of related units centered on a prototype. For grammatical purposes, the most important categorizations pertain to symbolic structures. It was argued in Chapter 3 that basic grammatical categories are definable with reference to the nature of their profiles. Thus a noun (in the most inclusive sense) is a symbolic structure whose semantic pole profiles a thing, whereas the semantic pole of a verb designates a process. The full characterization of such a class comprises a network of symbolic structures that includes an overall class schema (e.g. [[THING]/[X]]); subschemas described at various levels of specificity representing distinct subclasses (e.g. subschemas for the count-noun and mass-noun classes); the category prototype ([[PHYSICAL OBJECT]/[X]], a subschema within the count-noun category); and specific nouns established as conventional units (e.g. [[DOG]/[dɔg]]).

Describing grammatical patterns are constructional schemas, which specify conventionally established ways of combining (integrating) simpler symbolic structures to form more complex expressions. A constructional schema is merely a schematization of a set of specific expressions whose formation is parallel in some respect. The schema reflects their commonality; internally it displays the same symbolic complexity as its instantiating expressions--except that some or all of its symbolic components are schematic rather than specific--and details the nature of their integration to form a composite expression. A constructional schema can be used as a template for the assembly of novel expressions on the same pattern, or more generally, as a categorizing unit providing full or partial sanction for such expressions. An expression's categorization by sanctioning schemas constitutes its structural description (see Figure 7 of Chapter 1).

2.2. Syntagmatic combination

A predicate, internally, is an integrated system in which certain substructures are profiled. The same is true at higher levels of semantic organization. A composite semantic structure is derived by integrating the component structures in a very specific way, depending on their internal properties, and some facet of the integrated composite structure is selected as the profile of the whole. By way of illustration, let us go through the componential organization of *most of the pins*, following the constituency tree in Figure 2.[19]

It will be convenient to start with the constituent *the pins*. In Figure 2, of course, the various semantic units were all simply abbreviated with capital letters. To study their mode of syntagmatic combination, we must actually propose a rudimentary analysis of their internal structure, and operate with some more or less "pictorial" representation of that structure. Figure 4 is thus equivalent to the corresponding portion of Figure 2, but carries the semantic analysis to a greater degree.

Let us begin by examining the individual predicates [THE], [PIN], and [PL], which occur at the ends of branches in this constituency tree, since they correspond to nonanalyzable lexical units; the other two structures are composite and analyzable. All five semantic units are categorized by their profiles as things. The

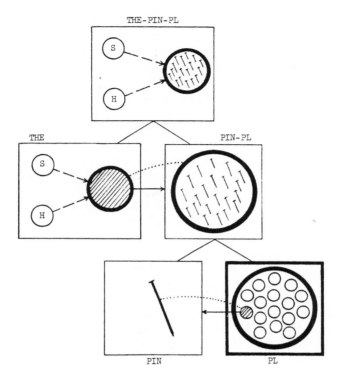

Figure 4.

diagram shows two levels of syntagmatic combination: in the first, [PIN] and [PL] combine to form the composite structure [PIN-PL]; this in turn combines with [THE] to yield [THE-PIN-PL] at the second level. The directionality of the arrows indicates that [PL] and [THE] are the dependent structures at the respective levels, while the heavy-line box (corresponding to an underscore in Figure 2) indicates that [PL] is also a profile determinant.

The representation of [PIN] is greatly simplified for pictorial ease; a fuller characterization would involve coordinated specifications in numerous domains (e.g. shape, material, function--cf. Figure 2 of Chapter 1). While [PIN] designates a simple, discrete object, the plural morpheme is more abstract: it designates a particular kind of mass object, defined as consisting of indefinitely many replications (in type) of a discrete object. The nature of this replicated discrete object is left unspecified within the plural predicate itself; only in syntagmatic combination with a count noun like *pin* is its nature specified. Note that the individual discrete objects are in the base of [PL], but are not profiled. Thus [PL] designates a schematic mass object, and a composite structure derived from it, such as [PIN-PL], designates a more specific mass object.

The definite article is what I refer to as a "grounding predication" (cf. Langacker 1978, 1985, *to appear*; Chapter 12). Both nominal and verbal elements take grounding predications, which specify their status in relation to the "ground", i.e. to the speech event and its participants. In the case of nominal structures, grounding pertains to questions of identification: whether or to what degree the speech-act participants can locate the thing referred to within the mass of objects populating their conceptual universe. A "nominal" (i.e. noun phrase) is a grounded expression that profiles a thing. In the case of verbal structures, grounding pertains to questions of time and reality. A "finite clause" is a grounded expression that profiles a process. With due allowances for the conceptual differences between things and relations, grounding predications for nominals and finite clauses show extensive parallels.

As for the definite article in particular, it suffices for present purposes to say that it profiles a thing (characterized with maximal schematicity) and further specifies that both the speaker (S) and the hearer (H) have each succeeded in establishing "mental contact" with that thing (i.e. in singling it out for individual conscious awareness), as indicated by the dashed arrows. If it seems strange to attribute to *the* the profile of a thing, recall that it corresponds to the first element of the demonstratives *this*, *that*, etc., which can function as nominal heads. It turns out that grounding predications as a class have a number of special properties. The most fundamental of these properties (discussed in Chapter 12) is that a grounding predication profiles the grounded entity rather than the grounding relationship itself. Hence *the* designates the thing whose epistemic status is being specified, whereas the mental contact which provides that status constitutes an unprofiled facet of the base.

Syntagmatic combination relies on correspondences established between subparts of the component structures; corresponding substructures (connected by dotted lines) are equated as referring to the same conceived entity. This overlap is what permits the components to unite in a coherent, integrated, composite structure.

When two component structures combine, normally an asymmetry exists between them, with grounds for regarding one as "conceptually autonomous" and the other as "conceptually dependent".[20] One structure is said to be dependent on another to the extent that it presupposes it as part of its own internal structure. More precisely, one structure, D, is said to be dependent on another structure, A, to the extent that a substructure (of type A) figures saliently in the internal composition of D, and is put in correspondence with A. We can illustrate this with [[PIN]-[PL]], where [PIN] is considered autonomous and [PL] dependent. As noted previously, [PL] designates a mass object defined as an indefinite number of replications of a discrete object. Thus [PL] makes salient internal reference to a schematically specified discrete object, and this substructure of [PL] is put in correspondence with the profile of [PIN] in the [[PIN]-[PL]] construction (observe the line of integration in the bottom layer of Figure 4). The situation is asymmetrical, since [PIN] does not make internal reference to a mass with anything near the salience that [PL] does to a discrete object. Hence [PL] is depicted as dependent on [PIN] in Figure 4.

We see, then, that when an autonomous and a dependent component combine to form a composite structure, some substructure within the dependent component corresponds to the autonomous structure as a whole (as determined by its profile) and typically stands in a schematic relation to it. This substructure is called an "elaboration site" (e-site), and is cross-hatched for ease of identification. The autonomous structure elaborates the content of the e-site to which it corresponds, specifying in greater detail this entity which the dependent component introduces only in schematic terms. The arrow from the dependent to the autonomous structure is therefore to be equated with the arrow of schematicity; observe that it connects the e-site within the dependent structure to the autonomous structure as a whole, for it is between these in particular that the relation of schematicity holds. This elaborative relation between the e-site in the dependent structure and the corresponding autonomous structure constitutes "grammatical valence" (see Chapter 6).

In Figure 4, then, the dependent [PL] bears a valence relation to the conceptually autonomous [PIN]. Because the individual discrete objects in the base of [PL] are specified to be replications of one another, it is arbitrary which one(s) we single out diagramatically as the e-site;[21] this substructure corresponds to [PIN] (to its profile in particular) and bears a schematic relation to it. This overlap between [PL] and [PIN] permits their integration to form a coherent composite structure. When an autonomous and a dependent structure combine syntagmatically, one of them is generally singled out as the "profile determinant" in the construction. The profile determinant is the component whose profile is inherited as the profile for the composite structure. Thus [PL] functions as the profile determinant in the [[PIN]-[PL]] construction, and the composite structure [PIN-PL] has the profile of a mass object instead of a discrete object.

It may be helpful, in considering syntagmatic combination, to think of the component semantic structures as being drawn on plastic transparencies. When the components are combined, the two transparencies are superimposed. The profile determinant goes on top, and corresponding entities on the two are lined up precisely, so that they merge into a single image when the stacked transparencies are viewed from above. What the viewer sees, when he looks at the stack from above, is the composite structure. Since the profile determinant is on top, its specifications are more salient; consequently the composite structure inherits its profile, which overrides that of the other component. Beyond this, the viewer is credited with the depth perception needed to observe the contribution made by each component to the integrated composite picture--this constitutes analyzability.

The valence relation between an autonomous and a dependent component is based on how a structure with the profile of the autonomous component can be made to fit into the scene provided by the dependent component, i.e. whether it matches some substructure within this scene, and can be taken as elaborating this substructure. Thus it is natural for the dependent structure to be the profile determinant, and this may in fact be the unmarked case. However, the opposite alignment is also very common; an example occurs in Figure 2. The distinction is a matter of considerable significance, since it allows a characterization of the traditional notion "modifier" that proves both workable and revelatory with respect to the underlying intuition behind the notion. The definition is quite simple: a dependent structure is a modifier of an autonomous structure in a syntagmatic combination when the autonomous structure is the profile determinant; i.e. D modifies A in the syntagmatic configuration D → A. A head-modifier relation thus involves a type of skewing, where structure A is able to combine grammatically with D because A fits into the scene D provides, but where their combination nevertheless organizes the composite scene along the lines suggested by A (the head), reducing the organization suggested by D (the modifier) to a tangential role. In terms of Figure 2, *of the pins* is a modifier of *most* in *most of the pins*, but the plural morpheme would not be considered a modifier of *pin* in *pins*. The contrast between *red cup* and *(The) cup (is) red* provides further illustration. In both examples, *red* and *cup* combine through a valence relation; *red* is dependent, and *cup* is autonomous.[22] *Red* qualifies as a modifier in *red cup*, since the autonomous *cup* is the profile determinant (*red cup* as a whole designates a thing, not a relation). In *The cup is red*, however, the dependent *red* is the profile determinant, since the clause as a whole is relational rather than nominal. Here *red* is not generally considered a modifier of *cup* (except in a very broad sense of the term): we speak of a subject-predicate rather than a head-modifier relation between them.

The second hierarchical level in Figure 4 should now be largely self-explanatory: [THE] is dependent, since it makes salient internal reference to a thing, which it grounds. This grounded entity corresponds to the mass designated by [PIN-PL]; it functions as the e-site within [THE], and [PIN-PL] elaborates the schematic specification. No profile determinant is indicated: since the components have profiles that correspond, either choice yields the same profile for the composite structure. The composite structure [THE-PIN-PL] therefore designates a mass object, identified to both speaker and hearer, which is characterized as consisting of an indefinite number of discrete objects each of which has the specifications of [PIN].[23]

Now that the constituent *the pins* has been examined, we are ready to look at *most of the pins*. The first step is to consider the semantic structure of *most*. Like *all* and *some* (among others), *most* is a "relative quantifier", so called because it expresses the quantity of a mass only in relative terms--in reference to a larger, landmark mass of which it is an inherent subpart.[24] I will go further and claim that they are relational nouns--i.e. they have the profile of a thing, but also have a salient, unprofiled landmark in their base--and that they serve as grounding predications. Their categorization as nouns is not terribly problematic, since they function overtly as nominal heads:

(14) a. *All agreed to cooperate.*
b. *Most proved to be rotten.*
c. *I only tried some.*

The fact that they are indefinite does not preclude their being grounding predications, since grounding can take the form of the absence (as well as the presence) of mental contact by the speaker and hearer. Moreover, they do specify the "epistemic" status of a mass object, in a broad sense that relates to its potential differentiation from a more inclusive background mass. Thus *most* specifies that the mass object which it designates comes reasonably close to exhausting the landmark mass it implies. This predication locates its profiled mass epistemically by saying in effect that the probability of finding a member of the profiled mass is quite high if one chooses at random a member of the landmark mass.

The predicate [MOST] is sketched in Figure 5(a). The conception serving as abstract domain for all the relative quantifiers involves the comparison of two mass objects, one of which is an inherent subpart of the other. Conceptually, the profiled mass is superimposed on the landmark mass and "stretched outward", as it were, to see how close its boundaries come to coinciding with the boundaries of the landmark. If we consider their boundaries as wholes, or some arbitrary segment of their boundaries, then the conceptual operation of comparison can be taken as defining an abstract scale, on which the landmark boundary functions as a goal or target of comparison that the boundary of the profiled mass can approach to varying degrees. This is shown in Figure 5(b), which corresponds to the portion of Figure 5(a) within the dashed lines. Here [MOST] specifies the profiled mass as falling in the "neighborhood" of the landmark along the scale of comparison. As

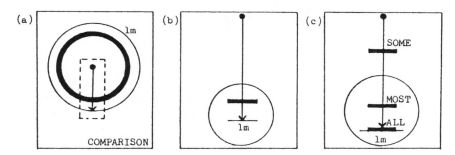

Figure 5.

seen in Figure 5(c), [ALL] is the same except that it instead involves an identity relation, while [SOME] falls outside the neighborhood of the landmark.[25]

Most of the pins is diagramed in Figure 6. At the first level of integration [OF] combines syntagmatically with [THE-PIN-PL], which corresponds to [OF]'s landmark and elaborates this e-site.[26] Since [OF] is dependent and also is the profile determinant, the relation between it and [THE-PIN-PL] is a prepositional-object relation, rather than a head-modifier one. The nonunit composite structure (OF-THE-PIN-PL) inherits from [OF] the profile of a stative relation. Its landmark is specified as a mass of pins identified to both speaker and hearer, and the trajector is some restricted submass of unspecified size.

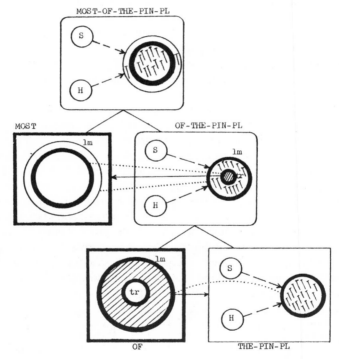

Figure 6.

At the second level of integration, (OF-THE-PIN-PL) is a prepositional-phrase modifier to the head [MOST].[27] There are two lines of integration at this level: the landmark mass of [MOST] corresponds to the landmark of the dependent structure, and the profile of [MOST] corresponds to its trajector, the e-site. [MOST] specifies the size of the trajector submass within the landmark mass, and since [MOST] is the profile determinant, (MOST-OF-THE-PIN-PL) designates this submass. *Most of the pins* thus profiles a mass of discrete objects (each with the specification of *pin*) whose boundary falls in the neighborhood of that of a more inclusive landmark mass predicated as being identified to both speaker and hearer.

3. The passive construction

There is no consensus in the generative tradition about the proper way of handling the rough synonymy of pairs of sentences like these:

(15) a. *Alice approached Bill.*
  b. *Bill was approached by Alice.*

However, several basic features of Chomsky's classic analysis (1957) have persisted, in one form or another, in many subsequent descriptions (e.g. Perlmutter & Postal 1983). One feature is that the synonymy is handled through a multilevel syntagmatic structure for passive clauses, in which the deep structure (or initial stratum) is basically active in organization. A second feature is that the object of *by* in passives is treated as a demoted deep-structure clausal subject. A third feature is that all or some of the grammatical morphemes marking the passive construction (*by*, *be*, and the perfect participial inflection) are meaningless entities, with purely formal or syntactic function.

The cognitive grammar analysis differs on all three points. Passive clauses do not derive from active clauses; though pairs like (15a) and (15b) have essentially the same composite structure, accounting for their rough synonymy, these composite structures are arrived at by different compositional paths, and the sentences are thus semantically distinct because of analyzability. All three grammatical morphemes are meaningful and figure actively in the semantic structure of passive expressions, contributing to their semantic distinctness from the corresponding actives. Finally, the object of *by* is simply the object of *by*: it is not demoted, and at no level is it the clausal subject (though it does correspond to the trajector of the verb taking the participial inflection).[28]

Before we examine the semantic value of the three grammatical morphemes, it will be helpful to review or introduce certain abbreviatory notations (cf. Figure 10 of Chapter 1). The notations in Figure 7 will allow us to represent crucial semantic relationships in diagrams of manageable complexity, but it must be remembered that they abbreviate highly elaborate semantic structures. Recall that an entity can be either a thing or a relation. A stative relation, or state, unites at least two entities, which may be either things or other relations. A complex relation is one consisting of a continuous series of component states (only a few of which can be explicitly represented in diagrams such as these). Such a relation is said to be atemporal when it is viewed holistically (i.e. when accessed primarily by means of summary scanning), even though the component states are conceived as being distributed through a continuous span of time. When a complex relation is scanned sequentially, it is termed a process; sequential scanning is indicated by a heavy-line segment of the time arrow. A process may be either perfective or imperfective, depending on whether or not the set of component states it profiles is bounded and homogeneous. Observe the notations used to indicate whether a state is specific or schematic, and whether a processual conception is perfective, imperfective, or neutral (schematic) in regard to this contrast.

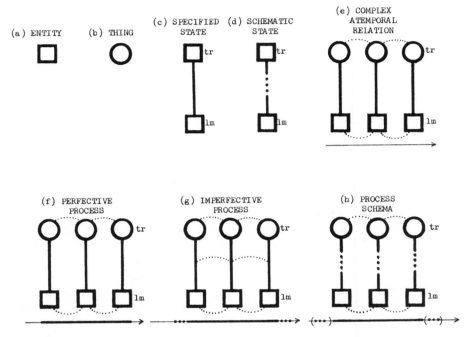

Figure 7.

Illustrating these and other notations is the construction representing the basic *V-er* nominalizing pattern (as in *hiker, diver, complainer, mixer*, etc.). Its semantic pole is sketched in Figure 8. One component structure is the verb stem (e.g. *hike*), which profiles a specific process. Observe that I have simplified the abbreviatory notation for a process even beyond what is shown in Figure 7, by explicitly indicating only one component state; nevertheless, the heavy-line portion of the time arrow signals that the profiled relationship in fact comprises a continuous series of such states. The predicate [ER] (i.e. the semantic pole of *-er*) designates a thing identified solely as the trajector of a process. Reference to this process is schematic internally to [ER], but specific in combination with the semantic pole of the verb stem. More precisely, [ER]'s base is a schematic process that functions as the elaboration site in this morphological construction. It is put in correspondence with, and elaborated by, the specific process profiled by the verb stem. [ER] is the profile determinant, so when corresponding entities are superimposed, the composite structure [V-ER] profiles the trajector of the specific process evoked by [V].

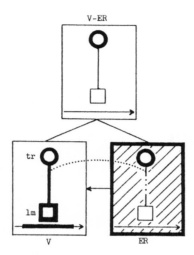

Figure 8.

3.1. The perfect participle

The perfect participial morpheme has a number of semantic variants, as do most common symbolic units. We will concern ourselves only with variation at its semantic pole, and will concentrate for now on three variants of the participial predicate (to be symbolized [PERF]) that occur with *be*.

Consider first these examples:

(16) a. *My wrist is all swollen.*
    b. *Janice is gone.*
    c. *The sidewalk is cracked.*

These illustrate a variant of [PERF]--call it [$PERF_1$]--that is purely aspectual in nature; specifically, it designates a state characterized as the final state in a process (e.g. *swollen* designates the final state in the process *swell*--see Figure 5(b) in Chapter 3). [$PERF_1$] is diagrammed in Figure 9(a). It takes as its base a schematic, single-participant process whose trajector undergoes a change of state or location (indicated by the squiggly arrow). Within that base, it profiles only the final, resultant state that comes about through the occurrence of that process; and because an expression's profile determines its grammatical category, [PERF$_1$] is not a verb but a stative relation (a type of adjective). When [PERF$_1$] combines syntagmatically with a verb stem, its schematic process is the e-site through which the valence relation is effected, and the stem elaborates the nature of the process which serves to define the state. Since [PERF$_1$] is the profile determinant in the construction, the perfect participle (*swollen; gone; cracked*) designates the final state in the process thus specified.

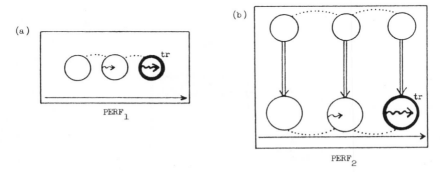

Figure 9.

The second variant of [PERF], labeled [PERF$_2$] and diagramed in Figure 9(b), is slightly more complex:

(17) a. *That watch you bought is probably stolen.*
     b. *The cathedral is totally destroyed.*
     c. *This slipper is all chewed up.*

As does [PERF$_1$], [PERF$_2$] evokes the conception of a change of state or location. It is more complex than [PERF$_1$] in that its base comprises a two-participant process whose trajector exerts a force (indicated by the double arrow) that induces the change in its landmark. With respect to this base, [PERF$_2$] profiles only the final state resulting from the change, and chooses as its trajector (figure within the profiled relationship) the participant that undergoes this change; it is the same as [PERF$_1$] in this regard, and like [PERF$_1$] it is categorized as a type of adjective. But unlike [PERF$_1$], [PERF$_2$] manifests a discrepancy between the trajector of its relational profile and the trajector of the schematic process that constitutes its base. There is consequently a discrepancy between the trajectors of the verb stem and of the adjectival participle formed when the verb stem elaborates the schematic base process of [PERF$_2$]. For instance, it is the landmark (not the trajector) of *steal* that corresponds to the trajector of *stolen*, which designates the resultant state of *steal*; the participial predication imposes a perspective on this state whereby the stolen object is viewed as figure.

People have the ability to transform one conceptual structure into another, and some semantic units are inherently transformational in this sense. For instance, if we take as point of reference the schematic process serving as base and e-site for [ER], this predicate can be described as transforming a process into a thing. Similarly, [PERF] transforms a process into a state; this is the sole value of [PERF$_1$], while [PERF$_2$] additionally effects a figure/ground reversal between the two things participating in the relation. It is important to observe that the transformational character of [ER] and [PERF] does not make them radically different from other predicates; they differ only in degree, and we need not set them apart as a special class of operators or grammatical morphemes. The conceptual transformations which they embody amount to nothing more than the imposition of figure/ground organization on a schematically specified scene. But all predicates actually derive their meaning from profile/base and trajector/landmark relationships, and all predicates can perfectly well be described as effecting transformations on their bases consisting of the imposition of differential salience on their substructures. Thus [ER] and [PERF] differ from typical lexical predicates primarily in that their bases are highly schematic. But specificity is a matter of degree for both lexical and grammatical morphemes, and hardly grounds for regarding [ER] and [PERF] as a different kind of animal. To do so would be to impose an artificial dichotomy on a continuum (cf. **1.5**).

We come now to [PERF$_3$], the variant that appears in the passive construction. Though [PERF$_2$] and [PERF$_3$] differ aspectually, as we will see below, they share the correspondence between the trajector of the profile and the landmark of the schematic process constituting the base. This "skewed" correspondence, the most distinctive feature of the passive construction, is treated as a central facet of the meaning of the participial morpheme. Because the "shift" from active to passive is internal to the predicate [PERF$_3$], its effect is already apparent in the contrast between *approach* and *approached*--the latter being formed by the syntagmatic combination of [PERF$_3$] with the verb stem at a low level in the constituency tree of a single clause. This analysis therefore contrasts with the standard multilevel account, in which a full active clause is transformed to a full passive by an operation bearing no intrinsic relation to participial inflection (often regarded as a grammatical marking without semantic value).[29]

The aspectual contrast between [PERF$_2$] and [PERF$_3$] is brought out by these examples:

(18) a. *My arm was (so) burned (I could hardly move it).*
    a′. *My arm was burned (as soon as I reached into the fire).*
    b. *The town was (already) destroyed (when we got there).*
    b′. *The town was destroyed (house by house).*

c. *The infield was covered with a tarp (all morning).*
c'. *The infield was covered with a tarp (in five minutes).*

Since both combine with transitive stems, and both occur in constructions with *be*, an expression is generally ambiguous unless additional material dictates a choice. Examples (18a)-(18c) involve [PERF$_2$]; they designate only the resultant state of the verbal process, and are therefore adjectival or stative in an obvious sense. Examples (18a')-(18c') are passive. It should be evident from intuition and from the disambiguating contexts that, in some sense, the passive expressions are processual--designating all the states within a process as it unfolds, not just the final state. The problem is to specify more precisely the sense in which [PERF$_3$] is processual.

One possibility would be to make the skewing illustrated in [PERF$_2$] the only difference between the base process and the profile in [PERF$_3$]; i.e. [PERF$_3$] would have the profile of a schematic process identical to the base process, except that the landmark of the base would correspond to the trajector of the profile. There are grounds for thinking that this may be too simple. At least two considerations suggest that passive participles with [PERF$_3$] are atemporal (hence nonprocessual), even though they profile all the states in a process. These considerations relate to the following general claims about the semantic structure of nominals and finite clauses (see Chapter 3):

(19) a. A finite clause always profiles a process.
    b. A nonfinite noun modifier is always atemporal.

In most of its standard uses, *be* combines with atemporal structures and merely furnishes them with the temporal extension and sequential scanning needed (in accordance with (19a)) to make them processual and thereby enable them to head a finite clause; this will be discussed more fully later. For instance, *tall*, *under*, and *playing* are, by themselves, atemporal and cannot stand as verbal heads in finite clauses. However *be tall*, *be under*, and *be playing* are (imperfective) processes, and can so function:

(20) a. *That building is tall.*
    b. *The wrench is under the sink.*
    c. *Those men are playing soccer.*

Because of principle (19b), though, *be* is superfluous with atemporal predications in nonfinite noun modifiers:

(21) a. *that (*be) tall building*
    b. *the wrench (*be) under the sink*
    c. *those men (*be) playing soccer*

Thus if [PERF$_3$] were processual, in the sense of being scanned sequentially
(having a temporal profile), then the *be* appearing in passive clauses would be
redundant, since the participle itself would satisfy principle (19a).[30] Moreover,
examples like the following would then be exceptions to (19b):

(22) a. *Anyone scrutinized inch by inch is likely to feel self-conscious.*
     b. *A baseball game played in under two hours is normally a pitchers' duel.*
     c. *A wagon train attacked while crossing the prairie would always form
        a circle.*

It seems fairly clear in each case that the participial modifier is formed with
[PERF$_3$] rather than [PERF$_2$], as indicated both by the accompanying adverbial
and by the semantic implausibility (given the overall sentential context) of
construing the modifier as designating only the final state in the participial process.
   Although these considerations are hardly overwhelming, I will tentatively assign
[PERF$_3$] the structure shown in the lower right section of Figure 10. It has for its
base a schematic process construed as being transitive; hence its central
participants are both things, and the lines indicating the component relations are
given as arrows to represent the asymmetry inherent in a transitive relationship
(prototypically this resides in the direction of energy flow--cf. Rice 1987a, 1987b).
The essential conceptual import of [PERF$_3$] resides in two aspects of the image it
imposes on this schematic base process. First, it chooses as trajector (relational
figure) the participant that serves as the primary landmark (not as the trajector)

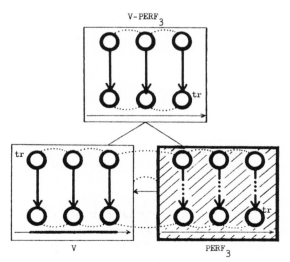

Figure 10.

within that base; it thus effects a figure/ground reversal with respect to the central relational participants. Second, while it profiles all the component states of the base process, [PERF$_3$] imposes an atemporal construal, viewing them holistically by means of summary (as opposed to sequential) scanning. It is thus a complex atemporal relation rather than a process (as indicated by the time arrow, no portion of which is drawn with a heavy line).

In all three variants of [PERF], its schematic base process functions as e-site for its syntagmatic combination with the verb stem (V). Further, [PERF] is both conceptually dependent and the profile determinant (hence not a modifier) in the participial construction; this is diagramed for [PERF$_3$] in Figure 10. Internally, [PERF] imposes a certain image on a schematic process, so when the verb stem elaborates this process, the composite structure [V-PERF] imposes the same image on a specified process. Figure 11 illustrates this more concretely. Figure 11(a) sketches the predicate [APPROACH], a perfective process in which the trajector moves from a position outside the neighborhood of the landmark to a position inside this neighborhood. When [PERF$_3$] combines with this predicate to form the passive participle *approached*, [APPROACH] furnishes a specified base process which is construed according to the dictates of [PERF$_3$]. The composite structure [APPROACH-PERF$_3$] is shown in Figure 11(b). It profiles a complex atemporal relation, whose trajector is the stationary entity serving as the goal of the motion.[31]

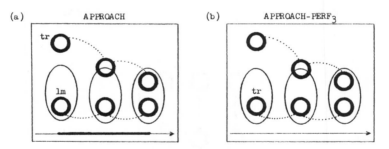

Figure 11.

In summary, [PERF$_3$], the pivotal predicate in the English passive construction, is one node in a lexical network that also includes [PERF$_1$] and [PERF$_2$], among others (see Langacker *to appear*, chapter 5). Their syntagmatic combination with verb stems (as in Figure 10) forms a similar network of morphological constructions. At a higher level of organization, these participate in a network of syntactic constructions, e.g. those of the form *be* plus participle (illustrated in (15)-(18)). The passive construction therefore does not stand in isolation, but rather is embedded in an array of interrelated constructions, involving interrelated senses of the participial morpheme. Consequently one must have grave misgivings about any analysis (e.g. Chomsky 1957) which pulls one particular construction out of this network and treats it in isolation from the rest by means of a device not applicable to them all, and which, moreover, ignores the semantic contribution of the morphemes uniting them.

3.2. The passive *be*

The forms *do* and *be* are ubiquitous in English grammar. Both have a number of related variants, some of which are given below:[32]

(23) a. *I did something terrible.*
   b. *Those clothes just won't do.*
   c. *What does she want?*

(24) a. *Don't be so noisy!*
   b. *He is tall.*
   c. *We were attacked by bandits.*

Though the semantic content of *do* or *be* is in each case limited and fairly abstract, I would argue that these morphemes are in fact meaningful, and I will state precisely the semantic values of those variants which concern us directly. All the variants under examination have the profile of a schematic process. They vary in regard to the type of process they designate, as well as in their degree of schematicity. There is also considerable overlap in the range of *do* and *be*.

Let us start with (23a), a canonical use of the "active" *do*. This variant of *do* designates a perfective process. It has subvariants (cf. Ross 1972), but prototypically it describes the exertion of volitional control over an activity that is objectified and construed as a landmark object; hence it has a value approximating 'execute' or 'carry out' with respect to that landmark. The other two variants of *do* extend or attenuate this sense in different ways. The one in (23b) is more abstract, meaning roughly 'suffice' or 'be suitable', and will not be considered further here. The auxiliary verb *do* of (23c) is still further attenuated: it can be regarded as a variant of the active *do* in which all sense of volitional control is bleached away (as well as that of physical activity), leaving only the process corresponding to the landmark within the active *do*. This process is specified only in the most schematic terms. In fact, it is the most abstract of the process predicates, designating a process but making no specification as to its nature, not even whether it is perfective or imperfective. Thus it sits at the top of the schematic hierarchy for processes, with the schemas for perfective and imperfective processes as immediate instantiations (see Figures 7(f)-(h)).

Let us now turn to *be*. The passive *be* of (24c) is our ultimate concern, but the variants of (24a)-(24b) will permit us to locate it in a broader context. Example

(24a) is perfective, and describes the volitional control of activity lending itself to characterization by an adjectival complement--in the present instance, *noisy*. It means approximately 'act in a particular manner', and is thus somewhat akin to the active *do* of (23a). The variant exemplified in (24b) is more common: it has the profile of a schematic imperfective process. Hence it corresponds exactly to Figure 7(g), and is also (at the semantic pole) to be equated with one of the immediate instantiations of the auxiliary *do*.

While one might quibble with some of the semantic characterizations I have offered, I hope they suffice to establish several points. First, in many (if not all) of their uses, *be* and *do* are clearly meaningful, though their meaning is fairly abstract. Second, their ranges of meaning overlap. One variant of each predicate designates the willful control of some kind of activity. Each also has less active, imperfective variants, without intimation of volitional control. Third, in view of these gradations, as well as the highly abstract and schematic content of many morphemes, it is at least not inherently implausible to claim that the auxiliary uses of *be* and *do* might represent limiting cases along the clines of activity and specificity, and that they have the values I attribute to them. If *be* in (24b) is indeed a fully schematic imperfective process, and *do* in (23c) a fully schematic process (neutralizing the difference between perfective and imperfective), the overlap in semantic range between *be* and *do* is quite extensive.

Internally, the auxiliary variants of *be* and *do* are virtually identical, differing only in that *do* is unspecified as to perfectivity. In other words, all the component states within *be* are presumed identical, but the states within *do* may or may not be identical. This difference may seem slight, but in fact it has important grammatical consequences, which emerge when we turn to the auxiliary constructions in which *be* or *do* combines syntagmatically with a predicate or a more elaborate semantic configuration. Note that the constructions are parallel to the extent that *be* and *do* are each dependent and serve as profile determinants (so they are not modifiers).

The primary difference lies in the choice of e-site. Because all the states within *be* are identical, in order to elaborate the schematic content of *be* it is sufficient to specify the nature of a single state, hence it has a single (arbitrarily selected) state for its e-site. Since *be* is the profile determinant, the composite structure [BE-STAT] (corresponding to expressions like *be tall*) designates a specified imperfective process. In contrast, not all the component states of *do* are necessarily identical, for *do* is not specifically imperfective. To elaborate the schematic content of *do*, then, one must further specify the nature of all its states. The e-site within *do* is consequently exhaustive of the contents of this predicate, which therefore combines syntagmatically with a processual rather than a stative structure. The composite structure [DO-PROC], corresponding to expressions like *do (...) run* or *do (...) want*, is a specified process which can be either perfective or imperfective, depending on the nature of the autonomous component (it is shown as perfective in Figure 12(b), below).

With these characterizations, we can begin to explain the grammatical peculiarities of *be* and *do*. Figure 12(a) shows precisely how *be* converts a stative predication into an imperfective process. Because of principle (19a) above, namely that a finite clause always profiles a process, combination with *be* is obligatory if stative predicates like *tall* and *under* are to function as lexical heads in such clauses.

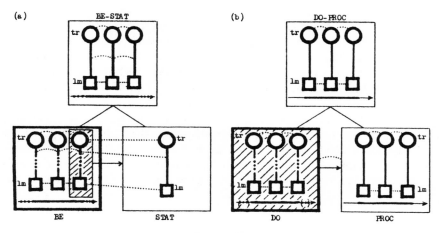

Figure 12.

With *do*, the situation is very different. Because the entire predicate functions as an e-site in Figure 12(b), this predicate as a whole is schematic for the autonomous processual structure with which it combines. All the specifications of *do* are also present in the autonomous structure, with the result that the schematic process of *do* is totally "swallowed up" when corresponding entities are superimposed to form the composite structure. This entails that the composite structure [DO-PROC] is identical to the autonomous component; i.e. *do* has no substantive effect on the meaning of the composite expression, despite its own (highly schematic) semantic value. Since a predicate like *run* or *want* is itself processual, it does not require *do* in order to serve as head in a finite clause. *Do* is thus optional in English, used only for emphasis or in special grammatical constructions which have conventionalized its inclusion.[33]

Now we are ready to examine the passive *be* of (24c). This is the predicate that combines with participles derived by [PERF$_3$] to form clausal heads such as *be attacked, be approached, be eaten*, etc.; let us symbolize it [BE$_p$]. We can assume that [BE$_p$] has the profile of a schematic process. The problem now is to determine the precise nature of this process, and to see how it cooperates with [PERF$_3$] in passive clauses. I will claim that the passive *be* has essentially the same meaning as the auxiliary *do*.[34] This is not so strange as it might seem, since we have seen that *be* and *do* overlap considerably in their semantic range; in any case, the only difference between the auxiliaries *be* and *do* in nonpassive expressions is that the former is specifically imperfective, and the latter neutral in regard to perfectivity. The passive *be* cannot be specifically imperfective, for it typically combines with participial structures formed on perfective verbs where the component states are not all identical.

The syntagmatic combination of [BE$_p$] with a passive participle is sketched in Figure 13(a). Recall that a passive participle with [PERF$_3$] is atemporal, consisting of an ordered series of states viewed holistically (by summary scanning). In the passive construction, these states elaborate the schematic states of [BE$_p$], which collectively serve as its e-site. The dependent [BE$_p$] is the profile determinant, imposing a processual construal (with sequential scanning) on the atemporal [V-PERF$_3$], while the specified states of [V-PERF$_3$] elaborate the corresponding schematic states in [BE$_p$]. The composite structure [BE$_p$-V-PERF$_3$] therefore designates a specified process whose essential content is inherited from the participle. Thus its perfectivity reflects that of the participle (and ultimately that of the verb stem), as does its trajector/landmark alignment (which reverses that of the stem). Figure 13(b) illustrates this concretely with the composite structure for *be approached* (cf. Figure 11).

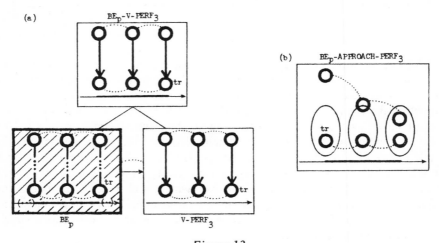

Figure 13.

Thus [BE$_p$] is seen to be intermediate between [BE] and [DO] as they normally function in auxiliary constructions. [BE$_p$] is like [DO] internally, in that there is no presumption that all its component states are identical. However it is like [BE] functionally, in that it combines with an atemporal structure and renders it processual (gives it a temporal profile). With [BE], this autonomous structure is stative (a simple atemporal relation), consisting of a single static configuration.

With [BE$_p$], on the other hand, it is a complex atemporal relation, consisting of a series of potentially distinct configurations viewed holistically.

3.3. By-phrases

Langacker and Munro (1975) argued that *by*-phrases are not an intrinsic part of the English passive construction. English passives frequently lack a *by*-phrase, and in many languages such a phrase is not permitted with passives at all. It was proposed that passives have unspecified underlying subjects, and that a *by*-phrase (when present) derives from a separate underlying conjunct. Thus (15b), *Bill was approached by Alice*, would have an underlying structure something like (25):

(25) *[△ approach Bill] and [[△approach Bill] by Alice]*

In the generative framework assumed in 1975 (at least for presentational purposes), this source for *by*-phrases was admittedly ad hoc and problematic. Cognitive grammar, by contrast, permits a treatment of *by*-phrases that preserves the spirit and advantages of this earlier analysis, but is fully workable and employs only broadly motivated descriptive devices. The analysis follows that of Hoard 1979 in treating *by*-phrases as normal oblique complements.

The first point to establish is that the passive *by* can reasonably be considered meaningful. The plausibility of this claim should be apparent from the sentences in (26), which exemplify numerous clearly meaningful variants of *by* forming an elaborate lexical network (see Hoard for additional arguments):

(26) a. *The willow tree is by the river.*
    b. *Jack is by himself upstairs.*
    c. *That's OK by me.*
    d. *That sculpture is by Zúñiga.*
    e. *He did it all by himself (i.e. without help).*
    f. *The applause was by everyone in the room.*
    g. *Bragging by officers will not be tolerated.*

In (26a) and (26b), *by* is a stative relation in the spatial domain. In (26c), a proposition (*That's OK*) is located in the neighborhood of a landmark (*me*) with respect to an abstract judgmental domain where judgments are attributed to individuals responsible for them. With the notion of responsibility comes the notion of the landmark being a source (not just a locative reference point). This more dynamic conception of the landmark as a source vis-à-vis the trajector is more pronounced in (26d) and (26e), which pertain to the creation of an art object or the execution of an act. The variant in (26f) and (26g) is very similar to the one in (26e), attributing responsibility for the execution of an act; it would be hard to argue that it is different from the *by* which appears in the passive construction. What we find, then, is a gradation in value--a chain of predicates symbolized with *by* in which the passive *by* finds a natural place. To treat the latter as a totally separate (and possibly meaningless) entity would be misguided.

The next step is to describe more precisely the internal semantic structure of *by*. It will be instructive to consider several variants of this predicate, as sketched in Figure 14. Diagramed in 14(a) is the simple locative sense of *by* illustrated in (26a). Its domain is physical space, and the profiled stative relation merely situates the trajector in the neighborhood of the landmark (i.e. [tr PROX lm]).[35] Diagram (b) represents the value of *by* in expressions like (26d), where the trajector's association with the landmark stems from an act of artistic creation. The process of bringing some entity into existence constitutes the base for this variant, which profiles the resultant state--it is by virtue of this creative act (rather than spatial proximity) that the trajector can be situated with respect to the landmark. The variant depicted in diagram (c) corresponds to example (26g). Like the artistic-creation sense of *by*, it evokes as its base the conception of a process. However, it differs from that sense in two basic ways. For one thing, the base process can represent any sort of activity (not just an act of creation). Moreover, the trajector --the entity located with respect to the landmark--is that process itself, under a nominal construal (Chapter 3). The profiled relationship holds between a reified activity (e.g. *bragging* in (26g)) and the actor construed as the source of that activity.

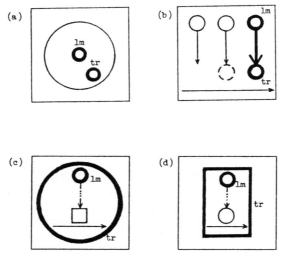

Figure 14.

That brings us to the passive *by*, diagramed in Figure 14(d). This variant is essentially the same as the one in 14(c). However, since this variant has evolved to combine syntagmatically with the passive participle, its trajector amounts to a schematic representation of passive participles, making it equivalent to [PERF$_3$]--a complex, schematic atemporal relation. (The trajector in Figure 14(d) can thus be compared to [PERF$_3$] in Figure 10.) Diagramatically, this trajector is enclosed in a box (rather than a circle) to indicate that it retains its relational construal.

Our final task is to show how the passive *by* combines syntagmatically with other structures in the overall grammatical organization of a passive clause. There are reasons to assume constituency trees having the general structure of Figure 15, corresponding to (15b), *Bill was approached by Alice*. We are directly concerned only with the lower portions of the tree, in particular as they pertain to [BE$_p$], [PERF$_3$], and [BY].[36] Although *be* and the passive participle are intimately associated synchronically and diachronically, the participle is a constituent that can appear independently of *be*:

(27) a. *A football game played by two good defensive teams usually turns out to be dull.*
　　b. *He ordered the town destroyed by a bomber squadron.*

This also shows that the combination of a passive participle and *by*-phrase can occur independently of *be*, suggesting the constituency shown, where the *by*-phrase is a prepositional-phrase modifier of the participle, and *be* combines with *approached by Alice* at a higher level of organization.

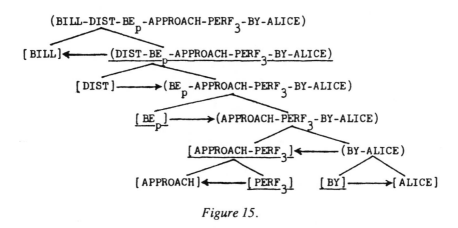

Figure 15.

Our principal interest is the syntagmatic combination of the passive participle and *by*-phrase to form expressions such as *approached by Alice*.[37] *Approached* was diagramed earlier in Figure 11(b). The composition of *by Alice* is shown on the right in Figure 16. As a regular instance of the prepositional-object construction, *Alice* (whose semantic specifications are abbreviated as A) elaborates the landmark of *by* (Figure 14(d)). Because *by* is the profile determinant, the composite expression *by Alice* designates a stative relation with a specified landmark and a schematic trajector characterized as a complex atemporal relation. *Approached* elaborates this schematic trajector at a higher level of constituency. And since *approached* is the profile determinant at this level, *approached by Alice* designates a complex atemporal relation in which one participant is schematic and the other--the actor--is specific owing to periphrastic specification by the prepositional phrase.

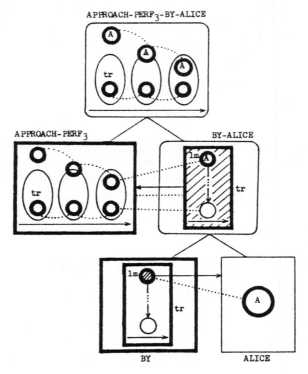

Figure 16.

In Figure 17(a) is sketched the composite structure of the entire sentence *Bill was approached by Alice*. From the composite structure in Figure 16, it is formed by successive integration with [BE$_p$], [DIST], and [BILL], as described in Figure 15. The effect of [BE$_p$] is to render the expression processual by imposing sequential scanning on the complex relational profile (see Figure 13). [DIST] locates the profiled relationship prior to the time of speaking, indicated diagramatically by the squiggly line labeled G (for "ground"). Finally, [BILL] then elaborates the schematic trajector in accordance with the regular construction for specifying clausal subjects.

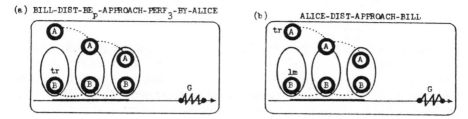

Figure 17.

The composite structure of (15a), *Alice approached Bill*, is presented for sake of comparison in Figure 17(b). The two composite structures are almost identical apart from figure/ground organization, specifically the choice of trajector (as elaborated by the subject nominal). This contrast ultimately represents the semantic contribution of the passive-participial morpheme. The two composite structures nevertheless designate the same objective process, and code it with much the same lexical content; this accounts from the approximate synonymy of the two sentences. They do however result from very different compositional paths and are semantically distinct.

3.4. Related phenomena

Synonymy between sentence pairs like (15a) and (15b) provided one argument for deriving passives from underlying (or initial) active structures. I have claimed that this synonymy is only approximate, and can be accommodated insightfully without resorting to a multilevel syntagmatic structure. Another argument for deriving passives from underlying actives was based on selectional restrictions. It should be evident that my analysis accounts automatically for the fact that the selectional restrictions on the active subject and object are identical, respectively, to those on the passive *by*-phrase object and subject: this is because the passive trajector corresponds to the landmark of the verb stem, and the landmark of *by* to the trajector of the verb stem, as specified by correspondences in the constructions describing the assembly of a passive expression. Selectional restrictions are semantic, and amount to nothing more than compatibility in the specifications of corresponding entities that are superimposed in syntagmatic combination to form a composite structure. The correspondences defining the passive construction assure that the proper restrictions are imposed, without special apparatus.

Sentences like the following have been used in another type of argument for deriving passives from actives:

(28) a. *There was believed to be a spy in their midst.*
  b. *It was believed to have rained during the night.*
  c. *Umbrage was taken at his insolent remarks.*

The discussion hinges on the claim that the surface subject in these passive sentences (either the "dummy" *there* or *it*, or else an "idiom chunk" such as *umbrage*) is meaningless, and could not have originated in its surface position. *There* and *it* must be inserted transformationally in the surbordinate clause, it is said, and raised to object position in the main clause, which is then passivized. *Umbrage* can occur only as part of the fixed idiom *take umbrage at*, and this implies that it must be the object in deep structure after lexical insertion. However, I do not accept the presuppositions of the argument. Neither passivization nor subject raising is a mechanical syntactic operation deriving one sentence type from another; rather, they represent separate constructions imposing their own imagery and perspective on a scene (see Chapter 7 and Langacker *to appear*, chapter 11). Moreover, *there*, *it*, and idiom chunks are considered meaningful entities that can perfectly well participate in such imagery.[38] I suggest that most idioms are analyzable to some degree, i.e. morphemes within the idiom are recognized as making specific semantic contributions (e.g. *umbrage* means something akin to 'anger' or 'offense'). The essence of an idiom does not reside in its form as a specific phonological sequence, but rather in its internal semantic and symbolic relationships. These relationships can easily be recognized despite perturbations in the ways that the components are woven into a grammatical structure.

In previous sections, I have emphasized how the grammatical morphemes of the passive construction function as nodes in lexical networks, and how the passive construction fits into a network of construction types. These networks are considerably more extensive than has been indicated thus far. The remainder of this section explores very briefly some further connections of the passive construction.

We have seen from examples like (22) and (27) that passive participial expressions, even with *by*-phrases, can occur without *be*. As shown in Figure 13(a), *be* is added to such expressions when a broader context requires a processual predication, but *be* is not the only predicate that can serve this function. The conventions of English also permit passives with *get*:

(29) a. *He got a hammer.*
  b. *He got his nephew elected mayor.*
  c. *He got (himself) elected mayor.*
  d. *He got stabbed.*

In (29a), *get* means 'obtain' in the sense of physical possession. In (29b), we see it extended to mean 'obtain' with respect to an abstract goal expressed by a passive participle: (29b) forms a paradigm with such examples as *He {wanted/ordered/had/saw} his nephew elected mayor*. Coreference between subject and object, as in (29c), makes *get* effectively intransitive and provides a bridge to cases like (29d), which are parallel in form to passives (*He {got/was} stabbed*).

As Lakoff 1971 observes, even the physical sense of *get* has a nonvolitional construal, e.g. (29a) can mean simply that the subject received a hammer. The other examples can similarly be interpreted nonvolitionally; the likelihood of this construal increases with decreasing transitivity, as one progresses from (29b) through (29d), and also with plausibility on pragmatic grounds. Thus we find a gradation along several parameters (abstractness, transitivity, volition), all of which see the semantic content of *get* impoverished as we move in the direction of (29d). If this impoverishment is pushed to its logical conclusion, *get* will amount to a fully schematic process--making it equivalent to the passive *be*, and erasing the difference between *get*-passives and *be*-passives. Lakoff has correctly noted, however, that *get*-passives still tend to imply greater action and volition on the part of the subject.[39]

In section **3.1**, our scope was limited to three variants of the perfect participial morpheme and their interaction with perfective process predicates. We saw that all three variants have a schematic process for their base, impose an atemporal construal, and select either the final state or the landmark of the base process for prominence (as either profile or relational figure). To round out our discussion of perfect participles, let us consider briefly their combination with imperfective processes.[40]

An unresolved problem concerning perfect participles is whether or not sentences like these are true passives:

(30) a. *The castle is surrounded by a moat.*

    b. *Those facts are known by all serious scholars.*

    c. *I am impressed by his grasp of world affairs.*

Somehow they seem more "stative" than prototypical passives; to back this up, it can be observed that (30a) describes a situation that must have obtained since the inception of the moat, which can hardly have surrounded the castle in the same, active sense that a group of hunters surround their quarry.

The reason for this "stative" feel is that the passives in (30) are formed from imperfective verbs. Their active counterparts, given below, are imperfective by the standard tests (Chapter 3), and describe a situation construed as constant through time:

(31) a. *A moat surrounds the castle.*
   b. *All serious scholars know those facts.*
   c. *His grasp of world affairs impresses me.*

When [PERF$_3$] combines with a perfective verb, which describes a change through time, the participle it derives profiles a series of partially distinct states, each corresponding to a particular point in the perfective trajectory. By contrast, when [PERF$_3$] combines with an imperfective verb, all the component states are identical: the atemporal profile is mass-like, consisting of an indefinite number of occurrences of a single state. Hence there is no change through time, and since an atemporal construal (involving summary rather than sequential scanning) deemphasizes temporal extension, there is little difference between a single occurrence of the state and multiple occurrences.

It follows that with imperfective verbs the contrast between [PERF$_2$] and [PERF$_3$] largely vanishes, which helps us explicate the following data:

(32) a. *His antics amuse me.*
   b. *I am amused at his antics.*
   c. *I am amused by his antics.*

Here (32a) describes an imperfective process, and it has both (32b) and (32c) as passive-like counterparts. Postal (1971) has argued that (32c), but not (32b), is a true passive, and I am inclined to agree. Given the preceding discussion, I believe we can go beyond this, accounting both for their differences and for their virtual semantic identity. The participle *amused* is adjectival in (32b), formed with [PERF$_2$], and passive in (32c), formed with [PERF$_3$], being based in each case on the imperfective stem *amuse*. We have just seen that the profile which [PERF$_3$] imposes on an imperfective stem is effectively equivalent to a single stative configuration, representative of any point within the processual profile of the stem. But just the same is true of [PERF$_2$] in combination with an imperfective stem. With perfectives, [PERF$_2$] designates the final, resultant state in the process, which may be quite distinct from the states leading up to it. In the case of imperfectives, however, all the component states are identical, so the final state (at which all the specifications of the process have been satisfied) can be equated with any state arbitrarily selected from the process. Just like the passive participle with [PERF$_3$], then, the adjectival participle with [PERF$_2$] is representative of any point within the processual profile of the imperfective stem.

It is, of course, only a matter of definition whether we consider sentences like (32b) to be passives. If we restrict the passive label to cases like (32c), with [PERF$_3$] and the possibility of a *by*-phrase, it is nonetheless true that the adjectival construction with [PERF$_2$] and other oblique phrases is closely related to the passive in networks of predicates and grammatical constructions. Though *at* predominates, various other prepositions are found in the adjectival construction:

(33) a. *I am amazed at his success.*
   b. *I am disgusted with your continual nagging.*
   c. *I am puzzled over those events.*

The adjective-preposition combination is conventionalized, and forms a close-knit unit. Nevertheless, I claim that in each instance the preposition is meaningful, and that in combination with the following nominal it retains some degree of analyzability as a prepositional phrase. To the extent that this is so, passive *by*-phrases take their position in a paradigm of oblique complements based on other prepositions, as well as a paradigm of constructions employing different variants of *by*, as illustrated in (26). In my view, this makes a special transformational source for the passive *by* highly dubious.[41] The *by*-phrase appearing in passives is simply a prepositional phrase, just as it appears to be on the surface. Its special role can be accounted for by the same descriptive devices needed for other oblique complements and for grammatical constructions in general.

5. Abstract motion

A well-known fact of language change is that verbs meaning 'go' often evolve into markers of future tense.* The French construction illustrated in (1) and its English translation are among the numerous examples that could be cited (cf. Givón 1973).

(1) *Il va finir bientôt.* 'He is going to finish soon'

This semantic shift is commonly attributed to spatial metaphor, wherein the meaning 'motion away from the speaker' is transferred from the spatial to the temporal domain. While accepting the basic validity of this analysis, I would nevertheless argue that as it stands it is insufficiently precise. For example, who should we take to be the mover, the speaker or the subject? In what sense is it meaningful to speak of 'motion through time'? My objective is to answer these questions, and to show how the shift from 'go' to 'future' is related to a variety of other phenomena. I will argue that the shift receives a natural and explicit characterization granted a number of independently motivated concepts and analyses of cognitive grammar.

1. Basic concepts and assumptions

My initial assumption is that meaning is properly equated with conceptualization, in a suitably broad sense of that term. Moreover, conceptualization can be analyzed at either of two levels: the phenomenological level (i.e. that of mental experience), and the level of cognitive events (i.e. neurological activity). I assume, in other words, that having a particular mental experience resides in the occurrence of some pattern of neural activation. Conceptualist semantics has thus far concerned itself primarily with the phenomenological level, as a matter of necessity. Still, the structures at this level must eventually be explicated with reference to neurological events. Though we can hardly hope to pin things down to the firing of specific neurons, we might at least hope to determine the functional architecture of those events whose occurrence could conceivably constitute a given experience.

In this spirit, I make the further (and I think quite plausible) assumption that any conception involving ordering or directionality at the experiential level implies some type of seriality at the processing level; an ordered conception necessarily incorporates the sequenced occurrence of cognitive events as one facet of its neurological implementation, and this sequencing is taken as being constitutive of the conceptual ordering. As an obvious and convenient example of an ordered conception, consider our ability to mentally recite the alphabet. The mental recitation of any individual letter must reside in the occurrence of some pattern of neural activation, which we can treat as a single cognitive event (despite its internal complexity). It is apparent, moreover, that our knowledge of the alphabet as an ordered structure reduces to our ability to recite the letters in proper sequence. Clearly, in performing this mental exercise of running through the sequence $[a > b > c > ... > x > y > z]$, we activate in serial fashion those cognitive events that constitute the recitation of the individual letters.

To avoid confusion, we must distinguish between the conception OF time, on the one hand, and the fact that conception takes place THROUGH time, on the other hand. I therefore speak of conceived time (symbolized t) and processing time (symbolized T), pertaining to the phenomenological and the event levels, respectively. Conceived time is time as an OBJECT of conceptualization; I conceive OF time when I consult my watch, when I use a word like *before*, or even when I see something happen (e.g. an object falling to the ground).[1] By contrast, processing time is time as a MEDIUM of conceptualization: every cognitive event requires some span of processing time for its occurrence (however brief it might be), including events that constitute the atemporal conception of static situations. Despite their obvious relationship, these two sorts of time are functionally distinct and must be separated for analytical purposes.

We also need a convenient way of referring to the relationship between a conceptualizer and the conceptualization he entertains at a given moment. I call this the construal relation, and adopt for it the notation in (2), where C stands for the conceptualizer, and Q for his immediate mental experience.

$$(2) \quad \begin{bmatrix} Q \\ C \end{bmatrix} T_i$$

Formula (2) simply indicates that conceptualizer C carries out conceptualization Q at moment T_i of processing time. Using this notation, we can now offer at least a partial representation of what happens when somebody mentally recites the alphabet:

$$(3) \quad \begin{bmatrix} a \\ C \end{bmatrix} T_1 > \begin{bmatrix} b \\ C \end{bmatrix} T_2 > \begin{bmatrix} c \\ C \end{bmatrix} T_3 > ... > \begin{bmatrix} x \\ C \end{bmatrix} T_{24} > \begin{bmatrix} y \\ C \end{bmatrix} T_{25} > \begin{bmatrix} z \\ C \end{bmatrix} T_{26}$$

The import of (3) is that C first activates the conception of a, then that of b, and so on; C's recitation of the alphabet occupies span $[T_1, T_2, T_3, ..., T_{26}]$ of processing time. Observe that conceived time has no intrinsic role in this exercise; at any one moment, C's conception is merely that of some letter in the alphabet. Though C may be aware of the passage of time, and may even pay heed to his own participation in a temporally-extended activity, neither sort of awareness is inherent in the recitation task per se.

Despite its subtlety, this matter of self-awareness is rich with implications for both semantic and grammatical structure (cf. Langacker 1985), and since it is central to our later concerns, we must find a way of dealing with it. It is helpful to start from the ideal (and possibly nonexistent) situation in which the conceptualizer manifests a total lack of self-awareness: C is completely absorbed in the conception of Q, to the extent that he loses all awareness of himself, and even of the fact that he is engaging in the conceptualization process (i.e. what C conceptualizes is simply Q, and not at all C *conceptualizing Q*). With respect to this idealized situation, I will say that the role of C is fully "subjective", whereas that of Q is "objective". Full subjectivity and objectivity thus stand in polar opposition, being defined for instances involving maximal asymmetry between the roles of conceptualizer and object of conceptualization. In practice, of course, the roles are commonly mixed, as the conceptualizer himself is often an object of conceptualization. To the extent that C creeps into the conceptualization, the subjectivity of his role declines; when C indulges his notorious egocentricity, and makes himself the focus of attention within Q, the basis for the subjective/objective distinction is eroded entirely.

The alphabet once more provides convenient illustration. Formula (3) represents the situation where C is totally absorbed in mentally reciting the alphabet and loses all self-awareness; the letters of the alphabet are thus fully objective entities (as I am using that term here), while C's role is maximally subjective. Suppose, on the other hand, that C not only mentally recites the alphabet, but also consciously monitors his facility and accuracy in doing so--in this case, C conceptualizes not only *the alphabet* (letter by letter), but also C *conceptualizing the alphabet*. There are consequently two levels of conceptualization:

$$(4)\ \left[\begin{matrix}\begin{bmatrix}\text{a}\\ \boxed{C}t_1\end{bmatrix}\\ C'\end{matrix}\right]_{T_1} > \left[\begin{matrix}\begin{bmatrix}\text{b}\\ \boxed{C}t_2\end{bmatrix}\\ C'\end{matrix}\right]_{T_2} > \left[\begin{matrix}\begin{bmatrix}\text{c}\\ \boxed{C}t_3\end{bmatrix}\\ C'\end{matrix}\right]_{T_3} > ... > \left[\begin{matrix}\begin{bmatrix}\text{z}\\ \boxed{C}t_{26}\end{bmatrix}\\ C'\end{matrix}\right]_{T_{26}}$$

Since all of (3) now functions as an object of conceptualization, it is embedded as such in a higher-order construal relation. Note that there are two conceptualizer roles, one for each level of organization: the conceptualizer's role in mentally reciting the alphabet (indicated by C), and his role in the self-monitoring of this process (indicated by C').

Because C is the object of self-observation in (4), this role is no longer a subjective one. Moreover, the processing time required for C to run through the alphabet qualifies as conceived time from the perspective of C', and is thus represented $[t_1, t_2, t_3, ..., t_{26}]$. Role C', by contrast, is purely subjective (provided that the conceptualizer does not add yet another layer of conceptualization by thinking about the fact that he is monitoring his recitation). Formula (4) can also be applied to the situation where C and C' are different individuals, which would be the case if C' were to imagine somebody else reciting the alphabet. The status of C in this situation depends on whose viewpoint is considered: from the standpoint of C', C is fully objective; from his own vantage point, however, C is simply running through the alphabet (without self-awareness), and is therefore subjectively construed.

2. The characterization of verbs

It was argued in Chapter 3 that a verb designates a complex relation, i.e. its profile comprises a continuous series of component states, each of which--taken individually--constitutes a simple, stative relation. How, then, does a verb differ from a preposition that describes a path (as opposed to a single, static location)? What is the difference, for example, between the verb *cross* in (5a) and the preposition *across* in (5b)?

(5) a. *A black dog crossed the field.*
    b. *A black dog walked across the field.*

It cannot merely be that the verb's component states are distributed through a continuous span of conceived time, for the same could be said of the preposition (see Figure 9(b) of Chapter 1).[2] I have therefore suggested that the difference perhaps does not lie in the conceptual content of the expressions, but rather in how this content is accessed.

My working hypothesis is that the difference between verbs and other complex relations is attributable to certain mental abilities that are both independently established and introspectively apparent. Suppose that somebody throws a ball, and that I watch it sail through the air. The flight of the ball represents a complex relation, as defined above: with the passage of time the ball occupies a series of distinct locations constituting a spatial path; the relationship of the ball to its surroundings does not reduce to a single consistent configuration (state). Now in observing this event, I may simply follow the ball's flight from its starting point to its destination, so that my conception at any one instant is focused on the momentary position of the ball in relation to its position an instant before. This mode of viewing an event constitutes sequential scanning--the states comprising the event are accessed in sequence, and the conception representing any one state is only momentary. However, I also have the ability to construe the process more holistically, either while watching it or during a mental "replay". I can pay specific attention to the ball's trajectory, seeing its trajectory "grow" from instant to instant as the ball sails along its path; at the end, I have built up a conception of the full trajectory that functions as a single gestalt and is manipulable as a simultaneously available whole (e.g. I can observe its shape and assess its degree of curvature). The term summary scanning refers to this second mode of tracking an event. The states comprising the event are still accessed in sequence, but once activated the conception corresponding to a given state remains active throughout. Thus the full conception grows progressively more complex, the end result being the simultaneous activation and accessibility of all the component states.

The notations previously introduced are capable of representing the difference between sequential and summary scanning. Consider the conception of an object falling to the ground, as diagramed in Figure 4(a) of Chapter 3. Only four component states are explicitly shown (labeled a, b, c, and d), but they stand for what is actually a continuous series.[3] The sequential scanning of this complex relation can be formulated as follows:

$$(6) \quad \begin{bmatrix} a \\ \\ C \end{bmatrix}_{T_1} > \begin{bmatrix} b \\ \\ C \end{bmatrix}_{T_2} > \begin{bmatrix} c \\ \\ C \end{bmatrix}_{T_3} > \begin{bmatrix} d \\ \\ C \end{bmatrix}_{T_4}$$

At moment T_1 of processing time, the conceptualizer activates the conception of state a; at T_2, he activates conception b; and so on. Observe that each conception begins to decay as the next one is activated, so that only one is fully active at any one instance. In summary scanning, by contrast, each state remains active as the next one in the series is accessed:

$$(7) \quad \begin{bmatrix} a \\ \\ C \end{bmatrix}_{T_1} > \begin{bmatrix} a \\ b \\ C \end{bmatrix}_{T_2} > \begin{bmatrix} a \\ b \\ c \\ C \end{bmatrix}_{T_3} > \begin{bmatrix} a \\ b \\ c \\ d \\ C \end{bmatrix}_{T_4}$$

The resulting conception grows progressively more complex, so that finally (at T_4) all the component states are superimposed and simultaneously active (see Chapter 3, Figure 4(b)). The directionality in this conception is due to the order in which the states are activated in building up to it.

The proposal advanced in Chapter 3 was that the difference between verbs and other complex relations is plausibly characterized in terms of sequential vs. summary scanning. Even if members of the two classes comprise the same series of states and thus have the same conceptual content, they differ in how this content is construed with respect to its pattern of activation through processing time.[4] A verb is said to profile a process: it scans sequentially through a complex relation whose component states are distributed continuously through a span of conceived time (referred to as the verb's temporal profile). Formula (8) is thus offered as a semantic characterization considered valid for all members of the verb class, where r_i stands for a stative relation, and $[r_i]t_i$ indicates that relation r_i holds at point t_i of conceived time.

$$(8) \quad \begin{bmatrix} [r_1]t_1 \\ C \end{bmatrix}_{T_1} > \begin{bmatrix} [r_2]t_2 \\ C \end{bmatrix}_{T_2} > \begin{bmatrix} [r_3]t_3 \\ C \end{bmatrix}_{T_3} > ... > \begin{bmatrix} [r_n]t_n \\ C \end{bmatrix}_{T_n}$$

A verb profiles a complex relation $[r_1, r_2, r_3, ..., r_n]$ extending through span $[t_1, t_2, t_3, ..., t_n]$ of conceived time. The conceptualizer C (identifiable as the speaker and/or hearer) scans sequentially through this complex configuration during span $[T_1, T_2, T_3, ..., T_n]$ of processing time.

Let us further recall the distinction between perfective and imperfective verbs. Roughly speaking, perfective verbs take the progressive, as illustrated in (9), but normally do not occur in the simple present tense; imperfectives do occur in the simple present, as in (10), but resist the progressive.

(9) a. *My neighbor is washing his car again.*
   b. *The coach is screaming at his players.*
   c. *A young couple was walking along the beach.*

(10) a. *I know that she understands the difficulty.*
   b. *Alice definitely likes tuna.*
   c. *Phil believes that Jason resembles his father.*

In a perfective, the component states constitute a bounded series, and generally they involve some change through time (i.e. there are adjacent states in the sequence where $r_i \neq r_{i+1}$). By contrast, imperfectives are not specifically bounded, and all the component states are construed as being identical. Formula (8) can be revised as follows to highlight the characteristic properties of imperfectives:

$$(11) \quad ... > \begin{bmatrix} [R]t_i \\ C \end{bmatrix}_{T_i} > \begin{bmatrix} [R]t_j \\ C \end{bmatrix}_{T_j} > \begin{bmatrix} [R]t_k \\ C \end{bmatrix}_{T_k} > ...$$

Formula (11) represents the special case of (8) in which no initial or final state is distinguished, and where $r_i = r_{i+1}$ throughout. An imperfective thus tracks through conceived time (by means of sequential scanning) the continuation of a stable situation, given as R in the formula.

3. Objective motion

We are now ready to consider verbs of physical motion, such as *trudge, walk, swim, climb, roll,* etc. The only facet of their meaning that directly concerns us is the mover's spatial trajectory; we may ignore such factors as the method and rate of locomotion. For our purposes, then, a motion verb can be regarded as a special sort of perfective process, namely one in which each component state specifies the relation between the mover and his immediate location. Starting from formula (8), we can therefore obtain the representation for a verb of spatial movement by substituting for each instance of r_i the more specific notation $[m]l_i$, which indicates that the mover m occupies location l_i:

$$(12) \quad \begin{bmatrix} [[m]l_1]t_1 \\ C \end{bmatrix}_{T_1} > \begin{bmatrix} [[m]l_2]t_2 \\ C \end{bmatrix}_{T_2} > ... > \begin{bmatrix} [[m]l_n]t_n \\ C \end{bmatrix}_{T_n}$$

Thus, m occupies location l_1 at moment t_1; he occupies l_2 at t_2; and so on. Through span $[t_1, t_2, t_3, ..., t_n]$ of conceived time, the mover traverses the spatial path $[l_1, l_2, l_3, ..., l_n]$. Formula (12) is highly schematic and expresses what all verbs of physical motion have in common. The meaning of *go* may well be limited to this schematic content when it functions as a maximally generic motion verb.

Consider now some uses of *go* that do not pertain to spatial motion:

(13) a. *Roger went through the alphabet in 7.3 seconds.*
   b. *This milk is about to go sour.*
   c. *The concert went from midnight to 4AM.*

Though one's first thought is to treat such sentences as instances of spatial metaphor, it is not obvious to me how strongly or consistently speakers perceive them as such; moreover, to describe a metaphor we must in any case characterize both the source and the target domains, together with the mapping between them (cf. Lakoff & Johnson 1980; Langacker 1987a, chapter 4). One way or another, we must therefore attribute to *go* a conventionally established range of values that indicate change in nonspatial domains.

Actually, there is no need to alter formula (12) to accommodate such examples --we need only interpret the notations in a suitably abstract manner. Under this generalized interpretation, $[l_1, l_2, l_3, ..., l_n]$ is not to be construed as a spatial path in particular, but simply as an ordered sequence of entities within the relevant domain, such that the "mover" m is capable of "making contact" with each of these entities individually; $[m]l_i$ then indicates the momentary contact of m with l_i in this domain. The notions *entity* and *contact* are admittedly vague, but their intended application to the present examples is reasonably straightforward: in (13a), the entities are letters of the alphabet, and Roger makes contact with a given letter by reciting it; in (13b), the entities are points along a scale for evaluating freshness/sourness, and the milk makes contact with such an entity by being fresh or sour to a specific degree; in (13c), the entities are points in conceived time, and the concert makes contact with a point when its duration extends to include it. What we have done, in effect, is to characterize a maximally schematic concept of motion, with respect to which physical movement through space is just a special case (though clearly prototypical). Let us speak of "abstract motion" when this schematic conception is applied to nonspatial domains, as in (13). Formula (14) thus describes the abstract motion of somebody going through the alphabet: the mover first recites the letter a at moment t_1 (this is represented formulaically as $[[m]a]t_1$), then the letter b at t_2, and so on.

$$(14) \quad \begin{bmatrix} [[m]a]t_1 \\ C \end{bmatrix}_{T_1} > \begin{bmatrix} [[m]b]t_2 \\ C \end{bmatrix}_{T_2} > ... > \begin{bmatrix} [[m]z]t_{26} \\ C \end{bmatrix}_{T_{26}}$$

For our later purposes, example (13c) holds particular significance. The concert is an abstract mover, making contact with an ordered series of points in time as its duration extends. The formulaic representation of this abstract motion is (15), which is exactly parallel to (14) except that the abstract path of motion is the temporal sequence $[t_1, t_2, t_3, ..., t_n]$ rather than the letters of the alphabet.

$$(15) \quad \begin{bmatrix} [[m]t_1]t_1 \\ C \end{bmatrix}_{T_1} > \begin{bmatrix} [[m]t_2]t_2 \\ C \end{bmatrix}_{T_2} > ... > \begin{bmatrix} [[m]t_n]t_n \\ C \end{bmatrix}_{T_n}$$

Observe that conceived time plays two distinct roles in (15). One is the role it has in any process, as defined in (8): the component states of the process are distributed through a continuous span of conceived time (and scanned sequentially through processing time). Its other role pertains to the internal structure of the component states: time serves as the cognitive domain with respect to which the profiled relation is characterized, and is thus analogous to space in verbs of physical motion, or the alphabet in (13a). Since the same span of conceived time is involved in both roles, it is perhaps superfluous to indicate t_i twice at each stage; $[[m]t_i]t_i$ could perfectly well be collapsed to $[m]t_i$. Still, it is important to emphasize this dual role and the parallelism of (13c) to other motion predications. The only thing special about this example is that conceived time is itself the domain in which the profiled relation manifests itself.[5]

A possible objection at this juncture is that the definition of abstract motion is so general that any change whatever could be construed as an instance. If so, I am inclined to believe that this consequence might be appropriate rather than unfortunate, for it is not at all obvious that change and motion are ever strongly dissociated in our conceptual world. It would be interesting in this regard to see if there are cases in which a verb meaning 'go' evolves into a pro-verb for the class of perfective processes, or conversely (see Langacker 1981 for a possible example).

4. Subjective motion

A perfective motion verb profiles change through time in the spatial location of the mover. There are also verbs that profile the static location of an entity:

(16) a. *A statue of Johanna Nichols stands in the plaza.*
   b. *The United States lies between Mexico and Canada.*

Here *stand* and *lie* are imperfective, i.e. they profile the continuation through time of a stable situation. In (11), the general formula for imperfective processes, the profiled relation scanned sequentially through conceived time was represented by R. To accommodate the special case where the profiled relation is locative, we need only substitute for R the more specific notation $[M]L$, indicating that entity M occupies location L:

$$(17) \quad ...> \begin{bmatrix} [[M]L]t_i \\ C \end{bmatrix}_{T_i} > \begin{bmatrix} [[M]L]t_j \\ C \end{bmatrix}_{T_j} > \begin{bmatrix} [[M]L]t_k \\ C \end{bmatrix}_{T_k} > ...$$

Though M does not move, it is analogous to a mover in being the entity whose location is specified. Observe that C's conception at any one instant is of the form $[[M]L]t_i$, which is basically the same as it is in the case of motion verbs, namely $[[m]l_i]t_i$ (cf. (12)). What distinguishes the two types of verbs is whether the locative specification differs from one state to the next, or remains constant throughout.

   Consider now the following pairs of sentences:

(18) a. *The roof slopes steeply upward.*
   b. *The roof slopes steeply downward.*

(19) a. *The hill gently rises from the bank of the river.*
   b. *The hill gently falls to the bank of the river.*

(20) a. *This highway goes from Tijuana to Ensenada.*
   b. *This highway goes from Ensenada to Tijuana.*

Like the ones in (16), these sentences describe stable situations in which nothing is portrayed as moving or otherwise changing. The felicity of the simple present tense confirms their analysis as imperfective processes: each profiles a single, constant configuration and follows its continuation through conceived time. Obviously, though, something more is going on. In (18)-(20) there is in each instance a clear semantic contrast between the two examples that cannot be attributed to objective properties of the profiled configuration, since precisely the same configuration is designated by the members of each pair. Intuitively, it seems evident that these sentences incorporate a sense of directionality that is lacking in (16)--each pair of sentences contrast semantically because they imply opposite directions. But how can we meaningfully speak of directionality when nothing moves or changes?

This is another instance where a semantic contrast does not reside in the conceptual content of two expressions, but rather in how that content is accessed (recall *cross* vs. *across*). For instance, (18a) and (18b) describe precisely the same situation pertaining to the spatial orientation of the roof, and both portray this situation as extending through conceived time without essential change; in this sense their conceptual content is identical. However, the profiled spatial configuration has a certain degree of internal complexity, because M (the roof) is itself an elongated, path-like object. We can reasonably suppose that the conception of such a configuration requires a certain span of processing time for its full activation: rather than springing instantaneously into full-blown existence, the conception might be built up incrementally, with all facets of it being active only at the conclusion of this "build-up phase". If so, the directionality we perceive in such sentences is attributable to the order in which the various facets of the configuration are activated. Moreover, since different orders of activation can lead to the same overall configuration, we have a way of accounting for the semantic contrast.

In Figure 1, I have sketched the overall locative configuration $[M]L$ whose continuation through conceived time is profiled by the sentences in (18). The domain for this conception is oriented space, i.e. space organized into the horizontal and vertical axes. The roof, M, is an elongated object whose alignment with respect to these axes is being assessed. Let us refer to the points along the spatial extension of M as $[m_1, m_2, m_3, ..., m_n]$; in the diagram, m_1 is equated with the roof's lower extremity, and m_n with its upper extremity. Each point m_i along the roof's extension occupies location l_i in oriented space; l_i reduces to the combination (h_i, v_i), where h_i is the horizontal projection of m_i, and v_i its vertical projection. L, the spatial location of M, therefore does not consist of a single point, but rather the path-like set of points $[l_1, l_2, l_3, ..., l_n]$.

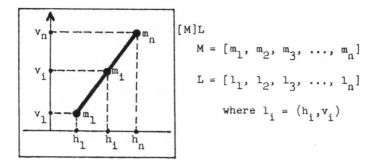

Figure 1.

I am assuming that every conception involving directionality at the experiential level implies some kind of seriality at the processing level. The directionality in (18) is attributed to the build-up phase leading to the full activation of configuration *[M]L*. For (18a), we may posit the following sequence of activation:

$$(21) \quad \begin{bmatrix} [m_1]l_1 \\ \\ C \end{bmatrix}_{T_1} > \begin{bmatrix} [m_1]l_1 \\ [m_2]l_2 \\ \\ C \end{bmatrix}_{T_2} > \begin{bmatrix} [m_1]l_1 \\ [m_2]l_2 \\ [m_3]l_3 \\ \\ C \end{bmatrix}_{T_3} > ... > \begin{bmatrix} [m_1]l_1 \\ [m_2]l_2 \\ [m_3]l_3 \\ \vdots \\ [m_n]l_n \\ \\ C \end{bmatrix}_{T_n}$$

That is, in building up to the full conception, C first activates subconfiguration $[m_1]l_1$, then $[m_2]l_2$, and so on. Summary scanning is employed, so once initiated each subconfiguration remains active throughout; as a consequence, the conception grows progressively more complex with the passage of processing time, until the full configuration *[M]L* is simultaneously active at T_n. Experientially, it is as if the roof "grows upward" starting from its lower extremity m_1, eventually reaching its full extension.[6] The analysis of (18b) is identical except that m_1 is equated with the roof's upper extremity, and m_n with its lower end. The sequence in (21) is then manifested experientially as the roof "growing downward" from top to bottom. But either sequence of activation results in the same overall configuration *[M]L*, whose extension through conceived time plays no inherent role in the build-up phase, as *[M]L* itself is atemporal. The perceived directionality of (18) derives instead from the order in which its subconfigurations are accessed through processing time.

We can of course speak of motion in sentences like (18), but motion of a special sort. As M "grows" upward or downward from its starting point, its leading edge can be thought of as moving through space in much the same way that the concert moves through time in (13c). However, as (21) shows, the position of M's leading edge changes only through processing time, not through conceived time; only by taking into account the time axis of the construal relation itself do we obtain the temporal component necessary for considering this to be a type of motion. Once we invoke processing time in this fashion, additional instances of motion can be discerned in (21). For these latter, the mover is not M, but rather C.

The conceptualizer can be thought of as moving along either of two paths: $[m_1, m_2, m_3, ..., m_n]$ $(= M)$, or $[l_1, l_2, l_3, ..., l_n]$ $(= L)$. This motion on the part of C is both abstract and subjective, as these terms were defined earlier. Let us focus on M (the case of L is exactly parallel). C's conception of M counts as an instance of abstract motion according to the following rationale: (i) $[m_1, m_2, m_3, ..., m_n]$ constitute an ordered set of entities; (ii) during the build-up phase, C accesses these entities in sequence, i.e. he first activates the conception of m_1, then that of m_2, and so on; (iii) by activating the conception of a particular entity m_i, C can be regarded as making contact with it mentally (just as one makes contact with the letters of the alphabet by reciting them--cf. (13a)); and (iv) each such contact occurs at a distinct point in (processing) time. We need only restate these interactions in the format $[[C]m_i]T_i$ to see that they qualify as an instance of abstract motion, with C as the mover.

C's motion in (21) is not only abstract but also subjective. The reason, quite simply, is that C does not conceive of himself as moving along a path: as (21) clearly reveals, C's conception at any instant is limited to some portion of the locative relationship $[M]L$, and his own role in this relation is purely subjective. It is only from the external perspective of the analyst that C moves abstractly along a path. Barring self-analysis (where C would play a dual role, as in (4)), the conception that C himself entertains is merely the directional construal of a static configuration.

5. Avenues of semantic extension

The sentences in (19), (20), and (22) illustrate a common type of semantic extension:

(22) *A white fence {runs/stretches/reaches/extends} from one end of his property to the other.*

In each case, a perfective verb of physical movement has developed an additional, imperfective value in which it describes the continuation through time of a static configuration. The conception of motion has not disappeared entirely, however; a shadow of it remains in the directionality with which the static configuration is construed, as characterized in (21). Whereas the basic meaning profiles physical motion by an objectively-construed mover (namely the subject), one (unprofiled) facet of the extended meaning is abstract motion by a subjectively-construed mover, specifically the conceptualizer. The pivotal factor in this type of semantic shift is therefore "subjectification": an originally objective notion is transferred to the subjective axis of the construal relation itself.[7]

A second common avenue of semantic extension is for the profile of a complex relation to be restricted to its final state; the extended meaning then constitutes a stative relation. The prepositions in (23) represent complex relations--each of them profiles a series of states that do not reduce to a single, consistent configuration.

(23) a. *The prisoner ran to the fence.*
   b. *Abernathy crawled through the tunnel.*
   c. *The scouts hiked over the mountain.*

The corresponding stative relations are illustrated in (24). Each preposition profiles only a single locative configuration, but one that is construed as the last in a series of configurations defining an extended spatial path.

(24) a. *The prisoner is already to the fence.*
   b. *Abernathy must be through the tunnel by now.*
   c. *The scouts were over the mountain by noon.*

The profile of a complex relation is similarly restricted to its final state in the case of adjectival past participles (e.g. *swollen* designates the final state of the process *swell*); here, of course, the relationship involves derivation rather than semantic extension.

Consider now the following sentences:

(25) a. *A stray dog walked across the plaza, through the alley, and over the bridge.*
   b. *The Linguistics Hall of Fame is across the plaza, through the alley, and over the bridge.*

Both incorporate the complex locative expression *across the plaza, through the alley, and over the bridge*, which describes an extended spatial path. Since (25a) profiles spatial motion by an objectively-construed mover, the occurrence of such a locative is quite natural. Why, however, should a path locative appear in (25b), which does not describe motion at all, but only the static, point-like location of its subject?

My proposal is that the locative in (25b) receives a special interpretation that combines the two types of semantic extension previously discussed. The normal value of a path locative, corresponding to the objective spatial motion of (25a), is depicted in Figure 2(a): with the passage of conceived time, the objective mover (i.e. the subject) occupies successively all those points that constitute the extended spatial path (indicated by the dashed arrow). The effect of subjectification is to replace the objective spatial motion of the subject with abstract, subjective motion on the part of *C* in building up to his conception of a stable objective configuration. We observed this effect in (18)-(20), and we observe it again in (25b). The difference between the two cases resides in whether or not the second type of semantic extension--profile restriction--also applies. It does not apply in (18)-(20), where the profiled objective configuration essentially "telescopes" all the component states of Figure 2(a); the subject is an elongated entity (a roof, hill, or highway) that simultaneously occupies all the points along the extended spatial path. In (25b), by contrast, the subject occupies only the endpoint of the path, corresponding to just the final state of Figure 2(a); we obtain this result by applying both profile restriction and subjectification to the basic meaning. The product of these two semantic extensions, as applied to Figure 2(a), is thus the structure represented in 2(b). Through time, the subject is stably located at the endpoint of a path anchored at the other end by the position of *C*, whose abstract and subjective motion along this path allows him to compute the location of the subject relative to his own.

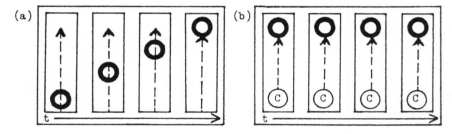

Figure 2.

Finally, let us consider sentences in which a finite motion verb takes an infinitival complement (see Lamiroy 1983 for insightful discussion):

(26) a. *Il monte se coucher.* 'He is going up to go to bed'
     b. *Il court le regarder.* 'He is running to look at it'

Semantically, it is specified that the subject traverses a spatial path, at the end of which he initiates the process indicated by the infinitival complement. Formally, these sentences are precisely parallel to those in which a verb meaning 'go' comes to indicate futurity. Thus, while (27) might be construed as indicating spatial motion that terminates in the process of door-opening, it is far more likely to be interpreted as a 'gonna'-type future, just as in the English translation:

(27) *Il va ouvrir la porte.* 'He is going to open the door'

This example brings us back to our original question: What is the proper way of describing the common semantic extension from 'go' to 'future'?

To account for this development, we need only combine the two avenues of semantic extension just considered with a third one that is massively attested in natural language: the application of a spatial term to the temporal domain (recall the discussion of (13c)). The extension from 'go' to 'future' is therefore captured by the difference between Figures 2(a) and 2(b), provided that the path of motion is interpreted as being spatial in the former and temporal in the latter. With the path construed as a spatial one, Figure 2(a) represents the movement sense of (27); at the endpoint of his motion, the subject initiates the process specified by the infinitival complement. With the path construed as a temporal one, Figure 2(b) represents the futurity sense of (27). Under this interpretation, (27) profiles the continuation through time of a stable configuration whose domain also happens to be that of conceived time. What is this temporal configuration? It is one in which the subject's initiation of the infinitival process lies downstream in time from the location of the conceptualizer; since C is the speaker and/or hearer, C's location is the time of the speech event. Moreover, C computes the position of the infinitival process relative to his own (the time of speaking) by sequentially activating, during the build-up phase, his conception of the temporal path linking the two.

In sum, it is not the subject who moves through time when a sentence like (27) indicates futurity, but rather the conceptualizer, whose motion is both subjective and abstract. It is argued in Chapter 12 that subjectification, as witnessed by the shift from 'go' to 'future', is a recurrent factor in the semantic attenuation that accompanies grammaticization.

6. Grammatical valence

A central feature of cognitive grammar is its treatment of valence and grammatical constructions.* Exemplification will be drawn from various American Indian languages of the Uto-Aztecan family (see Langacker 1977 for a survey). A common feature of these languages, and of languages generally, is the formation of complex verbs through the layering of "verb-like" derivational affixes. The Luiseño data in (1) is not untypical (the tense suffix -q indicates present or recent past).

(1) a. *noo ŋee-q*
     I   leave-TNS
     'I am leaving'

   b. *noo ŋee-viču-q*
      I   leave-want-TNS
      'I want to leave'

   c. *noo poy ŋee-ni-q*
      I   him leave-make-TNS
      'I made him leave'

   d. *noo poy ŋee-viču-ni-q*
      I   him leave-want-make-TNS
      'I made him want to leave'

   e. *noo poy ŋee-ni-viču-q*
      I   him leave-make-want-TNS
      'I want to make him leave'

   f. *noo poy ŋee-viču-ni-viču-q*
      I   him leave-want-make-want-TNS
      'I want to make him want to leave'

Perhaps the most intriguing aspect of such constructions is the tendency for morphological layering to correlate with "semantic scope", so that an inner layer of structure is semantically "in the scope of" the affix constituting the layer immediately external to it.

One approach to this phenomenon was afforded by the theory of generative semantics, as illustrated in Figure 1(a). Scope was explicated in terms of subordination in underlying structure; the surface complex verb was derived by repeated application of rules such as Predicate Raising and Equi-NP Deletion (cf. Langacker 1973b). In retrospect, several objections can be raised to this type of analysis. One pertains to the adequacy of the posited underlying structures as representations of meaning. Another is the absence of theory-independent motivation for treating the root and derivational affixes as deriving from clauses embedded to NP. Finally, the whole notion of deriving the surface form from a radically different underlying structure is rather suspect.

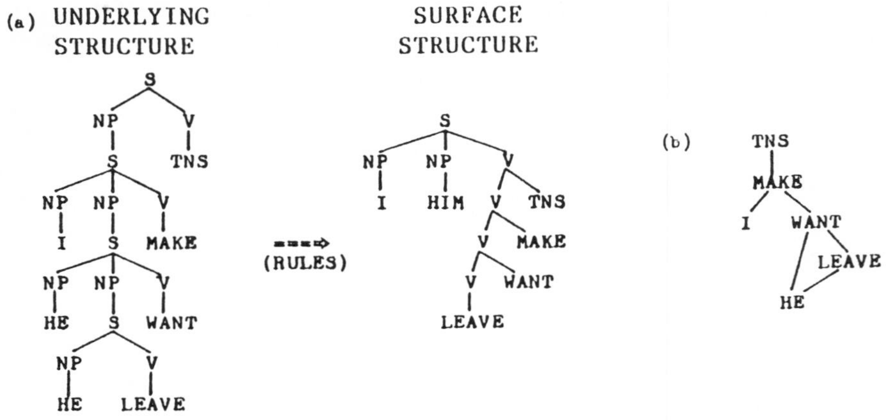

Figure 1.

Another alternative, which avoids at least one of the objections cited above, is to posit dependency trees like that in Figure 1(b). Such trees accommodate predicate-argument relationships without the arbitrary appeal to syntactic embedding under NP-nodes. However, they do not themselves address the matter of morphological layering; special provisions are required to provide for the grouping of predicates into words. I will argue, moreover, that predicate-argument representations of this kind are crucially inexplicit even with respect to pivotal semantic relationships.

This chapter approaches the correlation between semantic scope and morphological layering in the context of a broader conception of the nature of grammatical valence. It provides a reasonably explicit preliminary account of what permits morphemes to combine and of the relation their forms and meanings bear to those of the composite whole. It is suggested that predicate-argument structures like Figure 1(b) represent only a special (though prototypical) case in the spectrum of possible grammatical and semantic relationships. The correlation between semantic scope and morphological layering receives a natural explication in a theory which treats grammatical structure as an inherently symbolic phenomenon.

1. Canonical instances

Grammar is the combination of symbolic structures to form progressively more complex symbolic expressions. This combination is bipolar, with the integration of semantic structures standing in a symbolic relation to the integration of their corresponding phonological structures. Our main concern at present is the nature of this integration at the semantic pole. What precisely is the character of the semantic integration that forms a composite semantic structure from two or more component predications?

I emphasize at the start that I am not concerned with trying to predict the valence of a morpheme on the basis of its internal semantic structure. In fact, I do not think it is possible to predict valence in absolute terms. There is no reason to suppose, for instance, that the semantic pole of Luiseño *ŋee* 'leave' is substantially different in any crucial respect from that of English *leave*, yet *ŋee* is consistently intransitive, while *leave* optionally bears a valence relation of some kind to a nominal object complement (this very optionality establishes the point):

(2) a. *The man left.*
    b. *The man left the building.*

Instead of absolute predictability, we must settle for predictability of a weaker sort, one more generally appropriate for language: the semantic structure of a morpheme defines its valence potential and determines how readily it lends itself to certain kinds of valence relations exploiting that potential, but whether and how this potential will actually be realized is in some measure a function of linguistic convention (Chapter 10).

Our concern here, though, is with the nature of the valence ties (at the semantic pole) between two structures that do in fact combine in accordance with the conventions of the language. We will start with prototypical valence relations, turning subsequently to cases which deviate from the prototype in various ways.

Consider the following Hopi sentence:

(3) *taaqa moosa-t tɨwa*
    man cat-ACC see/find
    'The man found the cat'

(I will simplify matters by ignoring the accusative inflection on 'cat' as well as definiteness and tense/aspect.) In standard predicate-argument terms, the Hopi verb *tɨwa* is a canonical two-place predicate, for it designates a relation between two salient entities, a searcher/perceiver and the object sought/perceived. Figure 2 is a typical predicate-argument dependency tree representation for the lexical morphemes of (3), showing the valence relations between [FIND] and its arguments [MAN] and [CAT].

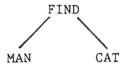

Figure 2.

Though Figure 2 is perfectly acceptable as a first approximation, it is undeniably inexplicit on many crucial points. For one thing, nothing of substance is indicated about the internal structure of any of the three predicates. Second, nothing explicitly shows that [MAN] and [CAT] have different roles with respect to [FIND], or what these roles are. Third, how [MAN] and [CAT] connect to [FIND], and what permits this combination in the first place, are left unspecified. Finally, there is no direct characterization of the composite semantic structure that results from integrating the three components.

The cognitive grammar account of grammatical valence can be regarded as an attempt to be explicit on all these points, i.e. to explicate the valid intuitions (pertaining to prototypical valence relations) that lie behind the widespread acceptance of some version of predicate-argument structure. We can begin with a characterization of the internal structure of the predicates, most crucially [FIND]. The matrix for this predicate is complex, involving not only the domain of physical space but also nonbasic domains pertaining to perception and cognition, including the knowledge that perceiving individuals, at a given time, have perceptual access to a limited area and make perceptual contact only with objects located within this perceptual field. I have conflated these different domains in Figure 3, which oversimplifies matters but is sufficient for present purposes.

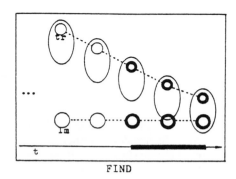

FIND

Figure 3.

[FIND] traces through time the evolution of a situation involving several entities. Two of these entities, both physical objects, are included in the relational profile as central participants: the trajector, corresponding to the searcher, functions as the figure within this profile; the object sought and found functions as the primary landmark. Less salient in this conception is a third entity, namely the perceptual field of the trajector, which I have given as an ellipse. The base of [FIND] includes a search process of indefinite duration. Only the final stages of that process are actually designated by the predicate and hence profiled, namely the transition into the situation where the landmark is located in the trajector's visual field. The dotted correspondence lines in Figure 3 indicate that the trajector is identical for all the component states, as is the landmark.

I will treat [MAN] and [CAT] in much lesser detail, using only a mnemonic sketch representing their shape specification in diagrams below. For our purposes, the relevant observation is that they designate prototypical things, bounded objects in physical space. Their full description also includes characterizations with respect to other domains (e.g. specifications of size, color, canonical activities, and so on).

Let us now consider the valence relations in Figure 2. A valence relation between two predications is possible just in case these predications overlap, in the sense that some substructure within one corresponds to a substructure within the other and is construed as identical to it. The dotted correspondence lines in Figure 4 therefore specify that the trajector of [FIND] is construed as being identical to the object profiled by [MAN], and that the landmark of [FIND] is construed as being identical to the profile of [CAT]. Establishing these correspondences is what permits [FIND] to combine with [MAN] and [CAT] in a grammatical valence relation. The lines of correspondence can also be thought of as specifying the integration of the component predications, i.e. as instructions for fitting these predications together to form a coherent composite structure. In Figure 4, they indicate that the specifications of [MAN] are to be superimposed on those of the

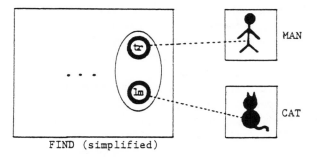

Figure 4.

trajector of [FIND], and the specifications of [CAT] on those of the landmark of [FIND]. [MAN] and [CAT] thus bear different relations to [FIND], since their profiles correspond to different substructures within it.

I claim that all valence relations are based on correspondences between subparts of the component structures. This is in fact the only constant factor in valence relations. However, there is considerably more that needs to be said about canonical relations like those in Figure 2 if we want to be fully explicit about their nature. For example, what is the nature of the asymmetry between [FIND] on the one hand and [MAN] and [CAT] on the other that leads us to put [FIND] on top in the dependency tree and the others on the bottom? What leads us to say, in predicate-argument terms, that [FIND] is the predicate, and [MAN] and [CAT] the arguments, rather than the converse? It would appear that this asymmetry is connected with the relational character of [FIND]. [FIND] introduces and organizes a scene in which salient participants interact in a specified way. [MAN] and [CAT] designate individual objects, and while it is part of our knowledge of these entities that they participate in relations with other objects, these external relationships are neither salient nor profiled within these predicates. [FIND] thus makes salient reference to two objects as part of its own internal structure--these objects function as the trajector and landmark within its relational profile--while neither [MAN] nor [CAT] profiles an external relation.

I speak of [FIND] as being conceptually dependent, while [MAN] and [CAT] are conceptually autonomous, with respect to the correspondences in Figure 4. [FIND] is conceptually dependent because it presupposes, as an inherent part of its own internal structure, the two things participating in the correspondences; [MAN] and [CAT] are conceptually autonomous because they do not similarly presuppose a salient external relationship. One cannot conceptualize the [FIND] relationship without conceptualizing the two things functioning as trajector and landmark of that relation (even if they are conceived only in the vaguest terms, say as blobs), but it is perfectly possible to conceptualize a man or a cat without mentally setting it in a relation with some external object. I would emphasize that conceptual autonomy and dependence are ultimately matters of degree, but in canonical instances of grammatical valence there is a fairly clear asymmetry between the dependent and autonomous predications along these lines. The dependent structure can be equated with the predicate, in predicate-argument terms, and the autonomous structures with its arguments.[1]

Though [FIND] introduces two relational participants which correspond to the profiles of the autonomous predicates, there is obviously a difference in the degree to which the corresponding entities are specified by the relational and nominal predications. [FIND] characterizes its trajector and landmark only in schematic terms--the former only as a thing capable of searching and perceiving, the latter only as a thing capable of being found--while [MAN] and [CAT] specify the corresponding objects in far greater detail. Hence there is a relation of schematicity between each of the profiled participants within [FIND] and the autonomous predicate whose profile corresponds to it. We can say that the dependent predicate organizes the scene, setting up a relation between schematically specified objects, and that the autonomous predicates fit into this scene and elaborate particular substructures within it. These substructures, called elaboration sites (e-sites), are cross-hatched in Figure 5 for ease of identification. The arrow leading from an e-site in the dependent predicate to the corresponding autonomous predicate thus stands for a relationship of schematicity.

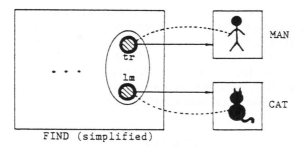

Figure 5.

Two further aspects of canonical valence relations must be considered. The first is constituency, which is treated here not as a separate dimension of linguistic organization, but merely as reflecting the order in which simpler symbolic structures successively combine to form progressively more complex ones. We may speak of a compositional path leading from individual morphemes, through intermediate composite structures at various levels of complexity, to the final composite structure representing the overall semantic and phonological value of the entire expression. Typically constituency is binary: at any particular level of organization, two component structures integrate to form a composite structure, which in turn can function as one of the two component structures at the next higher level of organization, and so on. It is important to observe that constituency per se is not employed in this framework for the characterization of basic grammatical relations. The subject and direct object of a clause, for example, are not defined in terms of a particular constituent-structure configuration--instead the subject is defined as a nominal which corresponds to the trajector of the clausal head, and the direct object as one which corresponds to its primary landmark (cf. Figure 5), regardless of the order in which these components are assembled. Different compositional paths (orders of assembly) often lead to the same overall composite structure, with no effect on our ability to characterize grammatical relations. Inherent to this account of grammatical valence, therefore, is the potential for constituency to be quite fluid and variable. The alternate constituency groupings suggested by phonological considerations (e.g. intonation breaks, different phonological phrasings) generally prove workable for the semantic pole as well.

Figure 6 shows the most likely constituency grouping for the example under discussion. At the lower level of constituency, [FIND] and [CAT] are integrated to form the composite structure (FIND-CAT). The schematicity arrow indicates that [FIND] is the dependent structure, and [CAT] the autonomous one; more specifically, [CAT] elaborates the landmark of [FIND].[2] At the higher level of constituency, [MAN] is integrated with the composite structure (FIND-CAT) to form the higher-order composite structure (FIND-CAT-MAN). At this second level, (FIND-CAT) is dependent, and the autonomous structure [MAN] elaborates its trajector. Note that rectangles and square brackets are employed to indicate that the enclosed structure presumably constitutes a unit (i.e. a fully mastered configuration) for a typical speaker; closed curves and parentheses are employed for novel structures. Thus, while all of the individual predicates in Figure 6 are obviously established units, the intermediate-level composite structure (FIND-CAT) may well be novel, as is the overall composite structure (FIND-CAT-MAN).

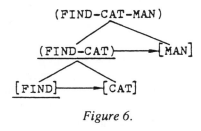

Figure 6.

The underscores in Figure 6 relate to the final aspect of canonical valence relations. Consider the lower level of constituency. [FIND], a process predicate, integrates with [CAT], which profiles a thing. What, then, will be the profile of the composite structure (FIND-CAT)? Will it designate a thing or a process? Clearly *moosat tɨwa* 'found the cat' designates a process, not a thing; it is the core of a clause, and a clause by definition is processual in nature. However there is no inherent reason why the composite structure would have to inherit the profile of the conceptually dependent component rather than the conceptually autonomous one --the choice must be specified as part of each grammatical construction. In a canonical valence relation, then, one of the component structures must be singled out as the profile determinant, which means that its profile prevails in determining the character of the composite structure. The underscores in Figure 6 mark the profile determinants. (FIND-CAT) is thus a process, for it inherits the processual profile of [FIND]. At the second level of constituency, similarly, (FIND-CAT) is marked as the profile determinant, so the composite structure for the entire expression is also processual, and (3) *taaqa moosat tɨwa* 'The man found the cat' qualifies as a clause.

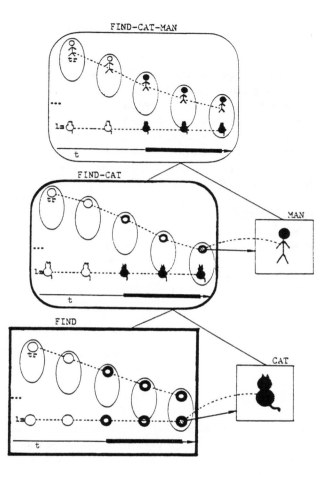

Figure 7.

Figure 6 of course abbreviates the semantic structures at each level. Figure 7 is a somewhat more adequate representation, depicting the internal organization of these structures within the limits of the notations introduced (obviously it is still quite informal). By now Figure 7 should be largely self-explanatory. At the lower level of constituency, [CAT] elaborates the landmark of [FIND], which serves as elaboration site and corresponds to the profile of [CAT]. [FIND] is the profile determinant--indicated by enclosing it in a box drawn with heavy lines. The novel composite structure (FIND-CAT) is formed by superimposing the specifications of [CAT] on the schematic landmark within [FIND], while retaining the processual profile of the latter. (FIND-CAT) is therefore a process with unspecified trajector. This trajector is elaborated at the second level of constituency, where it is put in correspondence with the profile of [MAN]. Since (FIND-CAT) is the profile determinant, the novel composite structure (FIND-CAT-MAN) is a process whose trajector receives the specifications of [MAN].

It should be apparent that the same composite structure would be obtained if the component structures were amalgamated in another order, i.e. if the constituency grouping were different. For instance, if [MAN] first elaborated the trajector of [FIND], the intermediate-level composite structure (FIND-MAN) would constitute a processual predication with a specific trajector and a schematic landmark. This landmark could then be elaborated by [CAT] at the second level of constituency, with the resulting overall composite structure being no different from the one shown in Figure 7. Regardless of the order of composition, *taaqa* 'man' would be identified as the clausal subject, since it elaborates the trajector of *tiwa* 'find' (whose processual profile is inherited by the clause as a whole); and *moosat* would be identified as the direct object, for it elaborates the primary landmark. It is reasonable to suppose that speakers do in fact employ this alternate constituency in sentences displaying object topicalization, as illustrated in (4).

(4) *moosat-t   taaqa   tiwa*
    cat-ACC   man   see/find
    'The cat the man found'

2. Noncanonical instances

The essential aspects of a canonical valence relation are summarized in Figure 8. It is a binary relation between two predications, one of which is conceptually autonomous and the other dependent. The dependent structure is relational and includes within its profile an entity, specifically a thing, which corresponds to the profile of the autonomous structure. This entity, only schematically specified within the dependent structure itself, functions as an elaboration site; this e-site bears a relation of schematicity to the autonomous structure, which serves to specify it in finer detail. Finally, the dependent structure is the profile determinant and hence imposes its relational profile on the composite structure.

This is the basic type of valence relation generally assumed in predicate-argument accounts of semantics, but among the cluster of properties defining it, only the existence of a correspondence between substructures of the components appears to be a universal property of grammatical valence relations. In this section we explore some of the ways in which such relations commonly deviate from the prototype.

When there is a clear asymmetry between two predications along the lines of conceptual autonomy/dependence, it is natural for the dependent structure to

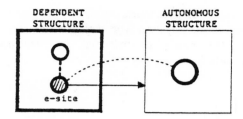

Figure 8.

function as profile determinant, as it canonically does. This is quite consonant with its function of organizing a scene, of establishing relations among schematically specified entities; the autonomous structure simply fits into this scene and elaborates one of these entities. Choosing the autonomous structure as profile determinant in such a situation amounts to a kind of skewing, where one component is intrinsically suited to play a scene-structuring role, but where the perspective of the other component is adopted by the composite structure.

This skewing is the basis for the cognitive grammar characterization of the head-modifier relation. We speak of such a relation when there is a clear asymmetry between a conceptually autonomous and a conceptually dependent predication, and where the autonomous structure functions as profile determinant: the autonomous component is then the head, while the dependent component is the modifier. In the canonical alignment of Figure 8, by contrast, where the dependent component functions as profile determinant, we speak instead of a head-complement relation.

Consider the Hopi expressions in (5).

(5) a. *taaqa wiipa*
 man tall
 'The man is tall'
 b. *wipa-taqa*
 tall-man
 'tall man'

Sentence (5a) is clausal, hence relational in character, and here we would normally speak of a subject-predicate relation between *taaqa* and *wiipa*, and refer to *taaqa* as a complement of *wiipa*. On the other hand, (5b) is nominal in character, and in this case it is customary to speak of a head-modifier relation. Yet in both instances [MAN] is autonomous and elaborates the trajector of the dependent [TALL], as seen in Figure 9(a). [TALL] profiles a relation between an object and an abstract scale of comparison. This scale pertains to the vertical extension of elongated

objects when they assume their canonical vertical orientation. [TALL] specifies
that the upper extreme of the trajector, with respect to this orientation, falls in the
landmark region of the scale's positive end, i.e. that portion beyond the
neighborhood of the norm (n).

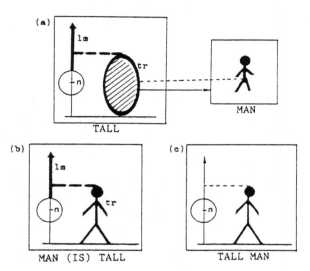

Figure 9.

The relationship depicted in 9(a) is valid for both (5a) and (5b), yet these
expressions are quite different in meaning. They differ precisely in that (5a) is
relational, while (5b) profiles a thing and is therefore nominal. Hence the
composite semantic structure in (5a) inherits the relational profile of [TALL], and
that of (5b) the nominal profile of [MAN]. These respective composite structures
are sketched in 9(b) and 9(c). Observe that in each instance a predication of
tallness is made with respect to the man--the only difference lies in whether that
relation is profiled (designated) by the overall expression, or whether it is merely
part of the base.

The difference between an adjectival and an adverbial modifier is simply that
the latter has a relation rather than a thing for its trajector and e-site. Consider the
expression *run fast*. With respect to a scale of rapidity, [FAST] situates a process
in that region of the scale which lies beyond the neighborhood of the norm in a
positive direction. This schematic process--the trajector of [FAST]--is elaborated
by [RUN] in a way precisely parallel to the way in which [MAN] elaborates the
trajector of [TALL] in *tall man*. [RUN] is clearly the profile determinant in *run
fast*, since this expression designates a type of running, not a type of rapidity--the
composite structure is quite analogous to Figure 9(c). Observe that the notion

"adverb" receives a very simple characterization in this framework: an adverb is a modifier whose head profiles a relation (as opposed to a thing).

We have now seen two ways in which valence relations can depart from the prototype: the autonomous structure may function as profile determinant, and the e-site within the dependent structure may be a relation rather than a thing. Additional kinds of departure from the prototype can be illustrated by a series of composite locative particles in Cora that were previously described in Chapter 2. The particular locative particles in question are specialized for topographical relations in mountainous terrain. Representative examples are given in (6a) and (6b).

(6) a. *yuu* 'right here at the foot of the slope'
    b. *mah* 'away up there to the side in the face of the slope'
    c. *y* 'proximal'; *m* 'medial'; $\emptyset$ 'distal'
    d. *u* 'inside'; *a* 'outside'
    e. *:* 'foot of slope'; *h* 'face of slope'; *n* 'top of slope'

These particles prove to be essentially regular combinations of three morphemes each. The alternatives for each position are given in (6c)-(6e).

The semantic structure of *mah* 'away up there to the side in the face of the slope' is sketched in Figure 10. The first component, *m* 'medial', marks distance from the speaker (S). The proximal range, indicated by a small, light circle, essentially encompasses the area within the speaker's physical reach. The medial range, which functions as a salient landmark and is shown in heavy outline as a major relational participant, basically includes the area within the speaker's visual field. The medial predication is thus a stative relation which locates the trajector within the medial range but outside the proximal area. Recall that the general contrast in Cora between *u* 'inside' and *a* 'outside' assumes a specialized value in this context. The relevant variants of *u* and *a* are defined relative to a domain which finds the speaker standing at the foot of a slope and looking straight up the face of this slope. The slope (including the foot, face, and top) is represented by a rectangle in the middle diagram at the bottom in Figure 10. The landmark for *u* and *a* is the area along the speaker's line of sight as he looks up the slope from this canonical position. The morphemes *u* and *a* also designate stative locative relations, situating the trajector either inside or outside the landmark region. Finally, *h* (yet another stative relation) indicates that the trajector is located in the face of the slope, as opposed to the foot or the top.

Lines of integration connect the three component predicates. It is an obligatory specification of this construction that the trajectors of the three predicates correspond. Moreover, the speaker is obviously the same in the first two components, and the slope is the same in the second two. The three predicates are therefore tightly integrated by correspondences connecting shared substructures. The composite structure is obtained simply by superimposing corresponding

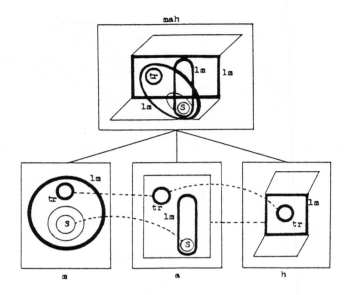

Figure 10.

entities. The result is a complex locative relationship in which the trajector is simultaneously located with respect to three parameters and three landmarks, one contributed by each component predicate. Taken together these add up to a fairly precise specification that can be glossed as in (6b).

This construction departs from prototypical valence relations in three ways. First, the construction is not binary. There is no apparent reason to break the three-morpheme sequence down into two levels of constituency; the three specifications are essentially coordinate. Second, there is no obvious sense in which any of the components is conceptually dependent relative to the others, hence there is no e-site. Finally, there is no basis for singling out any of the three component predicates as profile determinant. The composite expression *mah* does not designate any of the three component locative relations in particular, but rather the complex locative relation defined by coordinating the locative specifications along the three parameters. Because there is no profile determinant, nor any asymmetry in terms of conceptual autonomy/dependence, none of the component structures can be identified as a head, complement, or modifier with respect to the others.

3. Further departures from the canon

Additional types of departures from canonical valence relations can be illustrated by the Cahuilla data in (7) (from Seiler 1977: 300f).

(7) a. *ne-'aš̌ kiyul*
      my-pet fish
      'my fish'

b. *ne-'aš̌ tamawet*
      my-pet mockingbird
      'my mockingbird'

c. *ne-wes-'a   navet*
      my-plant-NR cactus
      'my cactus'

d. *ne-wes-'a   sandiya*
      my-plant-NR watermelon
      'my watermelon'

This is a type of noun-classifier construction frequently found in Uto-Aztecan possessive expressions. Instead of going directly on the possessed noun, the possessor prefix attaches to a more schematic noun, or classifier, to which the possessed noun stands in a sort of appositive relation. Cahuilla has a whole series of classifiers, only two of which are exemplified here. The classifier *'aš̌* is used for pets and other domesticated animals, and *wes-'a*, a nominalization of the verb stem *wes* 'plant', is used for crop plants sown in a row.

The semantic structure of (7a) is sketched in Figure 11. At the lower level of constituency, [MY] functions as a modifier of [PET]. I will assume that [MY] profiles a schematically characterized stative relation, whose landmark is identified with the speaker; it simply indicates that the trajector interacts with the speaker in some unspecified way. [PET] is a relational noun: it profiles a thing, identified schematically as some kind of animal (AN), but also makes salient internal reference to another individual, who participates in an unprofiled relationship of ownership with the designated animal and thus functions as a type of landmark (reference point) within this nominal predication. The valence relation between [MY] and [PET] involves two correspondences. First, the schematic trajector of [MY] is put in correspondence with the profile of [PET], and is elaborated by the latter predication. A second correspondence associates the landmarks of the two component predications--more precisely, the schematic relationship profiled by [MY] is equated with the ownership relation in the base of [PET]. Since [PET] is the profile determinant (head) in this construction, the composite structure [MY-

PET] is nominal rather than relational: it profiles an animal whose characterization is schematic apart from the specification that it is owned by the speaker.

Consider now the second level of constituency, where *ne-'aš* 'my pet' combines with *kiyul* 'fish'. The profile of [FISH] corresponds to the schematically characterized profile of [MY-PET], which is substantially elaborated by the former predication. The profile of [MY-PET] therefore functions as an e-site, and [MY-PET] can be regarded as conceptually dependent with respect to [FISH]. The composite structure (MY-PET-FISH), which designates a fish owned by the speaker, is surrounded by a closed curve rather than a box to indicate its presumed status as a novel expression (rather than a fixed unit).

This latter valence relation is noteworthy in two respects. For one thing, both component predications are nominal: [MY-PET] is dependent in the sense of being elaborated by [FISH] rather than conversely (cf. Figure 8), but neither component structure is a relational predication. The lack of a relational element is problematic in standard predicate-argument accounts of semantic structure (where predicates are considered n-place relations), but it poses no problems whatever in the present framework, where valence relations depend crucially only on the

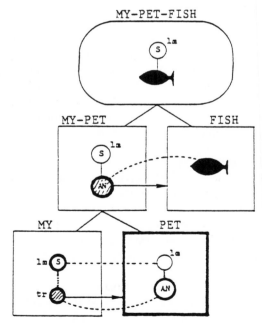

Figure 11.

existence of correspondences between substructures of the component predications. The second noteworthy feature of this construction is that neither component structure can be singled out as the profile determinant. We saw this situation previously in the Cora example, but here the reason is different: since the two component structures profile corresponding entities, the same composite structure would result regardless of which one we identified as the profile determinant. Because there is no clear-cut profile determinant, we lack the basis for positing either a head-modifier or a head-complement relation; the construction is basically appositional.

As a final example, Figure 12 sketches the semantic structure of *ne-wes-'a* 'my plant', the classifier portion of (7c)-(7d). At the lower level of constituency, the nominalizer *-'a* combines with the verb stem *wes* 'plant'. [PLANT] is a process predicate, represented with the abbreviatory notation introduced in Chapter 4. The nominalizing predication [NR] characterizes a thing by virtue of the role it plays in a process. The base of [NR] is thus analyzed as a schematic process, and its profile

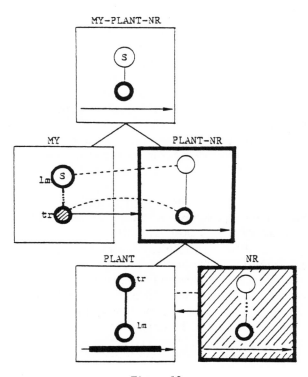

Figure 12.

is identified as the landmark of this base process. In the valence relation between [PLANT] and [NR], the entire schematic process constituting the base of [NR] functions as e-site; the specific process profiled by [PLANT] is put in correspondence with the base process of [NR], so that [PLANT] spells out in specific terms the process with respect to which the profile of the nominalization is characterized. [NR] is both dependent (being elaborated by the other component) and the profile determinant, so we must speak of a complement (rather than a head-modifier) relation. The composite structure [PLANT-NR] designates a thing identified as the landmark of the process of planting.

The integration of [PLANT] and [NR] illustrates two further departures from the canonical valence relation schematized in Figure 8. For the first time in our examples the e-site is neither the profile nor a subpart of the profile--rather it is a process in the base. Second, the e-site is not a proper substructure within the dependent predicate, but is in fact exhaustive of this predicate (apart from its profile specification). It is of course not unexpected, as a limiting case, that the substructure functioning as e-site might coincide with the whole.

At the second level of constituency, the trajector of [MY] corresponds to the profile of [PLANT-NR], being parallel to Figure 11 in this regard. A second correspondence associates the landmark of [MY] (the speaker) with the trajector of the process constituting the base of [PLANT-NR]; the interaction which [MY] predicates between its trajector and landmark is thus equated with the process of planting, and the speaker is identified with the trajector of this unprofiled process. [PLANT-NR] is conceptually autonomous relative to [MY] and also the profile determinant, so the two participate in a head-modifier relationship. The composite structure [MY-PLANT-NR] is a nominal predication which designates the landmark of the process of planting, whose trajector is the speaker. The resulting expression *ne-wes-'a* 'my plant/what I planted' is then capable of combining with an appositional noun like *navet* 'cactus' at a higher level of organization, as in our previous example.

We may now summarize the various ways in which a grammatical valence relation can depart from the prototype. A valence relation need not be binary, and it is not necessary that there be a clear asymmetry between an autonomous and a dependent structure. If there is such an asymmetry, the dependent structure need not be relational, and its e-site does not have to be a thing included in the profile: it can be a relation rather than a thing, and it can be an unprofiled facet of the base (or even subsume the base). Either the autonomous or the dependent structure can function as profile determinant, and in some instances the components contribute equally to the profile of the composite structure. Finally, a valence relation often involves multiple correspondences. The existence of at least one correspondence is perhaps the only invariant feature of valence relations.

4. Scope and morphological layering

We can now return to the problem posed earlier, namely the tendency for morphological layering to correlate with semantic scope, as illustrated by the Luiseño sentences in (1). The present conception of grammatical valence allows a straightforward account of the correlation and the expressions which display it. Let us focus on (1)(d). Limiting our attention for the moment to the verb, its constituency tree is given in Figure 13.

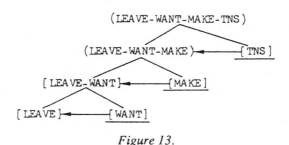

Figure 13.

Two factors combine to account for the correlation between morphological layering and semantic scope. First, at each level in the constituency hierarchy at the semantic pole, the conceptually dependent structure is also the profile determinant (hence we are dealing with head-complement rather than head-modifier relations). This is the canonical alignment, and it constitutes what was recognized as "semantic scope" in the generative semantic framework. At the lowest level, for instance, [LEAVE] elaborates the landmark of [WANT], hence [WANT] is dependent; [WANT] is also the profile determinant, since *ŋee-vicu* 'want to leave' is a kind of wanting, not a kind of leaving. Thus [WANT] imposes its profile on the composite structure, overriding the profile of [LEAVE], which serves to elaborate a substructure of [WANT]. This is the type of relationship people have in mind when they say that [LEAVE] is "in the semantic scope of" [WANT].

The second factor pertains to integration at the phonological pole, which we have largely ignored until now. The notions of autonomy and dependence are equally important at the phonological pole in valence relations as at the semantic pole. In the case of word structure, they amount to the distinction between "root" or "stem" on the one hand, and "affix" on the other. An affix is morphologically dependent in the sense that it is characterized in part by its position relative to a root or stem, and thus makes inherent reference to a schematically specified root or stem as part of its own internal structure. This schematic stem within each affix serves as e-site in a valence relation and is elaborated by a specified stem. A root or stem is autonomous in the sense that it makes no salient internal reference to another phonological entity relative to which it is positioned.

The phonological pole of *ŋee-vičʹu-ni-q* 'made want to leave' is sketched in Figure 14. At each successive level in the hierarchy, an affix (dependent) combines with a root or stem (autonomous) to form a higher-order stem or word (also autonomous). Observe, moreover, that at each level the autonomous semantic structure is symbolized by the autonomous phonological structure, and the dependent semantic structure by the dependent phonological structure. There is consequently a kind of "harmony" between the alignment of autonomous and dependent structures at the two poles, a perfectly natural phenomenon reminiscent of numerous other types of harmonization observable between different facets of linguistic organization.[3] It is hardly surprising that this parallel alignment of autonomy/dependence at the two poles represents a strong universal tendency (though exceptions can be found). When it also happens that the dependent semantic structure functions as the profile determinant (this too being the canonical situation), we obtain the usual correlation between morphological layering and semantic scope. As we work from the root outwards, each successive morphological increment symbolizes the introduction of a semantic predication which has the previously constructed predication "in its scope" (i.e. they participate in a head-complement relationship).

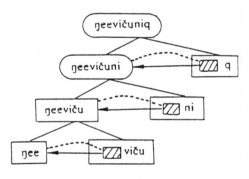

Figure 14.

Let us conclude by examining in specific detail how the complex verb *ŋee-vičʹu-ni-q* 'made want to leave' is assembled at the semantic pole. We must first consider the semantic poles of the component morphemes. [LEAVE] profiles a process in which the trajector, through time, moves from a position internal to the landmark to one external to it. The other three predicates are sketched in Figure 15. Each of them profiles a process, i.e. a series of relational configurations distributed through conceived time. Only a single configuration is explicitly represented in each diagram, which must nevertheless be interpreted as indicating the evolution of the profiled relationship throughout the temporal profile (marked by the heavy-line portion of the time arrow).

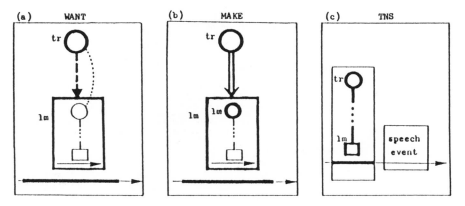

Figure 15.

The trajector of -*vicu* 'want' is a schematically characterized thing, and its landmark is a schematic process. I have used a dashed arrow to indicate the desire held by the trajector with respect to the landmark. Luiseño -*vicu* differs from English *want* in that its trajector is obligatorily equated with the trajector of the landmark process; hence the correspondence line connecting the two trajectors in Figure 15(a). The causative predicate -*ni* 'make' is diagramed in 15(b). The trajector is again a thing, but there are two salient landmarks, one nominal and the other relational. The relational landmark is the process induced by the overall trajector; the causative relationship between this trajector and the landmark process is represented by the double arrow. The nominal landmark is the same entity that functions as the trajector of the landmark process. [MAKE], in other words, is one of many predicates that has the potential for taking two nonsubject complements, one of them a direct object nominal and the other a relational complement having the direct object as one of its participants.[4] Lastly, the tense morpheme -*q* marks present or recent-past time (and also indicates that the subject is singular). In combination with -*ni* 'make', it receives the recent-past construal, as indicated in Figure 15(c). For reasons discussed in Chapter 12 (see also Langacker 1985), it is analyzed as profiling a schematic process, specified in the base as situated prior to the time of speaking (but in temporal proximity to the speech event).

The full constituency tree for the semantic pole of *ŋee-vicu-ni-q* 'made want to leave' is provided in Figure 16, which assumes that *ŋee-vicu* represents a familiar combination and has the status of a unit, while *ŋee-vicu-ni* and *ŋee-vicu-ni-q* constitute novel expressions. Observe that the three predicates described in Figure 15 all function as profile determinants, each at its own level of constituency. Moreover, each is conceptually dependent at its own level of organization, for it

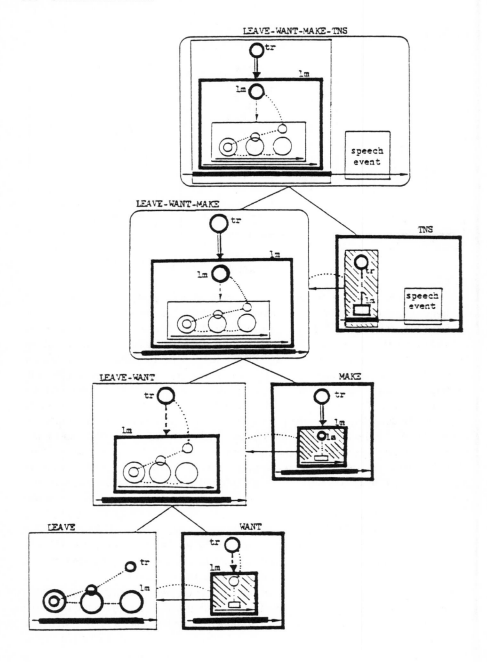

Figure 16.

contains a salient substructure that is elaborated by the stem it combines with. Each suffix is therefore semantically a head, and the stem it attaches to is a complement to that head.

At the first level of organization, the specific process profiled by [LEAVE] elaborates the schematic process serving as the landmark of [WANT], yielding the composite structure [LEAVE-WANT]. Recall that [WANT], as part of its internal structure, establishes a correspondence between its overall trajector and the trajector of the schematic process functioning as its landmark. As a result, when the specifications of [LEAVE] are superimposed on those of the processual landmark of [WANT] to derive the composite structure [LEAVE-WANT], the overall trajector of this composite predication is equated with that of the leaving, i.e. what the trajector wants is for himself to leave (rather than some other individual). The correspondence line internal to [WANT] therefore accomplishes what generative grammarians formerly achieved by their transformation of Equi-NP Deletion. No derivation from a hypothetical deep structure is required in this framework.

At the second level of organization, [LEAVE-WANT] elaborates the relational landmark of [MAKE] to form the composite structure (LEAVE-WANT-MAKE). This structure predicates a causal relationship between the overall trajector and the process of desiring to leave. At the third level, finally, the process (LEAVE-WANT-MAKE) elaborates the schematic process profiled by the tense predication, so that the composite structure (LEAVE-WANT-MAKE-TNS) situates just prior to the time of speaking the profiled process of one individual causing another to want to leave. Observe that both individuals are characterized only schematically at this level of organization.

The complex structure *ŋee-viču-ni-q* 'made want to leave' is categorized as a verb because its composite structure designates a process. As with any other verb, it is eligible to participate in further valence relations serving to elaborate the schematic things functioning as its trajector and landmark. The probable constituency tree for these further levels of composition is presented in Figure 17.[5] At the first level of organization, [HIM] (i.e. a third-person singular pronoun) elaborates the nominal landmark of (LEAVE-WANT-MAKE-TNS); since the latter predication is the profile determinant, the composite structure (HIM-LEAVE-WANT-MAKE-TNS) designates a process, one equivalent to the composite structure of Figure 16 except that its landmark is now more specific. At the second level of organization, the schematic trajector of (HIM-LEAVE-WANT-MAKE-TNS) is elaborated by [I]. Again we have a complement relation (i.e. the processual predication is the head), so the final composite structure (I-HIM-LEAVE-WANT-MAKE-TNS) also profiles a process, as does any finite clause.

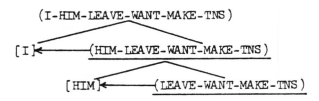

Figure 17.

Observe that the postulated constituency of this sentence, as depicted in Figures 13 and 17, is perfectly compatible with the one suggested by phonological and morphological considerations. [I] and [HIM] are added only after the entire complex verb has been assembled, as reflected by their status as separate words: *noo poy ŋee-vic̆u-ni-q*. Nevertheless, the correspondences which figure in the various valence relations (and those internal to certain predications) properly establish the speaker as the trajector of the causative relationship, and the third person singular individual as the trajector with respect to both the wanting and the leaving. All of this is accomplished without deriving the sentence from a hypothetical underlying structure posited solely to accommodate its supposed predicate-argument configuration (cf. Figure 1(b)), and without special rules like Predicate Raising and Equi-NP Deletion (Figure 1(a)).

As a general matter, this framework promises to reconcile semantic and grammatical constituency with the constituency one is led to posit on phonological grounds. Basic grammatical relations are not defined with respect to specific constituent structure configurations, but rather through correspondences and the trajector/landmark alignment internal to every relational predication. The same correspondences, and hence the same grammatical relations, can be established through alternate compositional paths leading to the same overall composite structure. This is why the conventions of a language often permit alternate word orders or phonological phrasings for otherwise equivalent expressions. Correspondences are essential to grammatical valence relations, but constituent structure is to some degree incidental and variable.

7. Active Zones

This chapter investigates a certain phenomenon, illustrated in (1), pertaining to the compatibility of a relational predication with its arguments.*

(1) a. *David blinked.*
   b. *She heard the piano.*
   c. *I'm in the phone book.*

All are perfectly normal expressions, yet they exhibit an apparent peculiarity when we think about what they actually seem to say. The subject of (1a) names a person, but the activity of blinking is not something carried out by a whole person--only the eyelid really does anything. In (1b), we encounter the seeming anomaly of a person hearing a physical object, when the only things we can in fact hear, quite obviously, are sounds. If (1c) is taken literally, moreover, we can only conclude that the speaker is either very small or quite cramped.

Examples like these have often been noted in one connection or another, but I am unaware of any comprehensive and unified treatment. Their implications are quite substantial, and go right to the heart of critical grammatical issues. I will claim, for instance, that the sentences in (2) illustrate the same basic phenomenon as those in (1).

(2) a. *Wombats are tough to catch.*
   b. *Tom is likely to succeed.*
   c. *I believe Donovan to be an honorable man.*

The sentences in (2) are commonly analyzed as manifesting the syntactic movement (or relation-changing) rules of Object-to-Subject Raising, Subject-to-Subject Raising, and Subject-to-Object Raising, respectively. I will suggest, on the contrary, that a reasonable account of the normal connection between relational predications and their nominal arguments, required even for single-clause expressions, obviates the need for special syntactic rules of this sort.

1. The phenomenon

Let us take the sentences in (3) as our point of departure. In each instance it can be argued that the central relational predication--[APPROACH], [BEYOND], or [NEAR]--profiles a relationship in which its trajector and landmark participate as integral, undifferentiated wholes. As the spacecraft approaches Uranus, for example, every part of it becomes progressively closer to every part of the planet, and no particular subpart of either one has special status in this regard.

(3) a. *The spacecraft is now approaching Uranus.*
   b. *Goleta is beyond Santa Barbara.*
   c. *Your dog is near my cat.*

(4) a. *Your dog bit my cat.*
   b. *Your dog bit my cat on the tail with its sharp teeth.*
   c. *?Your dog bit my cat with its teeth.*

When we examine (4a), a rather different picture emerges. Here it is evident that the relational predication [BITE] designates an interaction between its trajector and landmark that directly involves only selected aspects of these entities. For instance, the teeth of the dog are pivotal to the act of biting, but the contribution of its tail and kidneys to this process is at best negligible. With respect to the landmark, [BITE] itself does not specify which particular part of the cat is privileged to participate directly, but [BITE] strongly suggests that only restricted portions are affected.

Those portions of a trajector or landmark that participate directly in a given relation will be referred to as its "active zone" with respect to the relation in question. For some relational predications, like those in (3), the active zone of the trajector and/or landmark is coincident with the whole. For others, like [BITE], the active zone of the trajector and/or landmark is limited to a proper subpart of the whole. The active zone should not be thought of as a discrete or sharply bounded region within the overall entity--it is more accurate to think of it as the focal area of the relational interaction, the participation of a region becoming more tenuous the farther it lies from this focus. For example, the trajector's participation in the process designated by [BITE] is not strictly limited to its teeth: also involved are the jaws, the operative muscles, the nervous system, and so on. Pushing things to the extreme, one could argue that every part of the trajector is involved in the act of biting in one way or another, however marginal it might be, if only because all portions of the body are interconnected, so that no portion is totally unaffected by what happens to any other. I would not dispute this argument. The only point crucial here is that the participation of certain regions is obviously more direct and more central to the relational conception than that of others.

Linguistic form is often blind to these subtleties. Precisely the same expressions, namely *your dog* and *my cat*, are used to describe the trajector and primary landmark in sentences (3c) and (4a), even though these entities participate as integral wholes only in the former. On the assumption that the nouns *dog* and *cat* designate the entire animal (so that *dog*, for instance, would be an inappropriate expression to describe a disembodied set of teeth), we can observe that (4a) manifests a notable discrepancy between what is profiled by the trajector and landmark of [BITE] and the active zones of these entities with respect to the process. This discrepancy sometimes has overt linguistic consequences; it is possible, for example, to spell out the active zones explicitly by means of periphrastic expressions, such as the prepositional-phrase complements in (4b). Generally, though, such periphrasis is optional, and one resorts to it only when this additional specification is informative. This is the case in (4b), since [BITE] is vague about the active zone of its landmark, and since the adjective *sharp* provides information about the active zone of the trajector that would not otherwise be available. However the prepositional-phrase complement in (4c) adds nothing to the content conveyed by the verb, so this sentence is needlessly redundant.

The existence of a substantial discrepancy between the entity profiled by an expression and its active zone with respect to a given relational predication is not at all unusual. In fact, a bit of reflection reveals that a discrepancy between profile and active zone represents the NORMAL situation. It is in fact quite difficult to find convincing examples like those in (3), where all aspects of the designated entity participate equally in a relationship. In the overwhelming majority of instances the various facets of the profiled entity participate in a relationship to different degrees and in different ways. The examples in (5) afford some initial appreciation of the ubiquity of this phenomenon.

(5) a. *Roger blinked.*
   b. *Roger ate an apple.*
   c. *Roger heard a noise.*
   d. *Roger walked faster.*
   e. *Roger is digesting.*
   f. *Roger figured out the puzzle.*
   g. *Roger whistled.*
   h. *Roger peeled an orange.*
   i. *Roger licked the popsicle.*
   j. *Roger breathed hard.*

Considering the trajector of the main verb, we find that only selected facets of the designated individual participate directly in the process, and that these facets differ from one expression to the next. Roger's eyelids are the primary participants in (5a); in (5b), his hands, mouth, teeth, tongue, and the upper parts of his alimentary canal are more directly involved than, say, his kneecaps; his ears and central nervous system are pivotal in (5c); while the whole body moves in (5d), the legs in particular are of prime importance; and so on. In those cases where the landmark is distinct from the trajector, there is comparable variation. Thus the puzzle in (5f) participates holistically in the verbal process, but presumably only part of the apple is eaten in (5b) (most people do not consume the core), while in (5h)-(5i) only the outer surface of the landmark object is affected.

Some discrepancy between active zone and profile is thus the rule, not the exception. Our conception of grammatical organization must therefore be able to accommodate it as a normal situation rather than a pathological one, preferably without special apparatus. In fact, the problem is even worse than I have so far indicated. For one thing, even for those predications which appear to relate the trajector and landmark as integral wholes there is often an active-zone/profile discrepancy in specific instances. Consider [IN], whose trajector would seem to participate holistically in the inclusion relationship with its landmark. Yet this is very commonly not the case:

(6) a. *Abernathy is in the bathtub.*
    b. *Susan has a cigarette in her mouth.*
    c. *He has an axe in his hand.*

A normal construal of all three sentences situates only a portion of *in*'s trajector within the confines of its landmark.

A second exacerbating factor is that the active zone is often not even a subpart of the entity designated by a nominal expression. Frequently it is something merely associated with the designated element in some characteristic fashion, as we saw above in (1b)-(1c). In (1b), the subject does not hear the piano per se, as a physical object, but rather the sound emitted by the piano--canonically this would be the musical sound produced by playing the piano, but in context it could also be the crashing sound it makes when dropped from a helicopter. In (1c), of course, it is not the speaker as a physical object who occupies the phone book, but rather a symbolic representation of his name, address, and phone number. (7) provides some further examples.

(7) a. *I smell a cat.*
    b. *The ball is yellow.*
    c. *I need a red pen.*
    d. *This red pen is yellow.*

I might say (7a) when opening the garage door in the morning; what I actually smell is the odor emitted by certain excretions of the cat. In (7b), it is not the ball as a physical object that is capable of interacting with color space (a range of possible color sensations)--rather it is a color sensation associated with the ball's outer surface. The phrase *red pen* is ambiguous, and its ambiguity hinges precisely on the choice of active zone for *pen* with respect to the color predication. On the one hand, the active zone may be the color sensation associated with the outer surface of the pen (parallel to (7b)); on the other hand, it may be the sensation associated with the marks left on the page when the pen is used as a writing implement. By taking the notion active zone into account, we can explain why (7d) is meaningful and noncontradictory. The active zone of the pen with respect to the predication [RED] is the color of the marks it makes, while for [YELLOW] it is the color of the pen's outer surface.

Obviously, the permitted discrepancy between profile and active zone greatly increases the flexibility of a linguistic system. If the two were always required to coincide precisely, i.e. if the trajector and landmark of a relational predication had to be expressed with full accuracy and specificity, the result would be a vast proliferation of highly cumbersome locutions, a sample of which is offered in (8).

(8) a. *Roger's eyelids blinked.*
   b. *Roger's mind figured out the puzzle.*
   c. *Roger's lungs and oral tract whistled.*
   d. *Susan has the end of a cigarette in her mouth.*
   e. *He has a portion of the handle of an axe in his hand.*
   f. *The color sensation associated with the outer surface of this pen, the color sensation associated with the marks created by which is red, is yellow.*

The tolerance of profile/active-zone discrepancy is further quite natural in cognitive terms, for it permits the designation of linguistic expressions to focus on conceived entities that have substantial cognitive salience. The following principles can be seen at work in various examples: (i) a whole is generally more salient than its individual parts; (ii) discrete physical objects are generally more salient than abstract entities; and (iii) humans and (to a lesser extent) animals are generally more salient than inanimate objects (other things being equal).

2. Analysis

The apparent difficulty posed by profile/active-zone discrepancies is that what a sentence literally says conflicts with how it is actually understood, so that its compositional semantic value is either inappropriate or logically inconsistent. This is the type of situation for which generative theory has commonly posited logically consistent underlying structures, from which the surface form of an expression is derived by the application of transformational rules or some comparable device. For example, if it is granted that one can only hear sounds, not physical objects, the seeming anomaly of (1b) might be accommodated by taking (9a) as a deep structure and postulating an optional transformation that deletes the boldface portion of it.

(9) a. *She heard **the sound of** the piano.*
   b. ***The color sensation associated with the outer surface of** the ball is yellow.*
   c. *Roger's **hands, mouth, teeth, tongue, and the upper parts of his alimentary canal** ate an apple.*

Let us call this type of approach the "linguistic paraphrase analysis": an expression derives from an underlying structure that--when manifested without deletions--provides a logically accurate paraphrase of its actual meaning.

The linguistic paraphrase analysis is offered only as a straw man, not as a serious analysis on my part or anyone else's. There are obvious problems with it. While reasonable enough for cases like (9a), where a simple and obvious paraphrase readily suggests itself as a deep structure, its plausibility quickly evaporates when one tries to extend it to a representative array of instances: few linguists would be attracted by the deletions in (9b) and (9c) for the derivation of simple sentences like *The ball is yellow* and *Roger ate an apple*. The choice of a particular paraphrase to serve as underlying structure is arbitrary, moreover, and any paraphrase that is chosen is itself likely to prove inaccurate in more subtle ways; (9c), for instance, does not indicate that the various body parts mentioned participate in the process to different degrees and in different ways. Furthermore, the linguistic paraphrase analysis treats as problematic--as something to be remedied by abstract constructs--something that in actuality represents the normal situation rather than anything exceptional. A more natural account would be one in which the phenomenon is not a problem at all.

Actually, I would argue that the perception of the apparent difficulty rests on certain tacit and ill-founded assumptions. On what basis does one conclude that (9a), for example, is more accurate or logically valid than (1b), *She heard the piano*, as a characterization of the conceived situation? It is by virtue of the assumption--which I myself exploited in presenting the data--that *hear* has precisely the same meaning whether *sound* or *piano* occurs as its direct object; consequently the collocation of *hear* and *piano* should be anomalous, since a sense of *hear* which specifies that its direct object is a sound cannot combine felicitously with an object nominal designating a physical object. This line of thought prejudges the semantic value of the verb, however, treating it as nonpolysemous and attributing certain specific properties to its single meaning. The validity of these assumptions is not self-evident. Instead of saying that *hear* has a single meaning, designating the interaction between the perceiver and a sound, one could perfectly well say that *hear* has two semantic variants: the first designates the interaction between a perceiver and a sound, while the second designates the interaction between a perceiver and a sound-emitting object (the emission of sound being the basis for this interaction). (9a) and (1b) then involve different predications, both symbolized by the phonological sequence *hear*, and in neither expression does the meaning of the direct-object nominal conflict with the nature of the relational landmark implied by the verb. The linguistic paraphrase analysis avoids the necessity of postulating two separate predications associated with *hear*, but this is at best a Pyrrhic victory, as it engenders the need for highly abstract and highly problematic analyses like those in (9). Moreover, I take it as established that polysemy is the normal state of affairs for common lexical items. The truly heroic efforts that would be required to eradicate it in favor of abstract derivations in all instances would most certainly be radically misguided.

The analysis is rendered a bit more explicitly in Figure 1 (where AZ labels an active zone). The predication sketched in 1(a) corresponds to sentences like (9a), while that in 1(b) is illustrated by sentences like (1b). If the former is somehow more "basic" than the latter, as the argument for a transformational derivation of (1b) assumes, I would interpret this not as a matter of logical consistency, but rather as reflecting the greater entrenchment and cognitive salience of [HEAR], from which [HEAR'] may well originate as a semantic extension; all of this is perfectly consistent with the view of polysemy outlined earlier and is consonant with the general character of lexical items. Both predications have the same base, and differ only in the profile they impose on this base. Common to both predications, in other words, is the knowledge system that involves the full array of relevant concepts: that of sounds, including their emission from physical objects (or other sources); that of perceptual experience, implying a perceiving individual; and the knowledge that such experience relies on certain auditory apparatus within the perceiving individual.

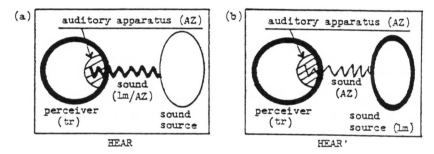

Figure 1.

The contrast between the two predications--the two senses of *hear*--comes down to a matter of imagery. Specifically, the predications differ as to the substructures they single out for special prominence as the trajector (figure within the relational conception) and primary landmark (the most salient entity other than the figure). However, the relative prominence of substructures, though it is definitely an aspect of meaning and constitutes a semantic difference between the two predications, is independent of what one might call the "content" of the predications as defined by their common base. In both instances, the perceiver as an integral whole is profiled as the relational trajector, even though selected facets of this individual are known to function more directly in auditory experience than others. Furthermore, in both predications the sound is conceived as mediating the relationship between this trajector and the sound source, regardless of whether it is the sound in particular or its source that is profiled as the primary landmark. [HEAR] focuses on the direct interaction between the sound and the perceiving individual, while

[HEAR′] profiles instead the mediated interconnection between the perceiver and the sound source, but both relationships are part of the meaning of both expressions, despite their differing salience. Observe that the two predications share a profile/active-zone discrepancy with respect to their trajector. [HEAR′] also exhibits such a discrepancy with respect to its landmark, whereas for [HEAR] the profile and active zone of the landmark coincide.

In short, the cognitive grammar framework accommodates the phenomenon with no special apparatus whatever. All of the constructs needed for this purpose are independently established features of the model, most notably its treatment of lexical polysemy, the profile/base conception of semantic structure, and the trajector/landmark asymmetry among the participants in a profiled relationship. Profiling and trajector/landmark alignment are matters of the relative prominence of substructures within a domain, and to some extent these aspects of semantic organization can vary independently of how the various substructures are intrinsically structured and interconnected. The entities accorded the status of trajector and primary landmark can therefore deviate from those that participate most directly and critically in a relationship, without this affecting its "content" or its "logical properties".

3. Grammatical implications

Since the nature of a predication's profile determines its basic grammatical category, lexical polysemy of the sort just described can extend across grammatical classes. A term like *yellow*, for example, can designate either a bounded region in color space, in which case the expression is nominal, or else a relationship of coincidence between this region and a light sensation, in which case the expression is adjectival. There are actually multiple adjectival senses. They differ as to whether the light sensation is itself selected as the trajector (relational figure), or whether that honor is accorded to some other entity, typically a physical object whose outer surface is the source of this sensation. The contrast between the *yellow* of *yellow flash* and that of *yellow ball* is therefore not unlike the one between the two senses of *hear*.

Another example of polysemy across grammatical classes is provided by modifiers like *fast* that can be used as either adverbs or adjectives (e.g. *work fast* vs. *fast car*). The adverbial predication is sketched in Figure 2(a). Its domain is the conception of a rate scale, and the region on this scale that lies beyond the neighborhood of the norm (n) functions as the primary landmark. Processes can be situated at various points along this scale, and the trajector of the predication is one such process, specified as being situated within the landmark region. What about the adjectival *fast*? A rate scale is clearly relevant, but a physical object like a car cannot, per se, interact with this scale. The active zone of a physical object with respect to a rate scale must be some process in which this object participates. This is made explicit in Figure 2(b), which has exactly the same base as 2(a). The contrast lies solely in the profiling, and specifically in the choice of overall trajector: the trajector of the adjectival [FAST] is not the process that occupies the landmark region of the rate scale, but rather the trajector of that process. The process is nevertheless a crucial part of the meaning of the adjective, as it mediates the relationship between the overall trajector and landmark.

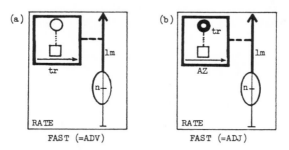

Figure 2.

We saw previously, in (4), that when the active zone of a predication diverges from its profile the former can be spelled out periphrastically if there is communicative motivation for so doing. This is true for the implicit process that functions as the active zone of the adjectival [FAST]. When the modified noun strongly implies a particular type of process, specifying this process periphrastically is superfluous, as seen in (10).

(10) *That {barber/runner/car/surgeon} is fast.*

(11) a. *When it comes to sweeping out the shop, that barber is really fast.*
   b. *That surgeon is fast at solving a Rubik's Cube.*

Periphrasis becomes necessary, however, when the process that functions as active zone is not the one derivationally or canonically associated with the modified noun, as in (11).
   A very similar analysis readily accommodates the seemingly unrelated data cited in Newmeyer 1970. The following examples are representative:

(12) a. *He began eating dinner.*
   b. *He began dinner.*

(13) a. *The orchestra started playing the next song.*
   b. *The orchestra started the next song.*

(14) a. *The author finished writing a new book.*
    b. *The author finished a new book.*

The problem is to account for the second sentence of each pair, where an aspectual verb like *begin*, *start*, or *finish* takes a simple direct-object nominal instead of the verbal complement we would "logically" expect. Newmeyer proposes something akin to the linguistic paraphrase analysis, but I would simply say that these verbs manifest a pattern of lexical variation hinging on a permitted discrepancy between active zone and profile. The basic analysis is presented in Figure 3.

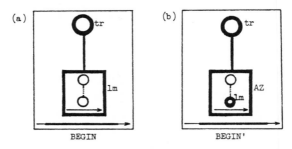

Figure 3.

I have nothing of a detailed nature to say about the semantic structure of verbs like *begin*, so instead of trying to diagram this structure I have simply employed an abbreviatory notation for a process predication. In a sentence like (12a), [BEGIN] profiles a process in which the trajector is a thing (spelled out by the subject nominal) and the primary landmark is another process.[1] In a sentence like (12b), on the other hand, the related predication [BEGIN'] profiles a process in which both prominent participants are things: the trajector is the same, but the primary landmark is not the initiated process as a whole, but rather the landmark of that process. The initiated process remains as a pivotal facet of the base--it is the active zone of the landmark with respect to the inceptive process designated by this predication--but it need not be spelled out explicitly when its character is apparent from context or the other lexical items in the sentence.

I would emphasize that the analyses presented so far in this section require no special apparatus. They employ precisely the same constructs introduced earlier and needed to handle the active-zone/profile discrepancies of simple sentences like those in (1). The only novel aspect of these latter analyses--one that is really nothing more than a special case of the general phenomenon--is the notion that the active zone of a thing with respect to a relationship may be a process in which that thing participates. This is necessary to account for the adjectival sense of *fast*, as well as examples like (12)-(14). Neither of these is generally thought to be associated with the raising constructions of (2), but it may already be apparent that the present analysis establishes a connection. In fact, the analysis I propose for raising constructions should by now be quite obvious.

Let us focus on Object-to-Subject Raising. The standard analysis derives the sentences in (15) from the respective deep structures that also underlie those in (16).

(15) a. *Hondas are easy to fix.*
    b. *Landscapes are tough to paint.*
    c. *Monopoly is fun to play.*

(16) a. *To fix Hondas is easy.*
    b. *To paint landscapes is tough.*
    c. *To play Monopoly is fun.*

Main-clause predications like *easy*, *tough*, and *fun* are claimed to have precisely the same meaning in the constructions of (15) and (16), one that selects a clausal subject at the deep-structure level. Object-to-Subject Raising then accounts for the superficial divergence from this pattern in cases like (16).

There are two basic classes of arguments that are generally advanced to motivate this type of analysis. One class--involving "idiom chunks" (e.g. *headway*) and "dummy" elements like *it* and *there*--I will ignore here, except to note in passing that they depend on certain assumptions that I do not accept (cf. Langacker 1987a). Instead I will concentrate on the second type of argument, which appeals to selectional restrictions and "logical" grammatical relations. In presenting the raising analysis to a class, I have often said something very much like the following: "What does (15a) mean? Logically, it is not Hondas that are easy, but rather the process of fixing them. The superficial form of the sentence obscures this relationship, but such relationships are captured explicitly at the deep-structure level if sentences like (15) derive by transformation from underlying structures like (16)."

Important and persuasive as such arguments were in establishing the transformational model, I would claim in retrospect that they are fallacious. The raising rules exemplify the linguistic paraphrase analysis, and the argument from logical grammatical relations is subject to the same criticism advanced in section 2 with respect to the putative derivation of (1b), *She heard the piano*, from (9a), *She heard the sound of the piano*: the argument prejudges the semantic value of the governing lexical item, assuming quite gratuitously that it has precisely the same meaning in both constructions, and that this meaning can be determined on some kind of (ill-defined) "logical" grounds.

Instead I suggest that *tough*, for instance, is polysemous, having the two semantic variants sketched in Figure 4 (among others). The base for both predications is a conceived scale of difficulty along which processes can be situated. The primary landmark is the region of this scale that lies beyond the neighborhood of the norm. In the case of [TOUGH], probably to be regarded as the more deeply entrenched variant (from which the other is extended), the trajector is a process that is located in this landmark region. All of these elements are present in the base of [TOUGH'], which differs only in its choice of overall trajector: the trajector of this predication is equated not with the entire process situated in the landmark region, but rather with the landmark of this process in particular. The full process is nevertheless crucial to the semantic value of [TOUGH'], for it constitutes the active zone of the overall trajector with respect to its interaction with the difficulty scale.

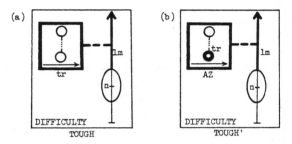

Figure 4.

In some respects my lexical variant analysis resembles the syntactic raising analysis. However the former straightforwardly accommodates certain types of data that cannot be handled in a purely syntactic account. I treat the *to*-clauses in (15) as periphrastic specifications of the trajector's active zone with respect to the scale of difficulty (or pleasure, etc.); parallel sentences lacking these clauses are thus not unexpected, but they are problematic in the raising analysis, since the missing clauses are the putative source of the subject nominal.

(17) a. *Landscapes are tough.*
   b. *Monopoly is fun.*
   c. *When it comes to fixing them, Hondas are easy.*

Sentence (17a) would be perfectly natural in the context of a painting class, where the process functioning as the active zone is too obvious to require periphrastic specification; the operative process is similarly quite apparent even out of context in (17b). Moreover, the lexical variant analysis is consistent with alternate types of periphrasis (though a *to*-clause is standard). Sentences like (17c) are thus anticipated, but they are problematic for the standard raising analysis.

The analysis of Subject-to-Subject and Subject-to-Object Raising differs only in specifics. Slightly different senses are thus attributed to *likely* in (18a) and (18b): a process serves as the overall trajector of [LIKELY] in (18a); the trajector of this process is specified instead as the overall trajector of [LIKELY'] in (18b), but the process remains in the base and functions as the active zone for the interaction of the overall trajector with the probability scale. The *to*-clause in (18b) elaborates the active zone periphrastically, but on occasion it can be omitted, as seen in (19).

(18) a. *For the dog to escape is likely.*
    b. *The dog is likely to escape.*

(19) a. *A war is likely.*
    b. Q: *Do you think anyone will come to the party?*
       A: *Well, Tom is likely.*

(20) a. *I would expect for the Clippers to lose again.*
    b. *I would expect the Clippers to lose again.*
    c. *When do you expect Tom?*

In similar fashion, slightly different predications are associated with *expect* in (20a) and (20b). A process functions as the overall landmark of [EXPECT] in (20a), but the trajector of this process has this status in the case of [EXPECT'] in (20b). The landmark process of (20a) is nevertheless an active zone in (20b), where it is elaborated periphrastically by the *to*-clause. While such elaboration is generally obligatory, sentences like (20c) show that it is optional with *expect* when the process is understood to involve nothing more than arrival on the scene.

8. The Yuman auxiliary

A prominent feature of all the Yuman languages is the "auxiliary verb" construction.*[1] Langdon (1978) offers the following reconstruction for Proto-Yuman, where V is the primary verb, -*k is the "same subject" switch-reference marker, and X subsumes a variety of inflections roughly describable as modal, aspectual, or predicational:

(1) V (-*k LOCATIONAL) (-*k BEHAVIORAL) - X

She further reconstructs locational auxiliaries with the meanings 'sit', 'stand', 'lie', 'stay', 'be there', 'arrive', 'go', 'come', and 'make noise', and behavioral auxiliaries with the approximate values 'be', 'do', and 'say'. A locational auxiliary may render an expression imperfective, while a behavioral auxiliary classes it as active or stative; both occur in (2):[2]

(2) ʔ-sik-k   ʔ-yak-k ʔ-yu-m   [Paipai]
    1-drink-SS 1-lie-SS 1-be-PRED
    'I am drinking (lying down)'

Each verb in the sequence takes a prefix indicating the person of the subject.

The proper analysis of this construction is a classic problem in Yuman studies. For one thing, there is not in general any morphological basis for identifying auxiliaries (cf. 'drink' and 'lie' in (2)). Moreover, the grammatical properties distinguishing auxiliaries from other verbs suggest "a continuum of degrees of grammaticization rather than a clear-cut division between incompatible types" (Langdon 1978: 101). It is therefore assumed that the major criterion for positing an auxiliary verb construction (as opposed to a sequence of separate clauses) is semantic, but here too there are difficulties. Norwood (1981: chapter 3) has argued that translation is an unreliable test, since the same verb group, e.g. Tipai ʔ-si: t-ʔ-yak, can often be translated as either 'I am drinking in a lying position' (suggesting an auxiliary use of 'lie') or else 'I am lying drinking' (implying nonauxiliary status). Even apparent redundancy is inconclusive as a test:

(3) ʔi:kʷič-v-č̌   w-ɬʸak t-u:-yaq   [Ipai]
    man-DEM-SUBJ 3-lie   PROG-3-lie
    'The man is lying down'

According to Norwood, this sentence can also be interpreted in some dialects with the biclausal meaning 'The man lay down and was lying there'.

Norwood also observes the awkwardness of accounting for such facts in any framework that employs standard phrase trees for syntactic description and accords discrete structural status to the auxiliary, e.g. by positing a special AUX-node. This type of analysis does not accommodate the graded character of the phenomena; for instance, there is nothing intermediate between the presence of an AUX-node and its absence. Substantially different syntactic structures are thus attributed to an expression on the basis of seemingly minor contrasts in meaning or translation (e.g. 'drink lying down' vs. 'lie drinking'). What makes this suspicious is the absence of formal corroboration for the putative differences in syntactic organization: a verb sequence commonly has the same morphological realization whether it is analyzed in terms of subordination, coordination, or a single-clause auxiliary verb construction. Indeed, the facts of Yuman lead one to suspect that any sharp distinctions along these lines might well be artifactual.

I suggest that these problems stem from certain standard theoretical assumptions, including the autonomy of grammar and the appropriateness of phrase markers for the representation of syntactic structure. They do not arise in the context of cognitive grammar, for it does not share these assumptions. Let us examine in general terms the type of analysis it makes available for the Yuman auxiliary and comparable phenomena.

We are concerned with grammatical constructions involving the integration of two verbs. Recall that a grammatical construction comprises two or more component expressions combining to form a composite expression. The component expressions are integrated by virtue of correspondences established between their substructures, with the composite expression obtained by superimposing corresponding entities and merging their specifications. At the semantic pole, one component expression typically elaborates a schematically characterized substructure within the other; this substructure is termed an elaboration site. Moreover, the composite structure generally inherits its profiling from one of the two components, which is thereby identified as the head.

Consider, for example, the integration of *the clock* and *on the desk* to form the composite expression *the clock on the desk*, as diagramed in Figure 1. The component semantic structures are sketched in 1(a). *The clock* profiles a thing, whose various specifications are abbreviated as *C*. The prepositional phrase *on the desk* profiles a stative relation; one participant (*the desk*) is characterized in some detail (*D* abbreviates its specifications), but the other is only schematic within the prepositional phrase itself. This schematic participant functions as elaboration site in the construction, and is identified by cross-hatching: the dotted line shows that it is placed in correspondence with the profile of *the clock*, and the arrow indicates that it is schematic for (and elaborated by) this latter structure. By superimposing the specifications of the corresponding elements, we obtain the composite structure sketched in 1(b). Observe that the composite structure inherits its profile from *the clock*, since *the clock on the desk* designates a thing rather than a locative relationship; the expression is therefore nominal, and *(the) clock* is its head. The locative relation vis-à-vis the desk is incorporated as an unprofiled facet of the base.

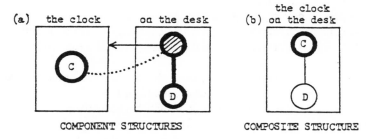

Figure 1.

The constructions that interest us here are those that figure in the composition of a finite clause, which cognitive grammar characterizes in terms of three semantic properties. First, a finite clause profiles a process. If it contains a number of verbs, the one from which it inherits its profile is by definition the clausal head; for instance, *try* is the head in *She tried to sleep*, since what this clause designates is an act of trying (not one of sleeping). Second, the profiled process is construed as constituting a single event (in the case of change) or a single situation (in the absence of change). In *She killed it*, for example, the causation and the dying are viewed as being subsumed in a single event (profiled by *kill*), but not in *She caused it to die*, where the profiled event is limited to the causation. Third, the profiled process is grounded (Chapter 4), i.e. some specification is made of its temporal, modal, and verificational status relative to the speech act and its participants (this is what makes a clause finite). Because the clausal head is directly tied in this fashion to the speech act participants, I have conjectured that the process it profiles is scanned sequentially (state by state) through its temporal evolution, whereas an unprofiled, ungrounded process--being accessed only indirectly, via the head--is construed more holistically.

Suppose that two verbs, V_1 and V_2, combine in the formation of a finite clause. Depending on the nature of their integration, there are several possibilities for the profile of the composite structure. One option is a "serial verb" construction, in which V_1 and V_2 are construed as separate phases or facets of a single overall process V_3 that is grounded and profiled as the clausal head. A second possibility is coordination: V_1 and V_2 are construed in parallel as conjunctive or disjunctive alternatives (*read and relax* vs. *read or relax*); each is separately profiled by the composite structure, and the resulting clause has two heads, both grounded. With a third option, illustrated by *She tried to sleep*, only V_1's profile is inherited at the composite structure level; *try* is thus the clausal head, and *(to) sleep* is a complement (i.e. it elaborates a substructure of the head). A final possibility is exemplified by the relation between *do* and *sleep* in *She did sleep (after all)*: V_1

profiles a highly schematic process that is placed in correspondence with the more specific process profiled by V_2. Being thus construed as schematic and specific representations of the same process, the profiles of V_1 and V_2 merge to form a single processual notion at the composite structure level. Since most of the conceptual content is contributed by V_2 in such cases, V_1 is commonly termed an "auxiliary". Still, V_1 is technically the grounded clausal head, while V_2--because it elaborates the head--is a complement.

In the cognitive grammar analysis, these distinctions are semantic, and do not entail any difference in constituency or grammatical form. The construction types are distinguished by the specific fashion in which two verbs are integrated at the semantic pole, and by the nature of the composite structure profile; phonologically, each type may simply be marked by the adjacency and temporal ordering of the verbs. Since nothing, moreover, prevents a single verb from occurring in more than one construction, the framework accounts very naturally for the semantic variability of the Yuman auxiliaries.

The behavioral auxiliary construction, illustrated in (4), has the form $V_2\ V_1\text{-}X$, where V_1 is the auxiliary (with the value 'be', 'do', or 'say') and X effects the grounding of the profiled process.

(4) *hatčoq ?-ka?a:-k ?-a?wi:-m*   [Mojave]
     dog   1-kick-SS 1-do-PRED
     'I kicked the dog'

Figure 2 diagrams the integration of V_1 and V_2. Each designates a process: schematic in the case of V_1, and specific for V_2. The dotted correspondence line specifies that these processes are construed as being the same, i.e. V_1 and V_2 are schematic and specific representations of the same event. V_2 therefore elaborates V_1, and all of V_1 is cross-hatched as an elaboration site. Since V_1 contributes no content not also found in V_2 (serving only to accentuate the active, stative, or communicative nature of the event), the composite structure profiles a single process equivalent to V_2.

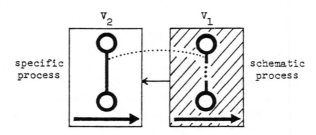

Figure 2.

Because V_1 and V_2 represent the same process, they have the same subject (represented by the upper circles in Figure 2). This motivates both the "same-subject" suffix on V_2 and the occurrence of matching subject-agreement prefixes on the two verbs. The subjects of V_1 and V_2 are also identical in the locational auxiliary constructions, with the same formal consequences. Three kinds of interpretation appear to be possible for sentences like (2) and (3). First, V_1 and V_2 can be coordinate, in which case each process is profiled and grounded at the composite structure level. The other two interpretations correspond to glosses such as 'drink lying down' vs. 'lie drinking'.

The locational auxiliaries ('lie', 'sit', 'stand', 'go', 'stay', etc.) profile processes that are "foundational" with respect to human experience: they involve a person globally, at least one invariably being applicable (a person unfailingly displays some posture, and is always either static or in motion); and more significantly, a particular status in regard to motion or posture is generally prerequisite to carrying out some other (often concurrent) activity. Owing to their foundational character and limited semantic content, verbs which profile such processes are very likely to assume auxiliary function. They do so, I suggest, to the extent that their role in supporting some additional activity comes to the fore as a salient aspect of their semantic value. For instance, the use of 'lie' as a locational auxiliary implies a value in which substantial prominence is accorded not only to the subject's prone posture, but also to a concurrent, schematically characterized activity by the same individual.

Figure 3 diagrams the locational auxiliary construction for those instances in which V_1 is construed as a "main verb" (e.g. 'lie drinking'). As just described, V_1 is internally complex: it profiles the continuation through time of a postural configuration (or else motion, etc.), but also invokes--as an unprofiled facet of its base--the schematic conception of an additional activity on the part of its subject. This schematic activity functions as elaboration site, and is put in correspondence

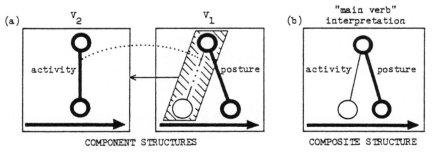

(a) V_2 V_1 (b)   "main verb" interpretation

activity   posture   activity   posture

COMPONENT STRUCTURES   COMPOSITE STRUCTURE

Figure 3.

with the specific activity profiled by V_2. The composite structure, shown in 3(b), inherits the profiling of V_1, and is obtained by merging the specifications of V_2 with those of the corresponding schematic activity internal to V_1. The so-called "main verb" interpretation of V_1 is simply a matter of the composite structure profiling the postural configuration rather than the associated activity.

What about the "auxiliary verb" interpretation of V_1, as suggested by such glosses as 'drink lying down'? Here it is reasonably claimed that the composite structure profiles the associated activity, with the postural configuration assuming secondary status as an unprofiled aspect of the base. One way of achieving this result, diagramed in Figure 4, attributes to V_1 a special semantic value in which the activity rather than the postural specification is profiled. For instance, V_1 would mean roughly 'do (while lying)', as opposed to 'lie (while doing)'; by comparing V_1 in Figures 3 and 4, we see that this semantic contrast is simply a matter of imposing alternate profiles on the same base. With V_1 so construed, the analysis proceeds as before: the schematic activity internal to V_1 serves as elaboration site and corresponds to the specific process profiled by V_2; and V_1 bequeathes its profile to the composite structure. The difference is that in this case the activity is profiled rather than the posture, both in V_1 and at the composite structure level.

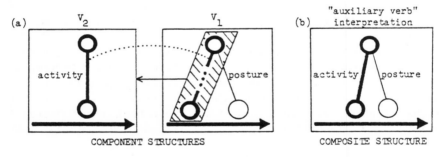

Figure 4.

Cognitive grammar thus affords a natural and revealing analysis of the Yuman auxiliary, and invokes no special apparatus to do so. In particular, it accommodates the various construals of locational auxiliaries without positing any necessary differences in either constituency or conceptual content--the contrasting interpretations merely reflect alternate profiling options, notably at the composite structure level. Since profiling amounts to nothing more than the relative prominence of substructures within a conceptualization, and is inherently a matter of degree, variability and even indeterminacy in the translation of locational auxiliary expressions is expected rather than problematic.

9. Transitivity, case, and grammatical relations

A central claim of cognitive grammar is that only symbolic units figure in the proper description of grammatical structure, and consequently that all valid grammatical constructs have some kind of conceptual import.* The present chapter explores the application of such a framework to the pivotal syntactic problems of transitivity, case, voice, and grammatical relations. It offers a preliminary sketch of what these phenomena look like in terms of the theory, and introduces certain constructs that seem necessary for their revealing description. (More detailed examination of these problems from the cognitive grammar perspective can be found in the following works: Cook 1988a, 1988b; Hung 1988; Janda *in press*, *to appear*; Langacker 1986, 1987b, 1988c, 1989, *to appear*; Maldonado 1988; Poteet 1988; Rice 1987a, 1987b, 1988; Smith 1985a, 1985b, 1987, 1989; Tuggy 1981, 1986, 1988, 1989.)

1. The conception of actions and events

Meanings are characterized relative to cognitive domains, many of which are what Lakoff (1987) refers to as "idealized cognitive models" (ICM's). We are interested specifically in the semantic values associated with case, voice, transitivity, and grammatical relations. Among the domains invoked by such elements are certain abstract but nonetheless powerful folk models pertaining to the make-up of our world, to the transmission of energy and its role in driving events (Talmy 1985a, 1988a), and to the nature of canonical actions. While the grammatical elements that concern us take these idealized cognitive models as the basis for their semantic characterization, the models themselves are not solely (or even primarily) linguistic.

We tend to conceive of our world as being populated by discrete objects, each of which (at a given moment) occupies a distinct location. Some of these objects are capable of moving about and interacting with others, particularly through direct physical contact. Motion is driven by energy, which some objects are capable of supplying internally and others must receive from outside sources. When physical contact is initiated with any degree of force, energy is transmitted from the mover to the impacted object; this may cause the latter to move also, and possibly to interact with additional objects. Let us call this archetypal conception the "billiard-ball model". Stark though it is, the billiard-ball model has substantial influence on our thought processes, and has been a significant factor in philosophical and scientific inquiry.

Our ability to interact perceptually with other entities gives rise to a second archetypal conception, which might be termed the "stage model". Though an explicit theater metaphor is not necessarily invoked, in many respects our role as observer is analogous to that of somebody watching a play. At any one time the observer is capable of attending only to a limited portion of the world around him, and generally his gaze is directed outward. The canonical viewing arrangement thus finds the observer focusing his attention on some external region, where actions unfold as upon a stage.[1] Moreover, just as actors move about the stage and handle various props, we tend to organize the scenes we observe in terms of distinct "participants" who interact within an inclusive and reasonably stable "setting". We further impose structure along the temporal axis, by chunking clusters of temporally contiguous interactions (particularly those involving common participants) into discrete "events". The stage model thus idealizes an essential aspect of our ongoing experience: the observation of sequences of external events, each involving the interactions of participants within a setting.

Additional cognitive models pertain to our experience as sentient creatures and as manipulators of physical objects. From countless instances of such experience, we develop a conception of certain typical roles that participants play in events. Descriptions of these roles read very much like Fillmore's classic definitions of semantic "cases" (1968), and some of the same terms are appropriate, but I must emphasize that we are not yet talking about specifically linguistic constructs. We can reasonably posit a number of "role archetypes" that organize our conception of events in much the same way that cardinal vowels serve as reference points in vowel space. However, there need not be any unique or exclusive inventory, for we are capable of extracting alternate and coexisting schemas to structure the same realm of experience.

The archetypal "agent" role is that of a person who volitionally carries out physical activity which results in contact with some external object and the transmission of energy to that object. The polar opposite of an agent is an inanimate "patient", which absorbs the energy transmitted by externally initiated physical contact and thereby undergoes some change of state. The "instrument" role is that of an inanimate object manipulated by an agent to affect a patient; it is through the instrument that energy is transmitted from the agent to the patient. A person engaged in mental activity instantiates the "experiencer" role. Other archetypes can be recognized, and finer distinctions can of course be made. For instance, we can recognize different types of experiencer, based on the kind of mental experience involved (intellectual, perceptual, emotive). We are also familiar with common deviations from these archetypes (e.g. nonhuman animate agents) and with certain hybrid roles (notably that of an animate experiencer-patient).

By combining the various models cited above, we arrive at a more complex conceptualization representing the "normal observation of a prototypical action", whose essential content is diagramed in Figure 1. The stage model contributes the notion of a viewer (V) observing an event from a vantage point external to its setting. In accordance with the billiard-ball model, this event consists of discrete objects moving about and interacting energetically through physical contact. The event constitutes a prototypical action when it focuses on two participants construed as instantiating the maximally opposed role archetypes, namely agent and patient. The transmission of energy is depicted by a double arrow, whose direction serves to distinguish the agent and patient participants. The squiggly arrow indicates the patient's resulting change of state.

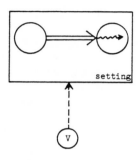

Figure 1.

2. Unmarked linguistic coding

Our attention now shifts to specifically linguistic phenomena. How are prototypical events, and other conceived situations, coded linguistically? In the unmarked case, there is a natural relationship between the structure of a conceived event and the grammatical organization of a finite clause that codes it. Considerable variation can nevertheless be observed even in such instances. If grammatical constructs are to accommodate the full range of examples, their characterization must therefore be suitably abstract.

2.1. Some basic grammatical constructs

The cognitive models described above are extracted from experience and help us to organize and interpret our mental world. Like any other conceptions, they are capable of serving as domains for the semantic characterization of linguistic structures. I will first suggest that the model in Figure 1 supports the description of certain grammatical constructs, including the notions "finite clause", "central participant", "subject", and "direct object".

Recall that all grammatical units are claimed to be symbolic, and thus to have conceptual import. This does not imply that a given element manifests a single meaning in all its occurrences--like a typical lexical item, a grammatical unit might perfectly well be polysemous, describable only as a network of distinct but related senses. For the constructs in question, the model in Figure 1 is most directly relevant to those values that are reasonably considered prototypical. These are the values observed in sentences like the following:

(1) a. *Gerald chopped the onion with a cleaver.*
   b. *The girl caught a fish at the lake.*
   c. *Yesterday Billy kicked his dog.*

Transitive sentences in the active voice describing physical interactions among third-person participants are highly unmarked. In their content, organization, and unmarked status, they naturally reflect the archetypal conception of Figure 1 (a prototypical action canonically observed).

The finite clause is a pivotal unit of grammatical organization. A sentence is generally built around a finite main clause, and often requires nothing further. Internally, a finite clause is the domain within which transitivity, case, and grammatical relations are determined. How, then, can this construct be characterized semantically? One requirement, irrelevant to immediate concerns, is that it contain some specification of tense or modality. Moreover, a finite clause invariably profiles a process, roughly definable as a relationship followed through some span of its temporal evolution. In the unmarked situation, the process designated by the clause as a whole is the same one that is profiled by the verb functioning as its lexical head.[2]

Though some processes involve nothing more than the perpetuation through time of a stable situation, most clauses with a finite head describe some kind of change. For unmarked clauses such as these, I believe it valid to claim that the profiled process is prototypically (if not always) construed as constituting a single event. Consider, for example, the oft-noted contrast between *kill* and *cause to die*:

(2) a. *Sir Abernathy killed his butler.*
   b. *Sir Abernathy caused his butler to die.*

As reflected in their finite heads, (2a) profiles the process *kill*, while (2b) profiles *cause*. Hence (2a) construes the causation and the dying as phases of a single event, while (2b) regards them as distinct but associated events, profiling only the former. This accounts for the "unity of time" and "unity of place" implied by *kill*, which precludes the occurrence of separate temporal or locative adverbs for the causation and the dying (cf. Fodor 1970; Wierzbicka 1975). If it is correct that a finite clause profiles a process construed as constituting a single event, this aspect of its organization reflects the ICM sketched in Figure 1. Recall that one facet of this model is the chunking into discrete events of temporally contiguous clusters of interactions observed within a setting.

A second facet of the model is the position of the viewer outside the setting in which the observed event occurs, with the consequence that the viewer is not himself a participant. In a recent paper (1985), I described a detailed and pervasive analogy between PERceptual and CONceptual relationships, wherein the relation between the perceiver and the scene he observes is treated as parallel to that between a conceptualizer and the idea he entertains. One highly significant linguistic application of this analogy equates the conceptualization with the meaning of an expression, and identifies the conceptualizer with the speaker and/or hearer. Construed in this fashion, the model of Figure 1 can be seen as corresponding to clauses with third-person participants, as in (1)-(2): despite their critical role as conceptualizers and deictic reference points, the speaker and hearer remain offstage and do not participate directly in the profiled event.[3]

Yet another facet of the model is the distinction it draws between the setting for an event and its participants. The setting is large enough to hold the participants and remains essentially constant; it provides the background for the unfolding of an event, but is not substantially involved in the interactions construed as comprising it. The event per se is limited to the interactions among participants, who are small and mobile relative to the setting and move around within it. This conceptual participant/setting organization is mirrored in clause structure by the distinction between the nominal arguments of a verb on the one hand, and certain clause-level modifiers on the other, notably adverbs of time and place. These adverbs are traditionally recognized as being quite "peripheral" within a clause. One factor in this assessment is their optionality. Another is their tendency to occur at the clausal extremities--in particular, their placement is external to a nominal argument when both occur on the same side of the verb (note the examples in (1): *...caught a fish at the lake*; *yesterday Billy kicked...*). Responsible for the peripheral status of temporal and locative adverbs, I suggest, is the conceptual naturalness of construing times and locations as settings.

Finally, the notions subject and direct object receive their prototypical values from the model in Figure 1. The participants so identified lie at opposite extremes in the chain of energetic interactions construed as constituting a single event: the subject is the volitional "energy source" who initiates the chain of activity, while the object is the "energy sink" that undergoes a resulting change of state. These are considered the "direct" or most central participants in the process profiled by a finite clause, and often they are morphologically unmarked. Any other participant is felt to be "oblique" or less central, and is specially marked, even if its role is actually quite pivotal (e.g. an instrument mediating the transfer of energy from agent to patient, as in (1a)).

2.2. Selection

Linguistic coding is highly selective. Typically, a conceived event comprises an intricate web of interactions involving numerous entities with the potential to be construed as participants, yet only a few of these interactions and participants are made explicit, and fewer still are rendered prominent. An example that should make this graphically apparent is the following, not at all implausible scenario: Floyd's little sister, Andrea, has been teasing him mercilessly all morning. Angry and desirous of revenge, Floyd picks up a hammer, swings it, and shatters Andrea's favorite drinking glass. The shards fly in all directions; one of them hits Andrea on the arm and cuts it, drawing blood. Hearing the commotion, their mother comes in and asks what happened. In response, Andrea utters these immortal words: *Floyd broke the glass.*

Consider the types of selection involved in constructing this finite clause. First, many aspects of the overall happening are excluded from the scope of predication, not being evoked or alluded to in any way: Andrea's teasing; where the hammer was lying before Floyd picked it up; Andrea's being wounded by a shard of glass; etc. Next, within the chosen scope of predication there are various options for profiling. Because the finite inflected verb determines the profile of the clause as a whole, by changing it we can shift the designated process from the complete act of breaking to a particular facet of it, such as the swing of the hammer or the change induced in the glass:

(3) a. *Floyd swung the hammer, thereby destroying the glass.*
    b. *The glass shattered from Floyd's hammer-blow.*

Moreover, there are many entities capable of being selected as the central participants. The choice depends not only on profiling, but also on how we opt to segment the world for expressive purposes. The entities construed as participants are not limited to concrete, "basic level" objects such as people, glasses, and hammers--some other possibilities are illustrated in (4).

(4) a. *Floyd's hammer-blow broke the glass.*
    b. *The force of the hammer hitting the glass caused shards to fly*
       in all directions.
    c. *Floyd's action generated fragments of glass.*
    d. *Floyd's arm brought the head of the hammer into contact with*
       the glass.
    e. *Floyd's strength overcame the structural integrity of the glass.*

Clearly, then, the objective properties of a situation do not mechanically determine the grammatical organization of a sentence or finite clause describing it.

Let us examine more abstractly the selective options that confront a speaker when he goes about constructing a finite clause to describe a conceived event. At the global level, he organizes his conception by distinguishing between the occurrence per se and the setting in which it unfolds, and further assumes some vantage point with respect to the scene (cf. Figure 1). He also determines what types of entities will be construed as participants: objects taken as wholes, subparts thereof, collections of objects, or entities of a more abstract nature (all of these are illustrated in (4)). The participants thus selected generally interact in myriad ways; they can be thought of as forming an "interactive network", schematized in Figure 2(a). We are most concerned with asymmetrical interactions, particularly those in which energy is transmitted from one participant to another. An interactive network often includes a series of energetic interactions, as sketched in Figure 2(b): one participant transfers energy to a second, thus inducing a reaction whereby it in turn transfers energy to a third, and so on indefinitely (until a participant is reached whose reaction entails no further energy transmission). I will use the term "action chain" for such a configuration.

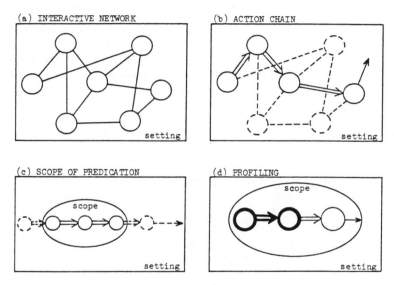

Figure 2.

The coverage of a finite clause is typically limited to certain facets of the interactive network it invokes. This is illustrated in Figure 2(c) with respect to the action chain in particular: portions of the chain lie outside the clause's scope of predication. Moreover, within the chosen scope there is further selection in regard to profiling--some substructure receives special prominence as that which the expression designates. In Figure 2(d), only the first segment of the action chain is profiled; the remainder nevertheless figures in the expression's meaning, provided that it falls within the scope boundaries.[4]

In a prototypical transitive clause, the profiled process constitutes an action chain that originates with a canonical agent (volitional energy source) and terminates with a canonical patient (energy sink). Moreover, the subject and direct object assume their prototypical values: the former codes the agent, and the latter the patient. But not every clause describes a canonical action, and one that does may still depart from the prototype by virtue of selection or other factors. The question then arises whether such grammatical concepts as subject, direct object, and transitivity are susceptible to semantic characterizations that are valid in general, not just for prototypical instances. I believe they are, and will offer specific proposals in due course. One should bear in mind, however, that universally valid definitions will necessarily be highly abstract (or schematic)--far more so than notions like 'agent' or 'energy source'.

2.3. Heads and tails

Let us confine our attention initially to energetic interactions that are easily construed as forming action chains. Suppose such a chain has three main participants that fall within the scope of predication of a finite clause. Suppose further that these participants instantiate the canonical agent, instrument, and patient roles, as diagramed in Figure 3(a). Prototypically, a clause which codes this situation profiles the full action chain, choosing the agent for its subject and the patient for its direct object. We have seen, however, that there are various other possibilities. The question we now address is whether there is anything we can say in general about the choice of subject and object in this type of configuration.

   Clearly, the notion subject or direct object cannot be equated with any single role archetype. Even in the active voice, either the agent, the instrument, or the patient can be chosen as subject:

   (5) a. *Floyd broke the glass (with the hammer).*
      b. *The hammer (easily) broke the glass.*
      c. *The glass (easily) broke.*

These respective possibilities are sketched in Figures 3(b)-(d). In (5a), *break* profiles the entire action chain connecting the agent and patient, and the agent is selected as subject. In (5b), which designates the interaction between the instrument and the patient, the subject is the instrument. Only the patient's change of state is profiled by *break* in (5c), and the patient is chosen as subject. We see, then, that the patient can be coded as either subject or object. Moreover, the direct object (if there is one) need not be the patient; in (6c) it is the instrument:[5]

   (6) a. *Floyd hit the glass (with the hammer).*
      b. *The hammer hit the glass.*
      c. *Floyd hit the hammer against the glass.*

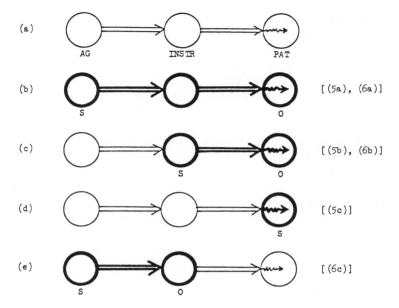

Figure 3.

Though an oversimplification, it is sufficient here to analyze (6c) as profiling only the first segment of the action chain, as shown in Figure 3(e); *hit* is thus attributed the approximate value 'wield in a hitting-type motion', and the prepositional phrase specifies the resulting contact with the glass. Except for the change from *break* to *hit*, (6a) and (6b) are parallel to their counterparts in (5).

It is evident from such examples that neither profiling nor the choice of clausal subject and object is strictly predictable from an action chain whose participants are assigned particular roles, even if the verb is specified; a given verb (like *break* or *hit*) may have several semantic variants, each imposing a different profile on the scene and making a different subject/object selection. It is equally apparent, however, that the choice of subject and object is anything but random. In fact, once the profile is known, the assignment of participants to these grammatical relations can be predicted (or conversely). The subject is consistently the "head" of the PROFILED portion of the action chain, i.e. the participant that is farthest "upstream" with respect to the energy flow. By contrast, the object is the "tail" of the profiled portion of the action chain: the participant distinct from the subject that lies the farthest "downstream" in the flow of energy. Though more abstract than 'agent', 'patient', or 'energy source', these characterizations are still semantic in nature. They invoke nothing more than the conception of an action chain (a schematic cognitive domain) and the notion of profiling, a facet of conventional imagery that is fundamental to semantic structure.

Recall that Fillmore (1968: 33), to accommodate sentences like (5) in case grammar, posited a hierarchy for the unmarked choice of subject: if an agent is present, it becomes the subject; otherwise, if there is an instrument, it becomes the subject; otherwise, the subject is the "objective" (= patient, for the present data). Whereas Fillmore simply stipulated this hierarchy, it follows as a consequence of the constructs and definitions I have proposed. The sequence AG > INSTR > PAT reflects the flow of energy in an action chain. Profiling allows different portions of a chain to be brought into prominence as the designated process, and if the subject is characterized as the head of the profiled portion, its choice will naturally conform to Fillmore's hierarchy. The precedence relations therefore derive from the inherent conceptual content of the role archetypes and their respective places in canonical instrumental actions.

The characterization of subject and object as head and tail of the profiled action chain is also applicable in more complex, less typical energetic interactions. Consider the following descriptions, all pertaining to the same episode in a baseball game:

(7) a. *Templeton hit the ball.*
  b. *The bat hit the ball.*
  c. *The ball hit the fence.*
  d. *Templeton hit the fence (with his line drive).*

The flow of energy follows the action chain TEMPLETON > BAT > BALL > FENCE. Using brackets to enclose the profiled portion of the chain, we have the following: (a) $[T > B > B] > F$; (b) $T > [B > B] > F$; (c) $T > B > [B > F]$; and (d) $[T > B > B > F]$. In each instance, the subject corresponds to the head of the bracketed sequence, and the object to its tail. We can think of profiling as a window looking out onto the scope of predication, through which only a part of the scene is directly visible. The subject and object are selected to lie at opposite extremities of the scene so framed.

We have now arrived at a generalized conception with respect to which the prototypical situation of Figure 1 represents a special case. In the general conception, the subject is identified as the head of the profiled action chain, and the direct object as its tail. Prototypically, the profile encompasses the full chain leading from a canonical agent to a canonical patient, so in this circumstance AG and PAT function as the respective semantic values of subject and object. These grammatical relations assume other specific values (e.g. INSTR or PAT for subject) when another profiling option makes the head or tail of the chain coincide with some other participant. However, the abstract characterization of subject and object in terms of the extremities of the profiled portion of an action chain does not specifically require that either participant conform precisely to any role archetype. For example, *ball* is the subject in (7c) even though it is not a canonical agent or instrument, and *fence*, hardly a prototypical patient (since it undergoes no change of state), is nevertheless the object.

2.4. Complexities

Though not yet sufficiently abstract, the definitions we have arrived at are nonetheless broadly applicable. They do however require certain points of clarification and elaboration, pertaining to both the participants in a process and the nature of their interaction.

Let us first observe that the tail of an action chain can represent any one of several role archetypes. We have focused thus far on entities that are patients, in the narrow sense that they absorb energy and thereby undergo an internal change of state. Some alternatives are illustrated in (8):

(8) a. *Jones threw a rock.*
   b. *Penelope tickled her little sister.*
   c. *Holmes severely injured his opponent.*
   d. *Holmes knocked his opponent against the ropes.*

In (8a), the force transmitted to the rock does not appreciably alter its internal state, but rather causes it to move with respect to its external surroundings; I will refer to such an entity as a "mover". In (8b), the effect of the profiled action is not so much to cause a physical change in the sister as to induce in her a particular type of sensory and emotional experience (which in turn has externally manifested consequences, such as squirming and giggling); hence the sister's role is primarily that of an experiencer. Frequently the action-chain tail instantiates more than one such role. The object in (8c) is both a patient and an experiencer, and in (8d) the object would normally be construed as an experiencer as well as a mover.

A slightly different phenomenon is for more than one position along an action chain (hence more than one role in an event) to be subsumed by what is construed as a single participant. Consider these sentences:

(9) a. *Greg scratched the elephant's back with a rake.*
   b. *Greg scratched Sheila's back.*
   c. *Greg scratched (his (own) back).*

The subject in (9a) is an agent, with the instrument a distinct participant, as per the billiard-ball model. By contrast, the default-case instrument in (9b) is part of the subject (his nails or fingertips), and is not separately coded. In (9c), the subject subsumes the roles of both instrument and experiencer, in addition to agent; an object is required only if one wishes to be precise about the part of the body affected. Some further possibilities are illustrated in (10).

(10) a. *Smedley switched off the TV.*
   b. *The frightened bird flew wildly about the room.*

In (10a), both Smedley's fingers and the TV's off-on switch serve to transmit energy along the action chain, so either is construable as an instrument (albeit a nonprototypical one). However, the sentence does not specifically portray these entities as instruments--it simply codes the agent and patient as undifferentiated wholes. The subject in (10b) subsumes the roles of agent and mover; secondarily, the agent-mover is also an experiencer, and its wings are a sort of instrument.

These observations are schematized in Figure 4. An entity portrayed linguistically as a single participant may nonetheless envelop multiple nodes in an interactive network. Moreover, the linguistically coded participant may include a substructure identifiable as that which plays a certain role or figures most directly in an interaction, but is not itself individually mentioned (cf. Chapter 7). The nodes of an interactive network are thus "chunked" into participants as one facet of the linguistic coding process. This chunking is cognitively natural (e.g. it reflects the cognitive salience of a whole relative to its parts), and is clearly decisive in determining the linguistically relevant structure of a network or action chain.

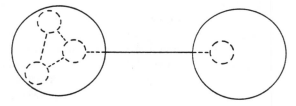

Figure 4.

A further dimension of complexity resides in the following obvious fact: not every process profiled by a transitive clause unfolds in physical space or involves the transmission of energy. Examples vary as to how closely they approximate the canonical conception of an action chain. In some instances, it is plausible to argue that this conception is extended metaphorically to nonphysical domains. Thus Talmy (1985a) extends his notion of force dynamics to certain social interactions.

(11) a. *They forced him to resign.*
   b. *Irving persuaded me to clean the garage.*
   c. *I urge you to give up that crazy idea.*

Overlapping with this class are verbs of transfer and communication, where the subject conveys some type of mover to a recipient:

(12) a. *Judith sent a package to her niece.*
   b. *I gave that information to all the neighbors.*
   c. *The bank transferred the deed to the new owners.*
   d. *He told those lies to anybody who would listen.*

Though physical energy need not be involved, the subject in each case instigates the movement of the object, and can thus be construed as an abstract energy source.

However, there are many transitive clauses that do not appear to involve the transfer of energy from subject to object, even in an abstract or metaphorical sense. Prominent examples include clauses describing perception and ideation:

(13) a. *Several witnesses saw the accident.*
   b. *I noticed a rip in the fabric.*
   c. *She remembered her childhood.*
   d. *I have carefully considered your offer.*

The subjects in these sentences are experiencers, i.e. they engage in some type of mental activity. We have previously examined cases, such as (8b), where mental experience is induced by the physical efforts of an external agent; the experiencer consequently lies downstream from the agent along the action chain, and is coded by the direct object. In (13), on the other hand, the experiencer appears as the subject, and while the experience may be externally induced or under volitional control, this need not be the case.

Though the notion of an action chain seems inappropriate in (13), there is nevertheless an abstract similarity between the role of the experiencer subject and that of an agent in prototypical actions. In both instances, we can speak of an "asymmetrical interaction" that is in some sense initiated by the agent or experiencer. In a prototypical action, the agent interacts with the patient through physical contact and the transmission of energy; this interaction is asymmetrical by virtue of the direction of energy flow, and also because the agent induces the contact by moving to the patient. The interactions described in (13) occur in the mental rather than the physical realm. A sentient creature is capable of generating an internal representation of the world around him, and also of entities that have no actual physical existence. By generating such a representation, the experiencer makes mental "contact" with the entities represented. We tend, in fact, to concretize our conceptualization of this process by construing the entity in question as external to the experiencer, who is conceived as mentally "moving" into contact with it.

Despite the abstract similarity, there is an important difference between these two sorts of asymmetric interactions. In a canonical action, both participants are involved in the energy flow, the agent as energy source and the patient as energy sink: AG===>PAT. However, in sentences like (13) we have no reason to posit any kind of energy transfer from the experiencer to the other participant. Hence the role of the second participant is nonenergetic, i.e. it is neither an energy source nor an energy sink. I will use the term "absolute" for such a participant. The interactions in (13) can therefore be represented as follows, where the dashed arrow indicates the mental contact that the experiencer establishes with the object of perception or conception: EXPER---->ABS. Their interaction is obviously asymmetrical, and the experiencer's role is energetic to the extent that we think of energy as being required for mental activity.

2.5. Subjective asymmetry

Even the abstract notion of asymmetrical interaction is not sufficient as it stands to accommodate the full range of data. There are numerous examples where this conception provides no apparent basis for the subject/object distinction:

(14) a. *The fifth floor contains a library.*
b. *A library occupies the fifth floor.*

(15) a. *Line A intersects line B.*
b. *Line B intersects line A.*

(16) a. *Marsha resembles Hilda.*
b. *Hilda resembles Marsha.*

Because these sentences describe static situations, it is not obvious that the notion of interaction is applicable. Furthermore, since the relationships of intersection and resemblance are symmetrical with respect to their intrinsic content, an analysis of (15) and (16) in terms of asymmetrical interaction seems more dubious still. An additional contrast with (13) is that neither participant is in any way energetic. The profiled relationships in (14)-(16) would thus appear to lack inherent asymmetry, serving to connect two absolute participants: ABS----ABS.

Nevertheless, it is intuitively evident that the members of each pair are semantically nonequivalent, and that some type of asymmetry in the portrayal of participants is responsible for the contrast. In (16a), for example, Hilda serves as a standard of comparison with respect to which Marsha is evaluated, while in (16b) these roles are reversed. It is a claim of cognitive grammar, as previously noted, that relational predications consistently single out some participant for special prominence; specifically, it is suggested that this element (the trajector) can be characterized as the figure within the relational profile. Since a finite clause is one type of relational predication, we expect as a special case that some participant will always be selected as figure/trajector at the clause level. I attribute this status to the clausal subject, and thereby explicate the perceived asymmetry in sentences like (14)-(16) in terms of figure/ground organization.

Under this analysis, such sentences are seen as limiting cases with respect to subject asymmetry. A finite clause always profiles a process, and its subject is in all cases analyzed as the processual figure. However, expressions form a gradation as to how strongly the choice of subject/trajector is suggested by their conceptual content. It is cognitively quite natural for the most energetic participant to stand out as a focus of attention, so in canonical AG===>PAT sentences the agent is the obvious candidate for selection as relational figure. In clauses like (13), of the form EXPER---->ABS, the asymmetry is perhaps less obvious because the profiled interactions occur in the mental realm; still, the experiencer is the only energetic participant and is thus the expected trajector. Sentences like (14)-(16) can be viewed as occupying the endpoint along this scale: the speaker imposes a choice of trajector that is essentially arbitrary from the standpoint of conceptual content. The selection of a relational figure can be motivated by content to a greater or lesser degree; zero motivation represents the limiting case.

The fact that figure/ground organization is itself a type of asymmetry suggests that the notion of asymmetric interaction may be valid after all for the characterization of transitive clauses, provided that the notion is correctly understood. Crucial in this regard are "subjectivity" and "objectivity", an important dimension of conventional imagery (cf. Langacker 1985, as well as Chapters 5 and 12). These terms pertain to the inherent asymmetry of a conceptual relationship. The role of the conceptualizer is maximally subjective when he himself does not figure in any way as part of the conceptualization, i.e. when he loses awareness of himself and his role as conceptualizer. Conversely, to the extent that reference to the conceptualizer is nonsalient or absent within a conception, the construal of its contents is said to be objective. In brief, full subjectivity and objectivity attach to the participants in a polarized conceptual relationship such that the roles of conceptualizer and object of conceptualization stand maximally opposed.

An expression's meaning is a conceptualization whose conceptualizer is the speaker (and secondarily the hearer). We are concerned in particular with the process profiled by a finite clause, and specifically with the suggestion that every transitive clause profiles an asymmetric interaction between its central participants. Though seemingly problematic for this characterization, sentences like (14)-(16) can be accommodated when subjectivity is taken into account. The profiled relationship is rendered asymmetrical by the very fact of one participant being elevated to the status of relational figure--what varies is whether this status is inspired by objective factors (i.e. the content of the conceived relationship), or whether its origin is purely subjective, in the sense of being imposed extrinsically as part of the conceptualization process itself. Moreover, it is in just this sense that the static relationships profiled in (14)-(16) can be said to constitute interactions. Recall that the conception of a relationship (either static or dynamic) resides in the occurrence of cognitive operations assessing the relative magnitude and position of entities within a domain. Thus, while a static relationship is not interactive objectively (i.e. in terms of content), its conception requires cognitive operations that establish interconnections between its participants and thereby render it subjectively interactive.

2.6. Subject and object

Semantically, a typical lexical item constitutes a complex category: it has not just one meaning, but rather a constellation of senses connected in various ways to form a network. Some of these senses represent extensions from other, more prototypical values. Some are schematic, and express the commonality observable across an array of more specific senses. The nodes and relationships comprised by such a network have varying degrees of cognitive salience. There need not be any node that is schematic with respect to all the others (i.e. an abstract characterization valid without exception for all category members).

Cognitive grammar maintains that grammatical structure is correctly described by means of symbolic units alone, and that grammar and lexicon form a continuum of symbolic structures. One therefore expects not only that grammatical constructs should be meaningful, but also that their meanings might resemble those of lexical items by forming networks of distinct but interrelated values. This is what I propose for such notions as subject, direct object, finite clause, and transitivity. It has come to be widely accepted that some or all of these categories have values that can be regarded as prototypical (cf. Hopper & Thompson 1980; Givón 1979, 1984). However, I take the further, more controversial position that these constructs have schematic characterizations as well, i.e. highly abstract descriptions applicable to the full range of instantiations.

These constructs receive their prototypical values in expressions describing canonical actions (Figure 1); here a finite clause profiles a process construed as constituting a single event, and its subject and object correspond respectively to the agent and patient role archetypes. Of course, transitive clauses are used for many other kinds of circumstances, and the farther they diverge from the prototype, the more abstract must be a schematic characterization capable of accommodating the full range of instances. The greatest divergence is observed in clauses describing static configurations, for which the notion event hardly seems appropriate; we can however say that such a clause profiles what is construed as a single situation.[6] The schema subsuming both possibilities specifies that a finite clause profiles a unitary process, where a process is defined abstractly as a relationship followed in its evolution through time (whether it changes or remains constant).

With respect to the notion subject, we have formulated successively more abstract (and hence more general) characterizations: agent; head of an action chain; energetic participant; and finally, figure within the profiled relationship. This last characterization is presumed to be universally valid--at the very least, it is apparent that any notional characterization applicable to all subjects will have to be comparably abstract. The common view that subjects are prototypically agents is of course accepted and accommodated. What about the equally prevalent idea that subjects are prototypically topics? The problem here is vagueness in describing the pertinent notion of topic; "what the sentence is about" remains a standard description (see van Oosten 1986 for a survey). While I have not yet given this matter the study it deserves, I am inclined to believe that this "aboutness" relationship is satisfactorily explicated by analyzing a subject as the figure within a profiled process.

The prototypical value for direct objects is that of a patient. More generally, a direct object can be characterized as the tail of an action chain, whether this be a patient, mover, experiencer, or some combination of these. A schematic characterization compatible with the full range of instances must be considerably more abstract, however, for it must further accommodate the unaffected, absolute object in sentences of the form EXPER---->ABS, and also the nonsubject nominal in sentences describing static situations. It should be apparent that a universally valid definition cannot pertain to the conceptual content of a clause; if one is possible at all, it must pertain instead to how this content is construed. Because a subject, as figure within the profiled relationship, is the most prominent clausal participant, it is natural to suggest that a direct object is the second-most prominent participant, i.e. the most prominent participant within the ground.[7] More precisely, I propose that a direct object be characterized schematically as a "prominent participant lying downstream from a participant subject", either in the flow of energy or in some abstract analog thereof. In extreme cases where conceptual content provides no inherent directionality, this abstract flow may be entirely subjective, involving nothing more than the order in which the conceptualizer accesses participants along a hierarchy of prominence.

A consequence of these definitions is that a clause may have a subject without having an object, but not conversely.[8] While every clause is presumed to select some entity as relational figure (hence as subject), an object occurs only if this entity is a participant and the profiled relationship happens to involve some additional, downstream participant. Intransitive clauses are thus accommodated: rather than associating two distinct nominal participants (in the fashion of the billiard-ball model), the profiled process holds between subparts of the subject, or between the subject and another type of entity (e.g. some facet of the setting or the domain). As for transitivity, the most schematic characterization refers only to the existence of participants meeting the specifications for subject and direct object. More specific characterizations refer to particular kinds of asymmetric interactions, prototypically the flow of energy from subject to object along an action chain.

3. Marked coding

The expressions examined thus far are unmarked, in that the subjective asymmetry coded linguistically in the choice of subject and object conforms to the most natural construal of an event on the basis of its conceptual content. However, to accommodate various communicative objectives, languages also permit the coding of events in a less straightforward fashion. We will consider several classes of phenomena: lexical variants, voice, and constructions in which trajector status is conferred on a nonparticipant.

3.1. Lexical options

A finite clause profiles a process involving a network of interacting participants within a setting (Figure 2). Though countless interactions are discernible in a typical event--depending on the domain of interest (e.g. physical vs. mental interactions), what sorts of entities are construed as participants, and so on--some are rendered far more salient than others by a particular linguistic coding. The choice of subject and object is a major factor in this regard. As figure within the profiled relationship, the subject is the most prominent clausal participant, while the object is the most prominent participant other than the subject. The salience of the subject and object naturally elevates the salience of those interactions that involve them directly, especially their interactions with one another. Hence the subject and object impose on the interactive network a "window of prominence" that highlights the path connecting them.

Suppose a conceived event approximates a canonical action: it incorporates an action chain with participants that straightforwardly instantiate the role archetypes of agent and (say) mover. Given the prototypical values of relevant constructs, the unmarked way of coding this conception linguistically is with a finite clause that profiles the portion of the action chain serving to connect the agent and the mover, these participants being selected as subject and direct object, respectively. There is no assurance, however, that this unmarked coding will conform to the speaker's communicative objectives. He may opt instead for some other choice of subject and object, thereby shifting the window of prominence away from the action chain to some other facet of the interactive network. In the resulting expression, such linguistic constructs as subject, object, and transitivity thus assume nonprototypical values.

A variety of lexical and grammatical resources allow marked coding. An oft-cited lexical example is the verb *receive*, which clearly, in contrast to *give*, imposes a marked construal on an act of transfer. Facets of the interactive network evoked by these verbs are sketched in Figure 5. The major participants are an agent, a mover, and the recipient. The recipient's role is complex--it is not only the final possessor, but typically perceives the change of possession and benefits as

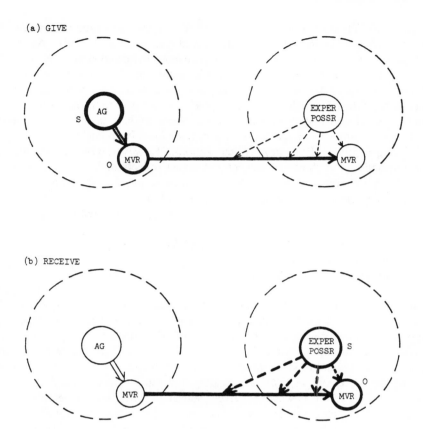

Figure 5.

well; I have thus adopted for it the abbreviatory label "experiencer-possessor". The dashed-line circles stand for arrays of entities over which the AG and EXPER-POSSR exercise dominion. For both *give* and *receive*, the AG exerts some force which impels the mover (physically or abstractly) from its own sphere of control to that of the EXPER-POSSR; the double arrow stands for the transmission of energy, as before, while the single arrow depicts the motion that results. The dashed-line arrows indicate the complex ways in which the EXPER-POSSR interacts with the MVR as it changes possession. A mixture of physical, perceptual, and emotive components (among others) generally figure in this relationship.[9]

The full scenario sketched in Figure 5 is a cognitive domain (ICM) supporting the characterization of both *give* and *receive*. Hence their semantic contrast resides less in conceptual content than in profiling and grammatical relations. As seen in 5(a), *give* effects an unmarked coding of the event: the profiled process coincides with the best exemplar of an action chain within the interactive network; the subject is an agent that heads the chain; and the object codes a mover. On the other hand, 5(b) shows that *receive* imposes on the overall event a window of prominence which highlights interactions peripheral to the primary flow of energy. It profiles a complex relationship that is not the most energetic within the scene and diverges greatly from prototypical actions. However, granted this marked profiling option, the choice of subject and object reflects their natural alignment. The subject is energetic relative to the object in the sense of establishing perceptual contact, being the locus of emotive experience, and exercising possessive control.

A more systematic device effecting marked coding is illustrated in (17):

(17) a. *The door opened only with great difficulty.*
   b. *A good tent puts up in about two minutes.*
   c. *This ice cream scoops out very easily.*

Such sentences have been analyzed in considerable detail by van Oosten (1977, 1986), who concludes that they portray the subject as being in some way responsible for the profiled activity, and are used when the role of any true agent is considered irrelevant. Though I agree with her analysis in essence, it seems apparent that sentences like these often do imply an agent--I do not, for example, imagine the ice cream in (17c) as wielding a scoop and lifting itself out of the container. The agent is however relatively nonsalient and is left unspecified.

The cognitive grammar analysis of this construction posits a pattern of semantic extension whereby the verb assumes a special semantic value. Consider Figure 6, which can be taken as representing three alternate senses of the verb *open*. Figure 6(a) represents its normal transitive value, as in *Andrea opened the door*: the agentive subject transmits energy to the object and thereby induces its motion. Depicted in 6(b) is the intransitive *open* of sentences like *The door opened*. On the relevant interpretation, neither an agent nor the transmission of energy is directly invoked, i.e. the motion is portrayed as absolute; being the only participant, the ABS-MVR is coded as subject. Figure 6(c) corresponds to sentence (17a). The efforts of an agent are included within the scope of predication, but remain unprofiled. The mover is once more selected as subject, there being no other participant in the profiled portion of the action chain. With the mover as relational figure, the interactions it participates in--especially those it initiates--receive augmented salience. In particular, the resistance it offers to the agent's exertions (or in other examples, its facilitation of those efforts) comes to the fore in this construction, as indicated in 6(c) by the double arrow internal to S. Though volition is not involved, this resistance (or facilitation) makes the mover agent-like to some degree.

Figure 6.

3.2. Voice

The sentences in (17) resemble passives, in that the head of an action chain remains unspecified, with a downstream participant assuming the role of subject/trajector. The subject is nevertheless chosen in conformity with our previous generalization, as it heads the profiled portion of the action chain (cf. Figures 3 and 6(c)). I therefore consider such sentences to represent an active-voice construction.

In a passive sentence, e.g. *The door was finally opened*, the choice of subject runs directly counter to the pattern observed so far--it is not the HEAD of a profiled action chain that is elevated to the status of trajector, but rather the TAIL, as shown in Figure 7. The two voices thus represent alternative philosophies with respect to the linguistic coding of events. By equating the relational figure with the most energetic participant, an active clause achieves the coalignment of two asymmetries, each of which presumably reflects the order in which conceived entities tend to be accessed at some level of cognitive processing: the ranking of participants in terms of their subjective prominence, and directionality in the objectively construed flow of energy. In a passive, by contrast, the most salient participant lies downstream in the energy flow. The resulting conflict in alignment is what makes the passive a marked construction; the profiled process receives an unnatural construal, being accessed through a focused participant representing the terminus (rather than the origin) relative to its inherent directionality. The communicative utility of this skewing is the *raison d'être* for the passive construction.[10]

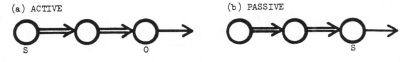

Figure 7.

Another facet of this skewing merits comment. The participant selected as direct object in an active clause is chosen instead as subject in the corresponding passive, but the converse is not true--the active subject is not expressed as the passive direct object. This follows directly from the previous characterization of a direct object as a prominent participant lying downstream from a participant subject. Consider this definition in relation to Figure 7(b). A passive is recognized as such by its effect on a nonpassive verb stem. This stem establishes the directionality of the profiled process, and thus determines the unmarked choice of subject. The effect of the passive is to impose a marked subject choice on the process so construed, equating the trajector with the terminus (rather than the origin) of the directed path linking the salient participants. The subject selection determines whether any other participant qualifies as direct object, which is not the case in 7(b): even if the head of the action chain has considerable prominence, it lies upstream from the subject rather than downstream. A passive is therefore intransitive, and the action-chain head is either left implicit or identified periphrastically (as an oblique).

3.3. Setting vs. participants

Recall that the stage model, an ICM underlying the canonical organization of finite clauses, makes a fundamental distinction between setting and participants. In the unmarked situation, entities construed as participants function as the clausal subject and object, while the setting is expressed by an adverbial modifier. Departures from this canon can nevertheless be observed, and have interesting grammatical consequences. Moreover, the setting/participant distinction is often a matter of degree and open to variable construal.

Based on such properties as size and mobility, some entities are most readily construed as participants, and others as settings. Status as participant or setting is not inherent to an entity, however, but depends on how a speaker conceives and portrays a situation in which it occurs. Consider these sentences:

(18) a. *In Oregon last summer, David caught a large brown trout.*
   b. *Oregon lies between California and Washington.*
   c. *I remember last summer very well.*

Among the entities most naturally construed as settings are geographical regions and extended time periods, such as *Oregon* and *last summer* in (18a); they tend to be stable and inclusive given the scope and scale of typical human interactions. Nonetheless, when we expand the scope of predication and consider relationships on a larger scale, these same entities can function as participants: in (18b) *Oregon* is the trajector in a locative relationship, while in (18c) *last summer* is the absolute participant in a mental interaction of the form EXPER---->ABS.

The grammatical significance of the setting/participant distinction becomes apparent when we review the definitions offered earlier for subject and direct object. At the most schematic level, a subject (clausal trajector) was defined as the figure within the profiled relationship. Importantly, this definition does not require that a subject be a participant; I will suggest, in fact, that trajector status is sometimes conferred on some facet of the setting. A participant generally is selected as subject, however, and as figure in the profiled relationship, it is then the most prominent participant in the scene. A direct object was characterized as the second-most prominent participant, and one that lies downstream from a participant subject. An object is therefore possible only in clauses that also have a subject (though it need not be overt--cf. footnote 8). Moreover, an object must be construed as a participant, and occurs only in clauses where the subject is also a participant.

Consider this characterization in relation to sentences like the following (due to Sally Rice):

(19) a. *Fred, who needed advice, rushed to Marsha.*
   b. *Marsha was rushed to by Fred, who needed advice.*
   c. *Fred, who needed a rest, rushed to the countryside.*
   d. **The countryside was rushed to by Fred, who needed a rest.*

At issue is whether the sequence V + P is capable of being analyzed as a complex verb $[V + P]_V$, with the following noun phrase becoming its direct object. The evidence of passivizability suggests that the sequence *rush to* permits this analysis, as seen in (19a)-(19b). Note, however, that passivization and (presumably) the complex-verb analysis are precluded in (19c)-(19d). This contrast can only be attributed to the character of the objects, *Marsha* vs. *the countryside*: people are prototypical participants, while the countryside--a canonical setting in all respects--is very difficult to construe in this fashion. Since participant status is part of the definition for direct objects, the behavior of *rush to* as a complex verb with *Marsha*, but not with *the countryside*, is predicted.[11]

Imposing figure/ground organization on a scene is something at which people manifest considerable flexibility. Thus, if a subject is correctly characterized as relational figure, it is hardly surprising that diverse elements can assume this function, including facets of the setting. In this regard, consider the contrast between (20) and (21):

(20) a. *Fleas are crawling all over my cat.*
   b. *Bees are swarming all through the garden.*

(21) a. *My cat is crawling with fleas.*
   b. *The garden is swarming with bees.*

Naturally, (21a) does not attribute any motion to the cat, nor does (21b) imply that the garden is buzzing about; instead, *{crawl/swarm} with* is interpreted as having the approximate value 'be the setting for {crawling/swarming} activity'. The semantic distinction between the sentences in (20) and their counterparts in (21) is diagramed in Figure 8. There is no substantial difference in conceptual content--in both (20) and (21), the insects move about (as indicated by the arrow) within a limited setting (the cat or the garden). The contrast resides primarily in the choice of subject, which is equated with the mover in 8(a), but with the setting in 8(b). It is thus a matter of conventional imagery.

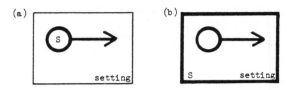

Figure 8.

Note that the contrast between 'crawl' or 'swarm' on the one hand, and 'be the setting for {crawling/swarming}' on the other, follows automatically from the choice of subject. A relational predication profiles interconnections among conceived entities, and the salience accorded a given entity largely determines that of the interconnections involving it. Thus the figure/subject and the second-most prominent entity define a window of prominence that serves as the focal point within the relational profile. When the setting is chosen as figure, as in Figure 8(b), the most prominent interconnections are consequently those between the setting and the mover. The center of prominence is no longer the crawling or swarming per se, but rather the relation borne by the setting to the actors and activity it contains.

In neither (20) nor (21) is the V + P sequence capable of analysis as a complex verb permitting passivization:

(22) a. **My cat is being crawled (all) over by fleas.*
  b. **Fleas are being crawled with by my cat.*

Since *my cat* is the setting rather than a participant in (20a), it resists being analyzed as a direct object, so (22a) is ill-formed. The deviance of (22b) cannot be explained in quite the same way, since *fleas* is definitely a participant in (21a), and hence the potential object of a complex verb. However, an object must not only be a participant itself, but must also lie downstream from a subject with participant status. Because the subject *my cat* lacks this status in (21a), *fleas* is not analyzable as a direct object. A passive based on (21a) is thereby precluded.

More strikingly, even a nominal that immediately follows a simple verb fails to be treated as a direct object (at least with respect to the passive construction) when the subject's role is exclusively that of a setting. For instance, the subjects in (23) are clearly settings, with *see* and *witness* assuming the approximate meanings 'be the setting for {seeing/witnessing}'; the corresponding passives in (24) are deviant (barring the anthropomorphicization of *arena*).

(23) a. *Tuesday saw yet another startling development.*
    b. *This arena has witnessed many thrilling contests.*

(24) a. **Yet another startling development was seen by Tuesday.*
    b. **Many thrilling contests have been witnessed by this arena.*

The analysis also explains data such as the following:

(25) a. *Brygida Rudzka stars in Fellini's new film.*
    b. *Fellini's new film stars Brygida Rudzka.*
    c. **Brygida Rudzka is starred by Fellini's new film.*

(26) a. *Fellini's new film features Brygida Rudzka.*
    b. **Brygida Rudzka is featured by Fellini's new film.*
    c. *Fellini features Brygida Rudzka in his new film.*
    d. *Brygida Rudzka is featured by Fellini in his new film.*

A film provides the setting for its actors; accordingly, the film is introduced in (25a) and (26c)-(26d) by a locative prepositional phrase. The verbs *star* and *feature* also allow this setting to be selected as subject, as we see in (25b) and (26a), but the postverbal noun phrase does not then constitute a passivizable direct object--note the deviance of (25c) and (26b). By contrast, the participant status of the subject in (26c) makes the postverbal noun phrase a direct object, with the consequence that (26d) is well-formed.

The nonobject character of a postverbal nominal is even more apparent in sentences like the following:

(27) a. *There is a salesman at the door.*
    b. *There are wasps in the attic.*

Bolinger (1977: chapter 5) has argued that the "existential" *there* refers to an abstract location, which may be equated with the "awareness" of the speaker or addressee. In similar fashion, Lakoff (1987) claims that *there* introduces a "mental space" (in the sense of Fauconnier 1985). I feel that something along these lines is undoubtedly correct, whatever the specific details. It is sufficient for present purposes to maintain that the *there* in (27) designates some type of abstract setting for the relationship specified by the postverbal elements. From such an analysis, it follows directly that the noun phrase after the verb is not a direct object.

A similar analysis may be proposed for German sentences like those in (29), which match the conceptual content of their counterparts in (28) but differ in conventional imagery:

(28) a. *Ein Kind spielt im Garten.* 'A child is playing in the garden'
   b. *Eine Vase steht auf dem Tisch.* 'A vase stands on the table'

(29) a. *Es spielt ein Kind im Garten.* 'There's a child playing in the garden'
   b. *Es steht eine Vase auf dem Tisch.* 'There stands a vase on the table'

From their grammatical behavior it is clear that the postverbal nominals in (29) are not direct objects--an automatic result if the subject *es* is considered an abstract setting roughly comparable to English *there*. If they are not direct objects, what are they? Relational grammar treats them as subject ''chômeurs'' created by the insertion of a semantically empty dummy. In the present analysis, they are simply prominent participants that qualify as neither subject nor object, while *es* and *there* are regarded as nonparticipant subjects with actual (albeit rarified) semantic content.[12]

4. Case

We have focused so far on the notions subject, direct object, transitivity, and finite clause. All languages require such constructs for their proper description, and universally valid schematic characterizations are reasonably sought. By contrast, case markings display substantial cross-linguistic variation: some languages dispense with them altogether, and case-marking systems are anything but uniform. Thus no specific inventory of cases can be posited as an absolute universal instantiated in all languages. Moreover, the search for all-encompassing schematic characterizations would not appear promising; case semantics is better approached in terms of language-specific families of senses organized around prototypical values.

4.1. General comments

Case markings are traditionally regarded as purely grammatical elements devoid of semantic content. There are several apparent reasons for this view: the role of case in signaling syntactic relations (notably subject and object) that are themselves denied semantic import; the fact that cases are often governed by verbs, prepositions, or constructions, leaving no option in their selection; the use of case for purposes of agreement, where by definition it is incapable of providing any independent semantic content; and the inability to isolate any single meaning appropriate for a particular case in all its occurrences.

From the perspective of cognitive grammar, these reasons are simply invalid. Markers identifying subjects and objects as such can be regarded as meaningful if these grammatical relations are themselves notionally grounded. The assumption that a governed morpheme is *ipso facto* semantically empty is erroneous: being obligatory is not the same as being meaningless, and the conventions of a language often specify the co-occurrence of particular meaningful elements. Likewise, the failure of a morpheme to contribute independent semantic content does not imply that it is semantically empty, but only that its contribution is redundant; semantic overlap is present to some degree in all composite expressions, and full overlap is an expected limiting case. Finally, polysemy is the normal situation for both lexical and grammatical morphemes; in neither instance does the absence of a single semantic value accounting directly for all of a morpheme's uses entail that it has no meaning at all.

Case markings thus conform to the fundamental generalization of cognitive grammar, namely that only symbolic units are required for the description of grammatical structure. They are not seen as mechanically induced, semantically empty grammatical markers, but rather as separate predications, whose value can either dovetail with that supplied by other elements or else provide supplementary semantic specifications. The meaning of a case marker reflects its function, which is to specify the type of role that a nominal entity plays with respect to some relation. Hence the cognitive domain supporting its semantic characterization is the schematic conception of an appropriate relation--let us call this the "base relation". The nominal entity whose role within the base relation is being specified may be called the "focused participant". In grammatical composition, the focused participant is equated with the profile of the nominal that the case marking attaches to; the schematically conceived base relation is generally identified with the process profiled by the clause in which the case-marked nominal appears (or with the relation profiled by the element that governs the case).

What does a case marker profile? There are two options. First, it may profile the focused participant (making it similar internally to a nominalizer like *-er* or *-ee*). Its effect on a noun phrase is then to derive a more elaborate nominal expression capable of serving as a subject or object. Alternatively, the case predication may be relational in character, profiling the interconnections between the focused participant and the base relation overall. In this event the case marker is very similar semantically to a preposition; accordingly, it converts a noun phrase into a relational expression of the sort that functions as an oblique complement. Note that both variants are possible for the same case, even in a single language. In Polish, for instance, some nominals marked instrumental are direct objects, while others are oblique.[13]

4.2. Role archetypes

We will consider only those categories that primarily involve the role of participants in the process profiled by a clause. Thereby excluded are such cases as the genitive, whose basic function is NP-internal rather than clausal; the vocative, which concerns an extraclausal relationship between the speaker and addressee; and locative cases, which generally pertain to the setting in which the profiled process unfolds. These distinctions are not always sharp, and the limitation is solely a matter of practicality.

As noted earlier, we conceive of processual participants with reference to an array of role archetypes. These archetypal notions derive from recurrent aspects of our everyday experience, and represent deeply ingrained categories organizing our conception of participant interactions. Thus role archetypes are not viewed as being solely or specifically linguistic in nature (despite their semantic and grammatical significance), but as part of our general conceptual apparatus. They differ in this respect from the constructs variously called "deep cases", "thematic relations", or "theta roles", as these are normally interpreted. The term role archetype is intended to underscore this difference in status.

The different status encourages alternate theoretical expectations. One is not led to anticipate (as with "deep cases", etc.) that linguistic theory should be capable of enumerating a small, fixed set of uniquely valued roles adequate for describing the nominal participants in any natural-language sentence. For one thing, our richly varied experience supports the extraction of numerous and multifarious schemas pertaining to types of participants and the nature of their involvement in a process. Those schematic conceptions that we single out for discussion as role archetypes may distinguish themselves by their degree of cognitive salience and utility, but they are nonetheless representatives of a far broader, even open-ended population. Moreover, I limit the descriptive function of role archetypes to providing the prototypical values of cases and other constructs (e.g. subject and object). A full description of such a construct requires a multiplicity of values related to the prototype by paths of semantic extension. The prototype itself may well be instantiated directly in only a minority of the sentences employing the construct.

As judged by their systematic cross-linguistic significance, only a handful of roles are sufficiently fundamental and cognitively salient to be considered archetypal: agent, instrument, experiencer, patient, mover, and absolute. The first two are manifested in the conception of a human actor volitionally wielding an object to physically affect some other entity (e.g. *Seymour sliced the salami with a knife*). I define an experiencer as an individual engaged in some type of mental process, be it intellectual, perceptual, or emotive; the subjects of *think*, *see*, and *fear* are examples. I will construe the term patient quite narrowly, to indicate an entity that undergoes an internal change of state, whereas a mover is an entity that changes position with respect to its surroundings; these are illustrated by the objects in (30a) and (30b), respectively.

(30) a. *Stanley melted the ice with a blowtorch.*
    b. *Abernathy hurled the discus nearly 70 meters.*

An absolute participant is one whose role in a process is viewed in isolation from the flow of energy and causal interactions. Both participants are absolute in a sentence like (31a), which portrays a static situation in purely configurational, nonenergetic terms.

(31) a. *A chain-link fence encloses his property.*
    b. *The weary ranger watched another lovely sunset.*
    c. *The ice slowly melted.*
    d. *The discus sailed nearly 70 meters.*

Sentences like (31b) are more dynamic, in that the subject is the locus of mental activity, but the object--unaffected by the process and insulated from the energy that drives it--is absolute. The subjects in (31c)-(31d) are also absolute, though not because their participation is intrinsically nonenergetic; in contrast to (30), these sentences simply abstract away from the triggering forces and focus on the change of state or position per se. Hence the subjects in (31c)-(31d) can be regarded as an "absolute patient" and an "absolute mover", respectively.[14]

It bears repeating that there is no unique or exclusive set of role conceptions. Those cited as archetypal are analogous to the highest peaks in a mountain range: they coexist with others that may be significant despite their lesser salience. A familiar example is the conception of inanimate, essentially autonomous forces capable of driving events:

(32) a. *The wind blew the door shut again.*
    b. *A flood wiped out the poverty-stricken village.*
    c. *An earthquake woke us up.*

Though such forces are neither agents nor instruments in any strict sense, a schematic conception of them is presumably invoked by speakers of English to represent the generalization that sentences like (32) are conventionally sanctioned. We have further noted the existence of hybrid roles that combine essential features of two or more archetypes, as illustrated by the subject of *jump* (AG-MVR) and the object of *injure* (EXPER-PAT). It should also be observed that processual participants need not conform precisely to an archetype or any other standard role conception. Pushing matters to the extreme, there is a sense in which every process defines a set of roles which reflect the specific details of that particular process and are consequently *sui generis*. That is in no way problematic in the present framework, and does not preclude either schematization or categorization.

Clearly, role archetypes amount to more than a structureless inventory of unrelated conceptions. By virtue of their intrinsic character, they participate in systemic relationships reminiscent of those observable among the phonemes of a language. One analogy is with the cardinal vowels, which are maximally differentiated with respect to the primary vocalic parameters, and thus make optimal use of the available phonological space. The agent and patient archetypes stand similarly opposed in regard to all their essential features: an agent is human, exercises volitional control, is an energy source, directs action outward, and remains basically unaffected by it; on the other hand, the archetypal patient is inanimate, consequently has no volition, serves as an energy sink, is the target for externally-initiated activity, and undergoes an internal change of state. Their polar opposition in this region of conceptual space lends a special salience to the agent and patient roles. The fact that AG and PAT represent the prototypical values for subjects and objects is one manifestation of their privileged status.

Role archetypes can also be arranged in hierarchies with respect to certain cognitively salient parameters. Each hierarchy constitutes a natural sequence for accessing the archetypes it comprises, and the ordering it imposes is exploited for linguistic purposes. We have already considered the hierarchy defined by the flow of energy along an action chain, namely AG > INSTR > PAT/MVR/EXPER, and noted its relevance to the unmarked choice of subject and object in English. Let us call this the "energy flow hierarchy". Also significant is the "initiative hierarchy", whose basic form is AG > EXPER > OTHER. This second hierarchy reflects the capacity of a participant to function as an original source of energy and thereby initiate contact with other entities. The archetypal agent ranks highest, since it is necessarily a source of energy in the physical domain. By contrast, an experiencer is not invariably construed as an energy source (some mental activity being externally induced), and *qua* experiencer initiates only abstract interactions with other entities (e.g. by imagining them or establishing perceptual contact). The initiative hierarchy correlates with the linear order of nominal participants in a sentence like *Tom showed Jill a turtle*, and also with their level of prominence as determined by grammatical relations.[15] The basic word order SUBJECT > INDIRECT OBJECT > DIRECT OBJECT found in many languages (e.g. Turkish, Japanese, Newari) is another manifestation of this hierarchy.

Additional systemic relationships are represented in Figure 9, which sorts role archetypes according to two binary oppositions. The distinction between "source domain" and "recipient domain" is based on energy transmission: by their very nature, agents and instruments pass energy along to participants downstream, whereas the other roles figure in the transfer of energy only as recipients, if at all (though an entity is often a patient, mover, or experiencer by virtue of energy absorption, these can also be construed as absolute--i.e. independently of energy flow). Within each domain, a further distinction is made between "active" and "passive participants". The active participant is in each case the one that ranks the highest on the initiative hierarchy.

	SOURCE DOMAIN	RECIPIENT DOMAIN
ACTIVE PARTICIPANT	AG	EXPER
PASSIVE PARTICIPANT	INSTR	PAT MVR ABS

Figure 9.

The groupings suggested by this chart are natural in other ways as well. As for the source domain, an instrument is naturally regarded as an extension of the agent: it implies an agent, who generally manipulates it directly (sometimes as part of his own body--cf. (9)). The grouping of AG and EXPER as active participants is motivated not only by their common initiative capacity, but also by their necessary sentience (required for either willful control or mental experience). Note further that an agent's experience of his action typically goes beyond volition (he may imagine it beforehand, perceive it, and recall it afterwards), and that purely mental activity is often subject to volitional control. Finally, the recipient domain appears to have a certain coherence. In sharp contrast to AG and INSTR, the roles in this domain--EXPER, PAT, MVR, and ABS--are all very commonly associated with direct objects. Moreover, they frequently coalesce to form hybrid roles (cf. (8)), any combination being possible.

4.3. Correlation with grammatical relations

Givón has rightly observed (1984: 136) that the diversity of case-marking systems derives from interplay in the coding of two kinds of information: what role archetype a nominal participant instantiates, and its grammatical relation in a clause (subject, object, or oblique).[16] There is of course a connection between the two, since archetypes figure in the description of grammatical relations (notably with respect to their prototypes). But there is also substantial divergence, as neither subjects nor objects invariably instantiate any particular archetype; their schematic characterization refers instead to figure/ground organization and degrees of prominence.

We can therefore envisage a spectrum of possibilities in regard to case systems. At one extreme, a system is "fully correlated" with grammatical relations, in that one case is devoted exclusively to marking subjects, and another to marking direct objects (with subjects and objects always being marked in this fashion). It is evident that a strict and wholly consistent nominative/accusative system has this character. The meanings of the nominative and accusative cases are then 'subject' and 'direct object', respectively, where these in turn are resolvable into the networks that define those relations semantically.[17] At the other extreme lies a "fully uncorrelated" system, i.e. one in which case categories have no direct connection whatever with the basic grammatical relations. Instead, each category is associated with a particular role archetype, which provides its prototypical value and anchors a network of conventionally established senses. Hence the only correlation between subjects and objects on the one hand, and cases on the other, resides in the fact that both are characterized (though independently) with reference to archetypal roles.

Fully correlated and uncorrelated systems should probably be regarded as idealizations--it is doubtful that pure examples are found in nature. For instance, even in strict NOM/ACC languages it is common for these cases to mark elements other than subjects and objects (e.g. certain adverbs might take ACC). Additionally, if a correlated system has more than two or three cases, some of them are sure to be characterized in terms of role archetypes; thus NOM/ACC systems often incorporate a dative case with EXPER as its prototype, an instrumental case centered on INSTR, and so forth. The reason for this role-oriented aspect of correlated systems is that there are more linguistically significant roles than there are grammatical relations distinguishable solely on the basis of prominence. Degrees of prominence alone could hardly be expected to support more than a three-member hierarchy: SUBJECT (relational figure) > OBJECT (the most salient participant other than the figure) > OBLIQUE (all remaining participants).[18] Hence just two cases (or three at most) are sufficient to accommodate prominence-based relationships, and in a larger system the remaining cases are dedicated to the coding of role archetypes.

Correlated and uncorrelated systems are therefore not radically divergent in character, especially in view of the fact that NOM and ACC take AG and PAT as their prototypes. The difference is that subject and object are prominence-based relations, whose association with AG and PAT is secondary (it stems from the inherent salience of these polar opposites, hence the naturalness of selecting them as the first- and second-most prominent participants). As a consequence, the networks representing conventionally established values of the subject and object categories extend beyond AG and PAT to subsume a variety of other archetypes. By contrast, since a role-based case is tied directly and specifically to an archetype, its values tend to cluster more tightly around it.

These notions suggest possible scenarios for typological change and the genesis of "mixed" systems. For example, a correlated system might arise when certain cases in an uncorrelated system "grammaticize" as markers for subject and object. We can see this as a matter of one network "capturing" or "entraining" another--e.g. the network for an agentive case might be expanded under the influence of the more inclusive network for subjects, resulting in their eventual coincidence. Such a process would have to be incremental, and at any intermediate stage one would analyze the system as typologically mixed. There is no reason, of course, to believe that a mixed system is inherently unstable, or that it is necessarily "caught in transition" between two pure (and thus ostensibly stable) types. On the contrary, all indications point to some kind of split or mixture being canonical, if not universal. The prevalence of languages split between nominative/accusative and ergative/absolutive organization is of course well known. Agent/patient languages also split in various ways (see Dahlstrom 1983).

But focusing for the moment on the (possibly nonexistent) ideal of unmixed languages, it is evident that nominative/accusative and agent/patient systems lie at opposite extremes of the spectrum. A strict and consistent NOM/ACC system is by definition fully correlated: these cases mark subjects and objects no matter what roles they instantiate. On the other hand, an ideal AG/PAT language is fully uncorrelated: one case consistently flags agentive participants, while a second marks patients (and maybe other roles in the recipient domain), irrespective of their status as subjects or objects. Where in this scheme do we fit an ergative/absolutive language? It would seem to fall near the correlated end of the spectrum. An ERG/ABS system cannot satisfy the definition of full correlation, since it violates the requirement that all subjects be marked by the same case. Nevertheless, to the extent that the ERG/ABS marking is predictable from the number of central participants (i.e. whether a clause has both a subject and an object, or just a subject), it is clearly sensitive to grammatical relations, and not to role archetypes per se.

4.4. Ergative/absolutive systems

Despite the foregoing remarks, we have not yet captured the spirit of an ERG/ABS system. If nothing were involved other than the identification of subjects and objects, it is hard to fathom why a language would ever depart from the NOM/ACC arrangement, which codes these relations directly and straightforwardly. If the subject and object relations are pivotal, why should a language mark them so inconsistently, with one case (ERG) used for certain subjects only, and the other (ABS) for both subjects and objects? We can pose the same problem by considering how the cases might be characterized semantically. The schematic value 'transitive subject' accommodates ERG--and in the present framework, this does constitute a meaning (albeit abstract). But what about ABS? What do the notions 'transitive object' and 'intransitive subject' have in common? Since ERG/ABS organization is anything but rare, there must be something conceptually natural about the grouping.

An initial clue is afforded by cross-linguistic tendencies in how the relevant cases are signaled phonologically: the predominant pattern in NOM/ACC languages is for NOM to be coded by zero, and ACC by overt phonological material; in ERG/ABS languages, ABS is generally the zero form, and ERG is marked overtly. While there are of course exceptions, the pattern is quite robust and thus indicative of deeper factors--perhaps NOM and ABS are the unmarked members of their respective case systems not just phonologically, but in some structural or semantic sense. My specific proposal is that NOM and ABS are characterized "autonomously", whereas ACC and ERG are characterized with reference to NOM and ABS. This has the distributional consequence that, while some nominal is marked NOM or ABS in every clause,[19] ACC and ERG occur only if there is some additional nominal meeting the appropriate conditions.

How this works for NOM and ACC is straightforward in light of previous discussion. NOM means 'subject', characterized schematically as clause-level relational figure. The characterization is autonomous (i.e. it makes no reference to other participants), and since figure/ground organization is inherent in relational predications, there is always some entity that qualifies. For ACC, which means 'direct object', the situation is very different. Recall that an object is characterized with reference to a subject: it is a prominent participant that lies downstream (typically along an action chain) with respect to a subject that is also a participant. These conditions are not always met, so not every sentence has an object. We can thus describe a subject as the "starting point" for calculating whether an object is also present. The calculation proceeds by (i) starting with the subject as point of origin; (ii) from there, tracing downstream along the action chain (or its analog); and (iii) ascertaining whether the profiled segment of this path terminates with a distinct participant having the requisite degree of prominence.

To the extent that NOM and ACC correlate with subject and object, a single calculation applies to both the cases and the grammatical relations. However, the same cannot be true of ERG/ABS languages, whose distinctive property is that the cases cross-cut the grammatical relations. The procedure as stated is presumably valid in such languages for grammatical relations, but some alternative is required for case marking.[20] As it turns out, the two procedures are very similar--one is essentially the inverse of the other. Transitivity and case are each determined by tracing a path along an action chain, but these paths proceed in opposite directions. Though each path is natural in its own way, their lack of coalignment is perhaps responsible for the minority status of ERG/ABS systems.

The procedure for determining case in an ERG/ABS language is as follows: (i) assign ABS case to the TAIL of the action chain (or its analog); (ii) from this starting point, trace an UPSTREAM path along the chain; and (iii) if a distinct participant is encountered that lies at the endpoint of this path (i.e. if it heads the profiled segment of the action chain), assign it ERG case. Observe that the characterization of ABS is autonomous, for it only invokes step (i), which does not refer to ERG. Moreover, ABS is always assigned, even if there is only a single participant; though degenerate, a one-participant relationship is still construable as an action chain, whose single member is both the head and the tail. On the other hand, ERG is characterized with reference to ABS, and will not occur in single-participant clauses, owing to the requirement that the ERG- and ABS-marked participants be distinct.

A consequence of this analysis is that ERG and ABS are not primarily or specifically markers of grammatical relations. The characterization of ABS, which is clearly pivotal, does not refer directly to subject or object, but rather to a participant's position on an action chain. There is of course an indirect (but nonetheless regular) connection between the cases and the grammatical relations, stemming from the fact that both are defined with reference to action chains or equivalent asymmetries. We can even admit that speakers exploit this connection and use the case markers to identify subjects and objects. The point remains, however, that the role-based value of ERG and ABS is fundamental, and that their relation-marking function represents a secondary overlay. The inconsistency of the correlation (subjects marked by both ERG and ABS; ABS marking both subjects and objects) is quite understandable from this perspective. Recall that case markers are treated in cognitive grammar as separate predications, i.e. they have their own semantic value, even when redundant or exploited for grammatical purposes. The semantic independence of role predications is obscured in fully correlated languages, where the meanings of NOM/ACC and subject/object essentially coincide, but it is more apparent in an ERG/ABS system (and quite obvious in an AG/PAT system).

What, then, are the meanings of ERG and ABS? A first approximation to their meanings is provided by the case-assignment procedure outlined above, which qualifies as a semantic description: it invokes a cognitive domain (the conception of an action chain) and specifies the relative position within it of the focused participants. The characterization can nevertheless be brought into sharper focus; our efforts along these lines will be rewarded by a deeper understanding of ergativity and associated grammatical phenomena. To achieve this, we must examine more closely the structure intrinsic to our conceptualization of canonical events.

4.5. The structure of events

A finite clause profiles a unitary process--that is, a process construed as constituting either a single situation or a single event. By definition, the conception of a process involves some entity and the evolution through time of a relationship in which it figures. In the case of situations, this relationship is conceived as a static configuration stable through time; for events, some kind of change is implied. This much conceptual content is the irreducible minimum for a processual predication.

Restricting our attention to this irreducible minimum, we must next consider the role an entity plays in the profiled process. For events, there are three basic possibilities: the entity either moves, has a mental experience, or undergoes an internal change of state (i.e. it is a MVR, EXPER, or PAT). These are diagramed in Figures 10(a)-(c), using abbreviatory notations that by now should be familiar. For situations, on the other hand, the entity may simply be viewed in relation to some domain or setting (e.g. *Wombats really exist*), and if so, its role is essentially vacuous in terms of conceptual content. There are advantages to treating this "empty" role as the degenerate instance with respect to MVR, EXPER, and PAT; in other words, the degree to which it undergoes motion, experience, or change of state represents the limiting or zero case. I thus refer to it as the "zero" role (Figure 10(d)).

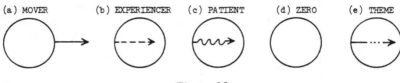

Figure 10.

I also posit a more schematic role conception that subsumes MVR, EXPER, PAT, and ZERO as special cases. The term "theme" is adopted for this generalized notion, and the notation of Figure 10(e) for its diagramatic representation. A thematic participant therefore undergoes some kind of change (possibly zero change, as a limiting case), but the characterization of TH is neutral as to whether the change is internal or external, and whether it occurs in the physical or the mental sphere. Observe that the roles subsumed by TH are essentially those of the recipient domain (Figure 9)--the only discrepancy is that ZERO replaces ABS. The difference is only apparent, however. The import of ABS is merely that energy is not considered a factor, hence this role is capable of being superimposed on any of the others; the combinations ABS-MVR, ABS-EXPER, and ABS-PAT have already been noted. To reconcile this inventory of thematic roles with those of the recipient domain, we need only recognize that participants previously treated as ABS *tout court* can in fact be analyzed as ABS-ZERO.

As its minimum conceptual content, therefore, a processual predication invokes a thematic relationship portrayed as either evolving through time (for events) or continuing unchanged (for situations). In the case of events, there are several basic ways of construing this minimal relationship with respect to the input of energy. One possibility is an absolute construal, sketched in Figure 11(a), which views the event autonomously by abstracting away from whatever energy might be required to drive it.[21] A second option is to conceive the requisite energy as being drawn from the theme's own internal resources, as shown in 11(b). Because the theme and energy source are thus collapsed in a single participant, a process construed in this fashion lends itself to coding by intransitive verbs; examples are *crawl* (for

MVR), *concentrate* (EXPER), and *burst* (PAT). A third alternative, given in 11(c), is for the energy to be supplied from some external source. Coding is then most naturally effected by a transitive verb taking the energy source as subject and the theme as object, e.g. *throw, tickle, squash.*

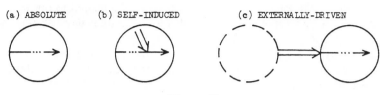

Figure 11.

Our capacity for imposing an absolute construal on events, even those that are inherently energetic, has many linguistic manifestations. Consider, for example, the nonreflexive verbs of French that take the auxiliary *être* 'be' rather than *avoir* 'have'. Essentially, they are intransitive motion verbs that limit themselves to describing direction of movement in a locative frame of reference: *aller* 'go', *venir* 'come', *monter* 'ascend', *descendre* 'descend', etc. Because these verbs are silent regarding such matters as rate and means of propulsion (which are closely associated with energy input), their construal of the profiled process is plausibly analyzed as absolute. Verbs which do specify the rate or manner of locomotion (*courir* 'run', *nager* 'swim', *voler* 'fly', etc.) take *avoir* instead of *être*, and so do *monter* and *descendre* when used as transitives or causatives.

More generally, the notions at hand permit a natural account of the verbs called "unaccusative" in relational grammar (Perlmutter 1978). I analyze unaccusatives as single-participant verbs whose construal of the profiled process is absolute, and though we cannot pursue the matter here, I believe this analysis will help account for their distinctive grammatical behavior. The sole participant of an unaccusative is characterizable as an ABS-TH. In other frameworks it is sometimes called an "inner argument", a term that is intuitively quite reasonable. We can now explain--on conceptual grounds--precisely why this description seems appropriate.

The reason is that a theme and the change it undergoes provide the minimum semantic content required for a processual predication, and thus constitute its irreducible conceptual "core". As such, a thematic relationship enjoys a certain autonomy vis-à-vis the agent and the flow of energy, even for inherently energetic processes (e.g. despite our knowledge that force is somehow involved, *The door opened* focuses exclusively on the mover's spatial trajectory--cf. Figure 6). The source domain is not similarly autonomous: it is far less natural to conceptualize the agent and energy flow independently of any reference to its downstream consequences (so that the agent, as it were, simply radiates energy "into the void"). This nonautonomy explains the peculiarity of sentences like **Andrea caused*, in which only the source domain is coded. Contributing to this difference in autonomy is a contrast between the source and recipient domains in the nature of their conceptual content, which tends to be richer and more concrete in the latter. Consider *Andrea opened the door*. Since there are many ways to open a door (in the ordinary way, by leaning on it, through magic or telekinesis, by pushing a button, etc.), all this sentence tells us for sure about the agent is that she somehow supplies the energy to initiate the process. Compared to our conception of the door following its spatial trajectory, this information is more abstract, harder to visualize separately, and less likely to be useful by itself.

The autonomy and semantic "weight" of a thematic relationship commonly allow it to stand alone as a complete event conception, hence as the process profiled by a finite clause. The clause is then intransitive, and its single participant is the subject. Alternatively, a thematic relationship can serve as the nucleus for assembling a more elaborate event conception.[22] Often this assembly is confined primarily to specifying the input of energy that drives the nuclear process (i.e. the source domain is invoked, and the theme--now construed as the recipient of energy input--is no longer absolute). This more elaborate conception is typically coded by a transitive clause, with the theme as object and the energy source as subject. The fact that objects are more "tightly bound" to the verb than transitive subjects (as witnessed cross-linguistically by word-order tendencies, noun incorporation, the prevalence of VO-idioms, etc.) is thus attributable to the conceptual status of objects as inner-layer participants.

As its irreducible conceptual nucleus, a thematic relationship is therefore the starting point for constructing a complex event conception, in the same sense that a root is the starting point for constructing a complex word, and a vowel the nucleus for assembling a syllable. Of course, there are many other ways in which an element is reasonably considered a starting point (cf. MacWhinney 1977): the agent is a starting point in terms of energy flow; as relational figure, the subject is a starting point with respect to the hierarchy of participant prominence; the first word in a sentence is its starting point along the temporal axis of phonological space; and so on. Each starting point represents the initial step in accessing certain elements of a complex structure in a cognitively natural sequence. These alternate "paths" through a clause can either dovetail or diverge, and their interplay is an essential aspect of grammatical structure.

4.6. Ergativity

We are now able to state more cogently the nature of the contrast between NOM/ACC and ERG/ABS languages. I will assume that grammatical relations are basically similar in all languages, and that our previous characterization is essentially valid: the subject is the most prominent clausal participant (prototypically an agent), while the object--the second-most prominent participant--has a thematic role and lies downstream from the subject. In both

NOM/ACC and ERG/ABS systems, then, the unmarked coding of a scene entails the coincidence of two kinds of starting points. The first is the starting point for the hierarchy of participant prominence (i.e. the subject). The second is the element suggested as the most natural starting point by the clause's conceptual content (e.g. an agent, action-chain head, or perceptual experiencer).

Against this common backdrop, NOM/ACC and ERG/ABS systems differ with respect to a third starting point, namely the one they adopt for the computation of case marking. Fully correlated with grammatical relations, a NOM/ACC system simply makes this third starting point coincide with the other two. The starting point for determining case is thus the subject, which is marked by NOM, and ACC-marking is invoked only if one encounters a second, distinct participant by following along the relevant paths (i.e. the prominence hierarchy, and the action chain or its analog). By contrast, the distinctive property of an ERG/ABS system is that the starting point it adopts for computing case diverges from the other two. Specifically, its starting point for case computation is the thematic relationship that constitutes the essential nucleus for the conception of a complex event or situation. This starting point is marked by ABS, and ERG is invoked only for a second, distinct participant encountered by continuing outward from the nucleus (hence upstream along the action chain or its analog).[23]

Thus, while they differ as to what counts as "initial" for purposes of case assignment, each system is natural in its own way. The choice of starting point is motivated in a NOM/ACC system by considerations of participant prominence and direction of energy flow; in an ERG/ABS system, it is motivated by conceptual autonomy and the inherently layered organization of a complex event conception. But in either type of system, the starting point is typically the zero form, with overt marking reserved for the possible occurrence of a secondary element. Moreover, both types of systems can be correlated with grammatical relations, so that only subjects and direct objects are accessed in the calculation.

What if there is only a single participant? Consider in particular a sentence like *She jumped* or *He concentrated*, in which the subject has both agentive and thematic properties. For purposes of case assignment, this participant qualifies as a starting point in either a NOM/ACC or an ERG/ABS language, but for different reasons: in the former, by virtue of being the subject and agent; in the latter, by virtue of being a theme. But in either sort of language, the lone participant typically remains unmarked, and for the same reason: the starting-point case (NOM or ABS) is generally zero.

A starting point is simply the initial element encountered when a complex structure is accessed via some cognitively natural ordering. As such, it is maximally "accessible" with respect to the parameter in question. If the starting points invoked for case do in fact initiate cognitively natural paths, we should expect this to be reflected in other sorts of grammatical behavior. That this is so for subjects, the starting point of the participant prominence hierarchy, is well known (cf. Keenan & Comrie 1977). The matter is not quite so obvious in regard to thematic relationships, the starting point in terms of conceptual autonomy, probably because the path involved is more abstract and of lesser cognitive salience. Nonetheless, ergativity outside the realm of case is quite common, even in languages with NOM/ACC systems.[24] It is likely that some phenomenon treating intransitive subjects and transitive objects alike (to the exclusion of transitive subjects) can be found in virtually every language.

The notion of starting points also helps to make sense of various types of split ergativity in the domain of case (cf. DeLancey 1981; Givón 1984: chapter 5). A frequent kind of split involves the "empathy" or "animacy hierarchy", where speaker and hearer outrank third-person participants, humans outrank nonhumans, animates outrank inanimates, and so on. Somewhere along this hierarchy there is a cut-off line, such that only those transitive subjects falling below the line take ergative case; the split most commonly divides the speech-act participants from the remainder, so that first- and second-person pronouns are the only transitive subjects to occur without ergative marking. One interpretation is that higher-ranking elements are inherently agentive, and that only for elements farther down on the hierarchy is agentivity sufficiently "newsworthy" to be marked overtly by ergative case. While this may well have some validity, it probably does not tell the whole story. Why, for instance, should third-person humans differ from the speech-act participants in regard to inherent agentivity?

Let me suggest an alternative (or complementary) account. The empathy hierarchy reflects a person's assessment of his relation to other sorts of entities. He perceives them as lying at different "distances" from himself in regard to such matters as likeness and common interests. The speaker is the ultimate starting point for computing these distances, but in the context of a speech event, the speaker and addressee (as coparticipants) are further construable as a joint, higher-order starting point established by the immediacy and inherent solidarity of the communicative act (the "us" vs. "them" syndrome). Ergative systems manifesting a split with respect to the empathy hierarchy receive a very natural description from this perspective: for a nominal to be marked with ergative case, it must lie beyond the starting point not only along the hierarchy of conceptual autonomy (which is characteristic of ergative case in general), but along the empathy hierarchy in addition. That is, an ERG-marked nominal must be noninitial on both parameters.

A second type of split is attested in Newari, a Tibeto-Burman language spoken in Nepal. One of the factors determining whether a transitive subject takes ERG case is its degree of focus. Thus (33a), with the subject marked ERG, is appropriate in response to the question 'Who's cooking the rice?', while (33b) answers the question 'What's the man doing?'.

(33) a. *wa manu-nan jaa thuyaa cona*
    the man-ERG rice cooking be
    'THE MAN is cooking the rice'

   b. *wa manu jaa thuyaa cona*
    the man rice cooking be
    'The man IS COOKING THE RICE'

This makes perfect sense in terms of our overall analysis, since the focused constituent represents the novel or informative part of the utterance, i.e. that portion of its semantic content which goes beyond what has previously been established in the discourse. At any given moment, the content already established serves as a baseline for evaluating that which is provided by the following utterance, whose focus consists of whatever information extends beyond this starting point. We can therefore analyze the ERG case marking in (33a) as indicating that the subject is noninitial (lies beyond the starting point) with respect to both the hierarchy of conceptual autonomy and the introduction of content in the flow of discourse.[25]

The analysis is also consistent with the standard account of other types of split, e.g. the common phenomenon of ERG/ABS morphology occurring only in perfective clauses. The usual explanation is that imperfectivity lessens the extent to which the object is affected by the action of the verb, and thus diminishes a clause's transitivity. Recall, in this regard, that ERG is characterized with reference to ABS--taking a thematic participant as starting point, ERG case is employed only for a second, distinct participant encountered farther along on the hierarchy of conceptual autonomy. Consequently, any factor that detracts from the salience of the object or its role in a clear-cut thematic relationship reduces its likelihood of being invoked as starting point for computing the applicability of ERG case marking.

4.7. *Other case phenomena*

The foregoing remarks provide at best a limited introduction to the rich domain of case semantics. For a glimpse at what remains, let us briefly consider some additional case phenomena. The discussion focuses on two broad issues: the systemic aspects of a case inventory, and the significance of regarding case markers as separate predications.

A case category is generally complex, comprising a network of alternate senses connected by relationships of schematicity and semantic extension. The specific array of senses associated with a particular case is a matter of linguistic convention and reflects the interaction of numerous factors. For one thing, the senses of a case tend to cluster around a particular role archetype, which provides its prototypical value and "center of gravity"; dative case, for instance, is normally centered on the experiencer role. A second factor is the number of cases in the system, and their competition for the privilege of coding the many possible role conceptions; clearly, in a small system each case will tend to subsume a broad range of values, possibly including more than one archetype. Finally, the relative naturalness of different schemes for apportioning the array of role conceptions to the various cases is determined by systemic relationships among the archetypes themselves.

Consider the systemic relationships represented in Figure 9, particularly the distinction between role archetypes in the source vs. the recipient domains. If (as previously maintained) this distinction is natural and has a conceptual basis, we can predict its relevance for the description of case in various languages. An example is provided by Newari, as illustrated in (34):

(34) a. *raam-an   cakku-n   laa   taala*
     Raam-ERG knife-ERG meat cut
     'Raam cut the meat with a knife'

  b. *phas-an   parjaa sankala*
     wind-ERG curtain move
     'The wind moved the curtain'

  c. *ji-n   baakas-an dhibaa kayaa*
     I-ERG   box-ERG   money   take
     'I took the money from the box'

It is evident that the Newari "ergative" case is not confined to transitive subjects in accordance with the strict characterization of ERG offered earlier. Nor is it limited to agents in any restrictive sense--we see it marking an instrument in (34a), an inanimate force in (34b), and even a locative source in (34c). Though its ergative/absolutive use can be regarded as central, the conventional values of this case essentially coincide with the roles of the source domain. 'Source domain element' is thus a schematic characterization that subsumes its conventionally sanctioned array of more specific senses.

Another systemic relationship involving role archetypes is the polar opposition between agent and patient. The cognitive salience of this maximal opposition has a variety of linguistic manifestations, one of which pertains to the distribution of zero marking (or the absence of a case predication). Very commonly, of course, subjects and direct objects--with AG and PAT as their respective prototypes--are indicated by zero, while noncentral participants bear overt case markings; it is apparently natural for a cluster of values around each pole of the opposition to be left unmarked, with any in-between value being signaled overtly. The clusters of zero-marked values sometimes cross-cut the subject and object relations. In Guarani, for example, zero marks both subjects and inanimate objects, whereas animate objects take the postposition *pe* (which also occurs with certain obliques). Similarly, subjects and objects are unmarked in Spanish, except for the "personal *a*" that occurs with objects which (roughly) are both animate and definite. Granted the notion of a polar AG/PAT opposition, this type of split in the marking of objects makes sense: inanimate patients stand maximally opposed to animate agents, so animate patients fall between the two extremes.[26]

These examples show a divergence between case and grammatical relations--i.e. the case system is less than fully correlated, since some objects are indicated by zero, while others take a case marker that also occurs with obliques. Such divergence is unsurprising in the present framework, for cases are treated as separate predications. Rather than being mechanically induced for the marking of grammatical relations, cases are attributed independent semantic content, which does not in general match the value implied by the grammatical relation of the case-marked nominal (though it may in particular instances). It is therefore common for the case borne by a nominal and its grammatical relation (however this might be signaled) to be sensitive to different factors, thus providing different kinds of information about the nominal's participation in an event.

This is nicely illustrated by the following data from Polish:

(35) a. *Rzucił   piłką   do   płotu.*
  he:threw ball:INSTR up:to fence:GEN
  'He threw the ball up to the fence'

  b. *?Rzucił piłkę   do   płotu.*
  he:threw ball:ACC   up:to fence:GEN
  'He threw the ball up to the fence'

  c. *Rzucił   piłką   w   mamę.*
  he:threw ball:INSTR at mother
  'He threw the ball at his mother'

  d. **Rzucił piłkę   w   mamę.*
  he:threw ball:ACC   at mother
  'He threw the ball at his mother'

Consider first grammatical relations. 'Ball' is evidently the direct object of 'throw', which profiles the transmission of energy from an agent to a theme and the resultant motion of the latter. With this verb, the object relation assumes a prototypical semantic value: 'ball' constitutes the tail within the profiled portion of the action chain, and lies downstream from a participant subject. Now if the Polish case system were fully correlated, objects would always be marked accusative, but in actuality the correlation is only partial. In simple expressions like 'He threw the ball', the object can take either accusative or instrumental case; with the addition of a goal-specifying prepositional phrase, as in (35), INSTR is either preferred or required. Clearly, case must be reckoned on some basis other than grammatical relations, at least for this range of data.

Prototypically, INSTR marks an intermediary with respect to the flow of energy along an action chain, and ACC the endpoint. What appears to be happening with 'throw' is that these cases retain the value of indicating an intermediary or an endpoint along a path, but that the path in question is not identified with the flow of energy from agent to theme--instead, the spatial path followed by the thematic object provides the basis for computing intermediary vs. endpoint status. More precisely, INSTR and ACC take on the respective values 'intermediate participant' and 'final participant' with respect to movement along a spatial path. When the mover's destination is a saliently specified individual, it is naturally construed as the final participant; 'mother' is thus the final participant in (35c)-(35d), making 'ball' (which moves from the subject to the prepositional object) an intermediary. As a consequence, the direct object 'ball' takes INSTR case, and cannot be marked ACC. The situation in (35a)-(35b) is slightly different because 'fence' is construable as either a participant or a facet of the setting. To the extent that this latter interpretation prevails, 'ball' can be regarded as the final participant and hence inflected for ACC case. When there is no prepositional phrase at all, either case is permitted on the object. The analysis then predicts a subtle semantic contrast: INSTR should evoke some conception (however tenuous and schematic) of the ball's destination, whereas with ACC, attention should be focused more narrowly on its flight.

Further illustration is provided by the dative case in Newari. In some of its uses, DAT codes classic indirect-object roles, such as recipient, benefactive, and target of communication:

(36) a. *ji-n   raam-yaata   kitaab biyaa*
        I-ERG Raam-DAT   book   give
        'I gave Raam a book'

     b. *gitaa-n   raam-yaata   jaa thuka*
        Gitaa-ERG Raam-DAT   rice cook
        'Gitaa cooked rice for Raam'

     c. *raam-an   gitaa-yaata   dhaala*
        Raam-ERG Gitaa-DAT   tell
        'Raam told Gitaa (something)'

Note that all of these roles involve some type of mental experience, and can thus be regarded as offshoots of the experiencer archetype, which anchors the DAT category. The Newari dative is further used to mark animate direct objects, either optionally or obligatorily (depending on the verb and other factors):

(37) a. *ji-n   wa misaa-yaata   khanaa*
     I-ERG the woman-DAT see
     'I saw the woman'

    b. *ji-n   wa misaa   khanaa*
     I-ERG the woman see
     'I saw the woman'

When there is a choice, as in (37), the contrast between DAT and ABS (zero) correlates with the salience of the object's role as experiencer; hence (37a) suggests some kind of interaction between the subject and object, whereas in (37b) the object is unaffected by the perceptual contact (i.e. its role is ABS-ZERO). To some degree, consequently, the EXPER archetype motivates the occurrence of DAT with animate objects in this language. However, even were this usage to be "grammaticized"--so that all animate objects took DAT, without exception--the implied semantic extension from 'experiencer' to 'animate object' would still be cognitively natural, since only animate entities are capable of experience.

Because cases represent separate predications, and correlate only partially and contingently with grammatical relations, it is hardly surprising that even subjects are sometimes marked with role-based cases, notably dative. Dative-subject constructions are basically limited, as one would predict, to clauses where the subject is readily construed as an experiencer. If the profiled relationship has the form EXPER---->ABS (or more precisely, EXPER---->ABS-ZERO), the experiencer is the unmarked choice for subject by virtue of being the locus of cognitive activity, and thus responsible for effecting the abstract interaction between the central participants. At the same time, the EXPER archetype functions as the prototype and center of gravity for DAT, so there is a natural tendency for the subject to be marked with DAT in such clauses even when subjects are normally indicated by some other case. Two kinds of optimality then find themselves in conflict: consistent marking of subjects by a single case (NOM or ERG) regardless of semantic role, versus consistent coding of the EXPER role (by DAT case) irrespective of grammatical relations. Some languages choose the latter option, or fashion a compromise position. The present framework affords an unproblematic analysis in either event.

Newari is a language that permits either option, and exploits the formal contrast to convey a difference in meaning. For example, (38a) might indicate that the speaker intends to include the addressee in his will, whereas (38b) simply describes a mnemonic experience:

(38) a. *ji-n   chan-ta   lumanke*
     I-ERG you-DAT remember:ACTIVE
     'I will remember you'

b. *ji-ta   cha luman*
I-DAT you remember
'I remember you'

In (38a), the subject is volitional and the object stands to be affected in some way by the profiled process; the formula AG===>EXPER is thus a rough approximation to its value, with ERG sensitive to the agentive character of the subject, and DAT to the experiential nature of the object. On the other hand, the contrasting formula for (38b) is EXPER---->ABS-ZERO; here DAT codes the experiential role of the subject, and zero (ABS) the absolute role of the object.

5. Causative constructions

Linguists have long recognized the significance of causative constructions to the study of case and grammatical relations. A survey of the relevant literature or even the central issues would be too ambitious for present purposes. Our sole objective is a brief and preliminary examination of how case marking in causatives can be approached from the standpoint of cognitive grammar.

5.1. Complex events

As noted previously, a thematic relationship evolving through time constitutes the irreducible nucleus of an event conception. The thematic process may be conceptualized autonomously, in which case its construal is said to be absolute. Alternatively, the process can anchor a more elaborate event conception that also makes reference to the energy that drives it. This complex event can in turn be conceived as resulting from an additional layer of energy input, and so on. Through successive incrementations of this sort, we can arrive at the conception of an action chain having any desired length, as diagramed in Figure 12.[27]

Depending on such factors as temporal and spatial contiguity, the links in an action chain are capable of being construed as either a single complex event or a sequence of separate (though causally related) events. A chain construed as a single event can be coded by a verb stem, whose morphemic composition may or may not reflect its semantic complexity: compare English *kill* with Nahuatl *mik-tia* (die-CAUS) 'kill'.[28] By contrast, an action chain chunked into separate events is usually (if not always) coded by separate verbs (e.g. *cause to die*). When one lexeme (be it an affix or a separate word) specifies an input of energy, and another codes the process driven by it, we recognize a construction as being (overtly) causative. Our concern here is with causative constructions in which the energy input and resulting activity are construed as a single event.

The interest of causative constructions for case and grammatical relations lies in

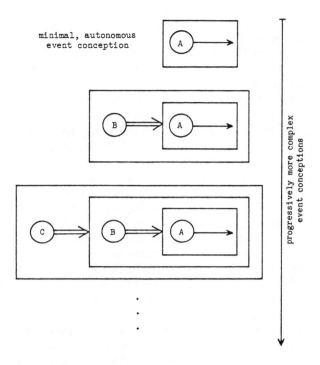

Figure 12.

their potential for creating single-clause expressions with more than the usual number of major participants, and with multiple participants instantiating a single role archetype (notably AG). Because the conventional clause-structure patterns of a language generally permit only a single subject and object, and may allow only one instance of a given case, the coding options available in terms of case and grammatical relations are stretched beyond their normal capacity. We gain added perspective on the meanings of these categories by observing how languages accommodate this strain.

Suppose that a complex event, e.g. one in which Paul induces a woman to throw a pebble, is to be coded in a single clause. There are three participants (two agents and a mover) instantiating roles that are normally coded by a subject or direct object, but in a single clause only two can be thusly accommodated. One common way of solving this problem is illustrated by French:

(39) *Paul a fait jeter le caillou par la femme.* 'Paul made the woman throw
                                                                                            the pebble'

That is, given the action chain [P===>[F===>[C→]]], the head of the chain (Paul) is coded as the subject and its tail (the pebble) as the object, leaving the intermediate participant (the woman) to be supplied periphrastically by means of a prepositional phrase. This solution is fully consonant with the schematic characterizations of subject and object proposed earlier on the basis of simpler expressions. Other solutions are of course conceivable--how a language does it is a matter of convention and not strongly predictable. Still, we can reasonably anticipate that the semantic values of cases and grammatical relations implied by their application to complex situations will either conform to their basic values or constitute natural extensions therefrom.

We will concern ourselves no further with grammatical relations, and focus instead on case marking, particularly in sentences parallel to (39). For present purposes, we can assume that the above solution holds for all the examples to be considered: the head and tail of the action chain are respectively chosen as subject and object, and take the case marking normally associated with these grammatical relations. The interesting problem pertains to the case that occurs on the intermediate participant, i.e. on what is generally referred to as the "downstairs" or "complement-clause subject", but which I will call the "causative pivot".

An insightful paper by Cole (1983) addresses this very issue. Cole claims that "the grammatical role in derived structure of the underlying complement subject is determined by [its] semantic role...in the complement clause" (116), and documents a number of specific patterns that languages follow in this regard. Though I accept his claim, and will show how his data can be accounted for in the context of cognitive grammar, our theoretical interpretations of the phenomena are quite different. What Cole refers to as "grammatical role" is consistently manifested by case marking in his examples. Moreover, he apparently attributes no meaning to either cases or grammatical relations per se (which makes the semantic determination of case somewhat mysterious), whereas I maintain that the occurrence and selection of a case marker is motivated by its semantic value. Finally, I do not posit underlying structures, analyze one-clause causatives in terms of complementation, or consider the causative pivot to be a clausal subject at any level of organization.[29]

5.2. Causatives derived from intransitives

When the basic verb is intransitive, matters are usually straightforward. Adding a causative predication expands the profiled relationship from a one- to a two-participant event, e.g. from [A→] to [B===>[A→]], and the grammatical devices employed in general for transitive clauses are sufficient. Participant B, the action-chain head, is chosen as subject and marked accordingly. Since the causative pivot, A, is also the tail of the action chain, it functions as direct object and takes the appropriate case (ACC or ABS).

Occasionally, however, there is more than one option for marking the causative pivot, as illustrated by these oft-cited Japanese examples:

(40) a. *taroo ga   ziroo o   ik-ase-ta*
      Taro NOM Jiro ACC go-CAUS-PAST
      'Taro caused Jiro to go'

    b. *taroo ga   ziroo ni   ik-ase-ta*
      Taro NOM Jiro DAT go-CAUS-PAST
      'Taro caused Jiro to go'

Cole notes that the choice between ACC and DAT is not semantically neutral: ACC is used when the subject is indifferent as to whether the pivot consents to go, whereas DAT intimates that the pivot goes willingly. In Hungarian, a similar contrast is marked by ACC vs. INSTR: ACC indicates that the subject personally conducts the activity (hence the pivot's role is involuntary), while instrumental case suggests that the subject effects the activity through instruction, so that the pivot has some responsibility for carrying it out. Cole's generalization, for these instances and others, is that DAT or INSTR is employed when the pivot is attributed a certain measure of agentivity.[30]

Following the spirit of Cole's analysis, I will say that DAT or INSTR marks the causative pivot as a "secondary agent". There are two essential facets to the characterization of this role. First, the pivot is not purely thematic--to some degree, it is responsible for initiating, executing, or furnishing the energy to drive the thematic process it undergoes (cf. Figure 11(b)). Additionally, the pivot's efforts are themselves induced by another, "primary agent" situated upstream along the action chain. A participant that satisfies these conditions thus finds itself in the situation diagramed in Figure 13(a). On the other hand, a pivot that fails to be marked as a secondary agent is simply a thematic object, as sketched in 13(b). It undergoes a thematic process driven by externally-supplied energy, but is not specifically portrayed as controlling or initiating this process.

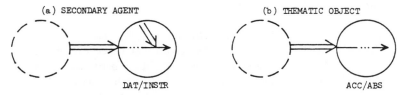

Figure 13.

I therefore maintain that 'secondary agent' is one conventional sense of DAT or INSTR case in a language which employs it (in contrast with ACC or ABS) to mark a causative pivot. While 'secondary agent' is obviously not the prototypical value of either DAT or INSTR, it is in each instance a natural semantic extension from the prototype; i.e. the similarities between 'secondary agent' on the one hand, and the experiencer or instrument role archetype on the other, are well within the range of those that motivate semantic extension in general. Whether this use of DAT or INSTR will occur in a given language is not claimed to be predictable--semantic extension is never subject to absolute predictability. It is merely suggested that when DAT or INSTR does in fact signal the agentivity of a causative pivot, this function reflects (or constitutes) a semantic value related nonarbitrarily to its other meanings.

First consider DAT. Our previous analysis of the experiencer archetype reveals a number of resemblances to the notion 'secondary agent' capable of motivating a semantic extension from the former to the latter. For one thing, several aspects of the secondary agent role belong to the realm of mental experience, including consent, volition, and the ability to carry out instructions. Recall, moreover, that EXPER ranks just behind AG on the initiative hierarchy (AG > EXPER > OTHER), which reflects the capacity of a participant to function as a source of energy. Finally, the characterization of EXPER as the active participant in the recipient domain (as opposed to the active participant in the source domain, or a passive participant in the recipient domain--see Figure 9) dovetails nicely with the intermediate status of a secondary agent.

This last consideration also holds for INSTR: the passive participant in the source domain is by nature intermediate, in contrast to the consistently initiative character of the active participant in the source domain, or the wholly noninitiative character of a passive participant in the recipient domain. More concretely, the positions of an instrument and a secondary agent are parallel with respect to the flow of energy through an action chain, in that each receives energy from an agent upstream but is also a type of energy source. Neither an instrument nor a secondary agent bears the ultimate responsibility for initiating an event, and each can be regarded as an extension of the primary agent.

5.3. Causatives derived from transitives

A causative based on a transitive verb, as in (39), has the abstract form [C===>[B===>[A→]]]. In contrast to the causatives based on intransitives, the action-chain tail (A) and causative pivot (B) are distinct participants. For the data that concerns us, the tail is selected as direct object and thus marked ACC or ABS. Our problem is to account for the case marking that occurs on the pivot, particularly in languages where more than one option is permitted.

Cole documents a number of attested patterns: DAT/INSTR/ACC (Quechua), DAT/INSTR (Kannada), DAT/ACC (Japanese, Modern Hebrew), and INSTR/ACC (Hungarian). He argues that agentivity is the primary factor determining case selection, but matters are in some respects more complex than with causatives derived from intransitives. For one thing, agentivity alone cannot account for a Quechua-type system with a three-way distinction. Furthermore, Japanese and Hebrew appear to make opposite uses of the same resources-- agentivity is associated with DAT in the former, but with ACC in the latter.

These complications turn out to be related, and both are resolvable with reference to the semantics of dative case. I have argued that the DAT category is centered in the domain of mental experience, with the EXPER archetype furnishing its prototypical value. It would therefore be natural for a language to mark a causative pivot with DAT case in just those instances where its role is primarily experiential, and to use some other case for nonexperiential pivots.[31] That this is true for Quechua is clear from Cole's discussion (though he does not specifically attribute DAT any meaning). He observes that the dative ending is found with causatives based on "verbs of experience" such as 'see', 'know', and 'remember':

(41) *nuqa runa-man rik^{h}u-či-ni*
    I   man-DAT see-CAUS-I
    'I showed it to the man'

In regard to Hebrew, Cole says that DAT marks nonagentive pivots, but his examples can also be accounted for in terms of experientiality. The causatives he cites with DAT (based on 'remember' and 'grasp an idea') clearly pertain to the realm of mental experience, whereas the experiential component of those taking ACC (based on 'swear a vow' and 'catch a ball') is decidedly less prominent.

I therefore propose that in some languages DAT case preempts the marking of causative pivots in those instances where the pivot's role approximates the experiencer archetype. Once such examples are set aside on the basis of this special treatment, the remainder lend themselves to an analysis which parallels that of causatives derived from intransitives: depending on the language, either DAT or INSTR acquires the extended semantic value 'secondary agent'; the degree of agentivity attributed to the pivot is then conveyed by whether it takes DAT/INSTR or some other case.

In Quechua, the pivot is marked as a secondary agent by instrumental case (DAT being reserved for experiencers). We thus find contrasts like the following:

(42) a. *nuqa fan-ta   rumi-ta   apa-či-ni*
       I   Juan-ACC rock-ACC carry-CAUS-I
       'I made Juan carry the rock'

     b. *nuqa fan-wan   rumi-ta   apa-či-ni*
       I   Juan-INSTR rock-ACC carry-CAUS-I
       'I had Juan carry the rock'

Cole describes the ACC as expressing direct, coercive causation, while INSTR indicates noncoercive, indirect causation. Now clearly, carrying a rock is inherently agentive, whether one does it under coercion or by consent. This content is not overridden by the case marking on the pivot, but rather provides the frame with respect to which the cases are semantically construed. Hence the ACC ending on 'Juan' in (42a) does not cancel its basic agentivity; it does however indicate that the pivot is only minimally agentive relative to the circumstances, i.e. that Juan exercises no independent judgment or volition, being an agent only from the standpoint of physically executing the activity. In (42b), on the other hand, the INSTR suffix specifies that to some degree Juan also manifests the mental aspects of agentivity. In short, though we can generalize that the INSTR/ACC contrast signals whether the pivot is construed as a secondary agent, the specific import of this notion is context dependent.

The only pattern noted by Cole that remains to be accounted for is the one witnessed in Kannada, where agentive pivots are marked with instrumental case, and nonagentive pivots with dative:

(43) a. *avanu   nanninda   bisketannu   tinnisidanu*
      he:NOM   me:INSTR   biscuit:ACC   eat:CAUS:PAST
      'He caused me to eat a biscuit'

    b. *avanu   nanage   bisketannu   tinnisidanu*
      he:NOM   me:DAT   biscuit:ACC   eat:CAUS:PAST
      'He fed me a biscuit'

Since the central values of either INSTR or DAT provide ample basis for a semantic extension to accommodate the role of a causative intermediary, it is not unexpected that in some languages both might undergo such a shift. The formal difference between the two cases is then exploited to code a contrast in the degree of agentivity attributed to the pivot--perhaps the very same contrast coded in other languages by INSTR vs. ACC or by DAT vs. ACC.[32]

Why should INSTR signal a higher degree of agentivity than DAT? This is natural in terms of role archetypes and their systemic relationships, because an instrument is the extension of an agent and belongs to the source domain, whereas experiencer is included among the thematic roles constituting the recipient domain. Of course, an equally good rationale can be offered for the opposite alignment: since the contrast in agentivity is largely confined to the mental sphere, a secondary agent could perfectly well be marked by DAT, and a nonvolitional intermediary by INSTR. The overall analysis therefore leads one to predict the existence of languages that mark the pivot in this fashion.

10. A usage-based model

The generative tradition has strongly emphasized the importance of "generality" in linguistic description.* The quest for generality is of course fundamental to the scientific enterprise; we may certainly accept its validity for linguistics. It is not necessarily obvious, however, how this abstract methodological imperative is best adapted and applied to the problems of our discipline, with its own distinctive subject matter. Generative theorists have applied it to linguistics in a specific manner that has had a powerful impact on their conception of linguistic theory and description. I believe their interpretation to be inappropriate for natural language, and its influence to have been a continuing source of difficulty in dealing with linguistic phenomena.

1. Two conceptions of generality

Summarized in (1) are three basic tenets of classic generative theory.

(1) a. Economy: A grammar should account for the widest possible array of
        data with the fewest possible statements.
    b. Generativity: A grammar is a set of statements specifying in full and
        explicit detail how expressions are constructed; it gives a
        well-defined set of expressions as output.
    c. Reductionism: If the rules of a grammar fully describe the composition
        of a particular structure, that structure is not itself individually
        listed in the grammar.

The economy principle holds that the shortest grammar is the best grammar, other things being equal; redundancy is therefore to be avoided. The generativity principle construes the grammar of a language as a self-contained algorithmic device, consisting primarily of rules for constructing well-formed expressions. The third principle follows from the other two: if a grammar is a set of rules for constructing expressions, and contains the fewest statements possible, then any expression constructed by these rules must itself be omitted from the grammar. Separately listing an expression computable by general rules would be redundant (and redundancy is evil).

Though initially this seems quite reasonable, in practice it has had some unfortunate consequences. One result is that virtually all research activity has been dedicated to searching for general rules and universal principles. Now obviously, the search for generalizations is a prime objective--the question I raise is one of balance, and whether the generalizations rest on adequate empirical foundations. It is apparent, for example, that generative grammarians have never dealt seriously with lexicon in its own terms. Nor do they often attempt, after stating a rule in general fashion, to document the actual extent of its applicability and the various factors that influence its felicity (cf. Gross 1979). The abstract systems of rules and principles constructed by theorists seldom emerge organically from the sensitive, fine-grained description of fully representative data (hence their mortality rate is high and their lifetime often tragically short). In brief, all the glory attaches to general principles and abstract theory; careful attention to the minutiae of language data is left for those without the insight and imagination to be good theorists.

These practical consequences are clearly a matter of judgment, and we will pursue them no further. More significant is the issue of whether the general methodological imperative of generality is appropriately implemented in linguistics by the positions in (1). One can argue, for instance, that generativity is purchased only at the price of arbitrary assumptions and apriori boundaries that exclude from the description substantial portions of the phenomenon that is putatively being described (a case in point is the distinction between semantics and pragmatics--cf. Haiman 1980; Langacker 1987a: chapter 4). One can also suggest that economy and reductionism, as defined in (1), are of dubious validity in any framework that makes a serious claim of psychological reality. We will focus on this latter point.

The assumptions in (1) constitute a "minimalist" conception of linguistic knowledge; the grammar of a language is reduced to the smallest possible set of statements, with all redundancy avoided. It is also a "top-down" conception emphasizing computation: anything which follows from general statements is omitted from the grammar, on the assumption that it is computed rather than being represented individually. However, we have no apriori reason to believe that the cognitive representation of a language conforms to this conception. It is plausible, psychologically, to suppose that speakers represent linguistic structures in different ways, with considerable redundancy built in. It is also reasonable to assume that many structures are learned as established units even when they also follow from general principles--the computability of a structure does not in principle preclude its learnability and inclusion as a distinct element in the cognitive representation of the linguistic system. The generative grammarian might reply that such considerations belong to the theory of performance, not a theory of competence. But at best the competence/performance distinction is unclear and problematic; as things stand, to invoke it in this manner is essentially vacuous. In actual practice, the effect of this distinction has been to insulate the framework from any possible attack based on its obvious psychological implausibility.

If claims of psychological reality are taken seriously, questions of economy assume the status of empirical issues, as opposed to methodological ones. Is it in fact true that a speaker arrives at any kind of redundancy-free representation of linguistic structure? Do speakers in fact avoid learning specific structures as separate units if they happen to conform to general rules? A description of linguistic ability that answers these questions negatively cannot legitimately be attacked on the grounds that the description fails to achieve maximum simplicity: the question of simplicity only arises for two descriptions of the same range of data, but the issue at stake is precisely that of determining what the relevant data is (i.e. what are the cognitive structures that we are trying to model?). One could just as well omit phonology from the grammar on the grounds that a grammar without a phonological component is simpler than a grammar with one.

For a specific example, consider such expressions as *dogs, trees, toes, pins, bells, walls,* and *eyes,* which instantiate a regular pattern of plural-noun formation. Clearly, a regular rule of plural formation can be given for English, and these expressions conform to the rule. According to the principle of reductionism, incorporating this rule in the grammar of English precludes the listing of individual plural forms like *dogs, trees, toes,* etc. The rules allow their computation from the noun stems, hence their inclusion in the grammar would be redundant.

The goal of cognitive grammar is to characterize those psychological structures that constitute a speaker's linguistic ability, i.e. his grasp of established linguistic convention. This notion inspires an alternate approach to forms like *dogs, trees, toes,* etc. A typical speaker uses frequently-occurring expressions like these on countless occasions; at least some of them must attain the status of units (i.e. familiar, thoroughly mastered structures--cognitive routines). In fact, the pattern itself can only be learned through the observation of instantiating expressions, some of which most likely become units before the pattern is extracted; it is implausible to suppose that these plural forms suddenly lose their status as familiar units when the rule is acquired, and must henceforth be computed from scratch.

Adopted instead is the alternative conception sketched in Figure 1. The grammar of a language is defined as a structured inventory of conventional

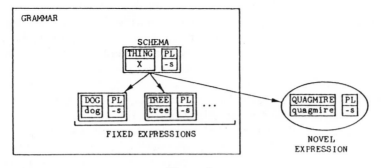

Figure 1.

linguistic units. Specific expressions are included in this inventory provided that they have the status of units--a reasonable assumption for *dogs, trees,* etc. Also included in the grammar are schemas extracted to represent the commonality observed in specific expressions (both units and nonunits). The schema corresponding to a grammatical pattern can be regarded as a template for the construction of instantiating expressions. Hence the schema for nouns like *dogs, trees,* etc. is a complex structure whose internal organization is exactly parallel to these plural forms, except that a schematic noun stem (given as [THING/X]) occurs in lieu of a specific noun stem. The schema therefore captures the pertinent generalization, and its categorization of instantiating expressions constitutes their structural description. The coexistence in the grammar of the schema and instantiations affords the speaker alternate ways of accessing a complex but regular expression with unit status: it can simply be activated directly, or else the speaker can employ the schema to compute it. Moreover, the schema is available for the computation of novel instantiations (e.g. *quagmires*); if such an expression is frequently employed, it may very well become established as a unit and thus be incorporated per se in the grammar. The specific array of instantiations having the status of units doubtless varies from speaker to speaker (and changes with experience for an individual speaker), but this is not considered problematic.

Generative grammarians have normally resisted the idea that regular expressions should be listed in a grammar, on the presumption that listing entails a failure to capture significant generalizations. I refer to this attitude as the "rule/list fallacy". It is fallacious because it tacitly presupposes only two options: rules vs. lists. But nothing in principle prevents a third option, namely positing both rules (i.e. schemas) and lists, as shown in Figure 1. By their very nature, schemas embody generalizations. The implicit assumption that rules and lists are mutually exclusive merely reflects the generative conception of economy, as described in (1), whose appropriateness for natural language is precisely what is at issue.

In describing cognitive grammar as a "usage-based" model of language structure, I have in mind the maximalist, nonreductive, and bottom-up character of the general approach (as compared to the minimalist, reductive, and top-down spirit of the generative tradition). The full import of this description will gradually become apparent. For now, let us briefly examine the basic thrust of each term.

The minimalist spirit of generative theory reflects an archetypal conception of the linguistic system as a self-contained and well-behaved set of general rules; though nobody believes that a language consists solely of general rules, this archetype strongly influences virtually every aspect of generative theory and descriptive practice. By contrast, the maximalist conception views the linguistic system as a massive, highly redundant inventory of conventional units. These units run the gamut from full generality to complete idiosyncrasy, and no special significance attaches to any distinctions one might draw along this scale. Valid generalizations are sought and captured (represented in the grammar by schematic units), but fully general statements are probably a distinct minority: rather than being prototypical for language, exceptionless rules are special, atypical cases. Moreover, the maximalist outlook leads one to anticipate a gradation between linguistic and extralinguistic knowledge; while it does not deny the possibility of innate structures specific to language, neither linguistic ability nor the grammar of a particular language is conceived as a discrete "module" with well-defined boundaries (*pace* Fodor 1983).

Cognitive grammar is nonreductive by virtue of recognizing both rules or patterns and the individual knowledge of specific structures that conform to them. A schema and its instantiations represent different facets of linguistic knowledge, and if they have the status of units, both are included in the grammar of a language. One advantage of this approach is its ability to accommodate, with no special apparatus, instances where a fixed expression is more detailed and elaborate than the structure that a rule or schema would allow one to compute.[1] The grammar is not conceived as a constructive device giving expressions as "output", but simply as providing a speaker with an inventory of symbolic resources that he--the speaker--can employ for the construction of novel expressions, using all the information and abilities at his disposal. As one such resource, the schema describing a pattern of composition is not itself responsible for actually constructing an expression. Instead it serves a categorizing function: it furnishes the minimal specifications an expression must observe to be categorized as a valid instantiation of the pattern it embodies. An expression may satisfy these specifications, and thus be judged compatible with the schema, even if its characterization is more precise and fully articulated than anything predictable just from the schema and the component morphemes.

Finally, the model is said to take a "bottom-up" (rather than a top-down) approach. What this amounts to is a redistribution of emphasis: instead of being almost solely concerned with general rules and principles, we must also give substantial weight to their arrays of conventional instantiations, investigating the actual extension of the patterns in question and the factors that influence it. Furthermore, since patterns are abstracted from specific instances, we need to investigate the schematization process. We know, for example, that speakers learn and manipulate specific expressions; but we do not know, in any direct way, precisely what degree of schematization they achieve, i.e. how abstract and general the rules are that they manage to extract from more specific structures. I suspect that speakers differ somewhat in this regard, and do not invariably arrive at the highest-level schemas that the data would support. In any event, the omnipotence of high-level generalizations is not a matter of apriori necessity. Though regularities are obviously noted and employed in the computation of novel expressions, it is quite conceivable that low-level schemas are more important for this purpose than highly abstract schemas representing the broadest generalizations possible. If high-level schemas are extracted, they may be of only secondary significance, serving more of an organizing function than an active computational one.

2. The network conception

Critical to the formulation of a usage-based theory is a coherent view of linguistic categorization. A particular model of categorization, the criterial attribute model, has generally been accepted without serious question in the Western intellectual tradition. More recently, the prototype model has been advanced as an alternative with greater claims to cognitive plausibility. My own proposal, the network model, represents a synthesis of prototype theory and categorization based on schemas. (For general discussion, see Lakoff 1982, 1987; Langacker 1987a: chapters 10-11.)

In a strict formulation of the criterial attribute model, a category is defined by a fixed set of properties or features. These attributes are necessary and sufficient conditions for category membership, affording absolute predictability in this regard: if an entity possesses all the criterial properties, it is a member of the class; otherwise it is not. Class membership is consequently an all-or-nothing affair; there are no degrees of membership, nor does a category display any significant internal structure.

The prototype model was pioneered by Eleanor Rosch, and has been presented and supported in numerous publications (e.g. Rosch 1973, 1975, 1977, 1978). In this model, a category is defined with reference to a prototype, i.e. a schematized representation of typical instances. Entities that conform to this prototype are accepted unproblematically as "central" members of the class. Nonconforming members may nevertheless be assimilated to the category as "peripheral" members provided that they are judged as being similar to the prototype in certain respects. A class is structured internally by virtue of its organization into central and peripheral members; moreover, class membership is a matter of degree, reflecting the distance of a member from the prototype. Because there is no specific checklist of criterial features, membership in a category is not subject to absolute predictability (indeed, there need be no significant features that are shared by all class members). Whether an entity qualifies depends on the judgment of the categorizer, and his tolerance in accepting members that diverge from the prototype. There is no fixed limit on how far something can depart from the prototype and still be assimilated to the class, if the categorizer is perceptive or clever enough to find some point of resemblance to typical instances.

The model I have adopted for cognitive grammar incorporates the prototype model as a special case. The members of a category are analyzed as nodes in a network, linked to one another by various sorts of categorizing relationships. One kind of categorizing relationship is extension from a prototype, which may either be a local prototype or the global prototype for the category as a whole. The notion of extension, symbolized by a dashed arrow, implies some conflict in specifications between the basic and extended values; hence [A] ---> [B] indicates that [B] is incompatible with [A] in some respect, but is nevertheless categorized by [A]. A second kind of categorizing relationship holds between a schema and a structure that elaborates or instantiates the schema. Symbolized by a solid arrow, e.g. [A] → [B], the relationship amounts to one of specialization: [B] conforms to the specifications of [A], but is characterized with finer precision and detail.[2] A third kind of categorizing relationship, [A] <---> [B], amounts to a perception of mutual similarity; it differs from extension only by lacking directionality. For any type of categorizing relationship, we can speak of the distance between [A] and [B], i.e. how much modification or elaboration of [A] is required to arrive at [B]. Beyond this, the nodes and categorizing relationships comprising the network vary greatly in their cognitive salience and degree of entrenchment.

The network model is conveniently illustrated by the alternate senses of a polysemous lexical item. A fragment of the network required for the English verb *run* is presented in Figure 2. With heavy lines (to indicate special cognitive salience) I have singled out the global category prototype, namely the conception of rapid bipedal human locomotion; this is presumably the meaning that is acquired first, and also the one most likely to be activated in a neutral context. We cannot be certain how far ''upward'' a speaker extends this network through the process of abstraction (schematization), and in particular, whether he extracts a ''superschema'' having all other nodes as direct or indirect instantiations. Nor do we know how far ''downward'' a speaker articulates the network into progressively more specialized notions. Speakers may very well differ in these respects, and also in the specific set of categorizing relationships they establish between nodes. But although the precise configuration of the network is variable and even indeterminate, the need to postulate some type of network is seemingly beyond dispute: the meanings of a commonly-used lexical item define a complex category, i.e. one that is not reducible to a single structure (node).

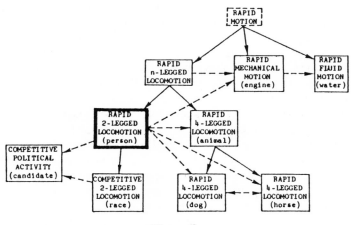

Figure 2.

A strict reductionist approach would seek maximum economy by positing only a single structure to represent the meaning of a lexical category. However, if our goal is to properly characterize a speaker's knowledge of linguistic convention, any such account is unworkable. From neither the category prototype alone, nor from an all-subsuming superschema (should there be one), is it possible to predict the exact array of extended or specialized values conventionally associated with a lexeme (out of all those values that are cognitively plausible). A speaker must learn specifically, for instance, that *run* is predicated of people, animals, engines, water, hosiery, noses, and candidates for political office; the conventions of English might well be different. Equally deficient is the atomistic approach of treating the individual senses as distinct and unrelated lexical items. The claim of massive homonymy implied by such an analysis is simply unwarranted--it is not by accident, but rather by virtue of intuitively evident semantic relationships, that the meanings are symbolized by the same form. A network representation provides all the necessary information: an inventory of senses describing the expression's conventional range of usage; the relationships these senses bear to one another; schemas expressing the generalizations supported by a given range of values; and specifications of distance and cognitive salience.

Some classic problems of lexical analysis are readily addressed in terms of the network model, namely the distinction between polysemy and homonymy, and that between ambiguity and vagueness. The first distinction hinges on whether the various senses associated with a given form are semantically related. In the network model, semantic relatedness is a matter of degree, so polysemy vs. homonymy does not reduce to a simple dichotomy. Two senses may be related directly, by a categorizing relationship, or else indirectly, through a chain of such relationships. Direct relationships range continuously along the distance parameter (e.g. the 'rapid 4-legged locomotion' sense of *run* lies closer to the prototype 'rapid 2-legged locomotion' than does 'rapid mechanical motion'). Moreover, relationships at a particular distance may differ in salience (consider the gradual "fading" of conventional metaphors). Since speakers are very adept at perceiving semantic relationships, and since comparison is encouraged by common symbolization, it is seldom safe to assume that no connection whatever is established between the alternate senses associated with a form. Even a tenuous relationship, dimly perceived, is still a relationship, and though certain phenomena may presuppose a close or salient connection (so that, for instance, *Tom and his dog are both running* is more felicitous than *Tom and the water are both running*), there is no basis for positing a specific cut-off point along the scale of semantic relatedness where polysemy abruptly stops and homonymy begins. Homonymy is better analyzed as the endpoint along the cline of relatedness--it is the limiting or degenerate case of polysemy, where the only relationship between two senses consists in their common phonological realization. Hence the actual descriptive problem is not to distinguish between homonymy and polysemy, but rather to characterize semantic networks as fully and accurately as possible.

Whereas the issue of polysemy pertains to whether two or more senses are semantically related, the distinction between ambiguity and vagueness depends on whether multiple senses should be posited in the first place. A commonly employed test concerns the number of interpretations supported by sentences like those in (2):

(2) a. *Tom has an uncle, and Bill does too.*
   b. *Tom has two ears, and Bill does too.*

A possible interpretation of (2a) is that Tom has a maternal uncle (i.e. a mother's brother) while Bill's uncle is paternal (a father's brother), or conversely; the anaphoric relationship between the clauses does not require that the two uncles be of the same type. By contrast, (2b) cannot easily be construed as meaning that Tom has two organs of hearing, while Bill has two cobs of corn--both clauses must be interpreted as referring to the same type of *ear*. From such observations, it is normally concluded that *uncle* displays vagueness rather than ambiguity: it has the single meaning 'parent's brother' (unspecified for the gender of the linking relative) rather than the two distinct senses 'mother's brother' and 'father's brother'. On the other hand, *ear* is ambiguous, with anaphora sensitive to the difference between the two meanings.

David Tuggy (1981) has argued that the felicity of interpretations involving a mixture of types is often a matter of degree. Thus (3a) seems peculiar if Tom is an artist doing a portrait while Bill is putting a new coat of paint on a fence, but the sentence is much less infelicitous if Tom is painting a massive mural instead.

(3) a. *Tom is painting, and Bill is too.*
   b. *Tom is talking, and Bill is too.*
   c. *Tom is writing, and Bill is too.*

If Tom is giving a formal lecture, and Bill is outside in the corridor chatting with a friend, (3b) is less than perfect, but much better than (2b) under the mixture-of-type interpretation; the same is true of (3c) if Tom is a novelist at work while Bill is simply writing a letter to his mother. Moreover, while (4a) is marginal (unless the bacon has burst into flames), the same mixture-of-type interpretation seems relatively natural in (4b).

(4) a. *?The fire is burning, and the bacon is too.*
   b. *Well, the fire is still burning. Oh my god! The bacon is too!*

Examples like these can be multiplied indefinitely, and suggest the inadequacy of a fully discrete analysis that posits either a single vague sense or two distinct senses.

Tuggy further suggests a promising way of handling these graded phenomena in a usage-based approach employing the network model. It is assumed, first, that schemas and instantiations may coexist in the grammar as different facets of a speaker's linguistic knowledge (cf. Figure 2). Thus, if the semantic network for *uncle* contains the schematic node [PARENT'S BROTHER], this does not preclude its also containing the instantiations [MOTHER'S BROTHER] and [FATHER'S BROTHER]. Moreover, the units of a grammar differ in their cognitive salience, which correlates with the likelihood of their activation. For seemingly clear instances of vagueness, we can hypothesize that the schema is quite salient relative to its instantiations; the reverse is postulated for clear-cut instances of ambiguity. This type of analysis is illustrated in Figure 3, where the supposed difference in salience is indicated by the use of heavy-line vs. dashed-line boxes. Because the gender of linking relatives is not a significant factor in English kinship terminology, it is plausible to assume that [PARENT'S BROTHER] is more salient in the network for *uncle* than either of its instantiations. For those speakers who associate the two senses of *ear*, a schema may well be extracted to represent their perceived commonality. However, this schema must be quite abstract (since the similarity is so tenuous), and would seem to be of little cognitive or communicative utility, so its salience is presumably quite low.

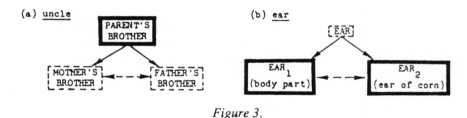

Figure 3.

Let us assume that the felicity of anaphoric expressions like those in (2) depends on the same semantic structure being activated in the construal of each clause. In the case of *uncle*, the large disparity in cognitive salience ensures that [PARENT'S BROTHER] is virtually always activated in preference to its instantiations; hence the common construal of *uncle* in the two clauses renders (2a) felicitous. By contrast, the specific senses of *ear* are far more likely to be activated than their schema, with the consequence that the felicity of (2b) varies depending on whether the same sense is activated for both clauses. For relatively clear examples like these, the network analysis is roughly equivalent to one that simply posits a single sense for vague expressions and two senses for ambiguous expressions. Its advantages are more apparent for examples of intermediate status, like those in (3) and (4). For these we need only assume that the specific and schematic senses have sufficient cognitive salience to compete for activation. *Talk*, for instance, has a specific value pertaining to formal oral presentations, another relating to informal conversation, and a schematic sense which abstracts away from the social context and focuses on the verbal activity per se. The felicity of a sentence like (3b) depends on which of these structures prevails when it is constructed or interpreted on a particular occasion. If Tom is giving a lecture and Bill is chatting with a friend, (3b) can nevertheless be judged felicitous when one is concerned primarily with the activity itself, so that the schema is activated for the construal of both clauses. When, instead, the emphasis lies on the social aspects of the two events, the specific values are activated in lieu of the schema; this difference in the construal of *talk* in the two clauses renders (3b) problematic (its degree of deviance reflecting the cognitive distance between the two senses). In principle, then, the fluidity of well-formedness judgments for sentences like (3)-(4) can be explicated in terms of a network whose elements range along a continuous scale of salience and ease of activation.

Let us conclude this initial discussion with some brief remarks on the growth and development of networks. There is an intimate connection between the "outward" growth of a network through extension, on the one hand, and its "upward" growth through schematization, on the other. The process of extension occurs because a speaker perceives some similarity between the basic value (i.e. the local or global prototype) and the extended value. This similarity perception represents the commonality of the basic and extended values, so it constitutes a schema having the two for instantiations, as depicted in Figure 4(a). The similarity perception per se need not be cognitively salient or achieve the status of a unit--it may be only a fleeting occurrence. Still, a category's outward extension from the prototype should tend to be accompanied by a certain amount of upward growth, as schemas are extracted to generalize over a more diverse array of category members.

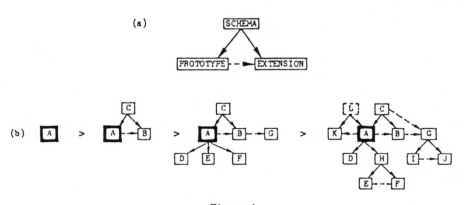

Figure 4.

In fact, the growth of a network from the category prototype probably involves a variety of phenomena, as depicted abstractly in Figure 4(b). Likely sorts of development include at least the following: (i) extension, with or without the implied schema achieving unit status (compare the extensions [A] ---> [B] and [B] ---> [G]); (ii) the "downward" articulation of a category as finer distinctions are made (e.g. the differentiation of [A] into [D], [E], and [F]); (iii) the extraction and interpolation of subschemas for nodes already present (note [H]); (iv) the incorporation of additional categorizing relationships, as direct comparisons happen to be made between indirectly-associated nodes (observe [C] ---> [G]); and (v) adjustments in the entrenchment and salience of elements, as determined by the vicissitudes of usage and experience.

3. General applicability

The semantic pole of a polysemous lexical item has served thus far as our prime example of a complex category, i.e. one whose characterization cannot be reduced to any single structure. I have proposed that a complex category be described as a network, where nodes with varying degrees of cognitive salience are connected by categorizing relationships. The network model subsumes the prototype model as a special case, and further accommodates taxonomic relationships based on schematization; it offers an integrated account of these modes of categorization, and holds considerable promise of empirical adequacy. I now suggest that the utility of these notions extends beyond the realm of lexical polysemy: linguistic categories are in general complex, and networks are required for their proper description. Clearly, the network model conforms to the maximalist, nonreductive, and bottom-up spirit of the usage-based approach. In fact, it is by adopting this model of categorization that cognitive grammar achieves and implements its usage-based character.

For a nonlexical example, consider the analysis of a phoneme as a complex category (cf. Nathan 1986). Let us suppose that the phoneme /a/ (in a particular language) occurs only in the syllables /a/, /pa/, /ta/, and /ka/. Each preceding consonant induces some phonetic modification of /a/, however minor it might be. This phoneme consequently has at least four allophones, namely [a], [^{p}a], [^{t}a], and [^{k}a] (where [^{p}a] is the allophone induced by /p/, and so on). The allophone [a], which stands alone as a syllable, is plausibly regarded as the basic allophone and equated with the category prototype; the others then function as context-induced extensions from this prototype, as diagramed in Figure 5. Moreover, speakers may well extract a schema to represent the commonality of the various allophones. Shown as [^{x}a] in the diagram, the schema is neutral as to whether and how the basic vocalism of [a] is modified by a preceding consonant.

The network model therefore reconciles two classic views on the nature of a phoneme: that which analyzes a phoneme as a set of allophones; and that which treats it as a unitary but necessarily abstract entity (i.e. a schema). The nonreductionist character of the analysis also accords with traditional phonemic

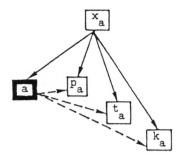

Figure 5.

descriptions, which provide a list of allophones for each phoneme, and state the environments that condition each derived or nonbasic allophone. The necessity for a nonreductionist account is readily apparent in this domain, since a speaker's phonetic ability does not reside in any single structure. A speaker who fully controls the phonetics of his language is able to pronounce not only the basic allophone, but also the full array of derived allophones, properly distributed. Each implies an articulatory (also an auditory) routine that a speaker masters as part of his internal representation of the linguistic system. These units are properly included in the grammar of a language, for they constitute one facet of a speaker's grasp of linguistic convention.

The inventory of conventional units comprising the grammar of a language is structured, in the sense that some units function as components of others. Often, in fact, a unit owes its specific character to a more inclusive structure in which it occurs, and is therefore confined to this structure (at least initially). For instance, the notation of Figure 5 should not be interpreted as implying that [^{p}a], [^{t}a], and [^{k}a] are free-standing units that can occur independently; they occur only in the context of the respective syllabic units [[p][^{p}a]], [[t][^{t}a]], and [[k][^{k}a]], since the preceding consonant induces their distinguishing phonetic properties. The categorizing relationship [a] ---> [^{p}a] of Figure 5 is thus more adequately represented in Figure 6(a), which shows the extended variant in the environment that determines and supports it.

The process of "accommodation", whereby a structure is adjusted to make it compatible with its context, is obviously a major factor in the evolution of complex categories. In this maximalist and nonreductive framework, a variant arising through accommodation is recognized as a distinct entity, a separate node in the network describing the category, regardless of how fully or automatically the context determines its specific properties. Let us suppose, for instance, that *run* is first learned with reference to the canonical, upright, 2-legged locomotion of

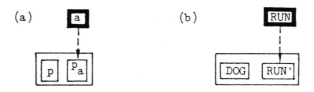

Figure 6.

humans. Hence the semantic pole of this verb is limited initially to a single value, [RUN] (which serves as the prototype of the fully-articulated category that eventually develops). What if the learner now observes the rapid locomotion of a dog? He may himself decide to use the verb *run* to describe this activity, or he may hear someone else describe it in this fashion. In either event, this usage implies and induces a sense that diverges from the prototype in readily observable respects: the actor is canine rather than human, it uses four legs rather than two, and so on. When predicated of a dog, *run* thus accommodates to its subject through the semantic extension [RUN] ---> [RUN'], as sketched in Figure 6(b). The accommodation is easily made, and essentially predictable from the specifications of the subject, but the extended value [RUN'] is nonetheless distinct from [RUN] and takes its place in the network constituting the semantic pole of the lexical item.

In similar fashion, I would posit numerous semantic variants of *eat*, accommodated to the nature of the food consumed and the specific activity required for its consumption. To be sure, I have no way of knowing just how finely articulated this category is, and it is doubtful that the lowest-level variants have any substantial measure of cognitive salience. It is nevertheless a conventional fact of English usage--not something a speaker must decide anew on each occasion--that *eat* is employed for such diverse activities as the consumption of meat, bananas, peanuts, and soup. There are standard objections to this analysis; they pertain to the proliferation of meanings, the mixture of pragmatic and semantic considerations, and the failure to extract a unifying generalization. However, all these objections reflect the minimalist, reductive bias of contemporary semantic theory, which is precisely what is at issue, and have little force from the standpoint of cognitive grammar. In particular, the postulation of specific variants does not prevent us from expressing the unifying generalization by means of a coexisting schema, which may very well have greater salience.

Like its semantic pole, the phonological pole of a lexical item is a complex category revealingly described as a network. Even an expression not generally thought of as having multiple allomorphs can nevertheless assume a variety of specific values (some of which may establish themselves as units) depending on such factors as tempo and prosody. The applicability of the network model is of course more obvious for expressions that do show allomorphic variation. Consider the noun *leaf*, whose phonological pole is diagramed in Figure 7(a). The basic allomorph, [lif], functions as the category prototype (it possibly subsumes more specific variants, as just noted). Since the plural is *leaves*, we must also recognize the allomorph [liv] (occurring only in the context of the plural construction), which constitutes an extension from the basic allomorph; representing the commonality of [lif] and [liv] is the schema [liF] (where [F] neutralizes the voicing contrast of [f] and [v]--i.e. it is equivalent to an "archiphoneme"). Though Figure 7(a) depicts only the phonological pole, observe that the context for [liv] requires bipolar characterization: the suffix triggering the phonological extension must be the plural morpheme [PL/z] in particular, and not the possessive.

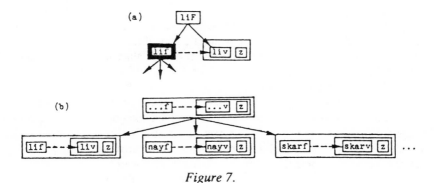

Figure 7.

The voicing of final [f] in the plural is of course not limited to *leaf*. Numerous other nouns display the same alternation, e.g. *hoof/hooves, life/lives, elf/elves, knife/knives, scarf/scarves, shelf/shelves, wife/wives, loaf/loaves*. Although the pattern is not productive (consider *fifes, reefs, puffs*, etc.), it does constitute a regularity that speakers may incorporate as part of their cognitive representation of the linguistic system. In the present framework, regularities are expressed by schemas. It is assumed that any configuration of structures--even a categorizing relationship--is potentially subject to schematization, should the proper circumstances arise. Here the conditions for schematization are indeed met: we find a series of nouns, all conforming to the schematic characterization [...f], which undergo parallel modifications in the context of the plural construction. The phonological network for each of these nouns includes a categorizing relationship between the basic allomorph ending in [f] and a secondary allomorph ending in [v], this latter occurring only in combination with the plural morpheme; thus, alongside [lif] ---> [liv] we find [nayf] ---> [nayv], [skarf] ---> [skarv], etc. A schema can be extracted to represent the commonality of these categorizations, as shown in Figure 7(b). Though abstract, this schema is itself a categorizing relationship of phonological extension, like any of its instantiations. Also like its instantiations, it contains a specification of the conditioning environment: the extended variant [...v] occurs only with [PL/z] (again, the semantic pole is not shown).

The schema depicted in Figure 7(b) is the cognitive grammar equivalent of a morphophonemic rule. It expresses a systematic relationship between the basic form of a noun and the special form it assumes in a particular morphological context. However, the asymmetry implied by the direction of the arrow, in either [...f] ---> [...v] or its instantiations, is not interpreted derivationally, i.e. as the relationship between an "underlying" and a "surface" representation. It is interpreted instead as the asymmetry inherent to comparison and categorization: [...f] is the standard of comparison (category prototype), while [...v] is the target of comparison (a peripheral member assimilated to the category through resemblance to the prototype). Apart from the type of structures that figure in the categorization, there is no fundamental difference between [...f] ---> [...v] (or [lif] ---> [liv], etc.) and the semantic extension of a lexical item.

The general applicability of the network model is starting to become apparent. With a limited set of constructs, this model offers a unified account of many facets of linguistic organization that are normally approached using very different techniques and descriptive devices. What distinguishes the various domains of linguistic structure is not the prevalence of complex categories requiring networks for their description, but rather the types of structures that function as nodes in these networks. In the case of a phoneme, these structures are single phonological segments (allophones and the schemas extracted from them). For a morpheme, the network at the semantic pole has individual senses as nodes, whereas allomorphs serve as nodes at the phonological pole. The network model is also adopted for the description of rules and their conventional instantiations, in which case the individual nodes of the network have a complex internal structure. In Figure 1, which depicts a combinatory rule (one pattern of plural-noun formation), the nodes include a schema and various instantiations; each node incorporates two symbolic units as component structures, together with the composite structure (not separately shown) resulting from their integration. The morphophonemic rule of Figure 7(b) is also modeled as a network; it is a different type of rule because the nodes comprising this network have a different type of internal structure: rather than a combinatory relationship between symbolic units, each node consists in a categorizing relationship between two phonological sequences (allomorphs).

The rule of Figure 7(b) is considered morphophonemic because it depends on a morphological context. The phonological extension [...f] ---> [...v] is limited to the plural-noun construction, which therefore figures in the characterization of each node. What if a pattern of phonological extension is not restricted to any particular morphological environment? In that case, no such environment is specified in the schema or its instantiations, and we recognize the rule as being purely phonological. For example, in words like *kitten, button, sentence*, etc., where [t] precedes the syllabic nasal [n̩], the [t] is commonly replaced by a glottal stop.

Hence each word has two phonological variants linked by a categorizing relationship, e.g. [kɪtn̩] ---> [kɪʔn̩]. From some array of specific categorizations of this sort, a schema is extracted to capture the regularity, as shown in Figure 8. This particular schema (unlike the previous one) is sufficiently salient or accessible to be readily invoked for the computation of novel instantiations. When activated in the context of a specific structure containing [tn̩], the schematic extension [...tn̩...] ---> [...ʔn̩...] yields a variant having [ʔn̩] in its stead; even nonsense words are likely to be pronounced in this fashion.

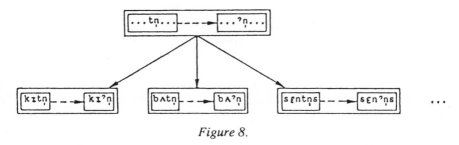

Figure 8.

A phonological rule is therefore analyzed in cognitive grammar as a pattern of phonological extension. Phonological and semantic extension are viewed as being directly analogous, with any differences between them attributable to inherent properties of the semantic and phonological domains. I will pursue their parallelism only to the point of noting that semantic extension is also subject to schematization and often follows conventional patterns. One such pattern, illustrated in (5), involves extending the term for an animal to indicate a person who resembles that animal in certain respects.

(5) a. *He's a pig.*
   b. *You're a rat.*
   c. *That lawyer is a real fox.*

Pig, rat, and *fox* are among the numerous animal names conventionally employed in this fashion; thus the semantic network associated with *pig*, for example, incorporates the categorizing relationship [PIG] ---> [PIG-LIKE PERSON]. Specific relationships of this sort give rise to the schema [ANIMAL] ---> [ANIMAL-LIKE PERSON], which is freely used for the computation of novel instantiations. When I call somebody an *ostrich*, a *fennec*, or even a *veritable brontosaurus*, I am thereby conforming to the conventions of English, even if these particular terms have never before been applied to people.

4. Distribution

Questions of distribution and productivity figure prominently in contemporary linguistic theory. Many theoretical constructs have at one time or another been invoked to deal with these matters (e.g. diacritics, rule features, major vs. minor rules, disjunctive ordering). Moreover, they are often cited in support of particular analyses and claims concerning the organization of linguistic systems. For example, it is not always possible to predict, on the basis of purely semantic or phonological properties, precisely which lexical items are eligible to undergo a given rule; this absence of absolute predictability is commonly taken as establishing the autonomy of grammar and the need for special, "grammatical" features and classes. It is also sometimes assumed that full generality is criterial for syntactic rules; any rule displaying only partial productivity is assigned to some other component of the grammar (e.g. lexicon or morphology).

Cognitive grammar's approach to these issues reflects its emphasis on naturalness, conceptual unification, and austerity in the adoption of theoretical constructs. The highly restrictive content requirement allows only three types of units in the grammar of a language: (i) semantic, phonological, and symbolic units that occur overtly; (ii) schemas for such structures; and (iii) categorizing relationships. A separate domain of specifically grammatical structure is thereby precluded, as are any descriptive elements (e.g. features or diacritics) devoid of both semantic and phonological content. A unified treatment is proposed for lexicon, morphology, and syntax: all are described by means of symbolic units exclusively; these traditionally recognized areas form a gradation of symbolic structures divided only arbitrarily into distinct components. To assume that productivity is coextensive with a particular structural domain, or delimits a coherent, self-contained body of phenomena, is at best gratuitous.

We must now consider how such a theory is capable of handling the problems of variable productivity and nonpredictable distribution. Granted that certain rules are applicable only to a limited class of structures, and granted further that membership in this class is not always predictable on semantic or phonological grounds, how does one specify the proper restrictions? As we will see, the answer lies in the usage-based character of the framework, together with the network model of complex categories.

Linguistic expressions are symbolic, each residing in the relationship between a semantic pole and a phonological pole. Grammar consists of patterns for combining simpler symbolic expressions to form progressively larger ones. In cognitive grammar, these patterns (i.e. grammatical rules) are analyzed as schematized expressions--they are themselves complex symbolic structures, parallel in formation to the expressions they schematize, but characterized at a level of abstraction that neutralizes the differences among them. These combinatory patterns are equivalent to grammatical constructions, so the schemas describing them are called constructional schemas. Each specifies the way in which two or more component structures are integrated, at the semantic and phonological poles, to form a bipolar composite structure. Constructional schemas capture generalizations, and serve as templates for the assembly of novel expressions.

I have already argued that constructional schemas coexist in the grammar of a language with those of their instantiations that have the status of units (cf. Figure 1). These instantiations need not be limited to specific expressions--we can also posit subschemas at various levels of abstraction, corresponding to subpatterns discernible in the data. In fact, these structures form a network, as they are linked to one another through relationships of schematicity, and possibly through other types of categorization as well. A grammatical construction can therefore be regarded as a complex category: it does not reside in any single structure, but rather in a family of structures connected by categorizing relationships. Internally, each node of this network is quite complex, comprising an entire constructional schema or subschema, or else a specific composite expression.

These notions are illustrated in Figure 9, which sketches the network corresponding to one pattern of past-tense marking in English. The maximal generalization is captured by the topmost schema, which says, in effect, that a verb stem containing [I] may form its past tense by ablauting this vowel to [æ]. In this abbreviatory notation, only the two component structures are explicitly indicated: [PROCESS/...I...] is the verb stem, and [PAST/...I...--->...æ...] is the appropriate allomorph of the past-tense morpheme; a more complete representation would also

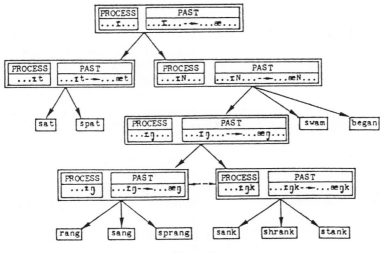

Figure 9.

show the nature of their integration at the two poles, and the composite structure that results (in this case [PROCESS-PAST/...æ...]). The two immediate instantiations of this schema are subschemas representing special cases of the general pattern, that in which the stem vowel [ɪ] is followed by [t], and that in which it is followed by a nasal ([N]); note that the component structures [PROCESS/...ɪt] and [PROCESS/...ɪN] elaborate the stem of the higher-level schema (the added detail is also reflected in the past-tense morpheme, which makes internal reference to the stem in specifying the ablaut pattern). Instantiating the first of these subschemas are the specific verb forms *sat* and *spat*, complex structures that I have rendered orthographically to simplify the diagram. The second subschema is instantiated by the specific verbs *swam* and *began*, and also by a lower-level subschema which identifies the nasal consonant of the stem as the velar nasal in particular. This subpattern in turn has two special cases (each with a number of instantiating expressions) that differ in whether the nasal is final or followed by [k].

The analysis is complicated, but I would argue for its cognitive and linguistic plausibility. It is certainly reasonable to suppose that forms like *sat, swam, began, rang, sank*, etc. are learned by speakers as familiar units.[3] All significant generalizations are captured, both the global generalization expressed by the topmost schema, and also the more limited generalizations reflecting the prevalence of certain types of stems as participants in this morphological construction. Whether speakers extract all available generalizations is an open question, but there is no particular reason to suppose that they proceed directly from specific forms to the highest-level schemas supported by the data, or that a category, should it develop in this manner, necessarily fails to undergo subsequent differentiation through the emergence of subschemas.

A network like Figure 9 brings out clearly the maximalist, nonreductive, and bottom-up nature of a usage-based approach. Revealing its maximalist character is the incorporation of structures representing all levels of generality, from specific forms to an all-subsuming schema. The analysis is nonreductive because it posits as units both schemas and specific expressions computable from those schemas. Its bottom-up orientation is reflected in the emphasis on low-level structures that provide the basis for higher-level schematization. By contrast, linguists are more accustomed to a minimalist, reductionist, top-down approach that achieves greater economy by including in the grammar only a rule equivalent to the topmost schema.

Either type of approach must somehow specify precisely which verbs participate in this construction, since most stems containing [ɪ] form their past tense in some other manner. A minimalist analysis would typically mark the proper verb stems with some kind of diacritic (e.g. a rule feature, or an indication of class membership), and condition the application of the ablaut rule on the presence of this marking. Because the diacritic has no intrinsic semantic or phonological content, it is considered a grammatical construct; and because the set of verbs in question is not semantically or phonologically predictable, it is taken as constituting a grammatical (specifically, a morphological) class. This apparent need to posit purely grammatical entities is then invoked as an argument for the autonomy of grammatical structure.

Diacritics are rendered unnecessary by the maximalist analysis of Figure 9. For example, the information that *sing* follows the [...ɪ...--->...æ...] ablaut pattern is provided directly, by (i) the inclusion of *sang* among the conventional units of the grammar, and (ii) its categorization by the schemas that define the pattern. Observe that the analysis obeys the content requirement, as it employs only symbolic units (both specific and schematic) and categorizing relationships. Though we can perfectly well speak of a grammatical (or morphological) construction, it is fully characterized in terms of symbolic relations between semantic and phonological structures--there is nothing that represents a separate domain, autonomous vis-à-vis semantics, of purely "grammatical" structure. Nor is the existence of an independent set of grammatical entities established by the impossibility of predicting the participating verb stems on semantic or phonological grounds. To assume so is to embrace the "type/predictability fallacy", i.e. the failure to distinguish between two issues that are in principle distinct: the types of structures that occur, and the predictability of their behavior (see Chapter 11).

We can now observe that the apparent argument cited above for the autonomy of grammar is in reality simply an artifact of the minimalist approach to grammatical description. If specific forms that instantiate a pattern are excluded from the grammar by the thesis of reductionism, they must be "constructed" by application of the relevant rule. If the lexical items that undergo this rule are limited to an arbitrary class, they must somehow be marked to undergo it. And since the requisite marking has no intrinsic semantic or phonological content, it must represent some other realm or dimension of linguistic organization. We have seen, however, that symbolic units are capable of furnishing the requisite distributional information provided that we take a maximalist, nonreductionist approach allowing schemas and instantiations to coexist in the grammar of a language.

In this usage-based framework, grammatical constructions are analyzed as complex categories. A speaker's conventional knowledge of a construction is not limited to a single, abstract rule or schema standing in isolation--it further embraces his knowledge of how the rule is implemented with respect to more specific structures. By its very nature, a high-level schema is compatible with a broad and structurally-diverse array of potential instantiations. Typically, however, conventional usage carves out for exploitation only limited regions within this field of structural possibilities. A full linguistic description must identify these regions, i.e. it must characterize the construction's conventional domain, as articulated by a hierarchy of lower-level structures. Providing this information are subschemas and expressions with the status of units: they specify the actual array of subcases and specific instances that support and give rise to the high-level generalization.

In the network for a grammatical construction, the individual nodes and categorizing relationships presumably differ in their cognitive salience and likelihood of activation, as they do in any complex category. There is no reason to assume that the highest-level schema is necessarily the most salient, or even that an all-subsuming schema is always extracted.[4] For the network of Figure 9, we can plausibly suppose that the highest-level schema is less readily activated (has a lesser degree of prominence) than specific forms like *sat, swam, began, rang, sank,* etc.; this would imply that such forms are generally accessed as units (as opposed to being computed from the stems by means of the schema). The opposite is no doubt true for other constructions: greater salience attaches to schemas (though not necessarily those at the highest levels), and relatively few instantiating expressions have the status of units; computation must therefore predominate. At least in principle, it is possible for behavioral evidence to be brought to bear on such matters--cognitive salience and accessibility are neither inherently mysterious nor beyond the reach of empirical inquiry.

This notion of accessibility is crucial to a usage-based account of distribution and productivity. The general problem can be formulated as follows: granted that a construction is a complex category, and properly represented as a network, how is this network invoked for the assembly (or evaluation) of a particular instantiating expression? We cannot assume that access to the network is random, or that all nodes are simultaneously and equally activated for this purpose--the resulting chaos would afford no basis for clear judgments of well-formedness or the assignment of structural descriptions. Instead, I suggest a working hypothesis that is basically compatible with a "connectionist" or "interactive-activation" model of cognitive processing (cf. Elman & McClelland 1984; McClelland & Rumelhart 1986; Rumelhart & McClelland 1986; Rumelhart & Zipser 1985; Waltz & Pollack 1985). This two-part proposal is formulated in (6).

(6) a. Uniqueness: When an expression is assessed relative to a grammatical construction, a single node (from the network representing the construction) is activated for its categorization; if this "active node" is schematic for the expression, the latter is judged well-formed (conventional).

   b. Selection: The likelihood that a given node will be chosen as the active node for categorizing a target expression correlates positively with its degree of entrenchment and cognitive salience, and negatively with its distance from the target (i.e. how far the target diverges from it by elaboration or extension).

The thrust of (6a) is that an expression's well-formedness depends on how it is structurally construed (i.e. what it is taken as being an instance of), and that a single episode of categorization (structural description) construes it in a particular way. Some factors that influence the choice of categorizing structure (active node) are suggested in (6b); they are matters of degree, and possibly antagonistic.

Let us consider these matters with reference to Figure 10, which represents the overall past-tense verb construction of English. At the semantic pole, both the topmost schema and all the subschemas specify the integration of [PROCESS] and [PAST] to form the composite structure [PROCESS-PAST] (not individually shown). However, at the phonological pole the topmost schema is so abstract that it is almost contentless; essentially, it characterizes the stem and inflection only as having "some phonological value". The reason for this extreme schematicity is that the various patterns of past-tense formation have very little in common phonologically. Schemas corresponding to four of these patterns are shown in the diagram. At the left is the subschema for the ablaut pattern [...ɪ... --->...æ...]; this is the same structure that functions as the highest-level node in Figure 9 (in this way the entire network of Figure 9 fits into the more inclusive network of Figure 10). The second subschema corresponds to the regular pattern of past-tense formation. At the phonological pole of the past-tense morpheme, [-D] stands for a schematized suffix having [-d], [-t], and [-əd] as instantiations (i.e. it specifies an alveolar stop and is neutral as to the presence of a preceding schwa). The three subcases of the regular pattern are represented by lower-level subschemas, which incorporate specific suffixes and specify the phonological characteristics of the stems they attach to; elaborating each low-level subschema is some array of instantiating expressions having unit status. The third and fourth major subschemas describe respectively the ablaut pattern of *brought, caught, fought, sought, taught,* etc., and the zero pattern of verbs like *cut, hit, slit, bet, spread,* and *bid.*

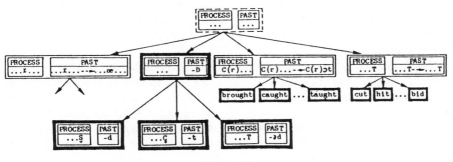

Figure 10.

Also represented in Figure 10 are rough hypotheses concerning the cognitive salience of the individual nodes. Among the schemas, the structures corresponding to the regular pattern are attributed the greatest prominence, as indicated by the heavy-line boxes; they can be regarded as the category prototype. Most of the specific expressions learned as units presumably have substantial salience as well. The schemas describing minor patterns are analyzed as having a lesser degree of prominence, while the topmost schema--considering the vacuity of its phonological pole--may well be the least prominent of all. Such differences in salience (likelihood of activation) are the device employed in this framework to implement the distinction between productive and nonproductive patterns (or between major and minor rules). Since prominence is a relative matter and varies continuously, we should expect in general to find a gradation between the two types instead of a strict dichotomy.

The contrast may nevertheless be quite pronounced in particular instances; a pattern that is distinctly more prominent than any potential competitor will almost invariably be selected for the construction and evaluation of novel expressions. The regular pattern of English past-tense formation is so identified precisely because it has this type of advantage. Consider a speaker who needs the past-tense form of *flit*, but happens not to have learned it as a unit. He must therefore select one of the schemas in the network for the past-tense construction to employ as the active node (basis for categorization) in assessing possible alternatives. Though all four patterns in Figure 10 are potentially applicable, he will most likely choose the regular pattern by virtue of its distinctive prominence. Within the regular pattern, moreover, the subschema [[PROCESS/...T]-[PAST/-əd]] will be chosen in preference to [[PROCESS/...C̦]-[PAST/-t]] on the basis of distance: the former characterizes the stem with greater specificity (alveolar stop vs. voiceless consonant) and hence is "closer" to the stem (such as *flit*) of potential target expressions. With [[PROCESS/...T]-[PAST/-əd]] selected as the active node, the target *flitted* is judged well-formed; it is fully compatible with the active node's schematic specifications. Other target expressions, e.g. *flat, flaught*, and *flit*, conflict with these specifications and are consequently judged ill-formed, despite being computable from other schemas. Given the selection of [[PROCESS/...T]-[PAST/-əd]] as the active node, their deviance is predicted by (6a), the uniqueness hypothesis.

The situation is quite different for specific expressions that are mastered as units, e.g. *sat, taught*, and *hit*. As units, they are themselves part of the network representing conventional knowledge of the past-tense construction, making them eligible for selection as the active node representing this construction. Suppose, for instance, that a speaker wishes to express the past tense of *hit*. If the past-tense expression *hit* has any substantial cognitive salience (which it must, as a frequently occurring form), the distance factor virtually assures its being chosen as active node: its distance from the target (i.e. the desired past-tense form of *hit*) is essentially zero. Only *hit* itself is compatible with this categorizing unit-- alternative expressions such as *hitted, haught*, and *hat* are deviant as the past-tense of *hit*, though computable via established schemas. In short, specific expressions with the status of conventional units sanction themselves (or occurrences of themselves) as being conventional, and thereby preempt the process of selecting an active node.

Though the selection process is described only vaguely at best in (6b), its general import can now be appreciated. The well-formedness (conventionality) of an expression is not absolute: it depends on what unit the expression is construed as instantiating, and on its compatibility with that unit (as evaluated by a categorizing judgment). The selection of a categorizing unit hinges on the dynamic interplay of factors that are frequently antagonistic. If specificity is held constant, the determining factor is entrenchment or cognitive salience; given a range of options, one of them may establish itself as the regular choice (the default-case option). Holding salience constant, the determining factor is cognitive distance, i.e. the extent to which the categorizing unit (active node) must be elaborated or extended to "reach" the target. The tendency for specific structures to prevail over patterns of greater generality has been noted in a variety of theoretical frameworks; examples include disjunctive rule ordering (Chomsky & Halle 1968), proper-inclusion precedence (Sanders 1974), and Hudson's priority-to-the-instance principle (1984). In the present framework, this tendency is naturally accommodated as one facet of a broader theoretical perspective emphasizing a nonreductive, bottom-up, usage-based account of language structure. Adopting this general orientation enables one to countenance with equanimity a far-reaching implication of (6b): for the most part, specific structures and low-level schemas are more significant than high-level schemas expressing the most inclusive generalizations. Even certain linguists who would resist this implication have, in formulating the precedence principles cited above, at least partially acknowledged its empirical force.

This conception gives rise to certain empirical predictions. One pertains to irregular forms, i.e. those that are idiosyncratic or follow a minor pattern: the more salient and deeply entrenched they are (as reflected in frequency of occurrence), the more resistant they should be to regularization. This correlation is in fact so firmly established that documentation would be otiose--let us focus instead on the basis for predicting it. Consider the past participle of *drive*. The regular pattern predicts *drived*, which a speaker immediately recognizes as being incorrect. The proper form, *driven*, exemplifies a minor pattern of little cognitive salience, but the form itself occurs frequently and constitutes a well-entrenched, easily accessible unit of English. If we attribute comparable salience to the unit *driven* and the schema describing the regular pattern of past-participle formation, the far greater specificity of the former determines its selection as active node whenever the past participle of *drive* is required. *Driven* thus sanctions itself as the correct expression, but *drived* is judged ill-formed (despite its regularity) when measured against this standard. By contrast, the verb *thrive* is relatively infrequent, and a typical speaker hardly ever has occasion to use its past-participial form. Those who use *thriven* must know it as a unit, but its status as such is only marginal; its rarity ensures its lack of prominence. Consequently, neither this unit nor the schema representing the regular pattern has an overwhelming advantage in the competition for selection as active node: the former is more specific, but the latter is far more salient. Hence the schema may well be selected, and if so, an occurrence of *thrived* will slip by unnoticed and be accepted as well-formed (which is quite unlikely in the case of *drived*).

A second prediction is that lower-level schemas should predominate in the computation of novel expressions. This prediction is based on the distance factor: because they are "closer" than high-level generalizations to the target expression, lower-level schemas should in general be selected as the basis for computation (active node). For illustration, let us return to the past-tense schemas of Figure 9, and consider the relative likelihood of innovative past-tense forms involving the ablaut of [ɪ] to [æ]. Though *brought* is well-entrenched as the past tense of *bring*, the sporadic occurrence of *brang* is at least conceivable (it is attested dialectally and in child language). We can explain this with reference to the low-level schema [[PROCESS/...ɪŋ]-[PAST/...ɪŋ--->...æŋ]] of Figure 9, extracted to represent the commonality of *rang, sang,* and *sprang*; not nearly so salient as the schemas for the regular pattern, it is nevertheless quite specific concerning the phonological shape of the verb stem, and thus stands a decent chance of being activated to compute the past-tense form of another stem meeting its specifications. Similarly, *shat* is sometimes encountered as a jocular or euphemistic past-tense form, and is computed from the low-level schema that expresses the commonality of *sat* and *spat*. On the other hand, the innovative past-tense forms *san* (for *sin*) and *hass* (for *hiss*) are unattested, uninterpretable, and inconceivable. Observe that the lowest-level schemas available for the computation of these forms are in fact quite abstract. *San* (if it occurred) would invoke the schema [[PROCESS/...ɪN...]-[PAST/...ɪN...--->...æN...]], which identifies the consonant following the ablauted vowel only as a nasal (not a specific segment), and is further neutral as to whether or not this consonant is stem-final. *Hass* would be computable only from the topmost schema in Figure 9, which is maximally schematic concerning the environment of the ablauted vowel.

To make the same point in another way, consider the topmost schema in Figure 10, which represents the maximal generalization concerning past-tense verbs in English. We have already noted that this schema is essentially vacuous at the phonological pole, because the various patterns of past-tense formation have virtually nothing in common. If this high-level schema were the one to be invoked for the computation or evaluation of novel expressions, it would have the effect of allowing any kind of stem to be marked for past tense in any way whatever--a maximally schematic characterization of the construction imposes no significant constraints on its possible instantiations. The actual work is obviously done by lower-level schemas.

A final example should reinforce and further clarify this notion. Postpositional endings in Classical Nahuatl vary in the type of noun stems to which they attach.

Certain postpositions, among them *-ko* 'in' and *-tew* 'like', attach only to lexical nouns (e.g. *siwaa-tew* 'like a woman'). Others, including *-waan* 'with' and *-pampa* 'because of', occur only with pronouns (e.g. *no-waan* 'with me'). A third class of postpositions, exemplified by *-pan* 'on' and *-caalan* 'among', suffix to nouns of either sort (e.g. *to-caalan* 'among us', $k^w aw$-*caalan* 'among the trees'). Each of these distributional possibilities implies a low-level constructional subschema, depicted in abbreviated form along the bottom row in Figure 11. For instance, the box at the lower left in this diagram stands for the constructional subschema expressing the generalization that *-ko* occurs on lexical nouns; the box at the lower right similarly expresses the generalization that *-pampa* combines with pronouns. Note that *-pan* and *-caalan* figure in two such subschemas each, one for each type of noun.

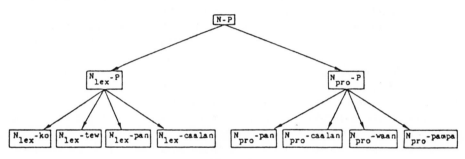

Figure 11.

From these low-level schemas, certain broader generalizations can be extracted. Since *-ko, -tew, -pan, -caalan,* and others occur on lexical nouns, a speaker could extract the intermediate-level subschema shown on the left in Figure 11; it specifies the existence of a compositional pattern whereby postpositions suffix to lexical nouns. Similarly, the intermediate-level subschema on the right in Figure 11, specifying the attachment of postpositions to pronouns, is supported by the occurrence on pronouns of *-pan, -caalan, -waan, -pampa,* etc. Moreover, since postpositions occur on both lexical nouns and pronouns, there are grounds for extracting the higher-level schema depicted at the top, which specifies that postpositions suffix to nouns. Each schema expresses the commonality of its immediate instantiations. It is clear, however, that only the lowest-level schemas could be invoked for the computation of novel expressions--it is only at this level that the distributional restrictions are apparent. If the topmost schema were activated for this purpose, it would sanction the occurrence of any postposition with either type of noun. The intermediate-level schemas would fare no better, for they specify the occurrence of any postposition with either a lexical noun or a pronoun.

5. Conclusion

Accepting the general principles of scientific inquiry does not itself resolve the more specific but nonetheless crucial issue of how these principles are appropriately applied to the problems of a particular discipline at a given stage of its development. I have argued, both on methodological and on empirical grounds, that the principle of generality has received in linguistics a commonly accepted interpretation that is in fact not appropriate to its subject matter. Current doctrine favors a minimalist account of linguistic knowledge, described in accordance with a complex array of theoretical apparatus featuring specialized devices for the various "components" of the linguistic system. By contrast, cognitive grammar pursues a maximalist account of linguistic knowledge, and tends toward austerity in the adoption of theoretical constructs; it seeks a unified treatment of the various facets of linguistic structure, attributing their differences to the content of the domains in question rather than the basic constructs invoked to handle them.

Prominent among these constructs are those comprised by the network model of complex categories. The network model affords an integrated account of categorization for the varied domains of linguistic structure. It accommodates not only those phenomena generally thought of as involving categorization, but also the nearest cognitive grammar analogs of rules, derivations, and structural descriptions. It is further responsible for the usage-based character of the framework; by tolerating the coexistence in a single network of specific expressions and schemas at varying levels of abstraction, it implements the maximalist, nonreductive, bottom-up orientation of the usage-based approach.

Problems of distribution and productivity are addressed by treating grammatical constructions as complex categories. A single, high-level generalization does not exhaust a speaker's conventional knowledge of a construction. A full description must also specify how this generalization is articulated through the supporting hierarchy of subpatterns and specific expressions. In this maximalist account, the structures that occur in a given construction are identified without the use of diacritics or other arbitrary devices. Moreover, specific expressions and low-level schemas are seen to be at least as important as higher-level schemas capturing the broadest generalizations. We have no assurance that speakers invariably arrive at high-level schemas, whose abstractness may render them essentially useless for the computation and evaluation of novel expressions; there is reason to think that lower-level schemas figure more prominently in this role. A major advantage of the usage-based conception is its ability to accommodate structures at this level of organization without the loss of valid generalizations.

11. Autonomy and agreement

A central theoretical issue is whether grammatical structure constitutes a distinct and autonomous aspect of linguistic organization.* It is widely believed that the autonomy of grammar has been securely established; among the factors that supposedly demonstrate its autonomy is the prevalence of arbitrary restrictions and grammatical markings, including patterns of agreement. However, consideration of this issue has been clouded by a certain amount of conceptual confusion and a simplistic view of the conceivable alternatives. One such alternative is cognitive grammar, which claims that grammatical structure is not autonomous but inherently symbolic. This chapter attempts to show that agreement and other kinds of grammatical marking can in principle be accommodated in such a framework. Hence their mere existence does not support the autonomy thesis.

1. The autonomy issue

Ever since the publication of *Syntactic Structures*, in which Chomsky argued that judgments of grammaticality are independent from judgments of meaning, the autonomy of syntax (and of grammar more generally) has been a basic dogma of generative theory. With the suppression of the generative semantic heresy, the autonomy thesis became virtually immune to challenge within the confines of the generative school itself. That has led in recent years to a strong emphasis on modularity, both in the broad sense of language overall constituting a separate mental faculty (Fodor 1983), and in the sense of the linguistic system consisting in a set of separate and autonomous components, or modules. Unsurprisingly, belief in modularity enables scholars to uncover evidence for it; these days, any phenomenon that might conceivably be interpreted in modular terms almost certainly will be.

The specific issue I am concerned with here is the autonomy of grammatical structure vis-à-vis semantics. By "grammar", I mean syntax together with any aspects of morphology considered grammatically relevant (cf. Anderson 1982); these include inflection and agreement at the very least (I myself posit no sharp dichotomy between inflectional and derivational morphology). The question, then, is whether grammar constitutes a separate level, domain, or dimension of linguistic structure--with its own primitives, representations, organizational principles, etc.-- that is properly described without essential reference to meaning. Now it is commonly assumed (e.g. in Newmeyer 1983) that the autonomy of grammar is established if any aspect of grammatical structure is less than fully predictable on the basis of meaning or other independent factors. That is, grammar is autonomous unless all grammatical patterns and restrictions fall out as automatic consequences of something else and thus escape the need of being listed or stated explicitly.

This line of thought embodies what I call the "type/predictability fallacy". It confuses two issues that are in principle quite distinct, namely (i) what KINDS of linguistic units there are, and (ii) the PREDICTABILITY of their behavior. Let us simply accept the obvious fact that grammar is NOT fully predictable from independent factors; although much of it is motivated rather than arbitrary, grammatical patterns and restrictions are not subject to absolute predictability and must indeed be stated explicitly in a linguistic description (for example, the particulars of an agreement phenomenon must be listed in a grammar in all their boring detail). If that is all one means by autonomy, then grammatical structure is certainly autonomous. It would be fallacious, however, to draw from this the further conclusion that grammar is autonomous in the sense of constituting a special domain of linguistic structure (with its own primitives, etc.) that is separate and distinct from semantics. It is logically coherent to admit that grammatical patterns and restrictions are less than fully predictable and do require explicit description, but to claim that all of the elements that figure in such a description are meaningful.

Such a position, I will argue, is not only logically coherent but also both workable and inherently desirable. The proposed alternative to the autonomy thesis--let us call it the "symbolic alternative"--holds that grammar is fully and appropriately describable using only symbolic units, each having both semantic and phonological import. This is a central tenet of cognitive grammar. More than any other framework, cognitive grammar offers conceptual unification and theoretical austerity, is highly restrictive in its adoption of descriptive constructs, and invokes only well-established cognitive abilities.

A prime objective of theoretical physics is to achieve a unified theory of the basic forces of nature, whereby the strong, weak, electromagnetic, and gravitational forces will be revealed as merely divergent manifestations of a single phenomenon. In the same spirit of unification, cognitive grammar posits for the description of linguistic structure only three basic types of units--semantic, phonological, and symbolic--which ultimately reduce to one. Lexicon, morphology, and syntax are all described in terms of symbolic units, which do not arrange themselves into discrete components but vary continuously along certain parameters. A symbolic unit is bipolar, reducing to a semantic unit (its semantic pole) standing in a symbolic relationship with a phonological unit (its phonological pole). A semantic unit is an established conceptualization of some sort, i.e. a fixed configuration in semantic space. A phonological unit can similarly be regarded as an established configuration in phonological space. Although the domains of meaning and form would seem to be a bare minimum for the description of language, in the final analysis phonological space is simply one region of semantic space (see Langacker 1987a: 2.2.1).

Cognitive grammar is highly restrictive due to the content requirement: the only units ascribable to a linguistic system are (i) semantic, phonological, and symbolic structures that are part of overtly occurring expressions; (ii) schematizations of permitted structures; and (iii) categorizing relationships between permitted structures. To take a phonological example, specific syllables such as [tap], [hɪs], [rʌn], and [lɛd] are part of overtly occurring expressions; the syllable canon [CVC] represents a schematization over such syllables; and [[CVC] → [tap]] is a categorizing relationship. The effect of this stringent requirement is to rule out any descriptive construct that is not derivable in a straightforward manner from data that is directly accessible (i.e. sound sequences and what they are understood as meaning). Proscribed, for instance, are "purely grammatical" constructs attributed neither semantic nor phonological value (e.g. empty diacritics, or phonologically zero syntactic dummies). The content requirement also implies that rules cannot be different in basic character from the expressions they describe--they can only constitute schematizations of expressions (or certain facets thereof). Arbitrary machinery such as the derivation of an expression from an underlying structure of radically different organization is thus precluded.

Cognitive grammar is also quite down-to-earth in the mental capacities it invokes as the basis for linguistic structure. Quite uncontroversially, it assumes that we have such abilities as the following: (i) to form structured conceptualizations; (ii) to perceive and articulate phonological sequences; (iii) to establish symbolic associations between conceptual and phonological structures; (iv) to use one structure as a basis for categorizing another; (v) to conceive a situation at varying levels of abstraction (schematization); (vi) to detect similarities between two structures; (vii) to establish correspondences between facets of different structures or elements in different domains; (viii) to combine simpler structures into more complex ones; (ix) to impose figure/ground organization on a scene; and (x) to construe a conceived situation in alternate ways (e.g. from different perspectives, or by according special prominence to different substructures). Abilities (i)-(iii) permit the formation of semantic, phonological, and symbolic units; (iv)-(vii) give rise to rules and linguistic categories; (vi)-(vii) are basic to metaphor; (vii)-(x) are crucial for grammatical structure; and (x) is fundamental to cognitive semantics.

Because of these virtues--unification, restrictiveness, and naturalness--cognitive grammar is intrinsically desirable from the standpoint of scientific method (not to mention esthetically and intuitively). Linguistic theorists thus ought to be vitally concerned with making this theory work if at all possible, abandoning it only with the greatest reluctance and only after exhausting all avenues for maintaining it in the face of apparent difficulties.

2. The symbolic alternative

I have outlined a theory in which grammar forms a continuum with lexicon, and only bipolar symbolic units--each with both semantic and phonological import--are posited for the description of grammatical structure. To be viable, such a theory must accommodate many phenomena often thought of as supporting the autonomy thesis, including grammatical classes, grammatical morphemes, constituency, grammatical relations, distributional restrictions, and grammatical rules. This section reviews how cognitive grammar handles each phenomenon. It is important to remember in this regard that we are not trying to predict grammar from meaning (especially not from meaning as conceived in objectivist terms); grammatical patterns and restrictions must be learned as a matter of linguistic convention and stated explicitly in a description. The claim instead is that only symbolic units are needed for this listing, provided that we learn to see both meaning and grammar in the proper way.

By ''lexicon'', I simply mean the inventory of fixed expressions in a language, regardless of size or the regularity of their composition. Lexical units vary in their level of specificity at both the semantic and the phonological poles. Semantically, such units run the gamut from the maximally schematic to the highly specific (e.g. *thing* → *animal* → *mammal* → *dog* → *beagle*). Although most lexical items are phonologically specific, here too there is variation. For example, a prefix might have the form *kV-*, with a specific consonant but a schematic vowel that harmonizes with the first vowel of the stem; in the case of full reduplication, both segments are schematic (*CV-*). Lexical units also vary in their degree of symbolic complexity, i.e. their decomposability into smaller symbolic units. A morpheme is symbolically noncomplex by definition. Progressively greater symbolic complexity is exhibited by a sequence of lexical items such as *sharp* < *sharpen* < *sharpener* < *pencil sharpener*.

These two parameters define a continuous field of possibilities, and the various sorts of symbolic units needed for lexicogrammatical description, though traditionally thought of as quite distinct, are more accurately seen as occupying different regions within this field. The units generally regarded as lexical items cluster in the region of specificity. So-called ''grammatical morphemes'' are symbolically minimal, and while often phonologically specific, semantically they are quite schematic. Basic grammatical classes (such as noun and verb) are characterized by symbolically minimal units that are highly schematic at both the semantic and the phonological poles. Grammatical rules and constructions reside in units that are both schematic and symbolically complex.

It was argued in Chapter 3 that basic grammatical classes are susceptible to abstract semantic characterizations applicable to all class members. Their semantic import pertains not so much to conceptual content as to the way in which that content is construed. Thus, when the verb *explode* is nominalized to yield the derived noun *explosion*, there is no real change in conceptual content; there is, however, a conceptual reification wherein the event described by the verb is construed as a thing, i.e. as a region in an abstract sense of that term. If that is so, we can posit a schema for the class of nouns, which we can abbreviate as follows: [THING/...]. This symbolic unit is maximally schematic at each pole; semantically, its only specification is that it profiles a thing, while phonologically it has no specific content. An expression is categorized as a noun by virtue of instantiating this class schema. For instance, *desk* is a noun because it participates in the categorizing relationship [[THING/...] → [DESK/desk]]. Similarly, every verb designates a process, as defined earlier. We can therefore postulate the class schema [PROCESS/...], together with categorizing relationships such as [[PROCESS/...] → [SEE/see]].

The elements usually regarded as grammatical morphemes are intermediate between class schemas, which are highly schematic at both poles, and run-of-the-mill lexical items, which are specific at each pole. Though quite variable, grammatical morphemes tend to be phonologically specific (since they have overt manifestation), while semantically they are often comparable to class schemas in their degree of schematicity. They may in fact be identical to such schemas. For example, I analyze the auxiliary verb *do* as being semantically equivalent to the verb-class schema, i.e. [PROCESS/do]. Similarly, the *thing* which occurs in expressions like *something* and *another thing* is perhaps the same in meaning as the noun-class schema: [THING/thing]. Derivational morphemes, at the semantic pole, are generally schematic for the class they derive. Thus *-er* is a schematic agentive noun; more precisely, it has for its base the schematic conception of the appropriate sort of process, and it profiles the trajector of that process. In like fashion, the stative participial morpheme (as in *broken*) invokes the schematic conception of a change-of-state process and profiles the final (resultant) state of that process.

Constituency is only a matter of simpler symbolic structures combining to form successively more complex symbolic structures. A constituent is formed when two component symbolic structures, [X/x] and [Y/y], are integrated at each pole to form a composite symbolic structure, [XY/xy]. Importantly, the integration of phonological structures symbolizes the integration of the corresponding semantic structures (see Figure 11 of Chapter 1). That is, the fact that [X] combines with [Y] in particular (and not with some other element) is signaled overtly by the combination of [x] and [y] at the phonological pole; in this regard, the only difference between morphology and syntax resides in whether the composite phonological structure [xy] is smaller or larger than a word. This entire configuration--bipolar component and composite structures, together with the relationships among them--constitutes a construction.

For concrete illustration, consider the expression *yellow balloon*, whose semantic and phonological poles are diagramed in Figures 1(a) and 1(b), respectively. At the semantic pole, the component structure [YELLOW] profiles an atemporal relation. Its trajector is characterized only schematically, as a physical entity of some sort, and its landmark is identified as the yellow region of color space (labeled *Y*). The profiled relationship (indicated by the dashed arrow) is one of coincidence between the landmark region and a color sensation associated with the trajector (cf. Chapter 7). The component predication [BALLOON] designates a particular kind of physical object; its detailed semantic specifications are abbreviated by a mnemonic sketch of its shape. The dotted line indicates that the trajector of [YELLOW] corresponds to the profile of [BALLOON], and the solid arrow, that [BALLOON] elaborates [YELLOW]'s schematic trajector. The composite structure, obtained by superimposing the specifications of corresponding elements, merges the conceptual content of [YELLOW] and [BALLOON] in such a way that the specific characteristics of the noun are associated with the trajector of the adjective. Observe that the balloon is profiled at the composite structure level, the color specification being an unprofiled facet of the base.

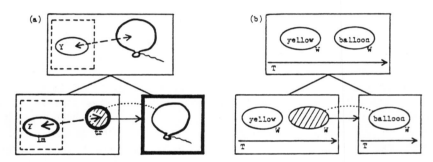

Figure 1.

At the phonological pole, the integration of [yellow] and [balloon] involves their adjacency in the speech stream and their occurrence in a particular temporal order. The arrow labeled *T* represents speech time, one dimension of phonological space, and *W* indicates that a phonological sequence is a word. The effect of the correspondence is to identify [balloon] as the word that follows [yellow], the composite structure thus being [yellow balloon]. Note that this phonological integration symbolizes the semantic integration of [YELLOW] and [BALLOON] described above (i.e. the temporal adjacency and ordering of [yellow] and [balloon] signals the fact that it is [BALLOON] which elaborates [YELLOW]'s trajector). Note further that the following formula is used to abbreviate the full construction: [[YELLOW/yellow][BALLOON/balloon]]. Although the composite structure is not separately shown in this type of abbreviatory notation, it must be understood as being present (and as determining the class membership of the overall expression).

The composite structure derived in this fashion can function as one component structure in another construction representing a higher level of constituency.[1] In this fashion, through successive cycles of bipolar integration deriving composite structures from simpler components, symbolic structures of indefinite complexity may be formed. Any intermediate structure along such a compositional path comprises what is generally recognized as a constituent; in cognitive grammar terms it is simply a bipolar structure of a certain size, consisting of an integrated conceptual structure standing in a symbolic relationship with an integrated phonological structure. Moreover, any structure along a compositional path belongs to a particular grammatical category by virtue of its profile at the semantic pole. For instance, both the component structure *balloon* and the composite structure *yellow balloon* are classed as nouns, since each profiles a thing and thus instantiates the noun-class schema. These categorizing relationships are not part of the compositional hierarchy per se, but rather orthogonal to it, as sketched in Figure 2.

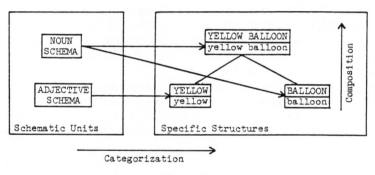

Figure 2.

In conformity to the content requirement, this mode of description employs only three kinds of structures: (i) symbolic structures that occur overtly (e.g. [BALLOON/balloon]); (ii) schematizations of such structures ([THING/...]); and (iii) categorizing relationships ([[THING/...] →ʻ [BALLOON/balloon]]). Specifically NOT posited are syntactic tree structures of the sort we have known and loved since 1957. The phrase trees of transformational syntax represent three kinds of information: constituency, linear order, and grammatical class (by means of node labels). Moreover, these phrase trees are regarded as purely grammatical or syntactic objects, belonging to a realm of linguistic structure distinct from both semantics and phonology; although rules of semantic and phonological interpretation refer to these phrase trees, they apply to the content provided by inserted lexical items--the trees themselves are not thought of as semantic or phonological entities, but as something quite different. Thus syntactic tree structures, as they are conceived in generative theory, stand in clear violation of the content requirement and cannot be employed in cognitive grammar.

Now I am not denying the need to accommodate the kinds of information represented in phrase trees: expressions do exhibit constituency, constituents do instantiate grammatical classes, and elements are linearly ordered. However, the need to represent these factors does not entail that phrase trees--conceived as autonomous syntactic objects--are the proper device for doing so, nor does it establish the autonomy thesis. We have in fact just seen how all of these factors are handled in a framework that posits only symbolic units and categorizing relationships. Constituency per se is just a matter of the step-by-step assembly (through bipolar integration) of progressively more elaborate symbolic structures. Class membership resides in the categorization of symbolic structures by class schemas (Figure 2), which are abstract symbolic units. What about linear order? More properly referred to as temporal order, it is simply one dimension of phonological space. Hence temporal ordering is specified within every symbolic structure, whether simple or complex, as one facet of the characterization of its phonological pole (Figure 1(b)). In a construction, therefore, linear ordering does not hold between the component structures, but is rather part of the internal phonological organization of both the component and composite structures. In summary, while the symbolic alternative makes available the kinds of information that originally motivated the adoption of syntactic tree structures, it views such trees as inappropriate and superfluous.

Eschewing syntactic tree structures does not prevent one from giving a reasonable account of grammatical relations, since the configurational approach to their characterization was misconceived in the first place. For subject and direct object, I have posited not only prototypical values based on the notions agent and patient, but also schematic values pertaining to the prominence of relational participants (Chapter 9). Recall that a relational predication singles out one of its participants as the trajector (figure within the profiled relationship), and that a distinct entity of secondary salience can be identified as a landmark. The subject and direct object relations are analyzed as clause-level manifestations of this asymmetry. Specifically, a subject is a nominal that elaborates the trajector of the process profiled by the clause as a whole, and a direct object is a nominal that elaborates its primary landmark. These relationships are diagramed in Figure 3 for the sentence *The girl entered the room* (note that tense and articles are omitted to simplify matters, and that *G* and *R* abbreviate the respective semantic specifications of *girl* and *room*).

What identifies *the girl* as subject is not any particular constituent structure, but rather the fact that its profile corresponds to the trajector of *enter*, the clausal head. In similar fashion, a correspondence between the landmark of *enter* and the profile of *the room* identifies the latter as direct object. These characterizations are independent of constituency, and indeed, I have omitted any indication of constituency from Figure 3; it is readily seen that the same composite structure results whether the object first elaborates the landmark, the subject first elaborates the trajector, or the two elaborations occur simultaneously. In this framework,

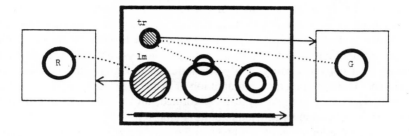

Figure 3.

there is no reason why constituency should not be free to vary within reasonable limits, even in a single language. I assume that the standard arrangement in which the verb and direct object form a constituent is indeed conventionalized as the prototypical pattern for English, but that the alternate grouping occurs in constructions like the following:

(1) a. *The girl entered, but the boy left, the room.*
   b. *This room, the girl entered (that one, she didn't).*
   c. *The room the girl entered was brightly lit.*

That is, the subject nominal elaborates the verbal trajector to form a subject-verb constituent whenever that grouping is required for higher-level structural purposes; there is no need to postulate a movement rule that derives the overt grouping from a hypothetical underlying structure with the regular *S(VO)* constituency.

The notions head, modifier, and complement also receive a straightforward characterization in this framework. In a construction, it is typical for the composite structure to inherit its profiling from one of the component structures, referred to as the profile determinant (indicated diagramatically by the heavy-line box). [BALLOON] is thus the profile determinant in Figure 1(a), since the composite structure designates the balloon rather than the color relation, while [ENTER] is the profile determinant in Figure 3, since the composite structure (not shown) inherits its processual profile. A head is defined quite simply as the profile determinant at a given level of organization (cf. Williams 1981; Zwicky 1985; Hudson 1984, 1987); hence *balloon* is the head in *yellow balloon*, and *enter(ed)* in *The girl entered the room.* Moreover, with respect to a particular construction a modifier is easily and accurately described as a component structure that is elaborated by the head, and a complement as one that elaborates the head. Examination of Figures 1 and 3 thus reveals that *yellow* modifies *balloon*, whereas *the girl* and *the room* are complements (or arguments) of *enter(ed)*.

The grammar of a language is not conceived as a generative or a constructive device, but simply as an inventory of conventional linguistic units. A grammar does not itself construct expressions or provide an exhaustive enumeration of the well-formed sentences of a language. It does however furnish the speaker with an array of symbolic resources that he can use in assembling expressions and assessing their conventionality. Only semantic, phonological, and symbolic units are posited. Through the bipolar integration of symbolic structures, expressions of progressively greater complexity can be formed, and a structure of any size is subject to categorization by schematic units (Figure 2).

Of course, the integration of symbolic structures does not proceed at random but in accordance with certain patterns and restrictions, which collectively constitute grammar in the traditional sense. In the present theory, grammatical patterns and restrictions are accommodated by means of symbolic units that are both schematic and symbolically complex. These units are nothing more than schematizations of constructions (i.e. symbolically complex expressions) and are thus referred to as constructional schemas. A constructional schema represents a conventionally established pattern of bipolar integration. It is abstracted from some array of specific expressions and embodies the commonality observable in their formation; hence it captures any generalizations inherent in the data, can be used as a template for the assembly of novel expressions on the same pattern, and provides a basis for assessing their conventionality (well-formedness).

In terms of its internal organization, a constructional schema is precisely analogous to the expressions from which it is extracted. It is in fact a construction with all of the structures and relationships previously described, differing only in level of specificity from the expressions it schematizes. Sketched in Figure 4, for example, is the constructional schema reflecting the commonality of such expressions as *yellow balloon, clever boy, large mansion*, etc. Comparison with Figure 1 reveals that this schema is exactly parallel in structure to *yellow balloon*, except that the noun and adjective are schematic rather than specific; observe, for

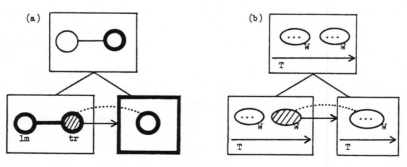

Figure 4.

instance, that in both diagrams integration at the semantic pole is effected by a correspondence between the adjectival trajector and the nominal profile. A constructional schema's semantic pole is functionally equivalent to a rule of semantic composition, for it represents an established pattern of conceptual integration. Of course, in this framework it constitutes an inherent and indissociable aspect of grammatical structure.

As schematizations of specific complex expressions, constructional schemas conform to the content requirement, and like such expressions, they may achieve any degree of symbolic complexity. For example, on the basis of derived nouns such as *opener, driver, complainer, grinder, mixer, swimmer,* etc. we must posit the constructional schema [[PROCESS/...][ER/-er]]; it incorporates the verb schema as one component structure, and its composite structure profiles the trajector of the schematic process thus introduced (the semantic contribution of *-er* is to impose this profiling). This entire schema is in turn incorporated as one component of the higher-order constructional schema required for expressions like *can opener, taxi driver, cement mixer, window washer, flame thrower,* and so on, in which the first noun elaborates the landmark of the process evoked by the second. This higher-order schema, [[THING/...] [[PROCESS/...][ER/-er]]], can in principle be incorporated as part of another constructional schema of even greater symbolic complexity.

A constructional schema such as [[THING/...] [[PROCESS/...][ER/-er]]] is not envisaged in cognitive grammar as standing in isolation or as constituting in and of itself a full characterization of the grammatical construction it describes. For one thing, specific expressions learned as fixed units are part of a speaker's knowledge of linguistic convention, even when they conform to a regular pattern; an expression like *pencil sharpener* is therefore included in the grammar, together with the schema and the categorizing relationship linking the two (see Figure 7 of Chapter 1). The network for the construction may also incorporate subschemas representing special cases of the general pattern; for instance, forms like *taxi driver, bus driver,* and *racecar driver* may give rise to a subschema that identifies the second word as *driver* in particular, i.e. [[THING/...] [[DRIVE/drive][ER/-er]]]. Expressions such as *sky writer, backseat driver, farm worker, deepsea diver, flagpole sitter,* etc. motivate another schema--an extension from the basic pattern--in which the first word specifies the location (rather than the landmark) of the process referred to in the second. Moreover, both these patterns (together with others) are subsumed by a higher-order schema for the overall class of *N+N* compounds: [[THING/...][THING/...]].

Hence the full description of a grammatical construction is analogous to that of the meaning of a lexical item. It does not reside in any single structure, but in a network of structures linked by categorizing relationships. Included in this network are any specific expressions learned as fixed units, low-level constructional schemas describing local regularities of limited scope, and higher-level schemas expressing broader generalizations at various levels of abstraction.

These structures have different degrees of cognitive salience (which translates into likelihood of activation), and there may or may not be an abstract "superschema" with respect to which all the other structures constitute special cases. Cognitive grammar is said to be a usage-based theory because of this bottom-to-top character and its emphasis on low-level structures (Chapter 10). The usage-based approach captures all valid generalizations--any regularity that a speaker might extract is expressed by an appropriate constructional schema. But it also recognizes that global generalizations do not exhaust our knowledge of linguistic convention. Within the space of structural possibilities consistent with a high-level pattern, typically only certain regions are conventionally exploited. Lower-level structures delimit these regions and specify the details of how a global pattern is actually implemented in conventional usage.

Any need for such problematic devices as rule features and empty diacritics is thereby eliminated. Let us admit that there are sometimes arbitrary restrictions on the occurrence of lexical items in a construction, so that one must somehow list the actual possibilities (selected from those compatible with the construction's conceptual import). The need for such listing does not establish the autonomy thesis, for it can be accomplished by means of symbolic units that conform to the content requirement, in particular by constructional subschemas. For example, consider the so-called Dative Shift construction, in which two nominals directly follow the verb (e.g. *I assigned him another task*). The most general schema for this construction simply specifies that a verb of transfer is followed by two nominal constituents: [[TRANSFER/...][THING/...][THING/...]]. However, this construction is for the most part limited to monosyllabic verbs; though semantically appropriate, polysyllables such as *transfer* and *communicate* are precluded (*I transferred him the deed*). Representing the major pattern--hence more salient and readily activated--is the subschema that makes this specification at the phonological pole: $[[\text{TRANSFER}/C_oVC_o][\text{THING}/...][\text{THING}/...]]$. Moreover, the fact that specific verbs like *give, send, tell*, etc. are conventionally established as occurring in the construction is indicated by lower-level subschemas that mention these actual verbs, e.g. [[GIVE/give] [THING/...][THING/...]].

How does a network of this sort give rise to judgments of well-formedness (conventionality)? I assume, first, that only one structure (node) from a particular network is activated to evaluate an expression (on a given occasion); this is called the active node. The expression's evaluation takes the form of categorization by the active node, and whether it is judged well-formed or deviant comes down to whether the categorizing relationship is one of schematicity ($A \rightarrow E$) or extension ($A \dashrightarrow E$), i.e. whether the expression merely elaborates the specifications of the categorizing structure, or whether it conflicts with them in some manner. In either case, the categorization thus effected constitutes the expression's structural description. What determines which node from a network will be selected as the active one? In line with recent work in parallel distributed processing, I assume that an expression tends to activate a structure for this purpose to the extent that they overlap in content, and that the nodes thus aroused compete in mutually inhibitory fashion for the privilege of effecting the categorization. The likelihood of a particular node being chosen is therefore a function of both its cognitive salience and its specificity; if salience is held constant, a low-level structure has the competitive advantage over a more schematic one, because its finer-grained characterization affords a more extensive basis for overlap with the target expression.

Hence low-level schemas may in general be more important than high-level patterns for the assessment of well-formedness. Indeed, a particular high-level schema may be too abstract and too nonsalient ever to be evoked as the active node. A likely example is [[TRANSFER/...][THING/...][THING/...]], representing the maximal generalization for the Dative Shift construction. Though it could in principle sanction such expressions as *I communicated them the information*, the role of active node is preempted by the far more salient subschema in which the verb is characterized as a monosyllable; when judged against that standard, the sentence is deviant.

3. Grammatical markings

Despite its synoptic character, the foregoing discussion should indicate that the symbolic alternative to autonomous grammar is internally coherent and capable in principle of representing many facets of grammatical structure. We are now ready to consider in more detail its treatment of grammatical markings, especially those that appear to be semantically arbitrary. We will see that even an extreme case of arbitrariness--namely, agreement involving such markings--is susceptible to symbolic description.

The issue of whether grammatical markings are meaningful has been obscured by various commonly-made assumptions, often tacit, that from the standpoint of cognitive grammar are both gratuitous and erroneous. The most basic and far-reaching assumption is that the objectivist view of meaning is appropriate for linguistic semantics. By adopting this view, one excludes (as either nonexistent or linguistically irrelevant) the subjective factors of construal that constitute the primary semantic contribution of grammatical structure. For example, the objectivist outlook affords no basis for recognizing figure/ground organization (trajector/landmark alignment) as an aspect of linguistic meaning; hence the truth-conditional equivalence of an active and a passive makes them semantically identical. Nor does objectivism allow one to describe the semantic contrast between *explode* and *explosion* in terms of conceptual reification.

Other common assumptions are implicit in the way constructions are generally analyzed and in the standard practice of distinguishing between "lexical" expressions on the one hand, and "grammatical morphemes" or "formatives" on the other. Often an element is regarded as meaningless if its occurrence is dictated by grammatical considerations or it fails to exhibit a single, independent, fairly specific meaning in all its uses. But such criteria are aprioristic and linguistically inappropriate. In fact, I consider all of the following properties to be consistent with the claim that an element is meaningful: (i) there is no single meaning that it displays in all its uses; (ii) its primary conceptual import resides in construal (rather than conceptual content or truth conditions); (iii) its meaning is highly abstract (schematic); (iv) its meaning is fully overlapped by that of co-occurring elements; (v) it serves an identifiable grammatical function; (vi) its occurrence is obligatory.

Property (i) does not imply meaninglessness unless we are willing to say that most lexical items are devoid of meaning. Polysemy is clearly the norm for lexical items that occur with any frequency, and there is no reason why a grammatical morpheme should not also display a variety of related senses describable as a network. For example, the past-participial morpheme has at least five semantic variants, as exemplified in the following expressions: *a cracked sidewalk*; *an excavated site; Her purse was snatched*; *They have resigned*; *a hooded sweatshirt*. Apart from being atemporal relations (as are countless other predications), there is no significant feature of meaning shared by all five senses, yet their family resemblance is quite apparent (and readily characterized using the constructs of cognitive grammar--see Chapter 4 and Langacker *to appear* (chapter 5)).

As for properties (ii) and (iii), it has already been argued that construal is an essential and ever-present aspect of linguistic meaning, and that lexical items vary enormously in their degree of specificity. It is therefore to be expected that certain expressions, representing the extreme, would be maximally schematic in terms of content yet semantically significant by virtue of the construal they impose on the content provided by other elements. A case in point is the derivational morpheme -*er*, whose base is a highly schematic process and which profiles the trajector of that process. In construction (see Figure 8 of Chapter 4), a specific verb stem (e.g. *complain*) elaborates the schematic base, providing the composite structure's major conceptual content, but -*er* determines its profile and hence its grammatical category. Though -*er* is often regarded as a grammatical operator, in this framework it counts as a meaningful element whose primary semantic value resides in an aspect of construal (profiling).

With respect to property (iv), it is important to distinguish between meaningfulness and nonoverlapping meaning. In every construction there is some degree of semantic overlap between the component structures; it is by virtue of this overlap that they merge to form a coherent composite structure. We can thus expect to encounter the limiting case in which the meaning of one component structure is fully subsumed by that of the other, which is thereby equivalent to the composite structure (i.e. when [A] merges with [AB], the composite result is also [AB]). Certain compounds have this character, e.g. *puppy dog*, *grizzly bear*, and *oak tree*. The second noun is in each instance schematic for the first (e.g. *dog* → *puppy*), so it contributes no information that the first does not also provide. The inclusion of *dog, bear*, and *tree* is therefore redundant, yet we would hardly want to say that these nouns are meaningless.

Nor does it follow from properties (v) and (vi) that an element is semantically empty. An expression with suitable meaning is not only capable of playing a role in grammar but may represent the obvious choice for a particular grammatical purpose; moreover, it does not magically lose all semantic value the moment it becomes the sole option and thus obligatory. For example, *by* serves the grammatical function of introducing the periphrastically specified agent in a passive, and in this role its selection is obligatory. Yet an analysis that failed to relate the passive *by* to such clearly meaningful uses as those in (12) would have to be judged inadequate.

> (2) a. *That painting is by Tamayo.*
> b. *The best jump of the day was by Lewis.*
> c. *She managed to do it all by herself.*

More generally, if the element introducing the passive agent were meaningless, one could not explain why expressions with particular sorts of values (e.g. 'from', 'through', 'with') are adopted for that role in language after language.

Even in combination, properties (i)-(vi) fail to demonstrate that an element is meaningless. The auxiliary verb *do*, for instance, is coherently analyzed as meaningful despite having at least four of these properties. Its occurrence in certain constructions is obligatory, and it is commonly described as serving the grammatical function of bearing a tense marker that would otherwise be stranded. I have characterized *do* semantically as being schematic for the class of verbs (i.e. it designates a process but is maximally nonspecific about its nature); this makes it suitable to function as a verbal pro form (e.g. *She did?*; *He does not!*). Because *do* is a schematic verb, moreover, its meaning is fully subsumed by that of a co-occurring main verb. The relation between *complain* and *do complain* is thus analogous to that between *puppy* and *puppy dog*, or *oak* and *oak tree*--in terms of conceptual content, the schematic element does not contribute anything to the composite semantic structure that is not also inherent in the more specific component. But although *do* is schematic and often redundant, it is not meaningless.

Granted cognitive grammar's more liberal conception of linguistic semantics and the conditions under which an element can be regarded as meaningful, one can formulate quite plausible analyses that attribute conceptual import even to classic examples of "semantically empty" grammatical markings. I would argue, for example, that case markers always have some kind of semantic value (Chapter 9). The standard reasons for denying this have all been shown invalid: that a single, invariant meaning cannot be posited for all uses of a case; that a verb or preposition often governs a particular case (making its selection obligatory); that the meaning of a case is sometimes quite abstract; and that it may be redundant (e.g. nominative case might simply mean 'subject', thus adding nothing to the semantic value of the grammatical relation it signals other than the salience due to explicit coding). By way of a positive demonstration, Smith (1987, 1989) has explored in great detail the dative and accusative cases of German, motivating for each a network of related senses that accommodate and illuminate its varied uses (both clausal and prepositional, governed and ungoverned). Janda (*to appear*) has proposed a comparable analysis of the Czech dative and the Russian instrumental.

We can also now appreciate the speciousness of arguing for the autonomy of grammar on the basis of the putative distinction between "grammatical number" and "semantic number". It is sometimes claimed (e.g. Hudson 1976: 6) that two levels of analysis have to be distinguished because of forms like *scissors, glasses, binoculars, pants, trousers, pliers, tweezers, shorts, tongs, scales, stairs, bleachers, catacombs*, etc., which are said to be "syntactically plural" but "semantically singular". The fallacy lies in the assertion that these nouns are semantically singular. Though it is certainly true that the entities they designate are in one respect unitary objects, it is equally true that they are characterized by internal multiplicity having substantial cognitive salience; I consider it intuitively obvious that the plural ending is conceptually motivated, for it reflects this multiplicity and enhances its salience. But if this is so obvious, why have linguists not entertained the analysis all along? Because their assumptions have not let them do so. For one thing, the notion that relative prominence (a matter of construal) might be an important aspect of meaning is foreign to objectivist semantics. More important is the tacit assumption that the plural morpheme must have a single meaning in all its uses. Prototypically, the plural designates a mass consisting of discrete entities all of which are instances of the same type, such that any one of those entities can be individually described by the singular stem. That is NOT the meaning of *-s* in *scissors, pants, bleachers*, etc., and since these forms are not semantically plural in the prototypical sense, it is concluded that they are not semantically plural at all but rather singular. However, we can perfectly well analyze the meaning of the plural inflection as a complex category comprising both the prototype and a number of extended values, one of which is to indicate the internal multiplicity of a unitary object. These forms are indeed semantically plural in this extended sense.

A comparable distinction is often drawn between "semantic" (or "natural") gender on the one hand, and "grammatical" (or "morphological") gender on the other. Indeed, the apparent arbitrariness of gender assignment over most of the lexicon in European languages is generally the first embarrassing fact to be thrown in the face of anybody with the audacity to suggest that grammar might be semantically based. Now it should first be noted that the arbitrariness of gender has been considerably exaggerated. For instance, Zubin & Köpcke (1986) have demonstrated that the German neuter is used with less than perfect but nonetheless impressive regularity for terms that neutralize some conceptual distinction. Also, it is widely recognized that gender distribution invariably shows redundancies, i.e. local generalizations (described in cognitive grammar by means of subschemas--

cf. van Hoek *in press*) such that virtually all nouns with a certain phonological, morphological, or semantic property have the same gender. But important though they are, these qualifications will not be our focus here. Let us make things as tough as possible by assuming (to some degree counterfactually) that, for all inanimate nouns in a language, gender is arbitrary and simply has to be learned.

The existence of arbitrary gender assignment does not establish the autonomy thesis and is fully compatible with the symbolic alternative. Recall the need to distinguish between what KINDS of structures there are--in particular, whether grammar constitutes a separate domain of linguistic structure with its own representations, primitives, etc.--and the PREDICTABILITY of their behavior. Inability to predict gender assignment on the basis of meaning does not entail that grammar is autonomous from semantics in the sense of representing an independently describable structural domain. Even if gender has to be listed for a large class of nouns, it is quite conceivable that the listing is effected by symbolic units alone, each of which is meaningful in some fashion. Such an account is perfectly feasible in the context of cognitive grammar.

As a concrete example, consider the Spanish nouns in (3)-(4), which represent the large set for which *-o* vs. *-a* signals masculine vs. feminine gender.

(3) a. *hermano* 'brother'; *muchacho* 'boy'; *gato* 'male cat'
    b. *hermana* 'sister'; *muchacha* 'girl'; *gata* 'female cat'

(4) a. *cerro* 'hill'; *palo* 'stick'; *libro* 'book'
    b. *mesa* 'table'; *casa* 'house'; *manzana* 'apple'

The nouns in (3) are typical of animates, where the *-o/-a* contrast correlates for the most part with natural gender and is commonly accepted as being meaningful. By contrast, natural gender is irrelevant for inanimate nouns like the ones in (4), and for these it is generally assumed that the gender marking is unpredictable and semantically empty. How, then, can one describe such data using only symbolic units, each with some meaning?

Examples like those in (3) are straightforwardly analyzed. Each noun is bimorphemic, consisting of a stem that is neutral in regard to gender (e.g. [CAT/gat]), together with an ending that specifies gender but is schematic with respect to the type of creature in which it is manifested. I will consider *-o* and *-a* to be noun-forming suffixes, which implies that they are themselves schematic nouns. Their meanings are roughly 'male creature' and 'female creature', or more simply, 'male' and 'female' (where the glosses are taken as nouns, not as adjectives): [MALE/-o]; [FEMALE/-a]. Represented in Figure 5(a) is the construction wherein *gata* 'female cat' derives from the bipolar integration of the component structures [CAT/gat] and [FEMALE/-a]. The phonological suffixation of [-a] to [gat] symbolizes the correspondence established at the semantic pole between the profiles of [CAT] and [FEMALE], whose specifications are both inherited by the composite structure profile. Note the following abbreviation for this construction: [[CAT/gat][FEMALE/-a]]. The composite structure [FEMALE CAT/gata] is not shown separately from its components in this format, but its presence is understood.

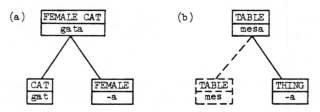

Figure 5.

With inanimate nouns like those in (4), the endings -*o* and -*a* certainly do not mean 'male' and 'female', nor is any specific value compatible with the full range of data. We have seen, however, that an element may be meaningful despite having multiple senses, and that the semantic value of a grammatical morpheme is often highly schematic. Furthermore, it is normal for a derivational morpheme to be schematic for the class it derives, as is the case for -*o* and -*a* with animate nouns (i.e. [MALE/-o] and [FEMALE/-a] are respectively schematic for the nouns in (3a) and (3b)). Now, since -*o* and -*a* are noun-forming endings even with inanimates, it is natural in the context of cognitive grammar to analyze them as being schematic for the class of nouns overall; semantically, each is then equivalent to the noun-class schema: [THING/-o]; [THING/-a]. The two morphemes are thus polysemous, each having a prototypical variant that occurs with animate nouns and specifies gender (e.g. [FEMALE/-a]), together with a variant that occurs with inanimates and is highly schematic at the semantic pole (e.g. [THING/-a]). Of course, neither the polysemy nor the schematicity renders them meaningless.

Two further points must be noted. First, inanimate nouns like the ones in (4) pose problems of morphemic analysis. Although the endings -*o* and -*a* clearly have structural significance and must be segmented as morphemes, there may be no basis for identifying the residue as a morpheme with the appropriate meaning. *Mesa* means 'table', for example, but *mes* does not occur independently with that meaning (by itself *mes* is a masculine noun meaning 'month'). The meaning 'table' is therefore associated with *mesa* as a whole, and it is not obviously justified to attribute that value to *mes* alone, or even to isolate that sequence as a morpheme (it would have to be a bound stem). While a situation of this sort is problematic from the standpoint of classical morphemic analysis, which is based on the building-block metaphor, the cognitive grammar conception of morphemes and morphemic analysis is considerably more flexible (Langacker 1987a: chapter 12). Suffice it to say that this framework permits the analysis sketched in Figure

5(b), where *-a* is identified as one component morpheme of *mesa* even if the remainder is so identified only weakly or not at all.[2]

Second, how does one know which inanimate nouns take *-o* and which ones take the homosemous *-a*? The choice cannot be predicted in any absolute way and must be listed as a matter of linguistic convention. How does the grammar (i.e. the cognitive representation of linguistic structure) specify this information? Not by tagging hypothetical stems like *mes* 'table' and *cerr* 'hill' with empty diacritics or rule features that will trigger the application of the proper morphological spelling rule. In accordance with the nonconstructive, usage-based nature of the framework, it is assumed instead that the information is provided directly through the speaker's knowledge of the full expression, including both the composite structure and its morphemic composition. That is, a speaker knows that 'table' is *mesa* rather than *meso* because he masters the full configuration of Figure 5(b). Hence the listing is accomplished by means of symbolic units alone.

4. Agreement

Agreement markings are perhaps the archetypal example of sentence "trappings" employed for purely grammatical purposes, and are supposedly inconsistent with any claim that grammar might have a semantic basis. Even when a doubly-marked feature seems clearly meaningful, as with number or the gender of an animate noun, the meaninglessness of the agreement marking is generally maintained on either of two grounds: by claiming that it is really "grammatical" (not "semantic") number or gender that is being signaled; or by saying that the agreement markings are not "independently meaningful", but simply copies of information provided elsewhere. As for the first claim, I have already argued that the grammatical vs. semantic distinction for number and gender is based on erroneous assumptions. The second claim confuses meaningfulness with nonoverlapping meaning. Semantic overlap is inherent in all constructions (even expressions like *yellow balloon*--see Figure 1), and although full overlap does produce redundancy, it simply does not follow that the overlapped element has no meaning at all and thus belongs to a special realm of grammatical structure. Agreement can in principle be accommodated by means of symbolic units.

In cognitive grammar, agreement markings are viewed as being predications in their own right. Let us first consider the matter abstractly. Suppose an agreement pattern has the basic form $A+x...B+x'$, where x is an inflection representing some property of A, and x' agrees with x (though they need not be formally identical); that is, even though x' is manifested on B, its selection is in some way determined by x and thus reflects an aspect of A.[3] It would be counter to both the letter and the spirit of cognitive grammar to describe this situation by a rule that "copies" x from A onto B, or in terms of features "percolating" up, down, across, around, or through. Instead, x and x' are both analyzed as meaningful symbolic units. Their co-occurrence may be required rather than optional, and it may be partially or even wholly redundant, but each has its own meaning and makes some kind of semantic contribution.

Two questions immediately arise: Why should a language bother to do this? And how can a pattern of agreement be specified in cognitive grammar? With respect to the first matter, the redundancy inherent in agreement makes it clear that the primary motivation does not lie in the ability of x' to supply additional conceptual content. To be sure, there are instances where x' is not fully determined by x and thus adds a semantic nuance that would otherwise be lacking. This is occasionally so with English verb agreement (which usually leaves no room for option and tells us nothing that is not also apparent from the subject):

(5) a. *Harvey's sheep {is/are} grazing on our lawn.*
   b. *The team {is/are} ready.*
   c. *Sweeping and dusting {is/are} hard work.*

In (5a), the verb inflection is informative to the hearer because it compensates for the neutralization by *sheep* of the singular/plural contrast. Some speakers can use the distinction in (5b) to indicate whether it is the team as a collective entity that is ready, or the individual players. And in (5c), the verb inflection signals whether the speaker regards sweeping and dusting as distinct activities or two facets of a single chore. Such phenomena should make one suspicious of a mechanical, feature-copying analysis. But suppose we concentrate on the presumably more frequent cases where x' is wholly subsumed by x and hence redundant. For these I have no quarrel with the traditional notion that the agreement serves the function of signaling grammatical relationships; it might indicate, for example, that B modifies A, or that A is an argument of B. I would only reiterate in this regard that serving a specifiable grammatical function is perfectly consistent with being meaningful.

How is an agreement pattern specified? Like any other aspect of grammatical structure, it is described by means of constructional schemas abstracted from specific expressions in which it is manifested. A pattern of the form $A+x...B+x'$ involves a number of elements, so the requisite constructional schema is symbolically complex and represents multiple levels of constituency. Taken individually, $A+x$ and $B+x'$ are themselves constructions with bipolar component and composite structures. If we translate $A+x$ into our standard abbreviatory format, it can be given as $[[A/a][X/x]]$, where $[A/a]$ and $[X/x]$ are the component structures (the composite structure $[AX/ax]$ is left implicit); $B+x'$ can similarly be given as $[[B/b][X'/x']]$. The agreement pattern is then characterized by a higher-order constructional schema that incorporates the other two as components and specifies how their composite structures are integrated at this second level of constituency: $[[[A/a][X/x]] [[B/b][X'/x']]]$ (the overall composite structure is again left implicit in the formula). Whether this pattern is optional or obligatory depends on what other constructional schemas might be available to sanction the combination of *A* and *B*, and on the relative specificity and cognitive salience of these structures. If there is no other candidate, the schema in question is necessarily selected as the active node for purposes of evaluating novel expressions; hence an expression that fails to show agreement (i.e. *A+x...B*) is perceived as ill-formed by virtue of violating its specifications (that is, it constitutes an extension rather than an elaboration vis-à-vis the categorizing structure). On the other hand, the same expression will be accepted as conforming to established convention should an appropriate schema with comparable salience be available to sanction it: [[[A/a][X/x]] [B/b]].

Convenient illustration is provided by gender agreement in Spanish between a noun and an adjective. The pattern exemplified in (6) can perhaps be regarded as prototypical.

(6) a. *gato blanco* 'white male cat'; *muchacho alto* 'tall boy'
    b. *gata blanca* 'white female cat'; *muchacha alta* 'tall girl'

Though not numerically preponderant, this pattern has the advantage of being both semantically and morphologically perspicuous: the *-o/-a* contrast clearly refers to natural gender, and agreement is manifested through phonologically identical endings on the noun and the adjective. Both the individual expressions and the constructional schemas they instantiate are readily described in cognitive grammar by means of constructs already introduced. Let us start by considering the formation of *gata blanca* 'white female cat'.

The assembly of *gata* 'female cat' from its component morphemes was previously described; its internal structure is represented by the abbreviatory formula [[CAT/gat][FEMALE/-a]], where the composite structure [FEMALE CAT/gata] remains implicit (cf. Figure 5(a)). Recall that [FEMALE/-a] is itself a schematic noun, whose profile (characterized only as a 'female creature') is put in correspondence with that of [CAT/gat]; the composite meaning is derived by merging the specifications of these corresponding entities. What about the *-a* of *blanca* 'white (female)'? There is no reason why *-a* cannot be attributed exactly the same meaning when it occurs on the adjective. Under this analysis, the semantic pole of *blanca* involves the integration depicted in Figure 6(a). *Blanc* 'white' profiles the relationship between the white region of color space (labeled *W*) and a schematic trajector. The other component structure, *-a*, profiles a thing that is also fairly schematic but is at least attributed the specifications (abbreviated *F*) that constitute the notion 'female'. Integration hinges on a correspondence between the trajector of *blanc* and the profile of *-a*; this elaborative relationship serves to identify the white entity as a female creature of some kind. And since *blanc* functions as the profile determinant, the composite structure *blanca* is adjectival. Shown on the left in Figure 6(b), it is exactly the same as *blanc* except that its trajector is characterized as a female (*F*).

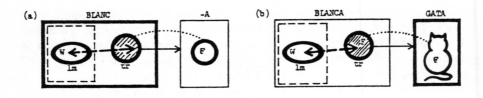

Figure 6.

Formulaically, I will represent the semantic pole of *blanc* as [**WHITE**(THING)], where the parentheses enclose the characterization of its trajector and the boldface indicates that what is profiled is the relationship between the trajector and a certain landmark. The bipolar representation of *blanc* is thus [**WHITE**(THING)/blanc], and that of *blanca* is [[**WHITE**(THING)/blanc] [FEMALE/-a]]. Implicit in this latter formula is *blanca*'s composite structure, namely [**WHITE**(FEMALE)/blanca], which--at a higher level of grammatical organization--combines with the composite structure of *gata* to derive the full expression. Sketched in Figure 6(b), their semantic integration is straightforward: once more, the schematic adjectival trajector is put in correspondence with the profile of the noun, whose characterization is more specific. At this level, however, it is the noun that functions as the profile determinant; hence the overall expression *gata blanca* designates the cat, not the adjectival relationship, which is nevertheless an important facet of the base in the overall composite structure (cf. Figure 1(a)). The formulaic representation of this composite structure is thus as follows: [WHITE(**FEMALE CAT**)/gata blanca].

The composition of *gata blanca* is summarized in Figure 7(a). In terms of the content requirement, this is a complex symbolic structure that occurs overtly.

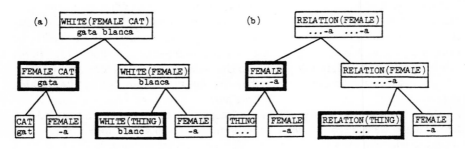

Figure 7.

Depicted in Figure 7(b) is a schematization of that structure: the symbolically complex constructional schema instantiated by *gata blanca* and an open-ended set of expressions formed on the same pattern. It is the schema that sanctions such expressions, and the categorizing relationship between the schema and a given instantiation constitutes the latter's structural description. We see, then, that the agreement pattern can indeed be specified by means of symbolic units alone.

Now that one agreement pattern has been described in fairly complete detail, the others can be discussed more briefly and represented more compactly. If we focus on the second level of constituency and employ the usual abbreviatory notation (in which the composite structure is left implicit), the constructional schema of Figure 7(b) can be given formulaically as follows: [[FEMALE/...-a][RELATION (FEMALE)/...-a]]. That is, a noun which designates a female and ends in -*a* can be modified by an adjective which also ends in -*a* as an indication that its trajector is female. In the same format, *gata blanca* has the representation [[FEMALE CAT/gata] [WHITE(FEMALE)/blanca]], which clearly reveals the parallelism between the schema and its elaboration. There is of course a directly analogous pattern for expressions headed by masculine nouns, such as *gato blanco* 'white male cat': [[MALE/...-o] [RELATION(MALE)/...-o]]. One can further envisage a more abstract schema that neutralizes the difference between these two and thus captures a higher-level generalization. Instead of referring to MALE and FEMALE in particular it invokes the schematic concept having these as special cases, and it refers schematically to a nonhigh back vowel rather than *o* and *a* specifically. Included in this high-level constructional schema is the specification that the gender and the vowel are the same in both component structures, whatever specific value they might assume.

A grammatical construction is a complex category describable as a network whose nodes are constructional schemas. For noun-adjective gender agreement in Spanish, the network is divisible into two parallel subparts, which comprise the constructional schemas involving masculine and feminine nouns. Each major schema in the subnetwork for masculine nouns stands in opposition to a corresponding schema for feminine nouns, as exemplified by the prototypes [[MALE/...-o] [RELATION(MALE)/...-o]] and [[FEMALE/...-a][RELATION (FEMALE)/...-a]]; moreover, each such pair supports the extraction of a higher-level schema that expresses their commonality. Having examined the prototype, we must now consider various extensions, i.e. corresponding constructional schemas within the two subnetworks that are less than fully perspicuous either semantically or morphologically. One such extension yields the schemas for expressions with animate nouns that do not show gender morphologically, e.g. *hombre rico* 'rich man' and *mujer alta* 'tall woman'. The adjustment is quite minimal--it is simply a matter of suspending the requirement that the noun be morphemically complex and that it end in -*o*/-*a*. The contrasting schemas are thus [[MALE/...] [RELATION(MALE)/...-o]] and [[FEMALE/...] [RELATION (FEMALE)/...-a]].

We must next consider forms like *cerro alto* 'high hill' and *mesa blanca* 'white table', where the agreement is phonologically overt but semantically opaque. Once again the description differs only minimally from the prototype: apart from the morphemic composition of the noun (see Figure 5(b)), the only difference is that *-o* and *-a* mean 'thing' rather than 'male' and 'female'. The requisite constructional schemas are thus [[THING/...-o][RELATION(THING)/...-o]] and [[THING/...-a] [RELATION(THING)/...-a]]; i.e. a noun can be modified by an adjective provided that both are inflected with *-o* or with *-a*. In examples like these, where there is no semantic contrast between the maximally schematic *-o* and *-a*, it is clear that agreement is motivated by functional considerations rather than conceptual content. Nevertheless, an analysis which treats these endings as symbolic units is perfectly coherent and fully consonant with the general principles of cognitive grammar. It is actually expected in this framework that certain grammatical markers should combine the properties of full schematicity, full redundancy, and having a specifiable function (none of which implies that they are meaningless).

The two previous extensions have rendered the agreement either morphologically or semantically nonperspicuous. There are of course expressions where it is nontransparent in both respects, for instance *lápiz corto* 'short pencil' and *flor roja* 'red flower'. These are readily described by constructional schemas in which the noun is fully schematic at both poles: [[THING/...] [RELATION(THING)/...-o]]; [[THING/...][RELATION(THING)/...-a]]. But if no restrictions are imposed on the noun, what ensures that a particular noun will take the proper form of the adjective? What prevents such combinations as *lápiz corta and *flor rojo? In other words, how does one specify grammatical gender in cases where neither form nor meaning determines the choice?

The usual approach is to mark each noun with a diacritic or a syntactic feature, but that is of course ruled out by the content requirement. Although the information that a given noun is masculine or feminine must be listed, only symbolic units can be employed for that purpose. Now to say that a noun is grammatically masculine is merely to say that it occurs in certain constructions, and in particular (since we are only concerned here with *N+ADJ* combinations) that it is modified by adjectives ending in *-o*. Hence the information that *lápiz* acts as a masculine noun (with respect to this construction) is provided by a subschema of [[THING/...][RELATION(THING)/...-o]] in which the noun is identified as *lápiz* specifically: [[PENCIL/lápiz][RELATION(THING)/...-o]]. In similar fashion, *flor* is marked as feminine by being incorporated in the constructional subschema [[FLOWER/flor][RELATION(THING)/...-a]]. The specificity of these subschemas ensures their selection as the active node whenever *lápiz* or *flor* takes an adjectival modifier. An expression like *flor rojo is therefore categorized as an extension vis-à-vis [[FLOWER/flor] [RELATION(THING)/...-a]]--and thus ungrammatical--rather than as a well-formed instantiation of [[THING/...] [RELATION(THING)/...-o]]. In the same way, *mujer alto 'tall woman' is judged deviant despite conforming to this latter schema because the role of categorizing structure is preempted by the more specific schema [[FEMALE/...] [RELATION(FEMALE)/...-a]], whose specifications it violates.

Many other constructional schemas will of course figure in an exhaustive description of gender agreement in Spanish. For example, higher-level schemas can be posited that generalize across the different classes of noun modifiers (adjectives, articles, quantifiers, and so on). Moving in the other direction, the pattern characterized by any of the schemas considered above can be further articulated by subschemas representing subpatterns with the status of conventional units, even down to the level of specific expressions of frequent occurrence. This type of system can, I believe, capture all valid generalizations while gracefully accommodating exceptions and idiosyncrasies. The noun *persona* 'person', for instance, is grammatically feminine though it refers to both males and females. This property is expressed by the constructional schema [[PERSON/persona] [RELATION(THING)/...-a]], a subschema of [[THING/...-a][RELATION (THING)/...-a]]. *Mano* 'hand', which is grammatically feminine despite ending in *o*, is likewise handled by the constructional schema [[HAND/mano] [RELATION(THING)/...-a]], which in this case is a subschema of [[THING/...] [RELATION(THING)/...-a]]. Observe that the final *a* of *persona* is analyzed as the schematic variant of the gender suffix (i.e. [THING/-a] rather than [FEMALE/-a]), whereas the final *o* of *mano* is simply part of the stem and not a gender suffix at all. Because nothing more is involved than different configurations of symbolic units, such distinctions are readily made in this framework.

5. Conclusion

I have by no means offered a complete analysis of gender agreement in Spanish. I hope to have shown, however, that agreement can in principle be handled by a system of this sort, and more generally, that a symbolic conception of grammatical structure is both coherent and potentially workable. If it is indeed workable--and I have yet to see any reason to doubt it--the symbolic alternative ought to be regarded as intrinsically preferable to autonomous theories of grammar on grounds of naturalness, restrictiveness, theoretical austerity, and conceptual unification. But regardless of one's attitude on this broader issue, I maintain that standard arguments for the autonomy thesis are invalid to the extent that they rest on the nonpredictability of grammatical structure. The essential claim of cognitive grammar is not that grammar is predictable from meaning or functional considerations, but rather that it inherently involves the structuring and symbolization of conceptual content. From this perspective, a description of grammar that pays no heed to meaning is as pointless as a dictionary that lists the forms without giving their definitions.

12. Subjectification

Inspired by formal logic based on truth conditions, semantic theory in the twentieth century has for the most part presupposed an "objectivist" view of meaning.* Indeed, semantics textbooks often devote considerable space to explaining why the student is wrong, if not hopelessly naive, in supposing that a meaning could be anything so mysterious as a thought or a concept (e.g. Kempson 1977: 15-20; Palmer 1981: 24-28). Recent years have nevertheless witnessed the emergence and continued elaboration of a reasonably explicit, empirically grounded "subjectivist" or "conceptualist" theory of meaning--in short, a true "cognitive semantics".[1] A foundational claim of cognitive semantics is that an expression's meaning cannot be reduced to an objective characterization of the situation described: equally important for linguistic semantics is how the conceptualizer chooses to construe the situation and portray it for expressive purposes. An expression's precise semantic value is determined by numerous facets of construal, including the level of specificity at which the situation is characterized, background assumptions and expectations, the relative prominence accorded various entities, and the perspective taken on the scene. It is one aspect of perspective that concerns us in this final chapter.

1. Perspective

The term perspective subsumes such factors as "orientation" and "vantage point". Many expressions invoke, not a "neutral" conception of the situation described (if such be possible), but rather one that embodies a particular viewing arrangement; the effects of that arrangement on the situation's appearance then constitute an inherent aspect of the expression's linguistic semantic value. The significance of orientation is most obvious in the case of *left* and *right*, whose use is determined by the direction in which the speaker, the hearer, or some other viewer is facing (cf. Vandeloise 1984, 1986):

(1) a. *Turn left at the next corner.*
    b. *Raisa was seated on Nancy's right.*

The import of vantage point is evident from deictics (e.g. *here* vs. *there*), from the Cora data discussed in Chapter 2, and from examples like (2), which is appropriate only if the tree is in the viewer's line of sight to the rock.

(2) *The tree is in front of the rock.*

The relevance of this construct is not limited to the spatial domain, as witnessed by tense markers and by terms like *yesterday* and *tomorrow*, whose assessment depends on a temporal vantage point. Moreover, for expressive purposes the speaker commonly assumes a vantage point other than his actual one (as in the "historical present").

Closely allied with vantage point is a further aspect of perspective that constitutes our present focus: the degree of "subjectivity" or "objectivity" with which the conceptualizer construes a particular entity or situation. Importantly, the terms subjective, objective, and their derivatives will be used here in a special, technical sense--though related, their values will not be taken as equivalent to those implied when speaking of a judgment being subjective vs. objective (i.e. 'personal, idiosyncratic' vs. 'impartial, based on solid evidence'), or even in referring to subjectivist vs. objectivist theories of meaning. The values that I will henceforth impute to them are best illustrated by a simple perceptual example. Consider the glasses I normally wear. If I take my glasses off, hold them in front of me, and examine them, their construal is maximally objective, as I will understand the term: they function solely and prominently as the OBJECT OF PERCEPTION, and not at all as part of the perceptual apparatus itself. By contrast, my construal of the glasses is maximally subjective when I am wearing them and examining another object, so that they fade from my conscious awareness despite their role in determining the nature of my perceptual experience. The glasses then function exclusively as part of the SUBJECT OF PERCEPTION--they are one component of the perceiving apparatus, but are not themselves perceived.

The contrast between subjective and objective construal therefore reflects the inherent asymmetry between a perceiving individual and the entity perceived. The asymmetry is maximized when the perceiver is so absorbed in the perceptual experience that he loses all awareness of self, and when the object perceived is well-delimited, wholly distinct from the perceiver, and located in a region of high perceptual acuity. Let us refer to this situation as the "optimal viewing arrangement". In this maximally asymmetrical arrangement, the entity construed subjectively is implicit and hence nonsalient--to use the theater metaphor, it remains offstage in the audience--whereas the objectively construed entity is salient by virtue of being placed onstage as the explicit focus of attention. Of course, such extreme polarization represents an ideal that may seldom be achieved in practice. To some extent, for example, I can perceive my glasses even while wearing them and looking at something else, and to that extent their perceptual construal is slightly objective and less than fully subjective. Subjectivity/ objectivity is often variable or a matter of degree, and it is precisely such cases that hold the greatest interest linguistically.

The optimal viewing arrangement is diagramed in Figure 1(a), using notations that should be largely self-explanatory. V is the viewer, P is the perceived object, and the dashed arrow stands for the perceptual relationship between them. The box labeled PF represents the full expanse of the viewer's perceptual field, while OS is the onstage region (also referred to as the "objective scene"), which can be characterized as the general locus of viewing attention. In the optimal arrangement, V has clear perceptual access to OS but is itself external to both OS and PF (self-perception being absent, as a matter of definition), whereas P is the specific focus of attention within OS. The construal of V is therefore subjective, and that of P objective, to the greatest possible extent. Diagramed in Figure 1(b) is an alternative that we can call the "egocentric viewing arrangement". I am probably not the first to observe that people are sometimes concerned with themselves and the relationships they bear to other entities. When this happens, V may not only be self-aware (hence included in PF), but can even go onstage, taking its place within an expanded, egocentrically determined OS region; at the extreme, V can itself become the focus of viewing attention (V = P). Each step along this path toward focused self-examination increases the objectivity of V's construal and diminishes that of P. It is only the optimal viewing arrangement, where the roles of perceiver and perceived exhibit complete polarization, that permits either full subjectivity or full objectivity.

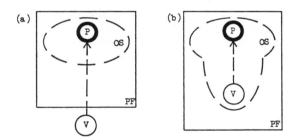

Figure 1.

Naturally, the scope of linguistic semantics extends beyond PERception to CONception overall, taken in the most inclusive sense. I will not speculate here on the extent to which nonperceptual aspects of cognition might actually be grounded in perception and shaped by perceptual principles (cf. Johnson 1987; Lakoff 1987: chapter 16). I do however believe that the notion of subjectivity/objectivity is applicable well beyond the perceptual sphere, narrowly interpreted. For one thing, even in the absence of actual perception I can easily imagine how an object appears when perceived with varying degrees of subjectivity. To take a less obvious case, suppose I experience an emotion, such as fear, desire, or elation. If I merely undergo that experience nonreflectively, both the emotion and my own role in feeling it are subjectively construed. But to the extent that I reflect on the emotional experience--by analyzing it, by comparing it to other such experiences, or simply by noting that I am undergoing it--the emotion and my role therein receive a more objective construal. Or compare how I conceive of my house when mentally tracing the route I take in driving to work, and when drawing a map showing the location of my house in relation to the campus. In the former instance, the house's location is construed subjectively, serving only as the implicit point of origin for the mental path. In the latter, by contrast, it has an objective construal by virtue of being put onstage as an explicit focus of attention.

The conceptualizations that concern us are the meanings of linguistic expressions (predications), and the various elements in Figure 1 can each be given a specific linguistic interpretation. Corresponding to V is the conceptualizer, who can be identified primarily with the speaker, secondarily with the addressee, and derivatively with some other individual whose perspective they adopt or otherwise take into account. The analog of PF is the overall scope of predication, defined as the maximal conception (or conceptual complex) that an expression specifically evokes and relies on for its semantic characterization. The correspondent of OS is the immediate scope of predication (e.g. the immediate scope of *elbow* is the conception of an arm, whereas its overall scope is the conception of the body as a whole). Analogous to P is the entity that the expression designates, i.e. its profile; for example, *elbow* takes the conception of an arm as its base, and within that base it profiles a major joint and the immediately surrounding area. The profile can also be characterized as the focal point within the immediate scope--it is onstage and objectively construed by definition. Finally, the perceptual relationship in Figure 1 corresponds to the construal relationship, which resides in the conceptualizer entertaining a certain conception and construing it in a particular fashion.

2. Grounding

I use the term "ground" for the speech event, its participants, and its immediate circumstances (such as the time and place of speaking). There is a rather tenuous sense in which the ground figures in the meaning of every expression: the very fact of being a linguistic expression implies a potential user, and in any actual use the speaker and hearer are likely to be at least dimly aware of their role in entertaining and construing the conception evoked. But if that is the extent of their involvement--as it is, say, for common nouns and verbs considered in isolation (e.g. *lamp, tree, toaster, day, twist, die, imagine, denigrate*)--then the speaker/hearer role is almost wholly subjective, and for descriptive purposes we can regard the ground as being external to the scope of predication. This configuration is diagramed in Figure 2(a), where G, MS, and IS respectively stand for the ground, the maximal scope, and the immediate scope (onstage region), and heavy lines indicate profiling. The class of "deictic" expressions can now be defined as those which necessarily do invoke the ground and thus include it in their scope. We can distinguish two broad classes of deictics. One class comprises expressions like *yesterday, tomorrow,* and *last year,* where the ground remains offstage as an implicit, unprofiled reference point, as sketched in Figure 2(b). Forming the other class are expressions such as *I*, *you*, *here*, and *now*, in which some facet of the ground is put onstage and profiled, as depicted in Figure 2(c). Naturally, as one goes from (a) to (c) the construal of G becomes progressively more objective.

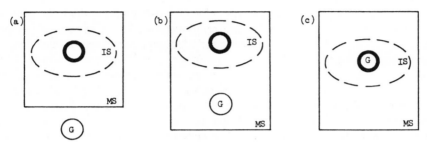

Figure 2.

Along another axis, linguistic expressions divide into two basic classes depending on the nature of their profile. A nominal expression profiles a thing, and (unsurprisingly) a relational expression designates a relation. Recall that thing and relation are used as technical terms whose characterization is highly abstract (see Chapter 3). A thing is conveniently represented by a circle and functions as the profile of nouns, pronouns, and full nominals (i.e. noun phrases). Such classes as adjectives, adverbs, prepositions, participles, verbs, and finite clauses profile relations; for present purposes, they can all be depicted by means of a line connecting the major participants (be they things or other relations), as shown in Figure 3(a). A relational expression usually manifests an asymmetry whereby one of its participants is singled out as that being located or assessed, or whose interactions are being followed through time. This is the trajector (tr),

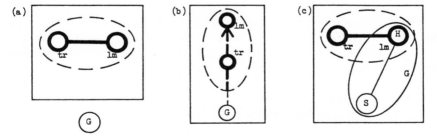

Figure 3.

hypothesized to be the figure within the profiled relationship. A salient entity other than the trajector is termed a landmark (lm). The subject/object distinction is just one, clause-level manifestation of trajector/landmark asymmetry, which is attributed to the internal structure of relational expressions at every level of organization (even single morphemes).

A profiled relation can occupy a number of different positions vis-à-vis the ground. Figure 3(a) represents a wholly objective construal in which the ground lies outside the scope of predication, as exemplified by such expressions as *under, chase, eaten, tall,* and *carelessly.* The ground (or some facet thereof) can also be included in the scope of predication as an offstage, unprofiled reference point. An example is *The tree is in front of the rock,* where the tree (tr) stands in the speaker's (and possibly the hearer's) line of sight to the rock (lm), as sketched in Figure 3(b). A third option is for a particular facet of the ground to be put onstage as one of the relational participants. Diagramed in Figure 3(c), for instance, is the configuration implied by an expression like *beside you:* the hearer (H) functions as an objective, overtly specified participant, whereas the speaker (S) remains implicit and subjective.

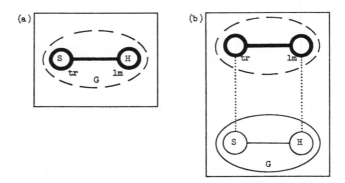

Figure 4.

Finally, the speech event itself constitutes a relationship capable of going onstage as the profile of a finite clause. In this case the immediate scope is identified with the ground, as shown in Figure 4(a). The resulting sentences are traditionally known as "performatives":

(3) a. *I tell you that she is innocent!*
   b. *I order you to go back to work immediately.*
   c. *I promise you that it will never happen again.*

It is well known that such expressions can generally be interpreted as either performatives or mere descriptions (unless disambiguated by an adverb such as *hereby* or *every morning*). Leaving aside the aspectual contrast (simple vs. habitual), we can characterize the difference between the performative and descriptive readings as residing in whether or not the ground and profile coincide. Figure 4(b) diagrams the descriptive interpretation, in which the profiled relation is distinct from the (offstage) speech event itself, even though its trajector and landmark correspond to the speech-act participants (as indicated by the dotted lines). Because the ground and profile remain distinct in 4(b), the former is to some degree construed subjectively, and the latter objectively. On the other hand, the coincidence of ground and profile in 4(a) removes the very basis for the subjective/objective asymmetry. Hence the speaker-hearer interaction designated by a performative clause has a degree of subjectivity that is the lowest possible for the ground, as well as a degree of objectivity that is the lowest possible for a profiled relationship.

It is well-established and uncontroversial that nominals (noun phrases) and finite clauses represent universal grammatical categories with special structural significance. I attribute the distinctive character of these constituents to the fact that they are "grounded", by which I mean that the profiled entity bears some relationship to the ground in regard to such fundamental issues as reality, existence, and speaker/hearer knowledge. In the case of English nominals, grounding is effected by articles, demonstratives, and certain quantifiers. Whereas a simple noun (e.g. *cat*) merely names a "type" of thing, a full nominal (*this cat*; *some cat*; *any cat*; *a certain cat*) designates an "instance" of that type and gives some indication of whether and how the speech-act participants have succeeded in establishing mental contact with that particular instance. Likewise, whereas a simple verb (e.g. *fall*) merely names a type of process, a finite clause (*It fell*; *It may fall*; *It would fall*) profiles a process instance and situates it with respect to the time and immediate reality of the speech event. Tense and the modals effect the grounding of finite clauses in English.

The grounding that derives a nominal or a finite clause need not be phonologically overt. For instance, both tense and modality are phonologically zero in a clause like *I see it*, yet in each case the absence of an overt marking has specific conceptual import ('immediacy to G' and 'location in reality'--cf. Langacker 1978 and *to appear*, chapter 6). At the same time, not every expression that satisfies the previous semantic description actually functions as a grounding element in the sense of being critical to the formation of a nominal or finite clause. A clause is not rendered finite by *tomorrow*, for example, even though this locates an event with respect to the time of speaking (*To work tomorrow would be inappropriate*). We can reasonably suppose that only "grammaticized" (as opposed to "lexical") elements can serve as true grounding predications. For the moment, it is sufficient to note that a grammaticized element is quite schematic semantically (i.e. it lacks the specificity and rich detail typical of lexical items) and tends to assume a "relativistic" or "topological" character rather than indicating a specific shape or value (cf. Talmy 1988b). Grounding predications do not necessarily constitute a homogeneous or sharply-bounded class, but there is no question that prototypical exemplars--such as articles, demonstratives, and tense markers--adhere to that characterization: their meanings are limited to general specifications concerning fundamental "epistemic" issues (reality, identification, etc.); moreover, they do not locate the profiled entity in terms of precise values or specific units of measurement ('at 3 PM'; 'with 83% certainty'; 'two miles past the horizon'), but only relative to the ground ('known to the speaker and hearer'; 'distant from the speaker'; 'prior to the moment of speaking').

Another trait of typical grounding predications--the one that most concerns us here--is that the ground itself receives a highly subjective construal despite its pivotal role. Indeed, I have argued elsewhere (1985) that a number of their grammatical properties are direct consequences of the ground being construed with maximal subjectivity, consistent with its inclusion in the scope of predication. It is instructive in this regard to compare the grammatical behavior of grounding elements to that of other expressions which appear to be semantically equivalent. Asked to provide a rough paraphrase of *this*, for example, one might well suggest the conjunction of *known to us* (i.e. 'definite') and *near me* ('proximal to the speaker'). Similarly, *before now* seems reasonable as a gloss for the past-tense predication, and *possible* for the epistemic sense of *may*. Observe that these seeming paraphrases represent such classes as adjectives, participles, and prepositional phrases, all of which are analyzed in cognitive grammar as atemporal relations. Judging from their behavior, however, the grounding elements do not belong to this category. For instance, whereas atemporal relations combine with *be* to form a clausal head, as in (4), we see from (5) that the corresponding grounding elements cannot.

(4) a. *The village is known to us and near me.*
   b. *The deadline was before now.*
   c. *A conclusive victory is possible.*

(5) a. **The village is this.*
   b. **The deadline was -ed.*
   c. **A conclusive victory is may.*

One can of course argue that (5b) is deviant because the past-tense morpheme cannot stand alone as an independent word, but even if we overlook this morphological deficiency the sentence is still quite bad. Nor does it matter that (5a) is marginally acceptable when *this* is interpreted as a predicate nominative-- the point is rather that (5a) cannot be taken as directly analogous to (4a), with *this* attributed the relational value 'known to us and near me'.

In brief, the evidence indicates that the grounding predication for a nominal profiles a thing and is thus itself a schematic nominal. This is fully consonant with the fact that many such expressions (*this, those, most, some, each, any*, etc.) are used independently as nominal pro forms--that is, as full noun phrases schematic in regard to type. Analogously, the grounding predication for a finite clause is best analyzed as designating a process, i.e. a temporal (rather than an atemporal) relation, as does a verb or a finite clause overall. Hence it is unsurprising that modals function as clausal pro forms (*She may*; *They could*; *You must*). We therefore want to say that a grounding expression is schematic for the constituent it derives, and that it designates a thing or a process even though it conveys the sort of content characteristic of atemporal relations. The distinction made in cognitive grammar between base (content) and profile (designation) allows a straightforward statement of the desired generalization: a grounding predication evokes as its base a GROUNDING RELATIONSHIP, but within that base it profiles only the GROUNDED ENTITY (a schematically characterized thing or process). When a grounding expression combines with other elements to form a specified (nonpro) nominal or finite clause, its profile--the grounded entity--is equated with that of the nominal or clausal head.

The crucial semantic contrast between a grounding predication and its atemporal counterpart is therefore not so much a matter of conceptual content as one of construal, specifically profiling and subjectivity. As shown in Figure 5(a), an expression like *identified to us* or *known to us and near me* profiles the grounding relationship (R_g): it is an atemporal relation (participial and/or prepositional) whose landmark is a facet of the ground, and whose trajector is the grounded entity. Note in particular that G is overtly coded as a central relational participant, hence it is salient and objectively construed. Diagramed in 5(b) is the corresponding grounding predication, such as *the* or *this*. Let us assume (though just for sake of discussion) that 5(a) and 5(b) incorporate precisely the same conceptual content. Even so, the alternative profiling they impose on this common base constitutes a semantic distinction entailing their membership in different grammatical classes. The grounding expression is nominal rather than relational because its profile is limited to the grounded entity, a thing; R_g remains unprofiled,

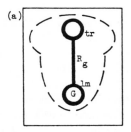 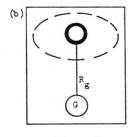 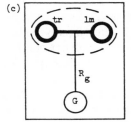

Figure 5.

while G is offstage and nonsalient. Likewise, Figure 5(c) represents the grounding predication for a finite clause, e.g. a past-tense marker. Here the profiled entity is a schematic process, which in construction is rendered specific by the inflected verb stem. The tense inflection is thus itself an abstract verb (just as *the* or *this* is an abstract noun), whereas an expression like *before now* or *prior to the time of speaking* designates R$_g$ and is atemporal rather than processual.

An essential property of grounding predications is that G is necessarily implicit despite its pivotal role as a reference point. For instance, there is no way to directly specify the landmark of *the* or *this*: expressions like **the us village* or **(the) village this me* are decidedly ill-formed (even uninterpretable). It is of course possible to specify the landmark indirectly, as in *the village identified to us* or *the village near me*. However, such periphrasis merely corroborates the contrast being drawn, since it relies on the very atemporal relations to which the grounding predications are being compared. The fact that these latter do not themselves permit explicit reference to the ground can be taken as indicative of a strongly subjective construal. Moreover, if we assume that G is construed with a high degree of subjectivity, the special profiling characteristic of a grounding element follows as an automatic consequence. Recall that a predication's profile is by definition the focal point within its immediate scope (the onstage region). By the same token, the trajector and primary landmark are twin foci within a relational predication, hence integral facets of the profiled relationship. But such a role is incompatible with strong subjectivity: if G is offstage and highly subjective, it cannot simultaneously be onstage anchoring a relationship (R$_g$) with the prominence and objectivity implied by profiling. The profile is thus restricted to the grounded entity. A grounding predication designates neither G nor R$_g$, essential though they are to its value.

3. The nature of subjectification

Having examined the nature of subjectivity and established its linguistic significance, let us now explore it from the diachronic standpoint. My central claim is that "subjectification" represents a common type of semantic change, and that it often figures in the process of "grammaticization", whereby grammatical elements evolve from lexical sources. It is of course a fundamental tenet of cognitive grammar that all grammatical units have some kind of conceptual import, so that lexicon and grammar form a continuum divisible only arbitrarily into separate components. As an element becomes grammaticized it therefore moves along this continuum rather than jumping from one discrete component to another, and it undergoes a change of meaning rather than becoming meaningless. Still, this change generally does involve some kind of semantic attenuation (or "bleaching", to use Givón's original term), which tends to be accompanied, iconically, by a reduction in phonological status (e.g. from an independent form to a clitic, affix, or inflection). These semantic and phonological developments are concomitant with the expression's conventionalization as one member of a relatively small set of contrasting elements systematically used for a particular structural purpose.

In the last few years, considerable progress has been made toward understanding the semantic attenuation inherent in grammaticization. We may note a number of recurrent factors, which are neither mutually exclusive nor sharply distinct. A frequent component of grammaticization (and semantic change in general) is transfer from a concrete to an abstract domain (cf. Sweetser 1984, 1987; Traugott & Dasher 1987). Also, a grammatical marker is usually quite schematic, its evolution marked by a loss of specificity that results in its applicability to a broader range of contexts (Bybee 1988; Bybee & Pagliuca 1985). Beyond this, grammaticization apparently preserves image-schematic structure and is presumably constrained by the "topological" or "relativistic" nature of grammatical meanings (Sweetser 1988; Talmy 1988b). Finally, grammaticized elements often shift from "propositional" to "textual" and "expressive" meanings, or from describing an external situation to reflecting evaluative, perceptual, or cognitive aspects of the "internal situation" (Traugott 1982, 1986, 1988). This last factor amounts to subjectification, under a broad interpretation of that term. My intent here is to show that at least some instances of grammaticization involve subjectification in the narrow sense, namely an increase in subjectivity as previously defined.

Subjectification in this narrow sense is represented abstractly in Figure 6. Its starting point, depicted on the left, is the canonical arrangement in which an external relationship, labeled XY, is construed objectively by the speaker and hearer. This relationship does not specifically invoke the ground as a participant or a reference point; in such cases, we will say that it runs along the "objective axis". The speaker and hearer do of course have a subjective involvement, for they entertain the conception even if they are not themselves a part of it. This

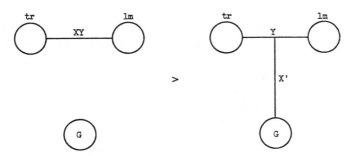

Figure 6.

construal relation between the conceptualizers and the object of conception is usefully thought of as being aligned along a "subjective axis", which leads from G to the profiled entity onstage and is thus orthogonal to the objective axis. Subjectification can now be characterized as the realignment of some relationship from the objective axis to the subjective axis. In Figure 6, the relationship thusly realigned is X, a facet or component of XY.[2] This results in the configuration shown on the right: in lieu of X, involving objectively construed participants, we find an analogous relationship, X', that holds instead between the objective situation and some aspect of the ground.

4. A spatial example

To clarify these notions, let us first consider a familiar spatial example. The preposition *across* has a number of established senses, two of which are illustrated in (6) and diagramed in Figure 7.

(6) a. *Vanessa jumped across the table.*
   b. *Vanessa is sitting across the table from Veronica.*

In (6a), *across* designates a complex atemporal relation, i.e. a sequence of locative configurations all involving the same trajector and landmark. Through time, represented in Figure 7(a) by the solid arrow (t), the trajector occupies a continuous series of positions with respect to the stationary landmark, thus defining a path leading from one side of the landmark to the other. This sense of *across* does not invoke the ground in any way: the profiled relationship lies wholly along the objective axis, while the ground is offstage and external to the scope of predication. The speaker/hearer role is maximally subjective, being limited to that of conceptualizer in the construal relation. The dashed arrows stand for a central facet of this construal, namely the conception of the trajector's sequential location at different positions along the spatial path.

In (6b), *across* profiles a simple atemporal relation. That is, it consists of just one configuration (not a series) and is capable of being fully instantiated at a single point in time (though the sentence as a whole attributes it a temporal duration coextensive with the immediate scope of predication). Sketched in Figure 7(b), this second sense of *across* represents a subjectification in relation to the first. Comparison of the two diagrams reveals that, with respect to the trajector and landmark themselves, the SINGLE locative relationship in 7(b) is identical to the FINAL one in the ordered sequence of 7(a). This shared relationship corresponds to Y in Figure 6: it is that portion of the original objective structure that is left behind when the remainder (X in Figure 6) is realigned from the objective to the subjective axis. The portion that undergoes the realignment is the conception of the trajector following a spatial path to arrive at this location. Although 7(b) does

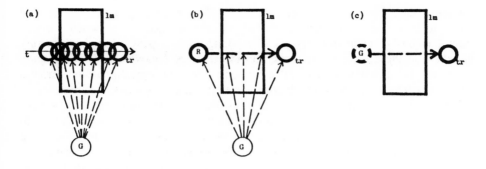

Figure 7.

not portray the trajector as moving in any way, it does involve a path-like notion pertaining to how the trajector's position is characterized. *Across* specifies that the trajector lies on the opposite side of the landmark from a reference point, R, which in (6b) is equated with Veronica. The use of *from* indicates that Veronica is conceived as the origin of a path, whose terminus is clearly the trajector; physical motion along this path would take one from Veronica's location to Vanessa's via the same trajectory followed by the moving trajector in 7(a). Yet nobody moves in (6b)/7(b)--at least not objectively. The only "movement" over this path is subjective, residing in the conceptualizer tracing along it mentally in order to locate the trajector vis-à-vis the reference point. This mental scanning is the manifestation of the realigned relationship along the subjective axis, and thus corresponds to X′ in Figure 6. Though analogous to the objective motion of (6a)/7(a), it is subjective because it only arises as part of the conceptualizing process.[3]

The foregoing instance of subjectification represents a general type characterized by the following central property: spatial motion on the part of an objectively construed participant is replaced by subjective motion (mental scanning) on the part of the conceptualizer. Let me mention just in passing that numerous English verbs have undergone an extension with this property:

(7) a. *The balloon {rose/fell/ascended/descended} rapidly.*
   b. *The hiker {went/ran/climbed} up the hill.*

(8) a. *Beyond the 2000 meter level, the trail {rises/falls/ascends/descends} quite steeply.*
   b. *The new highway {goes/runs/climbs} from the valley floor to the senator's mountain lodge.*

Whereas the subject in (7) in each case moves along a spatial path, the sentences in (8) describe static configurations in which a spatially-extended subject simultaneously occupies every location along such a path. The directionality inherent in these latter expressions, and the sense of "movement" they inspire, can only be attributed to subjective motion by the conceptualizer, who traces a mental path by scanning in a particular direction along the subject's expanse.

While these examples merit further discussion, for present purposes it is more relevant to call attention to two additional features shared by the extensions in (6) and in (7)-(8). First, when the conception of motion is realigned from the objective to the subjective axis, the objective situation that remains constitutes a single, static configuration. The resulting sentences are therefore imperfective, i.e. they follow the continuation through time of a stable relationship, even though their objective counterparts profile a change through time and are thus perfective (Chapter 3). Second, subjectification does not per se affect the choice of trajector and primary landmark. For instance, the same entity functions as trajector both in Figure 7(a), where it moves, and in 7(b), where it does not. Likewise, the objective entity that occupies all the points along the spatial path is chosen as the subject (clausal trajector) in both (7) and (8), despite being stationary in the latter. This is not only unproblematic in the present framework but is actually predicted. It is unproblematic because the notions trajector and landmark are characterized in terms of prominence (figure/ground organization) rather than any specific semantic roles (in particular, the trajector need not be a mover). It is predicted because the special prominence characteristic of the trajector and primary landmark is incompatible with subjectivity. Hence the conceptualizer cannot inherit the status of trajector (figure) when it becomes a subjective mover.

A second basic type of subjectification is exemplified by the following contrast:

(9) a. *Vanessa is sitting across the table from me.*
    b. *Vanessa is sitting across the table.*

Sentence (9a) is directly analogous to (6b), the only difference being that the reference point is identified as the speaker (*me* instead of *Veronica*). As for (9b), we will only concern ourselves with the default-case interpretation, where it too takes the speaker as reference point. Now the principles of cognitive grammar predict a semantic contrast between (9a) and (9b), even though they describe precisely the same spatial configuration. I have argued elsewhere (1985) that the formal distinction between overt and covert reference to the ground (as in *from me* vs. zero) iconically reflects its being construed with a greater or lesser degree of objectivity. Thus (9a) suggests a detached outlook in which the speaker treats his own participation as being on a par with anybody else's, whereas (9b) comes closer to describing the scene as the speaker actually sees it. For this reason (10a) is considerably more natural than (10b):

(10) a. *Look! My picture's in the paper! And Vanessa is sitting across the table from me!*

　　b. *?Look! My picture's in the paper! And Vanessa is sitting across the table!*

Examining a picture of oneself involves self-construal that has a high degree of objectivity, for it literally implies an external vantage point. This is consistent with the objectivity conveyed by the speaker's explicit self-reference in the final clause of (10a), but inconsistent with the subjectivity signaled by the lack of such reference in (10b).[4]

Across in (9a) can thus be attributed the same value it has in (6b), as diagramed in Figure 7(b). Through explicit self-reference (*from me*), the speaker puts himself onstage as an objectively construed participant (R). This may imply that the speaker "steps back" and views himself from an external perspective (in conformity with the noncoincidence of G and R in 7(b)); at the very least it involves the egocentric viewing arrangement, where the OS-region expands to encompass the ground (cf. Figure 5(a)). On the other hand, (9b) invokes a distinct sense of *across* in which the reference point is specifically equated with G (or the speaker's position in particular). Diagramed in Figure 7(c), this latter sense adds another degree and type of subjectification to that already observed in the relation between Figures 7(a) and 7(b). This further subjectification occurs when an originally objective reference point comes to be identified with a facet of the ground, which retains its subjective construal. Accordingly, the reference point is labeled G in Figure 7(c). Moreover, the circle representing it is drawn with a dashed line to indicate a certain measure of subjectivity: as the position from which the scene is viewed, G itself is either at the fringes of the OS-region (not a focus of observation) or perhaps offstage altogether (cf. Figure 3(b)).

The coordination of these two types of subjectification constitutes a productive pattern of semantic extension for path prepositions in English. That is, many path prepositions have a pair of established senses analogous to those of *across* diagramed in Figures 7(a) and (c): one sense describing spatial motion, objectively construed; and a second sense in which (i) spatial motion is replaced by subjective motion (i.e. mental scanning along a path leading from a reference point to the trajector's static location), and (ii) that reference point is identified with the ground, subjectively construed. Examples like the following are well known:

(11) a. *They hiked over that hill.*

　　b. *The village is just over that hill.*

(12) a. *She drove through the tunnel.*

　　b. *The guardhouse is through the tunnel.*

(13) a. *We strolled past the pet shop.*
    b. *The camera store is well past the pet shop.*

The same kind of extension occurs with complex path expressions formed by juxtaposing two or more prepositional phrases:

(14) a. *Fred walked through the yard, over the bridge, (and) across the field.*
    b. *The outhouse is through the yard, over the bridge, (and) across the field.*

Clearly, then, the pattern is applicable to an open-ended set of novel path expressions.

5. The future sense of 'go'

A further instance of this sort is the frequent evolution of motion verbs, 'go' in particular, into future markers displaying varying degrees of grammaticization (cf. Givón 1973; Ultan 1978; Bybee & Pagliuca 1987). Let us briefly review the analysis presented in Chapter 5, placing it in the context of the present discussion. Consider this French example (or its English translation):

(15) *Elle va fermer la porte.* 'She is going to close the door'

A sentence of this kind is ambiguous. On one reading, it describes objectively construed movement by the subject along a spatial path, at the end of which the subject initiates some activity. This sense is diagramed in Figure 8(a), where the squiggly arrow stands for the process thus initiated. As the goal of the trajector's motion, this schematically characterized process is a "relational landmark" of 'go'; the precise nature of this process is spelled out by the accompanying infinitival-clause complement. Additionally, (15) has a future reading in which the subject is not specifically portrayed as traversing any spatial path at all--she may already be at the door, for instance, or perhaps she can close it by remote control. Though it is not precluded that the subject moves, the sentence does not itself so indicate.

How does this future sense of 'go' derive from the original spatial sense? One might suggest that it constitutes a metaphorical extension from the spatial to the temporal domain: rather than moving through space in order to initiate the infinitival process, the subject moves through time. It does seem evident that the notion of a path receives a temporal interpretation. Nevertheless, this space-to-time transfer cannot be the only change involved. Observe, for example, that with the spatial reading the subject necessarily intends to carry out the infinitival process. However the temporal reading carries no such implication--instead we find a generalized conception of imminence or predictability, such that the speaker

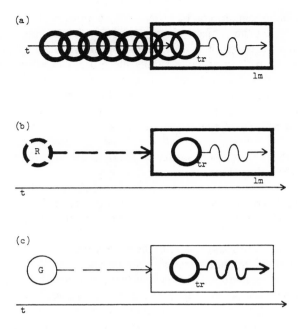

Figure 8.

(as opposed to the subject) foretells the event's occurrence. A sentence like (16) could therefore be uttered by a seismologist testing a predictive theory, or by any speaker willing to assume an air of prescience, but it does not imply that the earthquake moves through time with destructive intent:

(16) *Un tremblement de terre va détruire cette ville.* 'An earthquake is going to destroy that town'

Furthermore, in this example it is incoherent to analyze the subject as moving along a temporal path at the end of which it initiates the infinitival process. For all intents and purposes, the earthquake is coextensive with that process. Certainly its span of existence is not construed as extending from the moment of speaking until the future time at which the destruction occurs.

These considerations point to subjectification as a crucial factor in the extension of 'go' from its spatial sense to a marker of futurity. In fact, this extension is directly analogous to the one depicted in Figure 7, except that the two increments of subjectification (that leading from 7(a) to 7(b), and that leading from 7(b) to 7(c)) are accompanied by transfer from the spatial to the temporal domain. The effect of these modifications can be observed by comparing Figures 8(a) and 8(b). In the latter, it is not the subject who traverses a path--the subject merely carries out the infinitival process; it is instead the speaker/conceptualizer, who traces mentally along the path in order to situate the process in relation to a reference point. Moreover, this scanning proceeds through time (t) rather than space, and aligns itself with the flow of time, so the infinitival process is subsequent to the reference point (i.e. temporally downstream from R). Finally, there is a strong tendency for the reference point to be equated with the moment of speaking. This is especially so in French, where *aller* can only assume its future value when inflected for either the present (so that $R = G$) or the imperfect, as respectively illustrated in (15) and in (17a).

(17) a. *Elle allait fermer la porte.* 'She was going to close the door'
   b. *Elle ira fermer la porte.* 'She will be going to close the door'

The English *gonna* construction is more flexible, which we can take as indicative of a lesser degree of grammaticization. For instance, the English gloss in (17b) does permit a reading of future imminence (marginal though it may be), whereas the French example can only be interpreted as a description of future motion.

Thus Figure 8(b) represents a particular stage in the evolutionary process whereby a verb meaning 'go' grammaticizes to become a marker of future tense. Importantly, a verb at this stage is not yet a tense marker in the same way as English *-ed* or the inflectional future of French (e.g. *-a* in (17b))--that is, it is not yet a grounding predication that necessarily takes G as its reference point and constitutes the final, criterial step in forming a finite clause. Note that French *aller* and English *be going to* are themselves inflected for tense and do allow a reference point other than G. Despite their future value, they are themselves finite, inflected verbs that function as clausal heads (the future event being coded by an infinitival complement). What do they profile? Not the future event, but rather the relationship drawn with heavy lines in Figure 8(b): they designate the continuation through time of the (locally) stable configuration in which the landmark event (expressed by the infinitival complement) lies downstream in time from the reference point, as assessed by the speaker's mental scanning. Hence these verbs are imperfective, which we have already seen to be a consequence of the type of subjectification through which they arise. We have also seen that subjectification can occur without affecting trajector/landmark assignation. Observe that the same entities function as trajector and landmark in Figures 8(a) (the motion sense) and 8(b) (the future sense). Therefore, from the fact that the same nominal is the subject of 'go' on either the motion or the future interpretation, one cannot conclude that the latter construes it as the mover. I would claim instead that the future sense of 'go' profiles the relationship in which the trajector's participation in the landmark process lies at the end of a temporal path leading downstream from R.

A true future-tense marker has the value depicted in Figure 8(c). Recall that a grounding predication profiles the grounded entity rather than the grounding relationship. It is consequently the downstream event--a schematic process--that is profiled in 8(c), not its relation of temporal posteriority to the reference point (cf. Figure 5(c)). Moreover, in a grounding predication the reference point is specifically equated with the ground and construed with a high degree of subjectivity. The evolution of 8(b) into 8(c), i.e. of a 'go'-type future into a tense marker in the narrow sense, therefore involves two kinds of subjectification. We have already considered the first kind, wherein an originally objective reference point comes to be identified with the ground. In large measure, R and G are equated even in a 'go'-type future, as noted above; their identification is carried to completion in the further evolution producing a grounding predication. The second kind of subjectification is as follows: when G receives a highly subjective construal, a relationship invoking it as reference point loses its profiling to become an unprofiled facet of the base. Profiling implies a substantial degree of objectivity, and if G participates in a profiled relationship, it must at least be at or near the periphery of the onstage region. Thus, as G goes farther offstage, its construal becoming increasingly subjective, at some point the relation it anchors must also be considered offstage and hence excluded from the profile. It is for precisely this reason that a grounding predication fails to designate the grounding relationship, leaving only the grounded entity in profile. In the case of a tense marker, as in 8(c), that entity is a schematic process (which is spelled out in more specific terms by the clausal head).

6. Modals

This last type of subjectification can be further illustrated by the contrast between the English modals, which function as grounding predications, and the modals of German, which do not. To put the evolution of English modals into proper perspective, let us start at the period (Old English and beyond) at which they were main verbs whose essential content was purely objective. It is well known, for example, that *will* derives from a verb meaning 'want', that *may* imputed to its subject the strength or physical ability to do something, and *can* the requisite knowledge or mental ability. Verbs like these have certain properties, sketched in Figure 9(a), that make them appropriate sources for the development of modals. First, each invokes the conception of an associated process, which represents what it is that the subject wants or is somehow able to do. This schematic process is thus a relational landmark and is rendered specific by an infinitival complement. Second, the same individual functions as trajector of both the verb and the associated process; this identity is specified by the dotted correspondence line. Third, the trajector (manifested by the subject) is the locus of some kind of "potency" directed at the landmark process: a physical or mental force that, once unleashed, tends to cause its occurrence. This directed potency is represented by the double arrow. Finally, this arrow is drawn with dashed lines to indicate that the realization of the landmark process is potential rather than actual.

The evolution of the present-day English modals from sources of this kind can be seen as primarily a matter of progressive subjectification. The first major step in this evolutionary sequence comes about when the notion of directed potency is realigned from the objective to the subjective axis. In particular, the locus of this potency comes to be identified, not with the individual who carries out the landmark process, but rather with the speaker or with some other entity whose potency the speaker is in a position to report on. Thus in Figure 9(b) the objectively construed subject is no longer the source of potency, though it is still trajector of the landmark process. The potency directed at that process is an

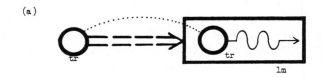

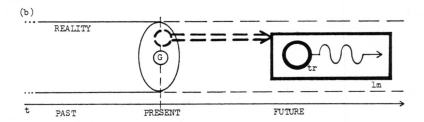

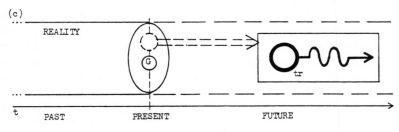

Figure 9.

abstract force such as obligation or permission (cf. Talmy 1988a), and its locus is some facet of current reality as assessed by the speaker. In the diagram, the speaker's conception of past and present reality is represented by a cylinder, which should be thought of as "growing" toward the future as reality evolves through time (following one potential path out of all those conceivable). The leading face of this cylinder defines the present, which by definition is where the ground is located.

The modals schematized in Figure 9(b) are main verbs (clausal heads) rather than grounding predications. They are directly analogous to the future 'go' of English and French (Figure 8(b)), in that the profiled relationship is the one that connects the landmark process to the ground (or to an associated reference point-- in this case, some other facet of present reality). Figure 9(b) thus represents a stage in the evolution of English modals at which they were comparable to the modals of modern German. Two basic grammatical properties indicate that the German modals are in fact main verbs rather than grounding predications serving to derive finite clauses. First, unlike the English modals they tolerate verb inflections whose specific effect is to render a verb nonfinite. Hence the German modals all have infinitival forms: *können* 'to be able to'; *sollen* 'to be supposed to'; *müssen* 'to have to'; *mögen* 'to like to'; *wollen* 'to want to'; and *dürfen* 'to be allowed to'. They also form past participles that occur in the perfect construction as complements to 'have': *Ich habe es gemusst* 'I have had to do it'. Second, the German modals themselves bear inflections for tense and person that I would analyze as grounding predications: *ich darf* 'I may'; *du darfst* 'you may'; *wir dürfen* 'we may'; *ich durfte* 'I was allowed to'; etc. Observe that English modals do not inflect for person. The reason is that they themselves have a grounding function: they combine with "tense" to form complex grounding predications that stand in opposition to those incorporating person inflections.[5]

From the configuration of Figure 9(b), the present-day English modals evolve through further subjectification. The crucial development is that the conception of directed potency loses its profiled status, the source of that potency (either the speaker or some other facet of present reality) being offstage and subjectively construed. The resulting expressions are grounding predications: as shown in Figure 9(c), they no longer profile the grounding relationship (directed potency), but only the grounded process serving as its target. Consider *must*, where the potency amounts to a kind of necessity. While it is certainly true that this notion of necessity provides the essential CONTENT, it is just the process deemed necessary--which *must* itself characterizes only schematically--that the modal actually DESIGNATES. The nature of the designated process is specified in finer detail by other clausal elements. Elaborating its trajector is a nominal which is thereby identified as the clausal subject (e.g. *She must*). The process overall is equated with the one profiled by the clausal head, so that in *She must leave*, for instance, the process deemed necessary is that of leaving.[6]

Hence the contrast between the German- and English-type modals (Figures 9(b) and (c)) is directly parallel to that between a 'go'-type future and a true future-tense marker (Figures 8(b) and (c)). It is important that this contrast not be confused with the distinction commonly drawn between "root" and "epistemic" meanings of the modals: since both root and epistemic senses are displayed by the main-verb modals of German, and also by the grounding modals of English, the two distinctions cannot be the same. Additionally, some of the German modals still have uses reflecting the configuration of Figure 9(a), as do English *can* and *will* (though I suspect that these latter no longer profile the relationship of potency). It is hardly surprising that senses corresponding to different degrees of subjectification might coexist for long periods of time.

How, then, can the root/epistemic distinction be characterized? Sweetser (1982, 1984) analyzes it as being a matter of whether the directed potency (abstract force) is manifested in the social sphere or the domain of reasoning. Without disagreeing, one can also see it as hinging on whether or not the locus of this potency can be identified with a particular individual, or at least with some delimited facet of present reality. For example, we speak of *should* having a root sense when the envisaged occurrence of the landmark process is construed as an obligation imposed by the speaker. A root sense may also involve the speaker reporting an obligation imposed by some other source of authority: it can be another person, an abstract entity such as a law, or even something as diffuse as societal norms or cultural expectations (e.g. *He shouldn't be so callous*). It thus seems natural to analyze an epistemic modal as representing a limiting case, that in which diffuseness of the locus of potency is pushed to its ultimate conclusion. In the senses we regard as epistemic, the locus of potency is the polar opposite of a focused, well-delimited source of authority--rather, it is identified holistically as the nature of evolving reality itself. Because the locus is undifferentiated and all-encompassing, factors that correlate inversely with objectivity, extension from a root to an epistemic meaning constitutes a type of subjectification. Moreover, construing the locus in this fashion entails a shift to another kind of potency, since authority or societal obligation can hardly be attributed to reality as an undifferentiated whole. Instead, reality itself--the way things are and the way they are going--is seen as having a certain "evolutionary momentum" that carries its future evolution in the direction of the landmark process and lends it a greater or lesser chance of actually reaching that target (cf. *The way things are going, we should finish by noon*).

Epistemic modals show an additional wrinkle that points to yet another layer of subjectification. At issue are expressions like those in (18).

(18) a. *You must be tired.*
     b. *He may be finished by now.*

Observe that these do not pertain to the likelihood of the target situation occurring in the future, but rather to the possibility that it already obtains. This usage reflects a shift in the domain where the notion of "momentum" is manifested: this conception is transferred from the evolution of REALITY ITSELF to the evolution of our KNOWLEDGE OF (PRESENT) REALITY. The sentences refer to an objective situation that already either is or is not part of present reality (*You are tired*; *He is finished by now*). What remains a matter of future potentiality is the revelation of this state of affairs to the speaker (and secondarily, to the hearer)--the modals express the likelihood that, as the speaker's knowledge of current reality continues to expand, the profiled situation will prove to be a part of it. Because reality is largely external, while knowledge of reality lies wholly within the province of the conceptualizer, the notion of evolutionary momentum is construed more subjectively when applied to the latter.

7. Possession and perfect aspect

Let us consider just one further example, namely the evolution of possessive verbs and their eventual grammaticization as markers of perfect aspect. It is well known that the typical source for such a verb is one describing a relationship of direct physical control (e.g. 'grasp', 'hold', 'keep'). A verb of this kind involves the configuration sketched in Figure 10(a), where the double arrow represents the transmission of energy from the subject (tr) to the object (lm). Now as a generalized verb of possession develops from this source, the notion of physical energy transfer becomes more and more attenuated. For one thing, a person who possesses an object does not necessarily hold it or make any other kind of physical contact: I do *have a shovel*, but I am not now using it or touching it; and if I *have a bar of gold*, I will probably store it in a vault and never touch it at all. Since the energy transfer implied by possession of this sort does not represent any actual instance but is only potential (or at most habitual), the arrow depicting it in Figure 10(b) is drawn with dashed (instead of solid) lines. There is further attenuation

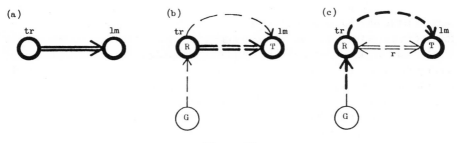

Figure 10.

when the notion of energy transmission is generalized and interpreted abstractly as applying to any kind of control or access. If I *have 10,000 shares of blue-chip stock*, I receive the income they generate and can dispose of them as I like, even though I may never interact with them in any physical way. Likewise, I *have certain rights, privileges, and prerogatives* that I can exercise as I choose; while this may entail physical consequences, it is only in an abstract sense that I can be said to interact with these entities per se. A nonphysical analog of energy transmission may predominate even with possession of a concrete object. If I *have a painting by Miró*, for example, physical control may be far less important than the visual access it affords.

The possessive uses considered so far all involve ownership, in either a basic or a metaphorical sense of that term. Possessive locutions are of course employed in many other ways, not all of which are obviously susceptible to such a description. Their use with expressions for body parts and kinship relations is universal and seemingly fundamental: although such possession does imply a certain kind of "potency" (we control our body physically, and the obligations attendant on kinship afford us a measure of social control), I very much doubt that we understand these relationships metaphorically in terms of ownership. In other examples, the possessor does not appear to manifest any kind of potency vis-à-vis the entity possessed:

(19) a. *Sam has a wart on his elbow.*
 b. *That theory has many serious problems.*
 c. *We have a lot of coyotes around here.*

Such considerations have led me to hypothesize that the linguistic category of possession has an abstract basis (i.e. a schematic characterization applicable to all class members) with respect to which ownership, part/whole, and kinship relations constitute special, prototypical cases.[7] What all possessives share, I believe, is that one entity (the "possessor") is used as a reference point (R) for purposes of establishing mental contact with another, the target (T). The reason that ownership, part/whole, and kinship relations are prototypical for possessives is that they in particular are central to our experience and lend themselves very well to this reference-point function. In the nature of human experience, people are far more likely to be known individually than their possessions and are thus more readily construed as reference points than as targets in the conception of their relationship (*The beggar has a cup*; *??The cup has a beggar*). Similarly, a part is characterized in relation to a larger whole, which usually has greater cognitive salience and is quite naturally chosen as a reference point (*The woman has long legs*; *??The long legs have a woman*). And for kinship terms, the possessor (ego) is a reference point virtually by definition.

The single dashed arrows in Figure 10(b) represent the mental path by which the speech-act participants establish mental contact with the target. I suggest that all possessives involve this reference-point function, even though it is commonly overshadowed by more objective notions with greater conceptual content (e.g. ownership). However, certain possessive uses show very little vestige of such notions, in which case the reference-point relationship becomes salient by comparison and may assume the status of relational profile. Consider (19c), roughly sketched in Figure 10(c). The subject (*we*) serves primarily as the point of reference for establishing a particular geographical area (*around here*) as the region within which the target (*a lot of coyotes*) is located. It would be too strong to claim that the role of *have*'s trajector in this construction is exclusively that of a reference point--also conveyed by (19c) is the idea that the presence of coyotes is potentially "relevant" to the trajector (e.g. we might conceivably see them or otherwise interact with them). Still, this notion of potential relevance seems decidedly secondary.[8] It is therefore shown as unprofiled in Figure 10(c), being depicted by the double-headed dashed arrow (r).

The extension leading from the configuration of Figure 10(b) to that of 10(c) can be regarded as a kind of subjectification, in that the prominence characteristic of profiling passes from an objective relationship of control, access, or potency to a reference-point relationship based on the subjective phenomenon of the conceptualizer establishing mental contact with the target. A precisely analogous change figures in the evolution of *have* into a marker of perfect aspect. In that case, however, the relevant sense of *have* is one in which the target is not a thing but rather a process construed atemporally and expressed by a past-participial complement. The hypothesized starting point is thus an expression such as *He has finished*, which is the same in form as the modern English perfect construction, albeit different in meaning. Specifically, the precursor of the perfect *have* is assumed to have profiled a relationship of relevance or potency between its trajector (specified by the subject) and the prior event described by the complement. On this interpretation, *He has finished* would indicate, roughly, that the subject stands in a relationship of accomplishment vis-à-vis the finishing, or that the prior occurrence of finishing remains relevant to him.

This hypothesized source is diagramed in Figure 11(a). The trajector participates in a profiled relationship of potency or relevance (r) with respect to a temporally prior event that constitutes a relational landmark. The dotted correspondence line indicates that the trajector of the profiled relation and that of the landmark process are the same. The landmark's temporal priority should perhaps be taken as a semantic contribution of the participial inflection. In any case, the construction does invoke time (t) as a central domain and takes the trajector--or more precisely, the time at which the trajector participates in relationship r--as a reference point for establishing the landmark's temporal location.

(a)

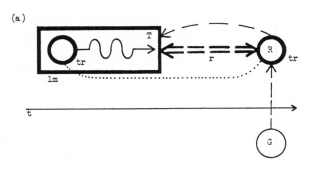

(b)

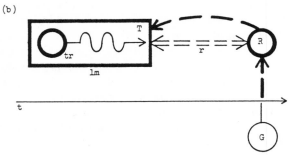

(c)

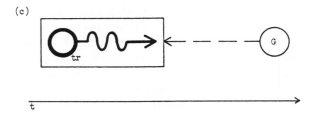

Figure 11.

Diagramed in Figure 11(b) is the perfect sense of *have*. It diverges from Figure 11(a) in only two respects, each of which we have observed in other instances of subjectification. First, the trajector ceases to be identified as the reference point, though it does continue its role as trajector of the landmark process (cf. Figures 8-9). The result is that the landmark event is no longer taken as being relevant to the SUBJECT in particular, but rather to SOME OTHER LOCUS (R), which often coincides with G.[9] Second, relation r becomes less salient, and as it does the reference-point function emerges as the profiled relationship (cf. Figures 10(b)-

(c)). The perfect *have* thus profiles the continuation through time of the stable situation in which the trajector's participation in the landmark process is located with respect to a temporal reference point (the participial inflection of the complement indicating that it precedes that reference point). As an unprofiled facet of its base, the perfect *have* further specifies that the landmark process bears to R a relationship traditionally described as one of "current relevance".

A construction of this sort is susceptible to further subjectification. For one thing, the notion of current relevance--the last vestige of the original objective relationship (Figure 10(a))--is rather tenuous and can fade away entirely; with r removed from Figure 11(b), all that remains is the reference-point function of temporal anteriority. The French perfect has in fact evolved to this degree, hence the *passé composé* is often translated into English with the simple past tense: *Il a fini* 'He finished'. Nevertheless, French *avoir* is still an inflected verb that serves as the head of a finite clause; it is not a grounding predication, for it designates the relationship of temporal anteriority rather than the prior event itself.[10] Subsequent evolution into a true past-tense marker can of course be envisaged. Required are two additional kinds of subjectification already described with respect to the emergence of other grounding predications (cf. Figures 8(b)-(c) and 9(b)-(c)): the coincidence of R and G becomes obligatory; and the relationship between G and the landmark process loses its profiling, with the consequence that only that process--the grounded entity--is designated. The resulting configuration is sketched in Figure 11(c).

8. Conclusion

At all three stages depicted in Figure 11, the trajector of the landmark process is also the trajector of *have* overall. Since analogous observations hold for all our previous examples (Figures 7-10), we can make the following generalization: the choice of trajector and primary landmark (subject and object) is not altered by subjectification per se, nor by the grammaticization that eventuates in a grounding predication. The trajector and the primary landmark (if there is one) are objectively construed, by definition serving as focal points within the profiled relationship onstage. Therefore, when one facet of a profiled relationship undergoes subjectification--starting with realignment from the objective to the subjective axis (Figure 6), followed by loss of profiling and (in some cases) eventual disappearance--the status of trajector and primary landmark can only be conferred on entities found within that portion of the original relationship that retains its objective construal. For example, there is no change in subject as *Il va finir* 'He is going to finish' evolves from a motion expression to a 'go'-type future (Figures 8(a)-(b)). The subject's role does however become more limited: no longer the mover (objective motion having been replaced by subjective motion on the part of the speaker), the subject is active only as indicated by its role as trajector of the landmark process. Similarly, the subject of a modal ceases to be the locus of directed potency (Figure 9), and the subject of the perfect *have* is neither the reference point nor the locus of current relevance (Figure 11). In each case the subject's active involvement is confined to its role within the target process.

This structure is perfectly consistent with the trajector's characterization in cognitive grammar as relational figure and hence as a kind of focal point within the objective scene (OS).[11] Moreover, it explains the semantic "transparency" of these grammaticized verbs, i.e. the fact that modals, the future 'go', and the perfect 'have' occur with any type of subject. Because the subject's actual participation is limited to the landmark process, it need only be semantically compatible with the infinitival, participial, or verbal complement expressing that process. This transparency was handled in transformational grammar by positing the rule of Subject-to-Subject Raising. One implication of the present analysis is that such a rule is artifactual, transparency being an inherent consequence of semantic factors, including subjectivity. Although it is beyond the scope of this chapter, the classic distinction between "raising" and "equi" verbs ought to be reexamined in these terms (cf. Newman 1981 and chapter 10 of Langacker *to appear*).

One of the "semantic-pragmatic tendencies" pointed out by Traugott as being characteristic of grammaticization is that "meanings tend to become increasingly situated in the speaker's subjective belief-state/attitude toward the situation" (1988: 410). In this chapter I have tried to build on that observation by examining certain instances in precise and explicit detail. I have argued that basic notions of cognitive grammar afford a coherent--and to some degree explanatory--account of the evolution and grammatical behavior of grammaticized elements. Among these notions are subjectivity and subjectification, whose subtlety and near ineffability should not be allowed to obscure their pivotal role in grammaticization and the semantic value of grounding predications. A broader conclusion is that the perspective taken on a scene, one facet of which is its subjectivity/objectivity vis-à-vis the conceptualizer, represents an important factor in both semantic and grammatical structure.

Final remarks

Though still unfamiliar to many linguists, cognitive grammar has rapidly and steadily developed. From a sketchy, programmatic conception of linguistic structure, it has evolved to become an increasingly well-articulated descriptive framework being applied to a substantial array of languages and grammatical phenomena. The foregoing chapters have applied it to a variety of languages from a number of different families and shown its utility for both synchronic and diachronic analysis. Detailed accounts have been provided of a broad spectrum of grammatical problems, including locatives, passive voice, raising constructions, agreement, case marking, ergativity, auxiliaries, aspect, transitivity, valence, grammatical relations, and the semantic characterization of basic grammatical classes. Beyond the present volume, moreover, fine-grained studies are now available treating such diverse topics as Samoan clause structure (Cook 1988a), English verb-particle combinations (Lindner 1981), locatives in French, English, and Cora (Vandeloise 1984, 1986; Hawkins 1984; Casad 1982), Russian aspectual verb prefixes (Janda 1984), case semantics in German and Slavic (Smith 1987; Janda *to appear*), transitivity and passivizability (Rice 1987b), and Nahuatl verb morphology (Tuggy 1981, 1986, 1988, 1989).

Interested scholars are therefore not without resources for assessing the theory's viability and potential insight. In making this assessment, three general considerations ought to be borne in mind that I regard as being of prime importance: naturalness, conceptual unification, and theoretical austerity. Cognitive grammar is natural in the sense that it relies only on well-established or easily demonstrable cognitive abilities (e.g. to categorize, to establish correspondences, to form complex conceptual and phonological structures, to forge symbolic links between the two, to impose figure/ground organization, to conceive of a situation at different levels of specificity, and so on). It is conceptually unified because it posits only semantic structures, phonological structures, and symbolic relationships between them. Lexicon, morphology, and syntax thus form a seamless whole consisting exclusively of symbolic structures, and semantics constitutes an inherent and indissociable aspect of grammar. The framework is theoretically austere by virtue of the content requirement. The only elements ascribable to a linguistic system are semantic, phonological, and symbolic structures that occur overtly as (parts of) linguistic expressions, schematizations of such structures, and categorizing relationships.

Descriptions conforming to these restrictions can, I think, accommodate the full range of structures encountered in natural languages. Perfecting the descriptive tools required for such descriptions is one of three related tasks involved in formulating a comprehensive linguistic theory. The second task is to specify the relative prototypicality of semantic, phonological, and symbolic structures, as determined by such factors as frequency of occurrence, order of acquisition, and degree of universality. The third task is to explain such prototypicality with reference to functional considerations. For this purpose, linguistic structure must be examined from the acquisitional, communicative, psychological, discourse, sociolinguistic, diachronic, and ecological perspectives. I believe that cognitive grammar offers a natural and revealing basis for studies of these kinds. It is therefore with great anticipation that I envisage the further interaction and progressive integration of cognitive grammar with functional approaches to language structure. The prospect of a comprehensive synthesis is both intellectually exciting and a realistic goal for the future evolution of cognitive linguistics.

Notes

Chapter 1: Introduction

*   The original version of this chapter appeared under the title "An introduction to cognitive grammar" in *Cognitive Science* 10: 1-40, 1986. It is reprinted with the permission of the Ablex Publishing Corporation.

1.   Observe that designation, in my technical sense of the term, does not pertain to the relation between a linguistic expression and the world--rather it is a relationship holding between a cognitive domain as a whole and certain of its subparts. I do not know whether profiling reduces to any independently established cognitive phenomenon. Possibly it constitutes one level of figure/ground organization, but not every figure is a designatum.

2.   In these expressions *eye* is evidently construed as the eye region, not the eyeball itself.

3.   The constructs needed to make this notion of subjectivity/objectivity precise are introduced in Langacker 1985 and 1987a, chapters 3 and 7. For vantage point and orientation, see Chapter 2 and Vandeloise 1984.

4.   Goldsmith 1980 presents a very similar analysis.

5.   The importance of conventionality should be emphasized. Often a speaker is led to employ a particular image simply because an alternative construction, which might seem more appropriate, happens not to be conventionally established. For instance, many verbs of transfer (e.g. *transfer* itself) are not employed in the double-object construction; the *to*-construction represents the speaker's only option with such verbs.

6.   At this level of organization, we can ignore the fact that *sharpen* is morphemically complex. The double-headed arrow labeled (e) in Figure 7 indicates identity of the associated structures.

7.   Fuller discussion is provided in Chapter 10. (See also chapter 11 of Langacker 1987a.)

8.   By reversing the trajector/landmark assignation, we obtain the predicate [BELOW].

9.   I omit the dashed line standing for the profiled interconnections, because the nature of these interconnections is implicit in the position of the major participants within the diagrams. Note that I regard these diagrams as heuristic in character, not as formal objects. They are analogous to the sketch a biologist might draw to illustrate the major components of a cell

and their relative positions within it.

10. Only for convenience do I speak of discrete states--a process is more accurately viewed as continuous.

11. The component structures are enclosed in boxes, to indicate that *above* and *the table* have the status of units. Closed curves surround the composite structure and the construction as a whole on the presumption that *above the table* is a novel expression (in the text, parentheses serve this purpose).

12. Omitted are the semantic contributions of the definite article and the verb inflection on *be*. Note that our concern is not the nature of agreement (cf. Chapter 11), but rather the issue of whether *the lamp* can be considered the subject of *be* in accordance with assumption (i).

Chapter 2: Inside and outside in Cora

*   This chapter was jointly authored with Eugene H. Casad. The original version was published under the title "'Inside' and 'outside' in Cora grammar" in the *International Journal of American Linguistics* 51: 247-281, 1985. It is reprinted with the permission of the University of Chicago Press.

1. Cora is a Uto-Aztecan language spoken by more than 10,000 people in the state of Nayarit, Mexico; Huichol is its nearest congener. The data in this article represents the dialect of Jesús María, Municipio de El Nayar. It was collected by Casad under the auspices of the Summer Institute of Linguistics between February 1971 and July 1977, both in the town of Jesús María and at the S.I.L. workshop centers at Ixmiquilpan, Hidalgo and Mitla, Oaxaca. Gratefully acknowledged is the aid and instruction of numerous Cora speakers, in particular Profesor Eusebio Zeferino Enriquez and the late Santos de Jesús. Casad 1977 is a preliminary description of the Cora locative system. A much fuller account is given in Casad 1982. Casad 1984 offers an overall description of the language.

2. Phonetic symbols are used with standard values, but note that ['] represents high tone, and [C^y] a laminal consonant. The following grammatical abbreviations are employed: PROX = proximal; MED = medial; DIST = distal; APPLIC = applicative; STAT = stative; EXT = extensive; ART = article; DUR = durative; SUBR = subordinator; PL = plural; REFL = reflexive; COMPL = completive. Hyphens are used for morpheme boundaries, and equal signs for clitic boundaries.

3. *e* is simply a phonetic variant of *a* 'outside'.

4. To emphasize that only two morphemes are involved, 'inside' and 'outside' are used throughout for the glosses of *u* and *a*. This should not be taken as a

denial of the polysemy outlined in the text.

5. This array may well include only a subset of the specific senses, and there need be no single structure that is schematic for all the other nodes in the network.

6. This position is in essential agreement with Fillmore (1977), who claims that meanings are always relativized to "scenes", and also with Haiman (1980), who argues persuasively that none of the apparent grounds for delimiting a restricted set of dictionary-type specifications for the description of a lexical item can be considered viable.

7. Let us avoid confusion by stating what the term "image" is not meant to imply. Most crucially, cognitive grammar makes no claim that all meaning reduces to visual imagery. (The frequent use of pictorial diagrams may have led some people to this erroneous conclusion.) Though visual imagery (and sensory imagery more generally) is indeed significant for semantic structure, it is certainly not exhaustive of it, and in fact the theory would be little affected if there were no such thing. Visual imagery probably does figure in the data considered here, which pertains primarily to spatial relationships. It should be noted, however, that a visual image is not in any meaningful sense a mental picture, nor is it anything mysterious: visual imagery has been shown by cognitive psychologists to be a viable topic of rigorous empirical investigation (see, for example, Kosslyn 1980).

8. The notions subject and object are special cases of trajector and landmark, respectively (see Chapter 9). Observe that the use of heavy lines to indicate the trajector alone is a convenient but ad hoc departure from the usual value of this notation (profiling). The same is true for the use of a circle to indicate the trajector even when the latter is a process rather than a thing.

9. As a general point, the location of a process is determined solely by the location of its participants and cannot be dissociated from it.

10. Alternatively, one could say that semantic specialization is the special case of semantic extension that obtains when all of the specifications of the original sense are compatible with the extended sense. The distinction between the two types of relation is not considered to be of prime importance; being a matter of degree, this distinction is often difficult to make, but nothing of substance hinges on the decision.

11. Note that semantic constituency correlates very well with phonological constituency, as generally proves to be the case in this framework.

12. We shall see later that an additional factor is also at work in motivating this *u/a* contrast.

13. A nonbasic domain is one that is not cognitively irreducible, i.e. a knowledge structure that can be analyzed into more fundamental notions.

14. This termination of the line of sight at the skyline simply reflects the fact that light travels in a straight line, so that something on top of a slope is generally not visually accessible to a viewer at its foot.

15. We have no basis for determining whether *h-* 'on a vertical surface' is a generalization of the topographical sense 'in the face of a slope' or whether the latter is a specialization of the former. The gloss 'face of slope' is used consistently in the examples simply for sake of uniformity.

16. The fact that the horizon does not actually enclose a trajector on the other side of it demonstrates that the 'inaccessible'/'accessible' sense of Figure 12 has become conventionally established and differentiated from the basic sense of Figure 1.

17. Lindner (1981, 1982) has found something very similar in the English verb-particle construction. Compare *The stars came out* with *The lights went out*. In the former *come out* indicates departure from a region of inaccessibility to the viewer, presupposing an external vantage point. In the latter *go out* indicates departure from a region of accessibility, presupposing an internal vantage point.

18. The 'inaccessible' construal does not seem plausible for (9a), which pertains to the inside of a house being all lit up by light visible through the windows. This constitutes evidence for positing penetration and accessibility as separate (though often correlated) parameters associated with the *u/a* contrast.

19. The other verb prefixes no doubt contribute to this contrast as well. The prefix *ka-* 'down' in (14a) renders the vertical dimension more salient, while $t^y a$- in (14b) highlights the position of the opening in the horizontal plane of the earth's surface.

20. Cf. the work of Friedrich on the role of shape in grammar (1969a, 1969b, 1970, 1971).

21. We are concerned with the verb prefix *u-* in (4a), not the particle *yú*. The 'inside' predication of this particle pertains to the region alongside the river; it represents an extension of *u* (from its topographical 'line of sight' value) that will not be further dealt with here.

22. If 'go' is considered to be neutral, focusing specifically on neither the origin nor the goal of the path, the choice of *a* still follows from the fact that *a* is the unmarked member of the *u/a* pair and occurs whenever the conditions for *u* are not fully satisfied; this matter is pursued below. These examples lend further support to the position that the trajector of *u/a* is best considered to be the verbal process itself rather than a participant in that process (the subject in particular). With the latter analysis we would in effect be claiming that the mover/viewer is located either in back or in front of

himself. This is not inherently contradictory (since the different locations pertain to different points in time), but it strikes one as less natural and needlessly contrived.

23. This discussion simplifies matters by conflating two notions distinguished in Chapter 1: scale (i.e. how large a region is included), and scope (i.e. which particular region is included, given a scale specification). A fuller discussion would also reveal that 'distance from the speaker' oversimplifies the value of the elements labeled PROX, MED, and DIST (but not in any way that affects the present analysis); see Casad 1982.

24. This discussion concerns deictic particles only and the scope of predication associated with them--it does not necessarily carry over to larger expressions containing these particles, such as the full phrases in (6) or the sentence as a whole. Since the explanation is based on the natural correlation between deictic specifications of distance from the speaker, on the one hand, and scope, on the other, it is at the level of the deictic particle that these scope considerations can be expected to prevail. The scope of predication may be greater at the phrasal or clausal level due to the presence of other expressions not tied so closely to deixis. Therefore, the presence in (6) of the postposition -ta'a 'in' does not contradict the analysis.

25. The occurrence of a in *mátavan ví ira' ata' a* 'right there across the river in the cornfield' is consequently doubly motivated. Based on the prototypical values of *u/a* (Figure 1), it is justified because the landmark overflows the scope of predication. Based on their extended values related to accessibility (Figure 13), it is justified because the trajector is on the same side of the horizon as the viewer.

26. Positing a single value and leaving the remainder for a separate "pragmatics" or "usage component" would amount to gratuitous compartmentalization and result in the removal from the domain of grammatical description of almost everything there is to say about these morphemes. Obviously nothing would be solved by an apriori decision of this sort.

Chapter 3: Nouns and verbs

* The original version of this chapter appeared in *Language* 63: 53-94, 1987. It is reprinted with the permission of the Linguistic Society of America.

1. To choose an example at random: "...no constant semantic effect is associated with the functioning of a morpheme as a noun, as a verb, or as any other part of speech" (Langacker 1973a: 87).

2.   This does not, however, establish the autonomy of grammar (see Chapter 11).

3.   See Lakoff 1982 and 1987 for comprehensive discussion of the prototype model (pioneered by Eleanor Rosch) and a devastating critique of the objectivist paradigm.

4.   This is pointed out by Lyons (1977: 440-441), and also by Jacobsen (1979), who argues persuasively that the noun/verb distinction is valid even for those languages commonly cited as lacking it.

5.   These terms are considered abstractly, as names for geometrical figures. When used for physical objects, they further invoke a notion of material substance, which introduces other (nonbasic) domains.

6.   Observe the contrast between the more schematic expressions *note* and *tone*: both designate a type of sound, but *note* specifically identifies this sound as being situated on a musical scale, while *tone* presupposes only the basic domain of pitch.

7.   I can say this based on previous knowledge (in which case the scope of predication includes more than the present extension of my visual field), but not to report my immediate perceptual experience.

8.   Cf. Langacker 1987a. Gentner (1981) explains certain psychological findings by suggesting that "noun referents" are very cohesive; they show a greater density of internal "links" or relationships than "verb referents", whose relations are more sparsely distributed through a domain.

9.   The individuation of a color sensation at some location presumably requires cognitive events (involving perception of contrast, etc.) above and beyond those that constitute the sensation itself.

10. Pluralization is one of the grammatical behaviors that identify count nouns, but its result is a type of mass noun. Plurals act like other mass nouns in many respects; e.g. they occur without determiners as full noun phrases (*She bought {fruit/peaches}*), and they take certain quantifiers that cannot combine with count nouns (*I ran into a lot of {trouble/problems/*problem}*). However, their behaviors contrast in regard to such factors as verb agreement and the selection of demonstratives (*These peaches are rotten* vs. *This fruit is rotten*). Wierzbicka 1985 provides extremely insightful discussion of the semantic factors which distinguish the mass-noun subclasses.

11. Confirming this reranking is the predicted change in domain of quantification: *three (good) wines* indicates three types, not three spatially distinct instantiations.

12. Evidence for this analysis is adduced in Langacker 1987a (chapter 6). Note that the trajector need not be construed as moving: the definition (relational figure) is abstract and thus broadly applicable. The notions subject and object are special cases of trajector and landmark, respectively.

13. Since *above* and *below* invoke the same domain (oriented space) and profile the same interconnections, the choice of trajector (figure) is solely responsible for their semantic contrast. The same is true for *before* and *after*.

14. Discreteness in the diagrams and formulas is simply for expository convenience. The mental experience is obviously continuous, and I make no claim that individual states are necessarily recognized as separate entities at any level of processing.

15. Infinitives and participles also have nominal variants (see section 11).

16. Recall that, by convention in diagrams of this sort, the upper participant is the trajector unless otherwise indicated.

17. Specifically excluded from (9b) are finite-clause relatives. The special status of finite clauses makes this a principled exception (cf. Langacker 1985).

18. The terms "active" and "stative" are more commonly employed; I resist them because "active" verbs often involve neither an action nor an agent, while "stative" is best reserved for single states (rather than the sequence of states that constitute a process). My imperfective class is equivalent to what Vendler (1967) calls "states"; his other three categories ("achievements", "activities", and "accomplishments") are subclasses of perfectives. (The contrast called "perfective"/"imperfective" in Slavic studies is not equivalent.)

19. Smith (1983) has drawn a similar conclusion; our analyses are basically compatible.

20. In saying that these sentences describe changes, I abstract away from the semantic contribution of the progressive construction, which serves to convert a perfective process into a type of imperfective.

21. The profile serves as the "focal point" within the (immediate) scope of predication.

22. I am concerned here only with the temporal use of the "past-tense" inflection. Langacker 1978 explains how this is related to its modal uses.

23. The progressive *-ing* and the *-ing* on noun modifiers are the same, though only the latter occurs with imperfectives (e.g. *anyone knowing his whereabouts*). The analysis explains this distributional contrast: the imperfectivizing function of *be...-ing* is nonvacuous only for perfectives, but either type of process requires the atemporalization effected by *-ing* to be

suitable as a modifier (generalization (9b)).

24. A comparable degree of abstraction is witnessed in mass nouns like *furniture* and in terms for superordinate categories (consider the plural *animals* used with reference to the diverse creatures found in a zoo).

25. Recall mass nouns like *grass*, whose homogeneity resides in the basically uniform distribution of easily discernible but more-or-less identical particles. My proposal treats *walk* as analogous to the count noun *lawn* (a bounded expanse of grass).

26. Since the imagery embodied by lexical and grammatical structures is to some degree conventional, another language might treat such processes as imperfective by focusing on their internal homogeneity. This would account for the corresponding verbs occurring in the simple present (e.g. French *Il dort* vs. English *He is sleeping*).

27. Equally important are standard assumptions about the proper role and level of predictability in linguistic analysis. Langacker 1987a (part I) argues for an alternative view.

Chapter 4: The English passive

* The original version of this chapter appeared under the title "Space grammar, analysability, and the English passive" in *Language* 58: 22-80, 1982. It is reprinted with the permission of the Linguistic Society of America.

1. Even when syntactic rules are restricted to small or arbitrary subclasses of lexical items, this has sometimes been stated in the lexicon through syntactic features on the lexical items, so that the rules could be given in fully general form in the syntactic component (cf. Chomsky 1965; Lakoff 1970). A complex formalism was thus invoked to save the thesis from its empirical liabilities.

2. It is structured in the sense that some units function as parts of other units (e.g. both *dog* and *-s* are components of the higher-order unit *dogs*).

3. The archetypal conception is wrong to claim that a generalization is necessarily missed if particular statements (content units) are listed in a grammar. This position implicitly assumes that the choice is between RULES ALONE and LISTS ALONE (in which case one must opt for the rules, as lists by themselves express no generalizations). However, the real choice, as I see it, is between RULES ALONE and BOTH RULES AND LISTS. In this conception, generalizations are captured (by rules, i.e. schemas) with either option. See Chapter 10 for further discussion.

4.   As a notational device, units are enclosed in rectangles or square brackets, while nonunit elements are enclosed in ellipses or parentheses.

5.   Figure 1 is a content structure with unit status. It instantiates a schema which embodies a general pattern of plural formation, and which is exactly parallel to Figure 1. It is obtained by replacing the specifications of [DOG] with the schematic semantic structure corresponding to the count-noun category, and by making a similar adjustment at the phonological pole.

6.   A distinction must be made between two kinds of componentiality, which might be termed "unipolar" and "bipolar". The former pertains to how complex structures are built up from components at the semantic or the phonological pole alone, apart from any consideration of symbolic units. Thus, at the phonological pole, unipolar componentiality involves natural phonological units, such as the organization of segments into syllables. In bipolar componentiality, the components are determined by symbolic considerations. The phonological units *dog* and *s* within *dogs* are of this sort, having structural significance only because of their symbolic associations. Bipolar componentiality is thus the same as analyzability, which is our present concern. Unipolar and bipolar components need not coincide (e.g. *dog* is not a natural phonological unit within *dogs*).

7.   Recall that the term image simply pertains to alternate ways of construing or structuring a conceived situation. It does not imply that meaning reduces to mental pictures or to visual imagery (e.g. as understood in Kosslyn 1980).

8.   As explained in Langacker (1976), my position is Whorfian in the sense of claiming that languages differ in the semantic structure which they impose on conceptualization, but not in the sense of claiming that conventional semantic structure has any tyrannical grip over our thought processes. We are perfectly capable of seeing through the conventional images of our language and of dealing nonlinguistically with conceptual structure. (Indeed, the fading of conventional imagery, leading ultimately to loss of analyzability and the consequent reanalysis of complex forms, is one of the major forces of language change.)

9.   Analyzability and the conventional imagery which it embodies are also important for diachronic considerations. It is well known that *peas* used to be parallel to *corn* in English, a simple unanalyzable mass noun. The back formation leading to the current structure can be represented in the formula [PEA-PL] > [[PEA]-[PL]]. It is of course much more common for composite expressions to gradually lose their analyzability.

10. Note that quantifiers like *some* function as nominal heads, and can be categorized as nouns.

11. The acceptability of such expressions as *almost all the peas* (pointed out to me by James McCawley) might seem to undermine this argument for the meaningfulness of *of*, but it would do so only in a framework where strongly predictive rules were being used to achieve economy. (E.g. a rule such as "Expressions of the form *QNT the N* are possible just in case QNT is universal" might be used to eliminate from the grammar explicit reference to such patterns as *all the N* and *both the N*.) Cognitive grammar is not such a framework. It is a "usage-based" model, where content units and low-level patterns with unit status are listed, and coexist in the grammar with whatever schemas can be extracted from them (Chapter 10). Even when distributional facts are clearly motivated by functional or semantic considerations, the grammar is not relieved of the burden of listing these facts. Thus *all the N* and *both the N* must both be listed as low-level patterns of English, despite the functional/semantic basis for their development--even if the higher-order schema *UNIV-QNT the N* is extracted to embody the generalization. Since schemas are permissive rather than restrictive, the existence of this schema does not prevent the lower-level pattern *all the N* from generalizing in another direction, giving rise to the schema *[(MDF) all] the N*, which sanctions expressions of the form *QNT the N* whenever the quantifier is *all*, with or without a modifier. This latter schema has such subschemas as *all the N, almost all the N, nearly all the N*, and *not all the N* as immediate instantiations, each reflecting an established pattern of English usage.

12. This emphasis on surface form is not, however, to be taken so strictly as to rule out the possibility of zero morphemes, or of grammatical morphemes whose semantic value is essentially vacuous in the sense of being overlapped by the meanings of other elements.

13. The constituency trees for grammatical constructions are always bipolar, as in Figure 1, but the phonological pole is often suppressed for ease of representation. The phonological pole of constituency trees is the functional equivalent of surface phrase structure in transformational grammar, though obviously there are substantial differences of conception and detail.

14. This mixture of novelty and unit status is typical of complex expressions. It helps explain how speakers are able to put together complicated "novel" expressions in real time--fluent speech would hardly be possible if every combinatory relationship in an expression had to be computed anew from rules or schemas.

15. This level-by-level amalgamation, coordinated at the semantic and phonological poles, is quite reminiscent of the relation between semantic interpretation rules and syntactic tree structure both in the Katz-Fodor semantic theory (1963) and in Montague grammar (cf. Partee 1975). To be

sure, the form-meaning correlation proposed here is embedded in a rather different overall framework, and my conception of semantic structure differs from that of those two models. It should be evident that cognitive grammar differs from Montague grammar in not conceiving of semantic structure as a logical representation in any standard sense of the term.

16. The situation is not drastically changed if, instead, we draw the line between stems (formed from roots by derivational processes), on the one hand, and all larger units (including words derived from stems by inflectional processes), on the other.

17. In fact, discord far more blatant than this between sanctioning and sanctioned expressions is tolerated, and often favored for expressive purposes. Metaphorical extension, a natural and pervasive feature of language use and change, differs only in degree from the present example. Though the point is not emphasized here, it can be seen that the present framework accommodates metaphorical extension as a normal, integral part of linguistic structure.

18. It is not claimed that this schematic notion invariably achieves unit status or cognitive salience. Nor is it claimed that a lexical network necessarily has a single superordinate schema bearing a relation of full schematicity to all other nodes in the network.

19. Phonological integration works very much like semantic integration (see Chapter 6). Recall that the syntagmatic combination at the semantic pole in Figure 2 is symbolized by corresponding syntagmatic relationships at the phonological pole.

20. Autonomy and dependence are matters of degree, and in some cases there is no basis for the designation. Note that my use of the term dependent is quite different from that in dependency grammar, and often at odds with it. This may seem perverse, but in fact there are good reasons for the terminology (see Langacker 1987a).

21. In a more precise formulation, the e-site would be equated with the type specification shared by all the discrete objects (see part I of Langacker *to appear*).

22. The adjective *red* makes salient internal reference to a thing (its trajector, which it locates in a particular region of color space) that corresponds to the profile of *cup*, but the internal reference of *cup* to a color specification is considerably less prominent. This same "valence potential" between the dependent *red* and the autonomous *cup* is exploited in both examples, but at different levels of organization. In *red cup*, the two morphemes combine directly; in the clause, however, it is actually the nominal *the cup* and the clausal predicate *is red* which combine as wholes, at a higher level of

organization. These examples show that the choice of profile determinant in a construction must be specified; it cannot be predicted from the direction of dependency or the internal properties of the components. Similarly, the choice of e-site (and whether a given substructure will ever be chosen to anchor a valence relation) is something specified as part of grammatical constructions, not an inherent property of individual predicates.

23. This semantic integration is symbolized by the phonological integration of *the* and *pins*. Specifically, *the* and *pins* are contiguous, with *the* preceding *pins* as a separate word.

24. Relative quantifiers contrast with "absolute quantifiers" with respect to a number of grammatical properties. For one thing, only absolute quantifiers can function as clausal heads: *We were {many/seven}*, but **We were {all/most}*. If relative quantifiers are grounding predications, as claimed, their inability to function as clausal heads follows from the general principle that such predications profile the grounded entity, rather than the grounding relationship itself. They will have a nonrelational profile because of the principle, whereas a clause requires a relational head. A second property distinguishing absolute and relative quantifiers is that only the former can occur in a simple nominal after a grounding predication like *the*: thus *the {many/seven} pencils that you broke*, but **the {all/most} pencils that you broke* (with *most* as nonsuperlative). This difference also supports the grounding nature of relative quantifiers.

25. Thus *all* and *most* instantiate the fundamental relational notions of coincidence and proximity discussed in Chapter 1. Figure 5(c) shows particular variants of *all* and *some*. *All* has a weaker variant, essentially equal to *almost all*, and *some* has a schematic variant which neutralizes the differences among *all*, *most*, and *some*, indicating only that the boundary of the profiled mass falls somewhere along the scale other than the point of origin (i.e. that the profiled mass is nonempty).

26. Phonologically, this integration is symbolized by the fact that *of* joins the phrase *the pins* to form a higher-order phrase.

27. At the phonological pole, *most* joins *of the pins* as a left sister in the higher-order phrase *most of the pins*. (I ignore here the alternate phrasing where *of* cliticizes to *most*.)

28. Within the transformational tradition, the analysis of Freidin 1975 is probably the most similar to the present account. However, a central issue in Freidin's paper is whether passivization is a lexical or a syntactic phenomenon; this is not a meaningful question from the cognitive grammar perspective.

29.   I do not claim that passive constructions in all languages involve a participial predicate of this kind or are to be analyzed as parallel to the English passive. The rubric "passive" is applied to a wide variety of constructions which, in one way or another, enhance the prominence of a landmark (cf. Givón 1979; Langacker & Munro 1975).

30.   This is admittedly not a strong consideration, since grammatical constructions do sometimes incorporate redundant material (see the treatment of *do* below).

31.   This is not contradictory, since the trajector is defined abstractly as the figure within a relational profile (not as a mover). It is of course easiest to conceptualize a scene by selecting the most active thing as figure, but this is a matter of image and perspective, and we can perfectly well do otherwise. *Approached* represents a marked way of construing the scene in accordance with its status as a marked (participialized) form of the verb stem.

32.   I have commented on the semantic values of *do* and *be* (and their relation to one another) in a number of publications, including Langacker 1975, 1978, 1981, and 1982.

33.   Note that meaningfulness is not the same as nonoverlapping meaning. It is possible and consistent to claim that *do* is meaningful, but that pairs of expressions like *run* and *do (...) run* are nevertheless substantially equivalent semantically. All syntagmatic combination depends on overlap of some kind; when that overlap is complete, as with *do*, the semantic value of the overlapped component is simply eclipsed by that of the more inclusive one. Note also that a specifiable grammatical function (e.g. serving to bear tense) does not render a morpheme meaningless, since a meaningful element (especially one with fairly unobtrusive semantic content) can perfectly well be conventionalized in a particular grammatical role. (See Chapter 11 for further discussion of these issues.)

34.   One minor difference is that $[BE_p]$, because it only occurs in combination with $[PERF_3]$, can be analyzed as profiling a schematic process that specifically involves two things as participants. This is not true of *be*'s basic variant (cf. Figure 12(a)).

35.   This partial characterization is sufficient for present purposes. I make no attempt here to determine how the simple spatial *by* differs from *near, with,* or *at*.

36.   For discussion of [DIST]--a grounding predication which is generally considered a marker of past tense, but which I label 'distal'--see Langacker 1978 and *to appear*, chapter 6.

37.   There appears to be a strong tendency for the landmark of a relational structure to be elaborated at a lower level of constituency than its trajector.

This corresponds to the traditional observation that an object is more closely bound to a verb than is its subject (as seen by word-order tendencies, the higher incidence of noun incorporation with objects than with subjects, the common occurrence of verb-object idioms as opposed to subject-verb idioms, etc.); it probably relates to the special status of the trajector as figure within the relational profile. In the case at hand, *Alice* elaborates the landmark of *by* at the lowest level, while *approached* elaborates the trajector of the composite structure *by Alice* at the next higher level. Note also that *Bill* elaborates the processual trajector at the highest level of constituency within the clause.

38.   Bolinger 1977 discusses the semantic value of *there* and *it*. For the analyzability of idioms, see Gorbet 1973 and Langacker 1987a.

39.   *Get* is restricted to atemporal complements: *get tall, get drunk, get a ladder, *get run, *get see a mirage*. Thus *get*-passives (e.g. *got stabbed*) provide another argument for the atemporality of passive participles.

40.   The variant of the perfect participle that appears with *have* (e.g. *We have finished*) is discussed in Chapter 12 and in chapter 5 of Langacker *to appear*. The occurrence of participial inflection on nouns (e.g. *one-eyed cat*) is also treated in the latter (cf. Hirtle 1970).

41.   The following sentence, quoted by Bolinger (p.c.) from the Boston *Globe*, provides further evidence against treating *by* as an incidental by-product (!) of a passive transformation: *The [caulking] gun is easier to use by amateurs.*

Chapter 5: Abstract motion

*   The original version of this chapter appeared in the *Proceedings of the Annual Meeting of the Berkeley Linguistics Society* 12: 455-471, 1986. It is reprinted with the permission of the Berkeley Linguistics Society.

1.   Though time may not be salient in such a conception, it is nonetheless invoked as an axis along which the action unfolds.

2.   One might argue that time is a primary domain for verbs but is absent (or quite nonsalient) within the complex matrix of path prepositions. However, the same argument cannot plausibly be made for infinitives or passive participles, since these derive from verb stems. The distinction between verbs and nonverbs is thus attributed to whether the conception of the component states is predominantly sequential or holistic.

3.   The discreteness implied by the diagrams and formulas is purely for expository convenience, and is not intended as a claim about cognitive

representation.

4. The subtlety of this contrast is consonant with the fact that languages often fail to make a formal distinction between verbs and complex nonverbal relations.

5. Many other expressions have time as their primary domain, e.g. *before* (*They finished before I got there*), which is a stative relation according to the definition given earlier.

6. Of course the entire sequence in (21) occurs in a matter of milliseconds; despite the seriality, it is almost instantaneous experientially.

7. Subjectification is discussed more fully in Chapter 12.

Chapter 6: Grammatical valence

* The original version of this chapter appeared under the title ''The nature of grammatical valence'' in Rudzka-Ostyn 1988, 91-125.

1. Recall that in the terminology of cognitive grammar, either the dependent or the autonomous structure can be a predicate--a predicate is defined as the semantic pole of a single morpheme.

2. Observe that the structure which I identify as conceptually dependent, in the sense described previously, is often not the same structure that is considered dependent in the sense of dependency grammar representations.

3. Note, for instance, the tendency for linear ordering to correlate with the sequencing of events.

4. Cf. *throw* in *He threw the clothes into the closet*--*the clothes* is construed as both the direct object of *throw* and the subject (trajector) vis-à-vis the relational complement *into the closet*.

5. This tree is exactly analogous to Figure 6, specifying the integration of subject and direct object nominals with a simple verb of Hopi.

Chapter 7: Active zones

* The original version of this chapter appeared in the *Proceedings of the Annual Meeting of the Berkeley Linguistics Society* 10: 172-188, 1984. It is reprinted with the permission of the Berkeley Linguistics Society.

1. Here and in what follows, I simplify matters in irrelevant respects by ignoring the semantic contribution of elements like *-ing* and *to*.

Chapter 8: The Yuman auxiliary

*   The original version of this chapter was written for a projected Festschrift to honor Margaret Langdon.

1.   Languages of the Yuman family (which belongs to the putative Hokan stock) are spoken in Arizona, southern California, and northern Baja California, Mexico.

2.   The following abbreviations are used in the glosses: 1 = first person; 2 = second person; 3 = third person; SS = same subject; PRED = predicational; DEM = demonstrative; SUBJ = subject marker; PROG = progressive.

Chapter 9: Transitivity, case, and grammatical relations

*   The original version of sections **1-3** of this chapter first appeared under the title "Settings, participants, and grammatical relations" in *Proceedings of the Annual Meeting of the Pacific Linguistics Conference* 2: 1-31, 1986. A version of the remainder first appeared in *Linguistic Notes from La Jolla* 14: 57-94, 1988, with the title "Case and grammatical relations in cognitive grammar (with special reference to Newari)".

1.   An alternative viewing arrangement, organized egocentrically with the viewer himself onstage, also has substantial cognitive and linguistic significance (Langacker 1985).

2.   We will not consider aspectual predications, which induce a departure from the unmarked situation by adjusting the profile contributed by the lexical head. Note that finite verb inflection attaches to that element whose processual profile prevails at the clause level.

3.   Though third-person sentences are in some sense canonical (as witnessed, say, by typical patterns of verb agreement), sentences with first- and second-person participants are obviously both natural and very frequent. These do not reflect the ICM of Figure 1, but rather an alternative, egocentrically organized model of comparable cognitive salience (cf. footnote 1).

4.   For illustration, consider the interactive network constituting our previous scenario. This network contains a lengthy action chain: Andrea's teasing induces Floyd to swing the hammer; this makes the glass break, sending shards flying; one of them strikes Andrea on the arm and causes blood to flow from the wound. Only those segments of the chain leading from Floyd to the disintegration of the glass fall within the scope of predication for *Floyd broke the glass*, which profiles this entire subchain. The profiling

shown in Figure 2(d) corresponds to sentence (3a): the finite main clause (*Floyd swung the hammer*) designates only the initial segment of the chain. Another option is given in (3b), where the profiled event (*shattered*) is confined to the fate of the glass.

5. This is Fillmore's (1970: 133) analysis of sentences like (6c), but I would argue that the object also has patient properties.

6. A static situation can be thought of as representing the limiting case of an event, that in which the extent of change falls to zero.

7. Similarly, Givón (1984: 138) characterizes subjects and direct objects as "primary" and "secondary clausal topics". I believe our analyses are complementary rather than incompatible: his description in terms of "clausal topic" aims at the category prototype (it seems doubtful that any independently established notion of topic can be attributed to every occurrence of a subject or direct object), while mine in terms of "figure" and "prominence" is maximally schematic. In any event, both accounts invoke some type of prominence (as opposed to specific conceptual content) to explicate the subject and object relations. (My own account is spelled out in considerably more detail in chapter 7 of Langacker *to appear*.)

8. To be more precise, a clause may have a trajector without having a primary landmark, but not conversely. Trajector/landmark asymmetry is inherent in a clause's semantic structure, regardless of whether these entities are spelled out by overt nominal expressions (thus identified as subject and direct object).

9. Many other elements and interactions could be added to this network, and might be important for particular expressions: the volitional control exerted by AG over his actions, the agent's own perceptual and emotive involvement with the process, the means through which the transfer is accomplished, the attitude of the EXPER-POSSR toward the AG, and so on.

10. There are obvious affinities here to the notions advanced in MacWhinney (1977) and DeLancey (1981). The independently developed analysis in Croft (1986) shows extensive parallels to my own. The reader will also note many similarities between the ideas presented here and various claims of role and reference grammar (Foley & Van Valin 1984). A more detailed analysis of the English passive was of course offered in Chapter 4, where it was argued that the full process designated by a verb stem remains profiled in the passive formed on it.

11. Also accounted for is the well-known fact that *This bed has been slept in* is felicitous only when the bed has been mussed up or otherwise affected by the sleeping: the bed must have participated in an interaction rather than simply being the location in which the sleeping occurred. Similarly,

whereas *England has been lived in by Fred* is deviant because there is no basis for construing England as a participant rather than the setting, parallel sentences are acceptable when such a basis is provided, e.g. *England has been lived in by many intellectual giants* (implying that they have left their stamp of greatness on the country).

12. Smith (1985a) has argued cogently that the failure of *es* to appear when a locative is preposed to the verb (e.g. *Im Garten spielt ein Kind*) reflects its nonparticipant status; being nothing more than a setting with presentative function, it becomes superfluous when another element assumes this role. By contrast, those instances of *es* that cooccur with preposed locatives (e.g. *Heute regnet es* 'Today it's raining' are plausibly claimed to be setting-like participants in the profiled process.

13. Katarzyna Dziwirek has contributed all my information concerning Polish. My source on Guarani was Rob Kluender, and the Newari data was elicited and analyzed by Ken Cook, Tony Hung, and Steve Poteet (cf. Cook 1988b; Hung 1988; Poteet 1988).

14. Note that the agent and instrument roles cannot be absolute, since they are defined with reference to the transmission of energy. The experiencer role is capable of an absolute/nonabsolute contrast, e.g. *Sheila was sad* vs. *Sheila was saddened (by the news)*.

15. I analyze *Jill* as the (true) direct object, hence the second-most prominent participant (after the subject). *A turtle* is treated as oblique, and more specifically as a complement expressing a relationship of possession (in a very general sense); this possessive relationship is not marked morphologically, but only by the juxtaposition of postverbal nominals (cf. Chapter 1).

16. Givón refers to these factors as "semantic" and "pragmatic case-roles". To avoid confusion, I restrict the term case to its traditional sense, i.e. surface case marked directly on nominals (whether by inflection, affixation, clitics, or particles).

17. These networks include the subject and object prototypes (AG and PAT, respectively), other conventionally sanctioned values (such as INSTR for subjects in English), and more schematic characterizations (e.g. 'head of action chain'; 'relational figure').

18. Similarly, one does not encounter languages with over three degrees of contrastive stress. However, tone systems exploit multiple parameters (pitch, contour, glottalization), and can therefore be considerably more elaborate; this richer phonological "content" is analogous to the conceptual content of cases based on role archetypes.

19. I simplify here by ignoring the possibility of participants remaining covert (cf. footnote 8).

20. I am assuming that the standard identification of participants as subjects and objects is correct for ergative languages. Though it merits serious investigation, I incline away from an obvious alternative, namely to analyze the absolutive-marked nominal as the subject in both transitive and intransitive clauses. I suspect the advantages of this approach (e.g. the greater cross-linguistic similarity of case-marking systems) do not offset its liabilities. For instance, grammatical relations would be substantially different for NOM/ACC and ERG/ABS languages (the ERG-marked nominal could not be considered a direct object). Moreover, in split-ergative languages the operative grammatical relations would vary according to aspect, person, etc., even for a single verb.

21. Recall that an absolute construal does not imply the absence or irrelevance of energy, but only its omission from the realm of explicit concern.

22. Its function is precisely analogous to that of a root in word formation: a word's root is its irreducible morphological core, which supports the addition of less autonomous elements in the formation of complex words. (For extensive discussion, see chapters 8 and 9 of Langacker 1987a.)

23. Note that absolutive case does not imply that a participant is absolute in the strong sense of being construed in abstraction from the flow of energy. However, since the case assignment procedure starts with the conceptually autonomous thematic core and works outward, energy input from the source domain is not yet a factor at the initial step when absolutive case is assigned.

24. Agreement often follows an ergative pattern. The Uto-Aztecan languages are strictly NOM/ACC in regard to case (if they have case marking), but generally have verb-stem suppletion showing ERG/ABS organization: intransitive verbs supplete for the number of their subject, and transitive verbs for the number of their object.

25. If the subject in (33b) is taken as bearing ABS case, the semantic description of this case category must be adjusted appropriately (e.g. by incorporating an additional sense defined with reference to the flow of information in a discourse). Alternatively, the zero marking can be interpreted as reflecting the absence of any case predication.

26. A further systemic aspect of case is the tendency for one member of the system to take on an exceptionally wide range of values, so that in essence it functions as what might be called (haplologically) a "default case". The dative assumes this role in German (see Smith 1987, 1989), and the instrumental in Polish.

27. A complex structure like [C===>[B===>[A→]]] can be viewed from either of two perspectives, implying different points of access: A (or [A→]) is the starting point in terms of building up the complex notion from its autonomous core, and C with reference to the flow of energy along the full action chain thus assembled. These two perspectives underpin the contrast between ERB/ABS and NOM/ACC organization.

28. A single complex event can also be coded by separate verb stems, as in (39) below.

29. The pivot is however the trajector of the predication representing the caused activity, and is thus the subject of the corresponding noncausative sentence.

30. Agentivity assumes many specific forms: consent, volition, secondary responsibility, etc. The subtle differences among them are not essential to either Cole's analysis or mine.

31. As with the dative-subject construction, two sorts of optimality find themselves in competition: consistent marking of the experiencer role vs. consistent marking of the causative pivot. How a language resolves this conflict is not predictable, but either solution is natural in its own fashion.

32. What case is selected to convey a particular extended meaning is variable and not strictly predictable. It is however expected that the various senses coded by a given case will be connected through cognitively plausible relationships.

Chapter 10: A usage-based model

* The original version of this chapter appeared in Rudzka-Ostyn 1988, 127-161.

1. For instance, an *eraser* is a particular type of object with specific properties, not just 'something that erases'.

2. Note that a schema is not viewed as a set of features or criterial attributes--it is an integrated structure whose internal organization is parallel to that of its instantiations.

3. Some, of course, are more frequent and deeply entrenched than others.

4. Indeed, the abstractness of a high-level schema is probably inimical to its prominence.

Chapter 11: Autonomy and agreement

* The original version of this chapter appeared under the title "Autonomy, agreement, and cognitive grammar" in Diane Brentari *et al.* (eds.), *Agreement in Grammatical Theory*, 147-180, Chicago, 1988. It is reprinted with the permission of the Chicago Linguistic Society.

1. For instance, *that* might combine with *yellow balloon* to form *that yellow balloon*, represented formulaically as follows: [[THAT/that] [[YELLOW/yellow] [BALLOON/balloon]]].

2. Comparable remarks hold for the *-s* of *scissors, binoculars, pants*, etc.

3. Alternatively, the pattern might simply be $A...B+x'$, with x' determined by A directly.

Chapter 12: Subjectification

* The original version of this chapter appeared in *Cognitive Linguistics* 1: 5-38, 1990. It is reprinted with the permission of Mouton de Gruyter.

1. See, for example, Brugman 1989; Fauconnier 1985; Fillmore 1982; Haiman 1980; Hawkins 1984; Herskovits 1985, 1986, 1988; Janda 1984, *to appear*; Kemmer 1988; Lakoff & Johnson 1980; Lakoff & Norvig 1987; Langacker 1988b; Lindner 1981, 1982; Maldonado 1988; Poteet 1987; Rice 1987b; Rudzka-Ostyn 1988; Smith 1987; Sweetser 1984, 1987; Talmy 1977, 1983, 1985b, 1988a, 1988b; Tuggy 1986; Vandeloise 1984, 1985a, 1985b, 1986, 1987.

2. As a limiting case, it may be exhaustive of XY.

3. It is not inherent in the objective situation, which one could just as well describe by saying *Veronica is sitting across the table from Vanessa*.

4. The latter is however acceptable to the extent that one "empathizes" with the speaker's image in the paper and imagines the speaker's experience at the moment the picture was taken.

5. The contrast is one of 'reality' vs. 'irreality'. For details, see chapter 6 of Langacker *to appear*.

6. The construction that integrates the grounding predication with the clausal head ensures that they and the resulting composite expression all designate the same process. As a consequence, *she* is simultaneously the trajector of *must*, of *leave*, and of the full clause.

7. See Langacker *to appear* for fuller discussion of possessives and the broader ramifications of the notions invoked to describe them.

8. Observe that *we* refers not just to the speaker and hearer but to all the people in the geographical area (cf. *They have a lot of armadillos in Texas*). With the subject construed "generically", the locus of experience and potential relevance is highly diffuse, implying a lesser degree of objectivity and salience.

9. The determining factor is the nature of the grounding predication: $R = G$ when *have* is in the present tense (e.g. *He has finished*), but not in the past (*He had finished*) or with a modal construed as referring to the future (*He may have finished by then*).

10. The French perfect is therefore directly analogous to a 'go'-type future (Figure 8(b)) or to the modals of German (Figure 9(b)).

11. That is, this schematic characterization makes no reference to any particular semantic role, only to figure/ground organization. This is not to deny that semantic roles are central to the description of category prototypes, as described in Chapter 9.

Bibliography

Anderson, Stephen R.
    1982   "Where's morphology?", *Linguistic Inquiry* 13: 571-612.
Bach, Emmon & Robert T. Harms (eds.)
    1968   *Universals in Linguistic Theory*. New York: Holt.
Barwise, Jon & John Perry
    1983   *Situations and Attitudes*. Cambridge, Mass. and London: MIT
                Press/Bradford.
Bates, Elizabeth & Brian MacWhinney
    1982   "Functionalist approaches to grammar", in: Lila Gleitman &
                Eric Wanner (eds.), 173-218.
Bever, Thomas G. & Peter S. Rosenbaum
    1970   "Some lexical structures and their empirical validity", in:
                Roderick A. Jacobs & Peter S. Rosenbaum (eds.), 3-19.
Bolinger, Dwight
    1977   *Meaning and Form*. London and New York: Longman.
Brugman, Claudia M.
    1989   *The Story of* Over*: Polysemy, Semantics, and the Structure of
                the Lexicon*. New York: Garland.
Bybee, Joan L.
    1988   "Semantic substance vs. contrast in the development of
                grammatical meaning", *Proceedings of the Annual Meeting
                of the Berkeley Linguistics Society* 14: 247-264.
Bybee, Joan L. & William Pagliuca
    1985   "Cross-linguistic comparison and the development of
                grammatical meaning", in: Jacek Fisiak (ed.), 59-83.
    1987   "The evolution of future meaning", in: Anna Giacalone
                Ramat *et al.* (eds.), 109-122.
Carlson, Lauri
    1981   "Aspect and quantification", in: Philip J. Tedeschi & Annie
                Zaenen (eds.), 31-64.
Casad, Eugene H.
    1977   "Location and direction in Cora discourse", *Anthropological
                Linguistics* 19: 216-241.
    1982   Cora locationals and structured imagery. [Unpublished Ph.D.
                dissertation, University of California, San Diego.]
    1984   "Cora", in: Ronald W. Langacker (ed.), 151-459.
    1988   "Conventionalization of Cora locationals", in: Brygida
                Rudzka-Ostyn (ed.), 345-378.

Chafe, Wallace L.
    1970   *Meaning and the Structure of Language.* Chicago: University of Chicago Press.

Chomsky, Noam
    1957   *Syntactic Structures.* (Janua Linguarum 4.) The Hague: Mouton.
    1965   *Aspects of the Theory of Syntax.* Cambridge, Mass.: MIT Press.

Chomsky, Noam & Morris Halle
    1968   *The Sound Pattern of English.* New York: Harper & Row.

Cole, Peter
    1983   "The grammatical role of the causee in universal grammar", *International Journal of American Linguistics* 49: 115-133.

Cole, Peter & Jerrold M. Sadock (eds.)
    1977   *Syntax and Semantics.* Vol. 8, *Grammatical Relations.* New York: Academic Press.

Cook, Kenneth W.
    1988a   A cognitive analysis of grammatical relations, case, and transitivity in Samoan. [Unpublished Ph.D. dissertation, University of California, San Diego.]
    1988b   "The semantics of Newari case-marking distinctions", *Linguistic Notes from La Jolla* 14: 42-56.
    1989   "A cognitive account of the Samoan *lavea* and *galo* verbs". Linguistic Agency University of Duisburg.

Craig, Colette (ed.)
    1986   *Noun Classes and Categorization.* Amsterdam and Philadelphia: John Benjamins.

Croft, William A.
    1986   Categories and relations in syntax: The clause-level organization of information. [Unpublished Ph.D. dissertation, Stanford University.]

Cruse, D. A.
    1979   "On the transitivity of the part-whole relation", *Journal of Linguistics* 15: 29-38.

Dahlstrom, Amy
    1983   "Agent-patient languages and split case marking systems", *Proceedings of the Annual Meeting of the Berkeley Linguistics Society* 9: 37-46.

Davidson, Donald & Gilbert Harman (eds.)
    1972   *Semantics of Natural Language.* Dordrecht and Boston: D. Reidel.

DeLancey, Scott
    1981   "An interpretation of split ergativity and related phenomena", *Language* 57: 626-657.

Efrat, Barbara S. (ed.)
    1979   *The Victoria Conference on Northwestern Languages.* (Heritage Record 4.) Victoria: British Columbia Provincial Museum.

Eilfort, William H. *et al.* (eds.)
    1985   *Papers from the Parasession on Causatives and Agentivity.* Chicago: Chicago Linguistic Society.

Elman, Jeffrey L. & James L. McClelland
    1984   "Speech perception as a cognitive process: The interactive activation model", in: Norman Lass (ed.), 337-374.

Fauconnier, Gilles
    1985   *Mental Spaces: Aspects of Meaning Construction in Natural Language.* Cambridge, Mass. and London: MIT Press/Bradford.

Ferguson, Charles A. & Carol B. Farwell
    1975   "Words and sounds in early language acquisition", *Language* 51: 419-439.

Fillmore, Charles J.
    1968   "The case for case", in: Emmon Bach and Robert T. Harms (eds.), 1-88.
    1970   "The grammar of *hitting* and *breaking*", in: Roderick A. Jacobs and Peter S. Rosenbaum (eds.), 120-133.
    1977   "The case for case reopened", in: Peter Cole and Jerrold M. Sadock (eds.), 59-81.
    1982   "Frame semantics", in: Linguistic Society of Korea (eds.), 111-137.

Fisiak, Jacek (ed.)
    1985   *Historical Semantics - Historical Word Formation.* Berlin: Mouton.

Fodor, Jerry A.
    1970   "Three reasons for not deriving 'kill' from 'cause to die'", *Linguistic Inquiry* 1: 429-438.
    1983   *The Modularity of Mind.* Cambridge, Mass. and London: MIT Press/Bradford.

Fodor, Jerry A. & Jerrold J. Katz (eds.)
    1964   *The Structure of Language: Readings in the Philosophy of Language.* Englewood Cliffs, N.J.: Prentice-Hall.

Foley, William A. & Robert D. Van Valin, Jr.
    1984   *Functional Syntax and Universal Grammar.* Cambridge: Cambridge University Press.
Freidin, Robert
    1975   "The analysis of passives", *Language* 51: 384-405.
Friedrich, Paul
    1969a   *On the Meaning of the Tarascan Suffixes of Space. International Journal of American Linguistics*, Memoir 23.
    1969b   "Metaphor-like relations between referential subsets", *Lingua* 24: 1-10.
    1970   "Shape in grammar", *Language* 46: 379-407.
    1971   *The Tarascan Suffixes of Locative Space.* (Language Science Monographs 9.) Bloomington: Indiana University Press.
Gentner, Dedre
    1981   "Some interesting differences between verbs and nouns", *Cognition and Brain Theory* 4: 161-178.
Givón, Talmy
    1973   "The time-axis phenomenon", *Language* 49: 890-925.
    1979   *On Understanding Grammar.* New York: Academic Press.
    1984   *Syntax: A Functional-Typological Introduction.* Vol. 1. Amsterdam and Philadelphia: John Benjamins.
    1989   *Mind, Code and Context: Essays in Pragmatics.* Hillsdale, N.J.: Erlbaum.
Gleitman, Lila & Eric Wanner (eds.)
    1982   *Language Acquisition: The State of the Art.* Cambridge: Cambridge University Press.
Goldsmith, John
    1980   "Meaning and mechanism in grammar", *Harvard Studies in Syntax and Semantics* 2: 423-449.
Goldsmith, John & Erich Woisetschlaeger
    1982   "The logic of the English progressive", *Linguistic Inquiry* 13: 79-89.
Gorbet, Larry
    1973   "The isthmus of anaphor (and idiomaticity)", *Stanford Occasional Papers in Linguistics* 3: 25-34.
Green, Georgia M.
    1974   *Semantics and Syntactic Regularity.* Bloomington: Indiana University Press.
Greenberg, Joseph H. (ed.)
    1978a   *Universals of Human Language.* Vol. 3, *Word Structure.* Stanford: Stanford University Press.
    1978b   *Universals of Human Language.* Vol. 4, *Syntax.* Stanford: Stanford University Press.

Gross, Maurice
 1979 "On the failure of generative grammar", *Language* 55: 859-885.

Grossman, Robin *et al.* (eds.)
 1975 *Papers from the Parasession on Functionalism.* Chicago: Chicago Linguistic Society.

Haiman, John
 1980 "Dictionaries and encyclopedias", *Lingua* 50: 329-357.
 1983 "Iconic and economic motivation", *Language* 59: 781-819.
 1985 *Natural Syntax: Iconicity and Erosion.* Cambridge: Cambridge University Press.

Haiman, John (ed.)
 1985 *Iconicity in Syntax.* (Typological Studies in Language 6.) Amsterdam and Philadelphia: John Benjamins.

Hawkins, Bruce W.
 1984 The semantics of English spatial prepositions. [Unpublished Ph.D. dissertation, University of California, San Diego.]
 1988 "The natural category MEDIUM: An alternative to selection restrictions and similar constructs", in: Brygida Rudzka-Ostyn (ed.), 231-270.

Herskovits, Annette H.
 1985 "Semantics and pragmatics of locative expressions", *Cognitive Science* 9: 341-378.
 1986 *Language and Spatial Cognition: An Interdisciplinary Study of the Prepositions in English.* Cambridge: Cambridge University Press.
 1988 "Spatial expressions and the plasticity of meaning", in: Brygida Rudzka-Ostyn (ed.), 271-297.

Heyvaert, F. J. & F. Steurs (eds.)
 1989 *Worlds Behind Words: Essays in Honour of Prof. Dr. F. G. Droste on the Occasion of His Sixtieth Birthday.* Leuven: Leuven University Press.

Hirtle, W. H.
 1970 "-Ed adjectives like 'verandahed' and 'blue-eyed'", *Journal of Linguistics* 6: 19-36.

Hoard, James E.
 1979 "On the semantic representation of oblique complements", *Language* 55: 319-332.

Hopper, Paul J. (ed.)
 1982 *Tense-Aspect: Between Semantics & Pragmatics.* (Typological Studies in Language 1.) Amsterdam and Philadelphia: John Benjamins.

Hopper, Paul J. & Sandra A. Thompson
    1980   "Transitivity in grammar and discourse", *Language* 56: 251-
                299.
    1984   "The discourse basis for lexical categories in universal
                grammar", *Language* 60: 703-752.
    1985   "The iconicity of the universal categories 'noun' and 'verb'",
                in: John Haiman (ed.), 151-183.
Hudson, Richard A.
    1976   *Arguments for a Non-Transformational Grammar.* Chicago:
                University of Chicago Press.
    1984   *Word Grammar.* Oxford: Basil Blackwell.
    1987   "Zwicky on heads", *Journal of Linguistics* 23: 109-132.
Hung, Tony
    1988   "Case and role in Newari: A cognitive grammar approach",
                Linguistic Notes from La Jolla 14: 95-107.
Jackendoff, Ray
    1983   *Semantics and Cognition.* (Current Studies in Linguistics 8.)
                Cambridge, Mass.: MIT Press.
Jacobs, Roderick A. & Peter S. Rosenbaum (eds.)
    1970   *Readings in English Transformational Grammar.* Waltham,
                Mass.: Ginn.
Jacobsen, William H., Jr.
    1979   "Noun and verb in Nootkan", in: Barbara S. Efrat (ed.), 83-
                155.
Janda, Laura A.
    1984   A semantic analysis of the Russian verbal prefixes ZA-,
                PERE-, DO-, and OT-. [Unpublished Ph.D. dissertation,
                University of California, Los Angeles.]
    1988   "The mapping of elements of cognitive space onto
                grammatical relations: An example from Russian verbal
                prefixation", in: Brygida Rudzka-Ostyn (ed.), 327-343.
    In press   "The radial network of a grammatical category--its genesis and
                dynamic structure".
    To appear   *A Geography of Case Semantics: The Czech Dative and the
                Russian Instrumental.*
Johnson, Mark
    1987   *The Body in the Mind: The Bodily Basis of Meaning,
                Imagination, and Reason.* Chicago and London: University
                of Chicago Press.
Johnson-Laird, Philip N.
    1983   *Mental Models.* Cambridge, Mass.: Harvard University Press.

Kachru, Braj B. *et al.* (eds.)
  1973   *Issues in Linguistics: Papers in Honor of Henry and Renée Kahane.* Urbana: University of Illinois Press.
Katz, Jerrold J. & Jerry A. Fodor
  1963   "The structure of a semantic theory", *Language* 39: 170-210.
Keenan, Edward L. & Bernard Comrie
  1977   "Noun phrase accessibility and universal grammar", *Linguistic Inquiry* 8: 63-99.
Kemmer, Suzanne E.
  1988   *The Middle Voice: A Typological and Diachronic Study.* [Unpublished Ph.D. dissertation, Stanford University.]
Kempson, Ruth M.
  1977   *Semantic Theory.* Cambridge: Cambridge University Press.
Keyser, Samuel Jay & Paul M. Postal
  1976   *Beginning English Grammar.* New York: Harper & Row.
Kimball, John (ed.)
  1975   *Syntax and Semantics.* Vol. 4. New York: Academic Press.
Klima, Edward S.
  1964   "Negation in English", in: Jerry A. Fodor and Jerrold J. Katz (eds.), 246-323.
Kosslyn, Stephen Michael
  1980   *Image and Mind.* Cambridge, Mass.: Harvard University Press.
Lakoff, George
  1970   *Irregularity in Syntax.* New York: Holt.
  1982   "Categories: An essay in cognitive linguistics", in: Linguistic Society of Korea (eds.), 139-193.
  1987   *Women, Fire, and Dangerous Things: What Categories Reveal about the Mind.* Chicago and London: University of Chicago Press.
Lakoff, George & Mark Johnson
  1980   *Metaphors We Live By.* Chicago and London: University of Chicago Press.
Lakoff, George & Peter Norvig
  1987   "Taking: A study in lexical network theory", *Proceedings of the Annual Meeting of the Berkeley Linguistics Society* 13: 195-206.
Lakoff, George & Mark Turner
  1989   *More than Cool Reason: A Field Guide to Poetic Metaphor.* Chicago and London: University of Chicago Press.

Lakoff, Robin
  1971   "Passive resistance", *Papers from the Regional Meeting of the Chicago Linguistic Society* 7: 149-162.
Lamiroy, Beatrice
  1983   *Les Verbes de Mouvement en Français et en Espagnol.* (Lingvisticae Investigationes Supplementa 11.) Amsterdam and Philadelphia: John Benjamins and Leuven University Press.
Langacker, Ronald W.
  1973a   *Language and its Structure.* (2nd edition.) New York: Harcourt Brace Jovanovich.
  1973b   "Predicate raising: Some Uto-Aztecan evidence", in: Braj B. Kachru *et al.* (eds.), 468-491.
  1975   "Functional stratigraphy", in: Robin Grossman *et al.* (eds.), 351-397.
  1976   "Semantic representations and the linguistic relativity hypothesis", *Foundations of Language* 14: 307-357.
  1977   *Studies in Uto-Aztecan Grammar.* Vol. 1, *An Overview of Uto-Aztecan Grammar.* (SIL Publications in Linguistics 56.) Dallas: Summer Institute of Linguistics and University of Texas at Arlington.
  1978   "The form and meaning of the English auxiliary", *Language* 54: 853-882.
  1981   "The integration of grammar and grammatical change", *Indian Linguistics* 42: 82-135.
  1982   "Remarks on English aspect", in: Paul J. Hopper (ed.), 265-304.
  1985   "Observations and speculations on subjectivity", in John Haiman (ed.), 109-150.
  1986   "Settings, participants, and grammatical relations", *Proceedings of the Annual Meeting of the Pacific Linguistics Conference* 2: 1-31.
  1987a   *Foundations of Cognitive Grammar.* Vol. 1, *Theoretical Prerequisites.* Stanford: Stanford University Press.
  1987b   "Grammatical ramifications of the setting/participant distinction", *Proceedings of the Annual Meeting of the Berkeley Linguistics Society* 13: 383-394.
  1988a   "An overview of cognitive grammar", in: Brygida Rudzka-Ostyn (ed.), 3-48.
  1988b   "A view of linguistic semantics", in: Brygida Rudzka-Ostyn (ed.), 49-90.

1988c   "Case and grammatical relations in cognitive grammar (with special reference to Newari)", *Linguistic Notes from La Jolla* 14: 57-94.

1989   "Absolute construal", in: F. J. Heyvaert & F. Steurs (eds.), 65-75.

To appear   *Foundations of Cognitive Grammar.* Vol. 2, *Descriptive Application.* Stanford: Stanford University Press.

Langacker, Ronald W. (ed.)

1984   *Studies in Uto-Aztecan Grammar.* Vol. 4, *Southern Uto-Aztecan Grammatical Sketches.* (SIL Publications in Linguistics 56.) Dallas: Summer Institute of Linguistics and University of Texas at Arlington.

Langacker, Ronald W. & Pamela Munro

1975   "Passives and their meaning", *Language* 51: 789-830.

Langdon, Margaret

1978   "Auxiliary verb constructions in Yuman", *Journal of California Anthropology Papers in Linguistics* 90-130.

Lass, Norman (ed.)

1984   *Speech and Language.* Vol. 10. New York: Academic Press.

Lehmann, Winfred P. & Yakov Malkiel (eds.)

1982   *Perspectives on Historical Linguistics.* Amsterdam and Philadelphia: John Benjamins.

Lindner, Susan

1981   A lexico-semantic analysis of English verb-particle constructions with UP and OUT. [Unpublished Ph.D. dissertation, University of California, San Diego.]

1982   "What goes up doesn't necessarily come down: The ins and outs of opposites", *Papers from the Regional Meeting of the Chicago Linguistic Society* 18: 305-323.

Linguistic Society of Korea (eds.)

1982   *Linguistics in the Morning Calm.* Seoul: Hanshin.

Lyons, John

1968   *Introduction to Theoretical Linguistics.* Cambridge: Cambridge University Press.

1977   *Semantics.* Cambridge: Cambridge University Press.

MacWhinney, Brian

1977   "Starting points", *Language* 53: 152-168.

Maldonado, Ricardo

1988   "Energetic reflexives in Spanish", *Proceedings of the Annual Meeting of the Berkeley Linguistics Society* 14: 153-165.

McClelland, James L. & David E. Rumelhart (eds.)

1986   *Parallel Distributed Processing: Explorations in the Microstructure of Cognition.* Vol. 2, *Psychological and*

Biological Models. Cambridge, Mass. and London: MIT Press/Bradford.

Miller, George A. & Philip N. Johnson-Laird
1976   *Language and Perception.* Cambridge, Mass.: Harvard/Belknap.

Moore, Terence & Christine Carling
1982   *Language Understanding: Towards a Post-Chomskyan Linguistics.* New York: St. Martin's Press.

Moore, Timothy E. (ed.)
1973   *Cognitive Development and the Acquisition of Language.* New York: Academic Press.

Mourelatos, Alexander P. D.
1981   "Events, processes, and states", in: Philip J. Tedeschi & Annie Zaenen (eds.), 191-212.

Nathan, Geoffrey S.
1986   "Phonemes as mental categories", *Proceedings of the Annual Meeting of the Berkeley Linguistics Society* 12: 212-223.

Newman, John
1981   The semantics of raising constructions. [Unpublished Ph.D. dissertation, University of California, San Diego.]

Newmeyer, Frederick J.
1970   "On the alleged boundary between syntax and semantics", *Foundations of Language* 6: 178-186.
1983   *Grammatical Theory: Its Limits and Its Possibilities.* Chicago and London: University of Chicago Press.

Norwood, Susan
1981   Progressives in Yuman and Romance. [Unpublished Ph.D. dissertation, University of California, San Diego.]

Oehrle, Richard T.
1977   Review of Green 1974. *Language* 53: 198-208.

Palmer, F. R.
1981   *Semantics.* (2nd edition.) Cambridge: Cambridge University Press.

Partee, Barbara
1975   "Montague grammar and transformational grammar", *Linguistic Inquiry* 6: 203-300.

Perlmutter, David M.
1978   "Impersonal passives and the unaccusative hypothesis", *Proceedings of the Annual Meeting of the Berkeley Linguistics Society* 4: 157-189.

Perlmutter, David M. (ed.)
1983   *Studies in Relational Grammar.* Vol. 1. Chicago and London: University of Chicago Press.

Perlmutter, David M. & Paul M. Postal
    1983   "Towards a universal characterization of passivization", in: David M. Perlmutter (ed.), 3-29.

Pick, Herbert & Linda Acredolo (eds.)
    1983   *Spatial Orientation: Theory, Research, and Application.* New York: Plenum Press.

Postal, Paul M.
    1971   *Cross-Over Phenomena.* New York: Holt.

Poteet, Stephen
    1987   "Paths through different domains: A cognitive grammar analysis of Mandarin *dào*", *Proceedings of the Annual Meeting of the Berkeley Linguistics Society* 13: 408-421.
    1988   "Causative constructions in Newari", *Linguistic Notes from La Jolla* 14: 108-146.

Ramat, Anna Giacalone *et al.* (eds.)
    1987   *Papers from the 7th International Conference on Historical Linguistics.* Amsterdam and Philadelphia: John Benjamins.

Rice, Sally
    1987a   "Towards a transitive prototype: Evidence from some atypical English passives", *Proceedings of the Annual Meeting of the Berkeley Linguistics Society* 13: 422-434.
    1987b   Towards a cognitive model of transitivity. [Unpublished Ph.D. dissertation, University of California, San Diego.]
    1988   "Unlikely lexical entries", *Proceedings of the Annual Meeting of the Berkeley Linguistics Society* 14: 202-212.

Rosch, Eleanor
    1973   "On the internal structure of perceptual and semantic categories", in: Timothy E. Moore (ed.), 111-144.
    1975   "Cognitive representations of semantic categories", *Journal of Experimental Psychology: General* 104: 192-233.
    1977   "Human categorization", in: Neil Warren (ed.), 1-49.
    1978   "Principles of categorization", in: Eleanor Rosch and Barbara B. Lloyd (eds.), 27-47.

Rosch, Eleanor & Barbara B. Lloyd (eds.)
    1978   *Cognition and Categorization.* Hillsdale, N.J.: Erlbaum.

Ross, John Robert
    1972   "Act", in: Donald Davidson & Gilbert Harman (eds.), 70-126.

Rudzka-Ostyn, Brygida (ed.)
    1988   *Topics in Cognitive Linguistics.* Amsterdam and Philadelphia: John Benjamins.

Rumelhart, David E. & James L. McClelland (eds.)
    1986   *Parallel Distributed Processing: Explorations in the Microstructure of Cognition.* Vol. 1, *Foundations.*

Cambridge, Mass. and London: MIT Press/Bradford.

Rumelhart, David E. & David Zipser
1985   "Feature discovery by competitive learning", *Cognitive Science* 9: 75-112.

Sanders, Gerald A.
1974   "Precedence relations in language", *Foundations of Language* 11: 361-400.

Seiler, Hansjakob
1977   *Cahuilla Grammar*. Banning, Calif.: Malki Museum Press.

Shepard, Roger N.
1978   "The mental image", *American Psychologist* 33: 125-137.

Shopen, Timothy (ed.)
1985   *Language Typology and Syntactic Description*. Vol. 3, *Grammatical Categories and the Lexicon*. Cambridge: Cambridge University Press.

Smith, Carlota S.
1964   "Determiners and relative clauses in a generative grammar of English", *Language* 40: 37-52.
1983   "A theory of aspectual choice", *Language* 59: 479-501.

Smith, Michael B.
1985a   "An analysis of German dummy subject constructions", *Proceedings of the Annual Meeting of the Pacific Linguistics Conference* 1: 412-425.
1985b   "Event chains, grammatical relations, and the semantics of case in German", *Papers from the Regional Meeting of the Chicago Linguistic Society* 21: 388-407.
1987   The semantics of dative and accusative in German: An investigation in cognitive grammar. [Unpublished Ph.D. dissertation, University of California, San Diego.]
1989   "Cases from conceptual categories: Evidence from German". Linguistic Agency University of Duisburg.

Sweetser, Eve E.
1982   "Root and epistemic modals: Causality in two worlds", *Proceedings of the Annual Meeting of the Berkeley Linguistics Society* 8: 484-507.
1984   Semantic structure and semantic change: A cognitive linguistic study of modality, perception, speech acts, and logical relations. [Unpublished Ph.D. dissertation, University of California, Berkeley.]
1987   "Metaphorical models of thought and speech: A comparison of historical directions and metaphorical mappings in two domains", *Proceedings of the Annual Meeting of the Berkeley Linguistics Society* 13: 446-459.

1988   "Grammaticalization and semantic bleaching", *Proceedings of the Annual Meeting of the Berkeley Linguistics Society* 14: 389-405.

Talmy, Leonard
1975   "Semantics and syntax of motion", in John Kimball (ed.), 181-238.

1977   "Rubber-sheet cognition in language", *Papers from the Regional Meeting of the Chicago Linguistic Society* 13: 612-628.

1978   "Figure and ground in complex sentences", in: Joseph H. Greenberg (ed.), Vol. 4, 625-649.

1983   "How language structures space", in: Herbert Pick and Linda Acredolo (eds.), 225-282.

1985a   "Force dynamics in language and thought", in: William H. Eilfort *et al.* (eds.), 293-337.

1985b   "Lexicalization patterns: Semantic structure in lexical forms", in: Timothy Shopen (ed.), 57-149.

1988a   "Force dynamics in language and cognition", *Cognitive Science* 12: 49-100.

1988b   "The relation of grammar to cognition", in: Brygida Rudzka-Ostyn (ed.), 165-205.

Tedeschi, Philip J. & Annie Zaenen (eds.)
1981   *Syntax and Semantics.* Vol. 14, *Tense and Aspect.* New York: Academic Press.

Traugott, Elizabeth
1982   "From propositional to textual and expressive meanings: Some semantic-pragmatic aspects of grammaticalization", in: Winfred P. Lehmann and Yakov Malkiel (eds.), 245-271.

1986   "From polysemy to internal semantic reconstruction", *Proceedings of the Annual Meeting of the Berkeley Linguistics Society* 12: 539-550.

1988   "Pragmatic strengthening and grammaticalization", *Proceedings of the Annual Meeting of the Berkeley Linguistics Society* 14: 406-416.

Traugott, Elizabeth & Richard Dasher
1987   "On the historical relation between mental and speech act verbs in English and Japanese", in: Anna Giacalone Ramat *et al.* (eds.), 561-573.

Tuggy, David
1980   "¡Ethical dative and possessor omission sí, possessor ascension no!", *Work Papers of the Summer Institute of Linguistics, University of North Dakota* 24: 97-141.

1981   The transitivity-related morphology of Tetelcingo Nahuatl: An
             exploration in space grammar. [Unpublished Ph.D.
             dissertation, University of California, San Diego.]
1986   "Noun incorporations in Nahuatl", *Proceedings of the Annual
             Meeting of the Pacific Linguistics Conference* 2: 455-469.
1988   "Náhuatl causative/applicatives in cognitive grammar", in:
             Brygida Rudzka-Ostyn (ed.), 587-618.
1989   "The affix-stem distinction in Orizaba Náhuatl". Linguistic
             Agency University of Duisburg.

Ultan, Russell
1978   "The nature of future tenses", in Joseph H. Greenberg (ed.),
             Vol. 3, 83-123.

van Hoek, Karen
   In press   "The organization of the Yiddish gender system".

van Oosten, Jeanne
1977   "Subjects and agenthood in English", *Papers from the
             Regional Meeting of the Chicago Linguistic Society* 13: 459-
             471.
1986   *The Nature of Subjects, Topics and Agents: A Cognitive
             Explanation.* Bloomington: Indiana University Linguistics
             Club.

Vandeloise, Claude
1984   Description of space in French. [Unpublished Ph.D.
             dissertation, University of California, San Diego.]
1985a   "Au-delà des descriptions géométriques et logiques de
             l'espace: Une description fonctionnelle", *Lingvisticae
             Investigationes* 9: 109-129.
1985b   "Les prépositions *sur/sous* et la relation *porteur/porté*",
             Leuvense Bijdragen 74: 457-481.
1986   *L'Espace en Français.* Paris: Editions du Seuil.
1987   "La préposition *à* et le principe d'anticipation", *Langue
             Française* 76: 77-111.

Vendler, Zeno
1967   *Linguistics in Philosophy.* Ithaca: Cornell University Press.

Wallace, Stephen
1982   "Figure and ground: The interrelationships of linguistic
             categories", in: Paul J. Hopper (ed.), 201-223.

Waltz, David L. & Jordan B. Pollack
1985   "Massively parallel parsing: A strongly interactive model of
             natural language interpretation", *Cognitive Science* 9: 51-74.

Warren, Neil (ed.)
1977   *Studies in Cross-Cultural Psychology.* Vol. 1. London:
             Academic Press.

Wierzbicka, Anna
    1975   "Why 'kill' does not mean 'cause to die': The semantics of action sentences", *Foundations of Language* 13: 491-528.
    1985   "Oats and wheat: The fallacy of arbitrariness", in John Haiman (ed.), 311-342.
    1988   *The Semantics of Grammar.* (Studies in Language Companion Series 18.) Amsterdam and Philadelphia: John Benjamins.

Williams, Edwin
    1981   "On the notions 'lexically related' and 'head of a word'", *Linguistic Inquiry* 12: 245-274.

Zubin, David A. & Klaus-Michael Köpcke
    1986   "Gender and folk taxonomy: The indexical relation between grammatical and lexical categorization", in: Colette Craig (ed.), 139-180.

Zwicky, Arnold M.
    1985   "Heads", *Journal of Linguistics* 21: 1-29.

Index

Horst Arndt · Richard W. Janney
InterGrammar

Toward an Integrative Model of Verbal, Prosodic and Kinesic Choices in Speech

1987. 14.8 x 22.8 cm. XVI, 458 pages. With 16 illustrations and 60 tables. Cloth. ISBN 3 11 011244 2
(Studies in Anthropological Linguistic 2)

This interdisciplinary research monograph deals with the production, coordination and interpretation of verbal and nonverbal behavior in American English Speech, as well as the communication of feelings and attitudes in face-to-face conversation.

InterGrammar is the name of the model of speech presented here, since it stresses the integrative approach of the model (inter) as well as the systematic order (grammar) in presenting patterns of verbal, prosodic and kinesic choice.

Research results from many fields are brought together into a conceptual framework that explains functional relationships between verbal, prosodic and kinesic speech activities from a unified point of view. The book explains how verbal and nonverbal signals are strategically combined to achieve different goals in different situations.

Thus, this work approaches speech from two perspectives: The first presents speaking as a unified human activity involving the entire body, and not just those parts of it used to produce "language". The second, the pragmatic perspective, views speaking as goal-directed human action involving speakers and partners in context, not just speakers in isolation.

mouton de gruyter
Berlin · New York